"I AM NOT ALONE"

A Study on the Son of God Doctrine by an Ex-Oneness Advocate

By Tom Raddatz

1Lord1Faith Publishing
Lancaster, Ohio

~~~

Visit us at:

1lord1faithpublishing.com

Copyright © 2017 by Tom Raddatz

All rights reserved. No part of this book may be reproduced or transmitted in any form or by any means, electronic or mechanical, including photocopying, recording, or by any information storage and retrieval system, without permission in writing from the copyright owner.

For permission to reuse content, please contact
tomr@1lord1faith.org

Artwork by Ken Etberg
https://kenetberg.wordpress.com/ken-etberg/

Print interior layout by Luca Funari at Wolfebook
https://tinyurl.com/y72l3ay3

Published by 1Lord1Faith Publishing, Lancaster, Ohio

Printed in the United States of America
ISBN 978-0-9854318-3-9 (paperback), 978-9854318-4-6 (pdf)

Library of Congress Subject Heading:
Religion – Doctrinal Theology – Christology
BISAC Subject Heading:
RELIGION / Christian Theology / Christology

~~~

For my daughters.

With special thanks to:
My wife, Deresa, for her invaluable support and spiritual insight.
Carol Wise, whose help, yet again, has been immeasurable.
Ken Etberg for all his great work and creativity.
Luca Funari, for bringing it all together.
Many friends and acquaintances,
for their input and encouragement
including but not limited to
J. Dan Gill, Joe Lake, Jeff Ellis, Chris Makowski,
Daniel Santangelo and Bill Williams.

And above all, God the Father,
and His Son, Jesus the Anointed One!

~~~~

FOREWORD

Tom Raddatz is among those few people who have done one of the most difficult things that we as human beings can do – he has honestly and selflessly reconsidered his own long held beliefs. As a result, he has made important changes in his understanding about God and Christ. With that same selflessness, and with love, he has written this book to his fellow Apostolic believers to encourage them to also sincerely reconsider those same matters.

Tom does not ask people to reassess their understanding based on dreams, visions or other revelations. Rather, he invites them to a reconsideration based on the Bible itself. There is no better way to measure ourselves than to look to the scriptures. Certainly, it is by the scriptures that we can see the accurate picture of what true Apostolic faith should look like: what true Apostolic believers should practice and teach.

Tom assures us that the doctrine of the Trinity does indeed come up short when it is tested against what the apostles taught in the Bible. What may come as a surprise to many is that Tom now believes that Oneness perspectives also fall short. As a longtime advocate and defender of Oneness, Brother Raddatz now tells his fellow Apostolics that there is a better way to understand the great issues about God and Jesus: a way that is more scriptural than either Oneness or the Trinity.

With that in mind, "I Am Not Alone" comes as a welcome opportunity. For all who have had questions about their Trinitarian or Oneness perspectives, and in my experience that is many people, this book brings them another, more scripturally sound way of looking at God and our savior Jesus. Clearly the Trinity and Oneness (as well as Arianism, Adoptionism, and a host of other "isms") actually present more questions than they solve. Tom walks his readers through the simplicity of the truth and gives them chapter and verse to help them come to a clear view of what our faith ought to be in light of the Bible.

Hence, he takes us through a rather methodic survey of the issues. He carefully addresses the various scriptures that are looked to by those who are of Oneness backgrounds. Tom gives us a fair and honest consideration of those scriptures and asks us the questions: "Have we been looking at these scriptures right?" "Is there a better way to understand these passages?" His answers are illuminating and helpful to any open minded inquiry.

I believe that this book presents both an opportunity and a responsibility for us. We as Apostolics say that our allegiance is to the scriptures. With that in mind, don't we owe it to ourselves, and to the world we want to reach, to be sure that the faith we hold so dear is pure from all of the insidious traditions of men which have plagued Christianity at large for so many centuries? Apostolics rightly ask the world to turn on the light of scriptural introspection and reconsider their long held beliefs. But we as Apostolics must ourselves always be willing to turn that same light on our own beliefs. We must not ask the world to do what we ourselves are not willing to do.

This book reflects Brother Raddatz's sincere effort to set before all Oneness believers a reconsideration of the very scriptures upon which we have said that our faith is based. Hence, we find scriptures discussed in this book from Genesis to Revelation and notably from the Acts of the Apostles. Every Apostolic believer should take advantage of this opportunity to test their understanding against the scriptural reasoning that is presented here.

Tom Raddatz is both my friend and a brother in Christ. As Apostolics ourselves, Tom and I did not know one another until recently. We had journeyed on our separate paths. However, by the kindness of God, we had independently arrived at the same important conclusion: We as individuals and as a movement still have farther to go to arrive at the faith of the original Apostolics in the Bible. I join Tom in inviting our fellow Apostolics to go forward with us and join us in that quest for more truth and a better understanding of our faith. This book presents a great opportunity for people to launch reconsiderations. You may not agree with Tom's view on every point. However, you may very well find yourself agreeing on far more than you would have thought. Perhaps it will be with you as it was with one dear brother who once said to me "I am now understanding things that I have not understood in all of my years as a minister."

"He who shows me where I err is not my enemy, he is my friend!" If that adage is true, then Tom Raddatz should become the friend of many through this book. Tom invites his readers to introspection and reconsideration of great issues. But he does so only after having set the example of doing that himself. I can say by personal experience that reconsidering our cherished beliefs is a hard thing to do no matter what our religious backgrounds may be. Yet, doing so helps to clear the way for a sounder, more wonderful faith. We can have a faith that is more pleasing to God, more beneficial to ourselves and that makes more sense to the world we seek to reach.

Have the heart of a Berean and "examine the scriptures for yourself" as to whether the things that Tom Raddatz writes in this book are true (Acts 17:10, 11). I believe that carefully reading this book will benefit your grasp of the issues and of the scriptures. I also believe that there are great blessings attached to walking in more scriptural light as God shines it to us. There is greater soundness of faith for those who do. I pray that all who read this book will be so blessed!

J. Dan Gill, Editor in Chief
21st Century Reformation
www.21stcr.org

Which of the following views
do you suppose describes a greater God?

Before all creation,
God foresaw and so foreordained, out of billions,
a certain man, whom He claimed as His own Son,
who would overcome all sin,
and live pleasing to God like no other man ever would;
and so, things having come to pass just as He planned,
God glorified and exalted that particular man
above all others...

Or

A God who clothed himself in humanity,
and did what would have been impossible for him not to do,
and then glorified Himself for it!

This book, very simply, is about the profound difference
in these two views.

This book explains why I now believe,
as did the apostles, on the former,
The Great God and His Son, Jesus the Anointed.

-Tom Raddatz

TABLE OF CONTENTS

FOREWORD	5
INTRODUCTION	9
PREFACE	15
SECTION ONE	
Biblical Rules For Interpreting God's Word	23
CHAPTER ONE	
A Plea For Bible-Based Standards	25
CHAPTER TWO	
"It Is Written Again" Rather Than Jumping To Conclusions	33
CHAPTER THREE	
The Schoolmaster That Brings Us To Christ	55
CHAPTER FOUR	
Biblical Arithmetic: Don't Add To Or Take Away From God's Word	73
SECTION TWO	
Jewish Prophecies: The True Foundations Of Messiah	89
CHAPTER FIVE	
Seed Of Eve, Abraham, And David	93
CHAPTER SIX	
The Son Of David Is The Son Of God	101
CHAPTER SEVEN	
Son Of Man	109
CHAPTER EIGHT	
A Man Like Unto Moses And His Brothers	117
CHAPTER NINE	
The Messiah = The Anointed One	125
CHAPTER TEN	
Isaiah 9:6: His Name Shall Be Called	137

Section Three
Pagan And Antichristian/Gnostic Views In Contrast To The Way Of Christ — 157

Chapter Eleven
A Question Of Coincidence, Or Influence Of Pagan Views? — 159

Chapter Twelve
Made Of The Seed Of David Vs. Dual Natures — 201

Chapter Thirteen
"Alone" Or "Not Alone" Vs. Dual Natures — 259

Chapter Fourteen
A Man Approved Of God Vs. Gods Come Down In The Likeness Of Men — 269

Chapter Fifteen
A Man Approved Of God — The "Therefore... Because" Passages — 279

Chapter Sixteen
Foreknowledge Vs. Preexistence — 291

Section Four
The New Testament Presentation Of Jesus Christ — 311

Chapter Seventeen
The Overwhelming Majority Of Passages Distinguishing Jesus From God — 313

Chapter Eighteen
The Synoptic Gospels — 327

Chapter Nineteen
The Gospel Of John — 351

Chapter Twenty
The Acts Of The Apostles — 367

Chapter Twenty-One
The Epistles — 389

Chapter Twenty-Two
The Book Of Revelation — 437

Chapter Twenty-Three
The Root And The Offspring Of David — 447

Section Five
Refuting Oneness "Proof-Texts" — 453
Chapter Twenty-Four
Laying Out The Plan To Refute Oneness — 455
Chapter Twenty-Five
Matt. 4:10 Worship God Only: Part 1, Old Testament Schoolmaster — 467
Chapter Twenty-Six
Matt. 4:10 Worship God Only: Part 2, Behold, Your King — 479
Chapter Twenty-Seven
John 1:1,14 The Word Was With God And The Word Was God — 493
Chapter Twenty-Eight
John 8:24 Unless You Believe That I Am He — 515
Chapter Twenty-Nine
John 8:58 Before Abraham Was, I Am — 523
Chapter Thirty
John 20:28 Thomas Answered Him, "My Lord And My God!" — 537
Chapter Thirty-One
Colossians 2:9 For In Him All The Fullness Of The Godhead Dwells Bodily — 561
Chapter Thirty-Two
1 Timothy 3:16 God Was Manifest In The Flesh — 567
Chapter Thirty-Three
Conclusive Summary Of Onenessianism — 579

Appendices — 583
Appendix - I
We Are Not Arians Or Jehovah's Witnesses ("Preexisters") — 585
Appendix - II
We Are Pentecostal — 599
Appendix - III
We Believe God Is Spirit And Incorporeal — 615
Appendix - IV
Baptism Into Jesus' Name — 621

PREFACE

As the title says, I once was a strong Oneness advocate. For those who don't know, being "Oneness" is to believe that Jesus is an incarnation of God the Father in the flesh. I wasn't *just* an advocate. I used to consider myself somewhat of a champion of Oneness. Around 2004 I felt inspired to seek out the early history of the Trinity dogma, with the idea of defending Oneness against it. I certainly did uncover the origins of the Trinity and how it was adopted and adapted from both pagan philosophy and Gnosticism.

What I didn't expect to find was that the very ideas and methods that enabled the evolution to the Trinity involved the same philosophical reasoning that caused some trains of thought to evolve into *modalistic monarchianism* (the ancient term for *"Oneness,"* or simply *"modalism"* for short). In other words, I discovered that if I were going to reject the Trinity, then in all good conscience I would also have to reject Modalism on the same grounds. This was not at all what I expected to find in my research.

This book is written to explain, as thoroughly and simply as I can, what I discovered, and why I no longer call or consider myself "Oneness." I am still very much Pentecostal. I still very much appreciate my Oneness Pentecostal background and still love my Oneness brothers and sisters. I'm not writing to condemn, but to bring others closer to "the knowledge of the Son of God" (Ephesians 4:13). As a Oneness advocate, I had long understood that its heritage was the result of many movements (Protestantism, the holiness movement, Pentecostalism, and baptism in the name of Jesus) away from post-apostolic traditions of men, whose intent was to restore apostolic teachings. It is in this same attitude of restoration of the faith once delivered that has led me to the knowledge of the true Son of God doctrine.

The book that covers my findings on the evolution of the Trinity is titled *God is One and Christ is All: Biblical Truth Against the Trinity*. The inspiration for this current book was emerging in my thoughts even as I wrote the last one.

My main intention in writing this book is to help us all be direct disciples of Jesus on the topic: who is Christ. This simply means *really listening to and hearing what he says* about himself. What I discovered and would like to share with you is this: what Jesus clearly says he is, and what is clearly and straightforwardly written in the Bible, is typically something *different* than what is found in most *traditional* forms of Christianity, including both Trinitarianism and Modalism. It is simply a biblical fact that nowhere did anyone in the Bible go around openly and clearly preaching either "the Trinity doctrine" or the "Oneness" message. No one in the Bible went around proclaiming, "Jesus is the second person of the Trinity," any more than they went around saying, "Jesus is the Father incarnated." But they did clearly preach *something* in the Bible, and that is what our goal is here: to clarify the Christ they preached and described.

It is my conviction that a biblical teaching should carry the same name as it is called in the Bible. So I was happy to discover that believers of this biblical doctrine call it simply "the Son of God" doctrine. That is exactly what the Bible calls this idea it teaches, that Jesus Christ is the prophesied Son of God. For the sake of full-disclosure, the teaching that we call the "Son of God doctrine" is virtually the same Christology that is also known as "Biblical Unitarianism," but I am not fond of that title.

There is a secondary purpose here. Since I formerly believed in the "Oneness" view, this work is also a refutation of the Oneness *theory*. But make no mistake. Embracing the biblical Son of God is not an acceptance of the Trinity by any means; in fact, far from it. This book will show you just how similar Modalism is to the Trinity, rather than to the true and biblical Son of God!

So let me point out a few of the beliefs I haven't changed by embracing the biblical Son of God teaching. In common with Oneness folks, we "Son of God" believers know the Trinity is a jumped-to conclusion that isn't clearly stated anywhere in the Bible. Together with Oneness, we also know that *the Trinity has lost sight of the Jewish roots and foundational principles* of God and Christ. Therefore, and still right along with Oneness, we are convinced that *the Trinity is an adding to and taking away from biblical definitions*. To make matters even worse, the trinitarian position didn't just appear out of thin air into the minds of its theologians; rather, it is an adoption of pagan views regarding God, which have been imposed upon the teachings of the Bible and functionally replaces what the Bible does clearly teach about God. These are just some of the many contentions against the Trinity proving it is not a biblical teaching. Certainly, its proponents adamantly believe and claim that it is biblical, but in actuality it is only a *derived* doctrine. It is derived by interpreting the Bible through pagan ideas, words, and concepts that are not ever spelled out in the Bible. In fact, such adoption of pagan thought is strictly forbidden in the Bible. These things against the Trinity we hold as much as Oneness folks do.

Where we depart from the Oneness view, and what has caused a change of my own heart away from Onenessianism, is that all of these basic issues I've just stated the Trinitarians are guilty of also hold true against the Oneness position. Therefore, in this book I will also compare the Oneness *interpretational methods* with many of the *similar faulty ways used by Trinitarians*. It is my hope that when Oneness folks see the similarity in methods and sources they and Trinitarians use, then they, like I did, will realize that Oneness/Modalism is no more biblical than the Trinity is.

I personally came to see this view of Christ mainly by doing what I now hope and recommend everyone learns to do: simply listen to what Jesus actually says about himself. The two biggest passages for me were John 5 and 8, and then the Bible as a whole. That open-mindedness to the Scriptures was coupled with researching the historical development of the Trinity. What I discovered along the way were the actual, extrabiblical sources of the Oneness view, right alongside those of the Trinity. It isn't a big mystery: what happened in either case is simply what the Bible calls being spoiled by philosophy and the traditions of men.

Certainly at this point most Oneness readers will be quite put off at the idea of someone challenging their favorite doctrine about Christ. In fact, Oneness folks will likely respond similarly to how Trinitarians respond to the Oneness message. So let me be clear: I have the same motive as Oneness advocates do when they assert their position against, say, Trinitarians; namely, I am simply responding to a serious and solemn call that is found in the Scriptures:

> Beloved, while I was very eager to write to you about our common salvation, I was constrained to write to you exhorting you to <u>contend earnestly for the faith which was once for all delivered</u> to the saints. (Jude 3)

I have done my homework and spent many years in research, and I can tell you quite assuredly that neither the Trinity nor Modalism is actually the faith that was once delivered by the apostles, or Jesus, or John the Baptist, or any Jew before them. The Trinity doctrine began in the mid-second century, although it was far from the developed form it would come to be in the fourth century; and the Oneness doctrine wasn't invented until after that, just before the turn of the third century. We know, historically, exactly who first presented each of these dogmas, and it wasn't the apostles or Christ.

> [6]I marvel that ye are so soon removed from him that called you into the grace of Christ unto another gospel: [7]Which is not another; but there be some that trouble you, and would pervert the gospel of Christ. [8]But though we, or an angel from heaven, preach any other gospel unto you than that which we have preached unto you, let him be accursed. [9]As we said before, so say I now again, If any man preach any other gospel unto you than that ye have received, let him be accursed. (Galatians 1:6–9, KJV)

So, even during the apostle's times there were teachers trying to pervert the simplicity of the message of Christ. How much more so in these last, most perilous of days? Therefore, let us set aside our emotional responses and come together and reasonably ask, what saith the Scriptures? For the Scriptures are not at all unclear if we would just take heed to the Lord's admonition that "those who have ears to hear, let them hear."

Next I want to explain how this book is arranged. The first section will lay the foundations of some simple, yet incontestable biblical rules for interpreting God's word. The second section will seek to restore and reestablish the simple yet powerful and unshakable Jewish roots of the Messiah (Christ). The third section will present the three greatest stumbling blocks that have effectively blinded both Trinitarian and Oneness theologians to the simplicity of Christ. The fourth section will demonstrate how clearly the apostles of Christ in the New Testament (NT) set forth basic descriptions of Christ that are and were in complete harmony with the Old Testament (OT) views of the Messiah. Having laid the evidence precept upon precept, the book will conclude with the fifth section, which provides direct rebuttals to certain key Oneness "proof texts." In this way, our topic will have been thoroughly covered.

I will be using an apparently new word that I believe I may have coined for use in this book: "Onenessian." Whereas "Oneness" is the term for a doctrine, we will use the word "Onenessian" for the adherents of that doctrine. Thus, "Onenessians" will be addressed in the same way as "Trinitarians" are addressed. This is not in any way intended to be disrespectful; rather, it is intended to be more grammatically correct, as is the word "Trinitarian." This word is also easier than saying "modalistic monarchians" and is intended to be more in line with their self-identity as "Oneness" believers.

I hope and pray that our Oneness readers will allow themselves to receive this biblically stated truth with the same open heart as they hope and expect their Trinitarian neighbors would open their hearts to their message; that is, to search the Scriptures whether these things be so. Any open and honest questions on the subject are wholeheartedly welcome.

Because knowing the truth, our Lord says, can, will, and does set us free.

Tom Raddatz

~~~

Unless otherwise stated, all scriptural quotes are from the World English Bible version (WEB), which is available on the Internet and is in the public domain. Other versions cited or referenced include: ASV (American Standard Version), CJB (Complete Jewish Bible), ESV (English Standard Version), ITB (Interlinear Transliterated Bible, Biblesoft 2006), JPS (Tanakh: A New Translation of The Holy Scriptures According to the Traditional Hebrew Text, The Jewish Publication Society, Philadelphia, 1985.) KJV (King James Version), NASB (New American Standard Bible), NASU (New American Standard Updated), NASV (New American Standard Version), NCV (New Century Version), NET (New English Translation), NIV (New International Version), NKJV (New King James Version), NLT (New Living Translation), NRSV (New Revised Standard Version), NWB (Noah Webster's Bible), RSV (Revised Standard Version), and YLT (Young's Literal Translation).

Generally, all spelling, punctuation, and capitalization will be maintained as found in the original quotes but won't necessarily match standards used in the text of this book. However, highlighting herein may have been added to the original.

All links or references to other sources are meant to point to the subject at hand only and are not meant, nor should they be taken, as any type of overall endorsement of those groups, links, or people.

There is considerable controversy over the Tetragrammaton, which is usually transliterated for us as YHWH. Since the exact pronunciation of this name of God is unknown, I will simply reproduce this name everywhere in this book in its transliterated form of YHWH.

Following is a brief glossary to define the key terms of our discussion; namely, "Oneness" and "Trinity," and the differences between the two.

Oneness means: Jesus is the person of God the Father, who has revealed Himself in human form as Jesus Christ.

- Modalistic Monarchianism (or Modalism) is the most predominant form of "Oneness." This term means the belief that God reveals Himself through "modes" rather than "persons" (as in the Trinity). Typically, these types of believers will say God was "the Father in creation, the Son in redemption, and the Spirit in sanctification."

Trinity means: There is one God, who exists in three distinct persons.
There are many variations, of which the following are just a few:

- The predominant view is stated in the formulation: "one substance (*ousia*) in three persons (*hypostasis*)."
- Another view is called "Arianism," which asserts the belief there was a time when the Son was not. To this camp belong all the Trinitarians before Origen, who invented the idea of the eternal generation of the Son.
- There are contentions between major schools of thought whether the Holy Spirit proceeds from the Father only, or from the Father and the Son.

Incarnationist means: Trinitarians, Arians and/or Onenessians, who have adopted the pagan idea of God being incarnated as a human in Christ.

Arian means: a view of Jesus (whether Trinitarian or not) which claims that Jesus literally preexisted his human birth as some form of spiritual entity. The original Arians of the fourth century claimed Jesus was made of "like" substance of God, whereas the opposing Athanasian Trinitarians claimed he was made of the "same substance" as God.

This book argues that none of these views are the original apostolic or biblical view of Christ. While concentrating on correcting the Oneness error with the truth, this book also often touches on the Trinity to show comparisons of how the two positions are arrived at. Ultimately, there are only two types of biblical "interpretation," Jesus' method or the devil's method. By exposing the devil's method and relying on Jesus' method, this book contends that we can know the truth of the matter. The truth has been stated and settled in the Scriptures, and indeed, knowing the truth does set free!

SECTION ONE

BIBLICAL RULES FOR INTERPRETING GOD'S WORD

CHAPTER ONE

A Plea for Bible-Based Standards

Whose Jesus Do You Believe In?

Pagan Philosopher's savior?   OR   Gnostic Christ?   OR   Jesus that the Apostles preached

☐   ☐   ☑

> I fear, lest... our minds may be corrupted from the simplicity that is in Christ. For if he who comes preaches *another Jesus whom we have not preached*, or if you receive a different spirit which you have not received, or a different gospel which you have not accepted—you may well put up with it! (2 Corinthians 11:3–4; NKJV)

We read in the Bible that Jesus said to beware because many false prophets have gone out into the world. So how can we make sure that our view of Christ is true to the Bible? Well, in the above passage we have an answer: stick with the simplicity of the Christ that the apostles *preached*, and don't be inclined to a different one. It is safe to say that all false teachings about Christ ignore this simply stated commandment from the apostle Paul.

To understand this verse we first need to know what the apostle meant by the word "preached." The word "preach" simply means *to proclaim*, or *to publish*. That is, it is something that is *openly stated or said*. The opposite of proclaiming is, of course, to conceal, or to hide, or even to deny. The word *preached* means that Paul is simply telling us to cling to the same Jesus that he and the other disciples *clearly and openly proclaimed*; thus, *not to a view that would appear to be concealed, or hidden, or denied.*

We see, then, that this passage gives us a simple biblical rule for knowing who and what the real Jesus Christ is. That is, we need to read what the apostles openly proclaimed Jesus to be! This also shows us that if we listen, the Bible itself tells us how to, and how not to, understand it.

Most Christians unkowingly ignore this simple, biblical command, as will be shown in this study.

But first let's ask, *what* did the apostles preach?

Invariably, they preached that Jesus was, "a man approved by God," as they did, for example, in Acts 2:

> ²²Men of Israel, hear these words! Jesus of Nazareth, <u>a man approved by God</u> to you by mighty works and wonders and signs which God did by him... ³⁶...*God has made him both Lord [King] and Christ [the Anointed One], this Jesus* whom you crucified. (Acts 2:22–23, 36; see also Acts 3:13–26, 5:29–32, 7:37, 7:54–56, 13:16–41, etc.)

The reason we look to Acts for what the apostles preached is because the other books were letters to those who had already received and believed the things the apostles preached, thus they are letters of intruction, or teaching, not proclomations. In the Book of Acts the apostles *never once strayed from preaching Christ as a man* who was foreknown and anointed by God, and who was born of the offspring of David. In fact, this same Son of God doctrine (that Jesus is a man, born of the seed of David) is the only view of Christ that can make *all* these claims:

- It is the *only* view of Christ that the apostles invariably *preached (openly declared or proclaimed).*
- It is the *only* view of Christ that was *clearly and invariably confessed* without any ambiguity whatsoever.

- It is the *only* view of Christ that you can find *clearly and thoroughly taught* (expressed, explained, and expounded upon) in the entire Bible.
- It is the *only* view of Christ that *doesn't require any extra-biblical words* and phrases to adequately express.
- It is the *only* view that is *clearly prophesied* throughout the OT.
- It is the *only* view that is *clearly* expressed in *the first mention and the last mention of Christ* in the Bible (in addition to every other clear passage in between)!

All of the preceding list is on the positive side of the Son of God doctrine! On the negative side:

- All other Christologies are based on pagan categories of incarnations (i.e., Acts 14:11).
- All other Christologies owe some of their main teachings to the antichristian Gnostics.
- All other Christologies resort to interpreting the Bible the way the devil does!

Neither Trinitarians nor Onenessians can even come close to making any of these claims, let alone every one of them! At best, both of those doctrines are shrouded in mystery, as if the Bible was ashamed to come out and simply express the claims of these two opinions!

> For I am not ashamed of the Good News of Christ, for it is the power of God for salvation for everyone who believes... (Romans 1:16)

Why would the Bible be ashamed to clearly and openly preach, proclaim, prophesy, confess, and explain such a saving doctrine as these groups claim of their positions? It's simply because those ideas aren't taught in the Bible; they have to be read into the Bible!

Such is far from the case with the Son of God doctrine. Again, quite frankly, taking any other position than the Son of God doctrine that the apostles preached is to claim Paul lied in 2 Corinthians 11:3–4!

We are going to cover the apostle's preaching of Christ more fully in Chapter Twenty. In the meantime, readers are encouraged to look up the following verses and see for themselves in their own Bibles whether the claim we made above is true: Acts 2:22–23, 36; 3:13–26; 5:29–32; 7:37; 7:54–56; and 13:16–41. Moreover, throughout this book we're going to show you just how true this doctrine is and how false, mistaken, misguided and misleading all other views are!

Methods of Interpretation

When hearing about the Son of God doctrine, Onenessians commonly respond, "well, what about Scripture x," and they'll quote their favorite proof text.

So, it won't do simply to state that Modalism is wrong. One of the first things we need to do, therefore, is to show you how clearly and obviously *wrong and disobedient their method of interpretation is* to begin with. What they and Trinitarians resort to is called "proof-texting." This is when a verse or passage is used to "prove" a doctrine when there are no passages that simply state what it is they are really trying to say. This method always leads to false teachings.

Here is an example of this proof-texting approach: the thief on the cross ploy. Every good Oneness Pentecostal knows that the thief on the cross is not a good example around which to build one's salvation doctrine. Let's read the passage...

> [39]One of the criminals who was hanged... [42]...said to Jesus, "Lord, remember me when you come into your Kingdom." [43]Jesus said to him, "Assuredly I tell you, today you will be with me in Paradise." (Luke 23:39–43)

As Pentecostals, we all know how frustrating it is when doubters fall for the "what about the thief on the cross?" tactic. Most Onenessians know what I mean; the Bible is so very clear in Acts 2:38: "Repent, and be baptized every one of you in the name of Jesus Christ unto (Gr. eis = unto) the remission of sins, and you shall receive the gift of the Holy Spirit!" Peter's words couldn't be clearer. And if you're a Pentecostal worth your salt, you know all the Scriptures about obeying the gospel by dying out to your sins in repentance, being buried with Jesus in water baptism and rising again in new life by receiving the precious gift of the Holy Spirit as you are born again as evidenced by speaking in other tongues as the Spirit gives the utterance! What a glorious salvation, which we also share with Oneness Pentecostals!

And you try to show someone the Scriptures testifying to this glorious salvation plan and explain that they could experience the same for themselves, and yet no matter what Scriptures you show them, some people still can't get over the idea that nothing was said about that thief being baptized in order to be saved.

But do you know what makes the thief on the cross excuse a subterfuge? It's that what they believe it means *isn't anything that the Bible actually says*! Nowhere does the Bible say a person can be saved if they *don't* submit to water baptism in Jesus' name! No Scripture says a person receives the promise of the Holy Spirit quietly and uneventfully. Do you see that? What the Bible does say is, "Repent and *be baptized*." It also says *"baptism does also save us"* (1 Peter 3:21) and that it is effective "by the answer of a good conscience toward God." In fact, it says baptism saves us in the same way that building an ark saved Noah! Yet the Bible says that Noah was saved by faith! Why? Because we are told that Noah obeyed through faith! (That's why, as Oneness Pentecostals know, we are also told we are "buried with Christ by baptism" in Romans 6:3–4). More precisely, by faith Noah saved his house by building an ark by faith (Hebrews 11:7). Would Noah have saved his house if he'd replied, "Oh, I don't need to build an ark. God is powerful enough to save me by grace alone through faith *alone*." Yeah, that would have gotten Noah a long way! No! It would have proven just how *dis*obedient he was, rather than displayed his obedient faith.

Many people get the idea of "obedient faith" wrong because they aren't hearing the whole counsel of God. *They are "cherry-picking,"* which means they pick the passages they want to hear and downplay and ignore the ones that don't fit their preconceived opinion. For example, in response to the misguided "faith alone" dogma, there is only one verse in the whole Bible with the words "faith" and "alone" in the same breath. This one:

> Even so *faith*, if it hath not works, is *dead*, being *alone*. (James 2:17, KJV)

Faith alone is dead faith, so why do people build their whole salvation plan on dead faith? This is one clear verse that plainly contradicts the "by grace alone through faith alone" rejection of water baptism for remission of sins.

Furthermore, the fact is, we don't really know if the thief was or wasn't baptized! In fact, chances are better that he was baptized than that he wasn't. Why? Because of what the Scripture says:

> ⁴John came baptizing in the wilderness and preaching the baptism of repentance for forgiveness of sins. ⁵*All the country of Judea and all those of Jerusalem went out to him. They were baptized* by him in the Jordan river, confessing their sins. (Mark 1:4–5)

If all were baptized, who's to say the thief was not baptized? Not only is it written that all the country of Judea and all those of Jerusalem were baptized, but we are also told what the state was of those who refused to be baptized:

> ²⁹When all the people and the tax collectors heard this, *they declared God to be just, having been baptized* with John's baptism. ³⁰*But the Pharisees and the lawyers rejected the counsel of God, not being baptized* by him themselves. (Luke 7:29–30)

The Pharisees and lawyers rejected the counsel of God by not being baptized. So then, even though they were on the other side of the cross, and thus under the Old Covenant, they could still be held ac-

SECTION ONE - RULES FOR INTERPRETING

countable for not submitting to God's latest command through His prophet John the Baptist!

By their mutual rejection of the necessity of water baptism, even for those "under the law," we see that those who use the thief on the cross as an excuse for not accepting the necessity of baptism for repentance *have more in common with the Pharisees than they do with the actual, true believers*! The believers, who did submit to baptism, declared, by that action, that God was just!

So, what we are seeing is that the "thief on the cross" ploy is just an excuse people use to keep from submitting to what God's word commands! Even though it is supposedly based on *building a doctrine from what the Bible implies, it is not founded on what the Bible clearly says; in fact, it actually opposes what the Bible does explicitly say! And that is exactly how the doctrines of both Trinity and Modalism were developed: by using the same method of interpretation* as those who use the "thief on the cross" ploy. In all three of these cases, *their doctrine isn't based on what the Bible clearly and explicitly says and explains*, but what they see implied and then presume it must mean, which then contradicts what is written somewhere else in the Bible.

This is why it is such a big deal that *only* the Son of God doctrine was openly proclaimed in the Bible, consistently confessed, and clearly spelled out and explained throughout the Bible, and it doesn't need any extrabiblical or nonbiblical terms or phrases to describe it!

Our challenge in convincing Onenessians is that they are trained and conditioned to respond to challenges to their man-made interpretation! In fact, they often respond in the same way that Trinitarians respond to challenges to the Trinity. And it's the same way the "faith only" groups respond with their pet Scriptures. Yet proof-texting as an interpretive method *goes against the biblical rules telling us how to properly interpret the word of God*. Yes, there is a right and a wrong way to interpret the Bible. And both are spelled out in the Bible. In fact, once you learn these rules, it doesn't matter what teaching you come up against; these same tools will allow you to biblically discern how any doctrine is formulated and whether it is truly biblical or not.

So our next point of business is to clarify this pivotal issue: how to rightly interpret the Bible, using biblical rules of interpretation that no one will be able to honestly refute!

CHAPTER TWO

"It is Written Again" Rather Than Jumping to Conclusions

> **Which type of interpretation method do you choose**
>
> The Devil's Method ☐ Provides False Doctrine
>
> Jesus' Method ☑ Says the Truth

> ¹...Jesus was led up by the Spirit into the wilderness to be tempted by the devil... ⁴ But he [Jesus] answered, *"It is written..."* ⁷ Jesus said to him, *"Again, it is written..."* ¹⁰ ...Jesus said to him, "Get behind me, Satan! For *it is written..."* (Matthew 4:1–10)

Did you notice that when Jesus was tempted by the devil's false interpretations of God's word, his response each of the three times was the same: *it is written*? Each time, Jesus was able to quote Scripture that clearly exposed the error of the devil's tempting interpretation. He didn't resort to deep explanations (*exegesis*) of the passage the devil quoted, or proof-texting (which is what the devil was doing); instead Jesus relied on what was actually and clearly stated. And when the devil tried quoting Scripture and basing an idea on it, Jesus responded by saying "it is written again" and supplied a verse that was clearer and more to the point than the devil's proof text.

In this way, based on his example, Jesus provides us with a biblical rule of interpretation:

> **Rule #1**: Don't jump to conclusions to define doctrine; instead, quote "it is written again" Scriptures, just as Jesus taught us by example.

Applying this rule is like learning to read, because this is where you learn to "read" or "discern" between true and false teachings. This rule supports the truth that the Scriptures thoroughly provide us with every good and true teaching.

> [16]Every writing inspired by God is profitable for teaching, for reproof, for correction, and for instruction which is in righteousness, [17]that the man of God may be complete, thoroughly equipped for every good work. (2 Timothy 3:16–17)

This rule teaches us that *all necessary Christian teachings are clearly written in the Scriptures*. These include doctrines such as Jesus Christ's virgin conception (Matthew 1:18–20); his death, burial, and resurrection (1 Corinthians 15:1–4); salvation by grace through faith (Ephesians 2:8); and many, in fact all, others. These teachings are *not hidden* in dark sentences or mysterious language that requires a "secret decoder ring" to decipher. They are simply and straightforwardly stated in the Scriptures.

On the other hand, *without exception*, all false teachings that are claimed to be *based on* Scriptures have at least this one thing in common: *they all jump to conclusions, just as the devil displayed in tempting Jesus*. That is to say, all false teachings are arrived at by some form of "interpreting" or "reasoning" other than simply quoting a Scripture that clearly states the teaching.

Keep in mind that no one is immune to falling for jumped-to conclusions. This is one of many temptations common to humanity (1 Corinthians 10:13). It is so common, in fact, that Jesus himself was tempted by and had to overcome it, as we've seen above! In Matthew 4:5–7, the devil quoted Psalm 91 to Jesus and actually tempted Jesus to jump from a pinnacle to show he was truly the Son of God. Because, the devil concluded, "it is written, 'He will give his angels charge concerning you... so that you don't dash your foot against a stone.'" How did Jesus respond? He answered by quoting Deuteronomy 6:16: "it is written again, 'you shall not test [or tempt] the Lord, your God.'"

Notice how the following graphic shows what the devil tried to do at the temptation of Christ:

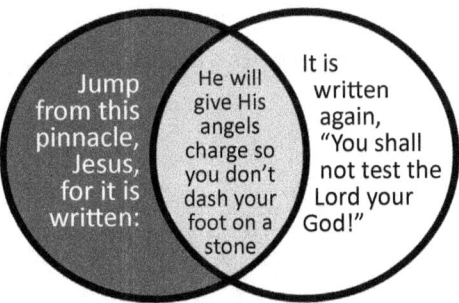

By quoting Scripture, the devil attempted to make his jumped-to conclusion appear completely within the contextual circle of God's written word. We could say he tried to create a "theological optical illusion." Thus, the circle on the left partially overlaps (in the gray area) the right circle. We could effectively call the Scripture in the gray area "the devil's playground." As Christians, we need not and must not be so naïve as to think such gray areas don't exist in the Scriptures. Accordingly, the Scripture exhorts us to study the Scriptures and to rightly discern them (2 Timothy 2:15).

"Gray area" Scriptures are any passage(s) that someone feels *need* to be *"explained in other words,"* when in fact those "other words" aren't found in the Bible in a way that clearly states the point the interpreter wants to make. (The key word is "need," not merely "can be.") The fact that their teaching or doctrine *needs* to be explained or rephrased makes it a gray area. This example of the devil's interpretation of Psalm 91 is the archetype for using a gray-area Scripture in a wrong way.

Let's look closer at the devil's gray-area Scripture. The Bible does promise protection, but it doesn't say that we can take that promise of protection and purposely use it to prove our faith in God and/or God's stamp of approval on our personal faith. That is why Jesus cited the commandment from Deuteronomy 6:16 not to tempt God, because it directly addresses the idea the devil proposed, which at best was only implied in the Psalm the devil quoted.

This is the critical part to understand: *Jesus' qualifying Scripture protected the gray-area passage within the right-hand circle, which is to say, strictly within a biblical interpretation.* At the same time, Jesus showed that the devil's interpretation sat clearly outside the circle of biblical truth. Here, displayed graphically, is what Jesus did:

The devil did the opposite of Jesus. He imposed his jumped-to, rephrased, redefined conclusion, which effectively negated the Scripture on the right. The Bible speaks precisely against this type of interpretation when it says "no prophesy of Scripture is of any private interpretation" (2 Peter 1:20).

The Bible also says that "the mind of the flesh is hostile towards God; for *it is not subject to God's law*, neither indeed can be" (Romans 8:7). The devil's temptation is the kind of action this verse refers to. It isn't that the devil didn't acknowledge God's word. It is that he found a way to wiggle out of being subject to God's complete word. What Jesus recognized was that the devil was trying to pit God's word against God's law. Since Jesus was subject to *all* of God's law, he wasn't willing to compromise one aspect in order to keep an exaggerated conclusion based on another aspect. There is a huge difference between what is actually stated in God's word versus what is added to it to make it appear to say something it never really states. This is the common error of both Trinitarianism and Onenessianism and all other "isms."

This is how people can seem to be in line with Scripture while they are actually being disobedient!

Here is what these circles are teaching us:

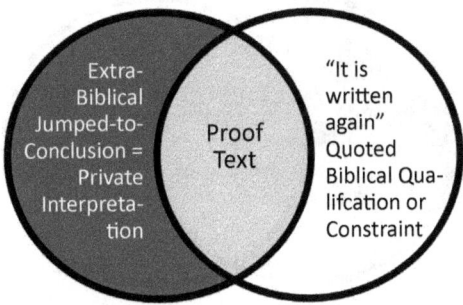

Notice that, while the center gray area could go either way, the far left conclusion and the far right Scripture cannot both be true. They are mutually exclusive. This shows how God's word really only teaches one truth, though other ideas are often "based on" Scripture without actually being "scriptural." *What makes the complete circle on the left wrong, and therefore evil, is that the conclusion stated on the far left negates certain explicit Scriptures that can be quoted in direct and clear opposition to that far-left opinion.* Only the whole right circle is truly *interpreting Scripture with Scripture* by encompassing "every word of God" (Matthew 4:4). Jesus was determined to be led, and *constrained* by, all the Scriptures. To the contrary, the devil and his followers are *not restrained by*, nor do they submit to, God's commandments; they merely give lip service to them like the devil did! *This is the difference between true and false Christian attitudes toward the Scriptures.*

> For this is the love of God, that we keep his commandments. His commandments are not grievous. (1 John 5:3)

And that is the takeaway lesson in our "Rule #1": those who are obedient *to every word of God* will not, knowingly, *disobey or diminish one passage or type of Scripture in order to keep a jumped-to conclusion of another*. For that is exactly the way the devil, the epitome of evil and wrong thinking, interprets God's words as given to us in the Bible.

Trinitarianism and the Circles of Discernment

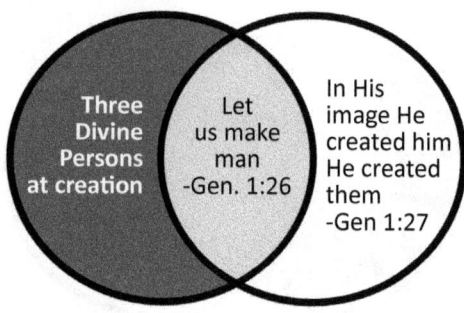

Look at how these circles of discernment reveal the Trinitarian interpretation of Genesis 1:26–27:

> ²⁶God said, "Let *us make* man in our image, after our likeness..." ²⁷God *created* man in *his* own image. In God's image *he created* him; male and female *he created* them. (Genesis 1:26–27)

Trinitarians claim the "let us make man" phrase indicates their proof that God is a Trinity of three persons. Note in the graphic the Trinitarian conclusion on the left and the biblical qualification on the right.

In opposition to the Trinity, nowhere in the Bible will you find where it explains that three deific persons were involved in Creation. The word for "to make" (v. 26) means something different than "to create" (v. 27). To the contrary of the Trinitarian conclusion, many passages, particularly in Isaiah, clearly explain that God was *alone* and *by Himself* when He created the heavens and earth. Using Jesus' words, these verses are our "it is written again" defense against the Trinitarian interpretation of Genesis 1:26. See for example Isaiah 41:20; 42:5; 43:1–3, 15; 45:6–9, 18. In particular, notice Isaiah 44:24:

> Thus saith the Lord, thy redeemer, and he that formed thee from the womb, I am the Lord that maketh all things; that stretcheth forth the heavens *alone*; that spreadeth abroad the earth *by myself*. (Isaiah 44:24 KJV)

So God says He was alone and by Himself when He created the earth. This is the opposite of a Trinity of persons. Trinitarians ignore the qualifying verses and assume that the "us" in Genesis 1:26 could mean three persons; and once they've latched onto the *possibility*, from then on it becomes the only interpretation acceptable to them. In this way, Trinitarians follow the devil's method of interpreting the Bible rather than Jesus' method.

Now it isn't as if Trinitarians ignore such passages as Isaiah; they simply take them as challenges that need to be reinterpreted to fit their preconception. And so, they conclude that such passages are talking about their view of One God in entirety (i.e., as in their formulation "one substance in three persons"), or some such thing. The main point is that they don't use such Scriptures the way Jesus did, by allowing such verses to qualify their "proof texts." The problem is that, at best, their proof texts only imply their conclusion.

On the other hand, it isn't extrabiblical on our part to say that God is personally one because *Jesus himself approved and authorized the Jewish understanding of the "what" of God.* He said, "You worship what you do not know; *We know what we worship, for salvation is of the Jews*" (John 4:22). The "what" emphatically known by Jews includes their understanding and knowledge of the truth that God is utterly one in personality! This is an irrefutable fact of history. Thus, the truth that God is *personally* one is part of God's first commandment *as interpreted for us by Jesus in Mark 12:29*: "The first of all commandments is, Hear O Israel; the Lord our God is one Lord: And you shall love the Lord your God with all your heart... this is the first commandment." Nevertheless, Trinitarians take their liberty to redefine the "what" of God based on jumped-to conclusions, seemingly *in spite of what Jesus says*! The Bible says not listening to Jesus is a really bad idea:

> For Moses indeed said to the fathers, "The Lord God will raise up a prophet for you from among your brothers, like me. You shall *listen to him in all things* whatever he says to you. It will be, that *every soul that will not listen to that prophet will be utterly destroyed* from among the people." (Acts 3:22–23)

Clearly, to be utterly destroyed is the opposite of Jesus' promise of eternal life though the salvation he offers. Yet Trinitarians, since the days of Justin Martyr, Tertullian, and even earlier, have refused to listen to the truth of Jesus' proclamation in John 4:22. Instead, they "deduce" that there are multiple persons in the godhead. But they didn't come up with the idea of "persons" out of the blue! They found that form of explanation in worldly philosophy. Here's how one scholar puts it:

> When Justin mentions that Christians believe in *the Triad*... he refers directly to the discussion among his contemporary Middle Platonists... There is a complete correlation between the two systems, that of Justin and that of Numenius (Table 1)...[1]

This scholar explains that the Trinitarians derived their view of God from pagan ideas that were already floating around, and not directly from the Bible or the apostles. This is simply an irrefutable historic fact that even reputable Trinitarian historians admit. But we don't need to rely only on current or latter day scholars. The early Trinitarians themselves also confessed this to be the case.

One such early Trinitarian was the theologian Gregory of Nyssa. Writing in his *Great Catechism*, he admitted and revealed the source of the concept and word of "persons" in the godhead. He said, "let... stand... *of the Hellenistic, only the distinction as to persons*..." Following is the passage where Gregory made this statement.

> But since our system of religion [wants] to *observe a distinction of persons* in the unity of the Nature... there is need...

---

[1] Marian Hillar, accessed 6/7/2015, at http://www.socinian.org/files/Numenius_GreekSources.pdf.

of a distinct technical statement in order to correct all error on this point... The mystery... is *separate as to personality yet is not divided as to subject matter.* For, *in personality, the Spirit is one thing and the Word another,* and yet again that from which the Word and Spirit is [i.e., the Father is], another [person]. But when you have gained the conception of what the [personal] distinction is in these, the oneness, again, of the nature admits not division, so that the supremacy of the one [pagan philosophic] First Cause[7] is not split and cut up into differing Godships, *neither does the statement harmonize with the Jewish dogma, but the truth passes in the mean between these two* [pagan and Jewish] conceptions, *destroying each heresy*, and yet accepting what is useful to it from each. *The Jewish dogma is destroyed* by the acceptance of the Word, and by the belief in the Spirit; *while the polytheistic error of the Greek school is made to vanish by the unity of the Nature...* While yet again, of the Jewish conception, let the unity of the Nature stand; and *of the [pagan/Greek] Hellenistic, only the distinction as to persons...* For it is as if the number of the [Trinity] were a remedy in the case of those who are in error as to the One, and the assertion of the unity for those whose beliefs are dispersed among a number of divinities.[2]

The word "Hellenistic" refers to Greek pagan thought—that is where Trinitarians got the concept of distinct persons in the godhead. He said this while claiming to have destroyed the Jewish understanding of God (which Jesus himself had upheld)! This is just the tip of the iceberg of reasons why the Trinity is simply unacceptable to those who truly value biblical teaching.

---

[2] Gregory of Nyssa, *The Great Catechism*, 1, 3, accessed 6/11/2015, at http://www.ccel.org/ccel/schaff/npnf205.xi.ii.v.html.

Onenessianism and Biblical Interpretation

**Dear Oneness Advocate:
Is your heart right toward the scriptures?**

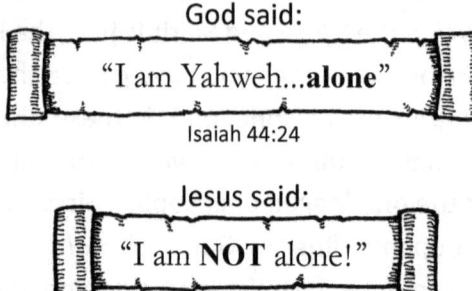

You want Trinitarians to listen to Isaiah, so
why won't you hear Jesus?

When we compare the method of interpretation used by Trinitarians with the method used by Onenessians, we find a match in methodology but not in their distinct conclusion.

Onenessians are quite correct in criticizing Trinitarians for jumping to conclusions in claiming that the "us" in Genesis means persons "in the godhead," when the Bible is so clear that God was alone in creation. Onenessians like to congratulate themselves for not falling for this Trinitarian adoption of pagan thought, while ignoring that they do the same thing!

The purpose here isn't to refute Trinitarianism as much as it is to show that Onenessians use the same false methods as Trinitarians do to reach their conclusions. The question is, if it can be shown that Onenessians are just as susceptible to jumping to conclusions against Jesus' words as the Trinitarians are, would you be willing to listen? Because it is just as important to teach the truth to Onenessians as to Trinitarians, and the same goes for us when we are in error.

How do you respond when your beliefs are challenged? Scripture demonstrates the range of possible reactions religious people have when confronted with truths that challenge what they believe: willingness, indifference, or indignation.

SECTION ONE - RULES FOR INTERPRETING

Willingness:	¹¹"Now these were more noble than those in Thessalonica, in that they received the word with all readiness of the mind, examining the Scriptures daily to see whether these things were so. ¹² Many of them therefore believed." (Acts 17:11–12) "Now when they heard this, they were cut to the heart, and said to Peter and the rest of the apostles, 'Brothers, what shall we do?'" (Acts 2:37)
Indifference:	"Then Agrippa said to Paul, 'You almost persuade me to become a Christian.'" (Acts 26:28, NKJV)
Indignation:	³³"They answered him, 'We are Abraham's seed, and have never been in bondage to anyone. How do you say, 'You will be made free?'... ⁴⁸Then the Jews answered him, 'Don't we say well that you are a Samaritan, and have a demon?'" (John 8:33, 48) "Now when they heard these things, they were cut to the heart, and they gnashed at him with their teeth." (Acts 7:54)

When Onenessians attempt to approach Trinitarians with their errors, the intention is not to condemn; it is to bring them into a more perfect understanding of Christ. Sometimes the Trinitarians are willing to test the words, and if they are noble like the Bereans in Acts 17, will study and find the Trinity is not in their Bibles. Others are completely indifferent, adopting the attitude of "you have your beliefs, and we have ours; let's just agree to disagree." And then there are the ones who instantly become indignant and defensive because their beliefs are being challenged for whatever reason.

Onenessians, in turn, respond in the same ways. It will be up to the reader to choose how he or she will respond. Only one way is actually biblically commanded and acceptable:

> Beloved, don't believe every spirit, <u>but test the spirits</u>, whether they are of God, because many false prophets have gone out into the world. (1 John 4:1)

This verse is a double-edged sword. Most people who believe they are already right with God tend to react like the believing Jews did in John 8:31–48 above. They initially become defensive and do not see that they are being approached with something legitimate. There is a psychological term for this kind of reaction: *confirmation bias*. Confirmation bias is the natural tendency to search for or interpret information in a way that confirms our preconceived ideas. This is not the reaction of a truth seeker, nor is it considered in a positive light in the scriptures. It is a natural tendency and not a spiritual one.

Instead, the noble reaction is to study whether those things are so, because you never know when your teaching is the one that God has sent someone to correct. Onenessians should recognize this since they are the product of a long line of restorations of apostolic teachings. First Luther caused a separation from the traditions of Roman Catholicism based on a renewed focus on grace; then the holiness movement emerged; later the Topeka, Kansas, Pentecostal movement; and then came the revelation of baptism in Jesus' name. God's restoration to the "faith once delivered" has not been a simple one-step process. Every move away from the traditions of men was met with resistance from those who had once accepted a previous move. And again, some moves weren't true moves of restoration. The point is, even false moves aren't effectively challenged by resorting to "gnashing" at people with their teeth, which is likely symbolic of an ad hominem type of attack where, instead of soundly addressing the issues, the character of the person is attacked.

What kind of response will you have, dear reader? Will you be inclined to nobly search the Scriptures whether these things be so? Or scoff at them as not worth your attention? Or instantly become defensive and indignant because someone has dared challenge your position?

With these questions in mind, let's examine the Oneness position for its jumped-to conclusions.

In his book, The Oneness of God, David Bernard jumps to a classic Oneness conclusion:

> Once, when Jesus was talking about the Father, the Pharisees asked, "Where is thy Father?" Jesus answered, "Ye neither know me, nor my Father: if ye had known me, ye should have known my Father also" (John 8:19)... *In other words, Jesus tried to tell them that He was the Father and the I AM*, and that *if they did not accept Him as God they would die in their sins*...[3]

Was Jesus "*trying* to tell them" he was the Father, as Bernard claims? Did Jesus actually say that, or does it require or need someone like Bernard to explain it that way to make it appear that's what Jesus said? The answer is that Jesus certainly did *not* say *"I am YHWH-God incarnate in the flesh,"* or Bernard wouldn't have had to say, "he *tried* to tell them that..."

Following are some of the words Jesus did say. Let's ask ourselves whether these support the idea that Jesus was "*trying* to say" he was the Father. Or, to the contrary, did he *explicitly* say he was personally distinct from the Father?

> ¹⁷It's also written in your law that the testimony of *two people is valid.* ¹⁸*I am one who* testifies about myself, *and the Father who* sent me testifies about me. (John 8:17–18)

Here in Jesus' *explicit* context of *two persons*—that is to say, *two individual* personalities—Jesus states that he is "one who" and in contrast to him is "the Father who," thus clearly indicating *two* "whos." So *according to Jesus, explicitly*, he and the Father are two "whos" *in the exact same manner in which two different and separate people* are two "whos" that are required as valid testimony. How much clearer would Jesus need to be for us to accept that he was teaching himself as a second or distinct personality from His Father?

---

[3] David K. Bernard, *The Oneness of God* (Word Aflame Press: Hazelwood, MO, 1983), 67.

Note that this is exactly the same conversation that immediately preceded the Jews' question and Jesus' reply, saying "Ye neither know me, nor my Father: if ye had known me, ye should have known my Father also." In other words, just exactly as Trinitarians ignore the context and wording of Genesis 1:27 to maintain their view of Genesis 1:26, so the *Onenessians ignore the context and actual wording of John 8:17–18 in order to uphold their theory* of what John 8:19 means.

Let's look at two additional verses where Jesus explains himself. Notice what Jesus says:

> Even if I do judge, my judgment is true, for *I am not alone*, but I am with the Father *who* sent me. (John 8:16)

> You will leave me alone. Yet *I am not alone*, because the Father is with me. (John 16:32)

These important verses speak clearly against the Onenessian view. How so? Onenessians argue against Trinitarians for ignoring the OT Scriptures that say *God is alone*, yet they are somehow unable to accept that Jesus clearly and often reiterates that he is "*not alone*" in the NT! This means that the Oneness argument *against* the Trinity in the OT is one of the biggest arguments *against* the Oneness view in the NT! Quite simply, in the OT, God *was* alone; in the NT, Jesus *is not* alone.

We could (and will) add many additional verses as evidence that Jesus is personally distinct from the Father. There are fifteen just in John 5 and thirteen just in John 8, which is already many more verses than can be found in Isaiah about God being alone.

Of course, *Onenessians don't and won't openly admit they "reject" the truth that Jesus is "not alone,"* any more than Trinitarians would openly admit they believe in three gods or that their position negates the Scriptures where God says he is one and alone. Rather, what they both do is simply reinterpret and redefine what those words and phrases mean until they can make them acceptable to their belief systems.

Trinitarians reinterpret "one God" to mean one in substance or essence rather than one in personality. Onenessians, on the other hand, by using some form of the unbiblical "two natures" doctrine, reinterpret the "not alone" and "two who" Scriptures to mean *modes or manifestations* of the one person of God rather than the plural personalities these passages clearly describe. Again, the problem is that neither of these two viewpoints is clearly described or explained *anywhere* in the Scriptures. Each is thus equally unbiblical in jumping to conclusions as the other is.

God Speaking	Jesus Speaking
"I am YHWH...*alone*" Isaiah 44:24	"I am **NOT alone**" John 8:16, 16:32
Trinitarians don't believe Him!	Onenessians don't believe him!
Same display of **DISBELIEF** in different manifestations	

These last two Scriptures are among Jesus' "I am" statements. Onenessians claim to love the "I am" statements of Jesus, except, apparently, ones like these two. These two are very descriptive and to the point. Just how clear was Jesus? What if Jesus were to say something like, "Most assuredly, I tell you, the Son *can do nothing of himself...*" (John 5:19), or something like, "*I can of myself do nothing*" (John 5:30)? Why can't Onenessians allow these self-descriptions of Jesus to be just as important as any other? Answer: if they did, like I have, they would no longer accept a Oneness interpretation.

The simple truth is, Jesus saying "*I can do nothing of myself*" and God saying, "*I am that I am*" are ways of stating *two mutually exclusive sets of personal abilities*. The former describes Jesus' *personal* utter helplessness, whereas the other denotes God's *absolute, utterly unlimited, personal, self-reliant power*. So where did Jesus get his power and authority if not from "himself"? In speaking of his "self" as being incapable of doing anything, was he, "trying to say" he was *self*-reliant? No, rather he was just as clear about that as anything else for anyone really willing to hear him. He said, "All authority <u>has been given</u> to me in heaven and on earth" (Matthew 28:18). *This is also saying the exact polar opposite of what God meant when He said, "I am that I am"* (Exodus 3:14). Being "given" authority is another opposite from being absolutely self-reliant. That's because "given" authority by definition means it is a *derived* authority and thus an authority not originating within one's self. In this way we can see that *what is actually "spelled out" and clearly explained by Jesus himself differs considerably to what is imposed by jumping to Onenessian conclusions.* Now we can begin to see that what Jesus actually did say, in many places, is as opposite to Onenessianism as the Trinity is to Jewish monotheism.

We also need to ask *why* Jesus would *"try* to say" one thing when he was clearly and actually saying the exact opposite in the same discussion? Was Jesus, who is described as the word of God made flesh, not able to say what he really meant? Was Jesus, who is also called the Truth, telling lies to teach truth? For example, why would someone say, "I work busing tables," if he *were trying to say*, "I am the president of the USA"? What Jesus did say was actually even more opposite than this because these are both jobs that are done by humans! So again, by saying he "can do nothing of himself," he *absolutely and clearly stated the exact opposite of what it means to say, "I am that I am."* So he certainly did not say, nor was he even trying to say, that he was "I am that I am," because he had already clearly denied that he could do anything at all *of himself*.

So who is telling the truth here, Jesus when he said he could do nothing of himself, or the Onenessians when they say he "tried to tell them that He was the Father and the I AM" *even though he had already told them he could do nothing of himself?* We have chosen to reject handling the word of God deceitfully in that way and have chosen instead to believe Jesus and the whole word of God.

Onenessianism and the Circles of Discernment

Here is the Oneness position as viewed in our circles of discernment:

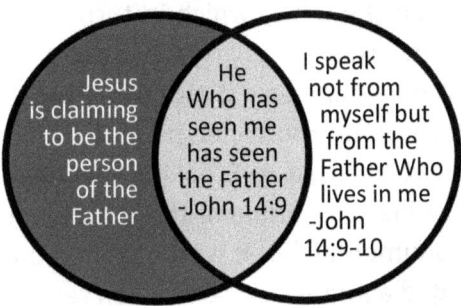

Again, in no way did Jesus simply say, "I am the person of the Father incarnate." Rather, in saying he did *not* speak from his "self," and then saying the Father was a different "who," Jesus was explaining himself with very clear and *meaning*ful terms. In this way *he actually clearly ruled out the Oneness jumped-to conclusion* that there is only one personal "self" in Christ. Onenessians simply refuse to hear him.

Certainly, we are *not* denying that God the Father dwelled in Jesus to a unique degree. What we are saying is that no Scripture teaches that "indwelling" equals or means "sameness of personality." In fact, *indwelling* means precisely the opposite. By searching the Scriptures we learn that all true Christians are also indwelled by God's Spirit (e.g., Romans 8:11; 2 Corinthians 6:16; Ephesians 3:17), but that doesn't make us the same personal "self" as the Spirit that is *dwelling* in us. In fact, it quite purposely means the exact opposite, that we are not to think we are the God who dwells in us. The truth is that Jesus was indwelt by God more completely than we are, but that is a matter of degree; it was still an indwelling, and being an indwelling it specifically did not mean *identification*. (We will cover indwelling again and quote these verses in Chapter Thirteen).

On the other hand, what the Oneness doctrine is implying is that *indwelling* means he is an *incarnation* of God the Father. The problem is that *indwelling* means something completely different. This Oneness interpretation (that *indwelling,* as it relates to Christ, really means *incarnation*) is yet another man-made tradition that is never, ever clearly spelled out in Scripture. Instead, the Oneness position is imposed on the text of the Bible *in the same exact way as the Trinitarians impose their extrabiblical and innovative description of their god* on the Bible, which in turn is the same way the devil tried to tempt Jesus.

Now that last paragraph said a mouthful, but it also brings this first rule of interpretation into perspective. Let me demonstrate just how important this rule is. Breaking this rule is actually what enabled the very first sin, bringing the whole world into sin and death. This is monumental, but it is true! When the serpent tempted Eve, he provided a jumped-to conclusion regarding God's word:

> [3]He said to the woman, "Has God really said, 'You shall not eat of any tree of the garden?'"... [4]The serpent said to the woman, "You won't surely die, [5]for God knows that in the day you eat it, your eyes will be opened, and you will be like God, knowing good and evil." (Genesis 3:1–5)

That was how the serpent tempted Eve—by jumping to the conclusion and proposing the idea that God "meant" (or as some would put it, God supposedly "was trying to say" but didn't say) that her eyes would be opened and she would become more like God by knowing good and evil.

Let's look at what Jesus had to say about the devil's jumping to conclusions (presumably in the Garden):

> [42]Therefore Jesus said to them... [44]... "You are of your father, the devil, and you want to do the desires of your father. *He was a murderer from the beginning*, and doesn't stand in the truth, because *there is no truth in him*. When *he speaks a lie*, he speaks on his own; *for he is a liar, and the father of it*. [45]But because I tell the truth, you don't believe me. [46]Which of you convicts me of sin? If I tell the truth, why do you not believe me? [47]He who is of God hears the words of God. For this cause *you don't hear, because you are not of God*." (John 8:42–47)

Most Christians understand clearly that lying and committing murder are sins, but in this passage Jesus directly links both of those sins to the original lie of the devil in the Garden of Eden. Thus, *according to Jesus,* it is murderously devil-like to interpret God's word the way Satan does. The serpent's lie caused death to pass upon all mankind, so Jesus was right to call him a murderer. Likewise, false doctrines negate the true teachings that lead to salvation—through the man God ordained to lead us unto eternal life—thus turning words that were meant for life into words of death.

We can describe what Satan did in the Garden in many ways. We can say he put words in God's mouth, as if God had meant something God never said. He made God out to be unclear—as if God tried to say one thing and really meant another—and thus made it appear that people need a religious expert (theologian) to interpret God for them. He implied that the way to interpret God is to lean on your own understanding, which the Bible denounces. He implied that God's word was hopelessly difficult to interpret correctly, and on and on we could go.

Most important, though, is Jesus' position toward the devil's defiance. In fact, we could say Jesus was calling what the devil did in the Garden the granddaddy of all evil, because *that lie* was what enabled all sin, including murder. In this light, when we think of how evil it is to lie, steal, or murder, we should think the same thing of the devil's method of interpreting God's word. It is a sin to use that method, and whoever does so has become a servant of sin and not of God (Romans 6:16). Oneness folks have no problem pointing out to Trinitarians that their teaching breaks the first commandment of God and is thus idolatry. But are Onenessians willing to examine whether or not their own method of interpreting the Bible follows the devil's example rather than Christ's?

In the final analysis, *those who follow the devil's technique* of jumping to conclusions are not doing themselves or their followers any favors. We as Christians need to be able to discern what teachings are derived by following Jesus' way, and which are derived by following the opposite way. The Bible gives us this dire warning:

> [13]For such men are false apostles, deceitful workers, masquerading as Christ's apostles. [14]And no wonder, for even Satan masquerades as an angel of light. [15]It is no great thing therefore if his ministers also masquerade as servants of righteousness, whose end will be according to their works. (2 Corinthians 11:13–15)

Those aren't my words; those are Scriptures. And don't Onenessians use this same verse in contending against the errors of Trinitarianism and other false teachings? So should Onenessianism be held to a double set of standards? Is Onenessianism so fragile as to be afraid that close scrutiny will wreck it? Doesn't truth fear no questions? If so, then let's ask the hard questions of Onessianism and see whether or not it was developed in a biblical manner or after the devil's way of interpretation.

While the purpose in this chapter is to introduce the proper rules of interpretation, hopefully you see how this first rule has exposed the error of using John 8:19 as a proof text for Onenessianism. The Oneness interpretation is not considering Jesus' words in a truly "it is written again" manner. The Oneness position jumps to a conclusion over this passage in the same way as their arch-rivals the Trinitarians do with Genesis 1:26.

Now look what remains if we move the jumped-to conclusions of Trinitarianism and Onenessianism away from their respective biblical interpretations.

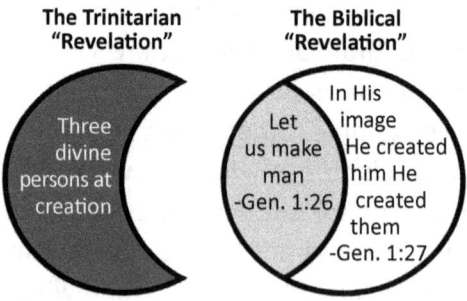

SECTION ONE - RULES FOR INTERPRETING

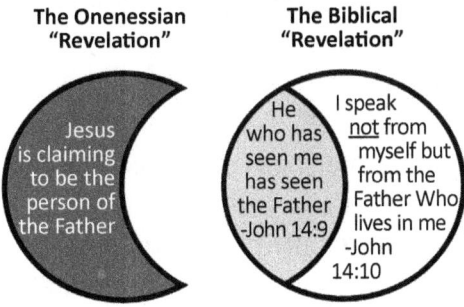

Notice that what they call "revelations" are really nothing more than man-made interpretations! When we hear Onenessians claim that Oneness is a "revelation," we can now clearly see that doesn't necessarily mean their "revelation" is a scriptural one.

> [19]*We have the more sure word of prophecy; whereunto you do well that you take heed*, as to a lamp shining in a dark place, until the day dawns, and the morning star arises in your hearts: [20]*knowing this first, that no prophecy of Scripture is of private interpretation.* [21]For no prophecy ever came by the will of man: but holy men of God spoke, being moved by the Holy Spirit. (2 Peter 1:19–21)

We uphold that *the "more sure word of prophecy" on the right of each graphic is both explanatory and revelatory, so who has the true biblical revelation?* Others claim such extrabiblical ideas on the left are "necessary" teachings even though *such explanations are nowhere found as such anywhere in the Scripture.* That is simply because the biblical writers never meant their words to teach such conclusions.

Although this single example may not instantly convince you of the error of the Oneness position, you should be able to recognize the error in the method used *in this example*. And then once you see the sheer *volume of repetitions of just such instances* we are going to present, we hope you will come to see that jumping to conclusions; that is, *interpreting the way the devil does, is, ultimately, the only method that Onenessians use (indeed that they can use) to support their theory* that God was personally incarnated as Jesus the Anointed One.

In Summary: This chapter has contrasted jumping to conclusions with legitimate quoting of Scripture in interpreting God's word. Our conclusion is that all core Christian doctrines *are clearly spelled out and explained* in the Christian Scriptures. This statement is never so apparent or so true of any other doctrine as when the Bible teaches about the Messiah/Christ, the Son of God and Son of Man.

When considering any teaching, whether from us or from your spiritual leaders or circles, or wherever, you need to prayerfully ask, does it fit with what the Bible clearly says, or is it in direct opposition to one or more verses that just don't fit that conclusion? In other words:

> Man does not live by bread alone, but *by every word* that proceeds out of the mouth of God. (Deuteronomy 8:3 and Matthew 4:4)

CHAPTER THREE

The Schoolmaster That Brings Us to Christ

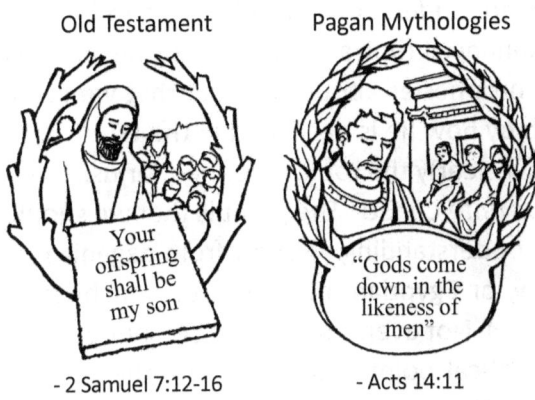

But this I confess to you, that... I serve the God of our fathers, *believing all things which... are written in the prophets*. (Acts 24:14)

But before faith came, we were kept under the law, shut up unto the faith which should afterwards be revealed. Wherefore *the law was our schoolmaster to bring us unto Christ*, that we might be justified by faith. But after that faith is come, we are no longer under a schoolmaster. (Galatians 3:23–25, KJV)

These verses tell us two things. First, Christianity began as a continuance of worshiping the God of the OT. Second is the idea that constitutes our second rule.

Rule #2: It is a simple, vital truth that *the OT law is the schoolmaster, our "elementary school" if you will, that brings us to Christ.*

Learning basic Bible interpretation can be like learning to read, write, and do arithmetic. That exact concept is spelled out in the above Scripture.

Now, in considering this rule, don't forget the first rule and jump to conclusions about the OT. Notice in the same passage, Paul says that we are *no longer under* the schoolmaster, which he identified as the law. He means that *the OT is no longer the Covenant that God's people are under*. So Paul isn't trying to bring us back under the law's ordinances (nor are we); rather, his point is that the OT teaches and prophesies about Christ so that we can recognize the true Messiah by how he is described in the OT.

Notice how clearly the topic is defined for us: "the... schoolmaster *to bring us unto Christ*." The point is that we shouldn't learn the basics of our understanding of *Christ* from paganism, or humanism, or philosophy, or Egyptian mysticism, or antichristian Gnosticism, or any other *ism*. Not even from leaning on our own understanding!

This is a critical point, because along the way we're going to show you how Oneness theologians have lost sight of this simple biblical rule and in its place have allowed their ideas to be heavily influenced (whether admittedly or knowingly or not) by *each and every one of* those *isms* listed in the last paragraph.

It is typical for Onenessians to point out to Trinitarians that their teachings are just modifications of ancient beliefs in three gods. Unfortunately, Trinitarians rarely seem to listen; at least we've all failed to eradicate that false teaching once and for all. *The reason seems to be because Trinitarians are usually so conditioned to "see" the Trinity in their proof texts that their biases and preconceptions won't allow them to examine their beliefs critically.* In Jesus' words, they often don't have "ears to hear," as it were. Thus, Trinitarians often claim that they see the Trinity in the Bible, and that settles it for them.

It is as if modern Trinitarians have each inherited a pair of pagan-philosophy-shaded prescription lenses from Justin, Tertullian, and others. This seems to be the best way of explaining why they still insist on interpreting the Scriptures in line with philosophical concepts and ideas. The First Commandment's "one" has become as blurred as if they had taken a big red marker and crossed it out and added the word "three" in its place! This is how that notion looks graphically:

Note: if you are reading this in black and white, the word "one" and "Deut. 6:4" on the right are both struck through with a red line which will appear white.

Now, consider our discussion from the last chapter in light of the rule of this chapter. Instead of using the OT to understand the NT, Trinitarians use ideas from philosophy to interpret both! The graphic illustrates what happens to those who attempt to interpret the Bible through the wisdom of the world. To be fair, Trinitarians have noticed verses in the NT where personal distinctions between God the Father and his begotten son are indeed clearly stated. Yet they took such NT verses as liberty to impose plural personalities *within the godhead*, thereby changing God Himself to be something He never was, if we look at God as defined in the OT. They say they are interpreting the OT through the NT, but they were never given such authority to change God into a Trinity of persons in the godhead, and certainly the apostles never spelled out the Trinity doctrine.

In the last chapter we discussed how philosophy influenced the development of theology, which is the study of all things about God. We quoted Jesus' view of God when he said, "You worship what you do not know; *We know what we worship for salvation is of the Jews*" (John 4:22). In the beginning of this chapter, we quoted Galatians 3:23–25, thereby switching to the topic of Christology, which is the study of all things about Christ. According to Paul, the OT was our schoolmaster to bring us to Christ (Christology), and according to Jesus, the "what" of God (theology) is and was known and understood by the Jews. Putting these two verses together tells us that both the study (and our understanding) of God and the study of Christ have their firm basis in the OT, which means not in worldly or pagan views.

Concluding that Jesus was YHWH incarnate is problematic in two ways. First, it is *not a biblically accurate view* of the *Jewish* Messiah, since *the OT was not a schoolmaster that taught or explained that concept.* No Jew ever understood the Messiah that way.

Secondly, *it is a view that comes directly from paganism, which makes paganism, rather than the OT, the schoolmaster to bring us to "that" Christ!*

This we can see clearly in our Bibles by simply reading Acts 14:8–15:

> ⁸At Lystra a certain man sat, impotent in his feet, a cripple from his mother's womb, who never had walked. ⁹He was listening to Paul speaking, who, fastening eyes on him, and seeing that he had faith to be made whole, ¹⁰said with a loud voice, "Stand upright on your feet!" He leaped up and walked. ¹¹When the multitude saw what Paul had done, *they lifted up their voice, saying in the language of Lycaonia,* "<u>The gods have come down to us in the likeness of men</u>!" ¹²They called Barnabas "Jupiter," and Paul "Mercury," because he was the chief speaker. ¹³The priest of Jupiter, whose temple was in front of their city, brought oxen and garlands to the gates, and would have made a sacrifice along with the multitudes. ¹⁴But when the apostles, Barnabas and Paul, heard of it, *they tore their clothes,* and sprang into the multitude, crying out, ¹⁵"Men, why are you doing these things?" (Acts 14:8–15)

The writers of the Bible knew how to form a sentence that reads, "the gods have come down to us in the likeness of men." But *nowhere in the whole Bible will you read such a clearly stated sentence about the biblical YHWH "coming to us in the likeness of men."* Looking for such a phrase or statement in the Scripture is just as fruitless as looking for the word "Trinity" or a definition of the Trinity in the Bible. Onenessians are quick to point this out to Trinitarians. But that doesn't stop the Onenessians from interpreting the Bible the same way Trinitarians do through their mutually held pagan idea of incarnations of deity!

The prescription-glasses analogy shows us that the Trinitarian view reads certain passages within a narrowly prescribed "lens" or "filter" that distorts the image of what those words were meant to say. The issue is, what was the original intent of the passage? And then, what "filter" or preconceived notion or jumped-to conclusion is being used to alter that intent and arrive at a nonbiblical conclusion. This is what we mean by saying they use theological lenses, or filters, through which to interpret the biblical descriptions of God and Christ.

The problem is that filters aren't merely used to view an image; they are actually used to creatively *change* an image! When Trinitarians and Onenessians interpret the Scriptures, they are using their "gods come down in the likeness of men" or their "Gnostic dual-nature" shades, or some combination of those or other "filters." Whatever lens they are using, the effect is changing the view of the OT Schoolmaster. Unfortunately, the more they *practice* using these filters the *more creative* they get at doing so. This is why the apostles warned, "impostors will grow worse and worse, deceiving and being deceived" (2 Timothy 3:13). Both positions believe they are getting better at explaining their position, when in reality they are just getting more sophisticated in their deceptions, as this passage warns.

In a manner of speaking, those others are "Photoshopping" the biblical doctrines of Christ in order to "doctor them up." Even after they have managed to "noticeably alter" their "image," they still claim their views are biblical. But honestly, this just isn't the case. Pre-Photoshopped images may form the basis of a final product in photography, but once the original has been noticeably altered, it is dishonest and deceptive to pass off the change as being identical with the original. This type of "change" being made to the understanding of Christ is precisely what we are warned against because it moves us away from the original Jesus to another Jesus.

The proper "shades" would be the OT-as-schoolmaster shades; that is, the "lens" the good physician of the Bible prescribes! Rather than darkening our view, the prescribed shades work to lend clarity and magnify the truth of God's words!

Since the OT is to be our foundation, or "lens," when interpreting the NT Scriptures, then it stands to reason that worldly philosophy and pagan ideas and myths are to be *soundly rejected* as views used to interpret the Bible.

Trinitarians seem to be oblivious to the magnitude of what it would have taken to transform Christianity into a Trinitarian religion from its beginnings in strict Jewish monotheism. They want us to believe that this transformation happened without any discussion whatsoever *in the biblical records*. In fact, *all the discussions about the Trinity appeared after the apostles because the idea of God in three persons wasn't even invented, as far as Christianity was concerned, until after they were gone!* So, in effect, Trinitarians want us to believe that such a fundamental doctrine as the Trinity was transmitted in only a few gray-area biblical verses that the apostles gave us for the purpose of negating the fundamental concept of Jewish monotheism. This is simply theological dishonesty and deception on a grand scale!

By the same token, Oneness theologians assert the same thing about their view of God the Father incarnating Himself into a man. Both groups want us to believe that only they (or those who have had their same special revelation) can interpret the Scriptures correctly for us so we won't be confused. And they both condemn us as being blind if we don't share their interpretation of these scant proof texts. If that doesn't sound like con-artistry, pray tell what does?

Furthermore, Trinitarians want us to believe that what was finally hammered out in the fourth century was what apostolic Christians had always believed, even though we can see in the historical records every step in the *evolution* of the doctrine, moving them step by step away from the "One God" faith once delivered. Imagine if evolutionists could produce a complete skeleton of every transitory life form they claim emerged in their theory that humans evolved from amoebas. It would be irrefutable evidence of their theory. But they don't have such observable, irrefutable evidence; all they have are their jumped-to conclusions derived from how they interpret the data of the fossil records.

The reverse is true of the development of the Trinity. We have a *record of every single step* of its evolution from pure Jewish monotheism to full-blown Nicene, coequalist/coeternalist Trinitarianism. And there are some absolutely incompatible thought forms they had to go through to get to Nicaea. They even admit it! See, for example, newadvent.org under "Monarchians" for this little gem: "There was much that was unsatisfactory in the theology of the Trinity and in the Christology of the orthodox writers of the Ante-Nicene period." In other words, before Nicaea, the so-called orthodox writers did not know how to properly speak of the Trinity! None of them!

Onenessians don't acknowledge that the idea of the incarnation of deity is clearly one of those extrabiblical steps that led to Nicene Trinitarianism. When Onenessians resort to using the incarnation theory to interpret the Bible, they also have to resort to a step in the development of the Trinity for "opening their eyes" to the idea. The truth is that adopting the incarnation idea didn't open their eyes, but rather meant putting on the dark shades of paganism, which clouded their clear vision to the words and teachings of the Scriptures.

Again, it isn't as if Onenessians and Trinitarians don't have their proof texts; it's that they don't have any clear biblical statements that God personally incarnated Himself into a human being. Probably the closest proof text they have is John 1:14.

> The Word became flesh, and lived among us. We saw his glory, such glory as of the one and only Son of the Father, full of grace and truth. (John 1:14)

It is very clear that John did *not* say "God was made flesh, became Himself human, and lived among us" or that "God was incarnated." The following graphic shows how Onenessians and Trinitarians believe John should have written it. By means of the graphic, we can see they really don't believe it the way it was written:

Recall that the phrase "God has come down in the likeness of men," from Acts 14:11, was a false, pagan-inspired response to the gospel. We could even say it is a pagan confession in the sense of a statement of belief, or conviction. Paul was appalled at such a response; he found nothing redeemable about it.

You see, John 1:14 purposely doesn't say "God was made flesh." It says the word was made flesh. It is only by imposing an artificial interpretation that the passage is made to appear to say God was incarnated in Jesus.

How do we know that? How can we be so sure? For two reasons: first, no biblical writer ever clearly said that is what it means; and secondly, they did describe something different. We know this by looking at the "it is written again" Scriptures. None of these next passages is compatible with the idea that Jesus was the "person" of God incarnate:

> The words... I <u>speak</u> not from myself; but the Father who lives in me. (John 14:10)

> The <u>word</u> which you hear <u>isn't mine</u>, but the Father's who sent me. (John 14:24)

> He who sent me is true; and the things which I <u>heard</u> from him, these I <u>say</u>... (John 8:26)

> ... I do nothing of myself; but *as my Father taught me, I speak* these things. (John 8:28)

> For *I spoke not from myself, but the Father... he gave me a commandment*, what I should *say*, and what I should speak... The things therefore which *I speak, even as the Father has said* to me, so I speak. (John 12:49–50)

> Now... *the words which you have given me I have given to them*, and they received them... (John 17:7–8)

> For he whom God has sent *speaks the words of God*... (John 3:34–35)

> For Moses indeed said to the fathers, 'The Lord God will raise up a prophet for you from among your brothers, like me. You shall *listen to him in all things whatever he says to you*. It will be, that *every soul that will not listen to that prophet will be utterly destroyed* from among the people.' (Acts 3:22–23)

If Jesus is "the word incarnate," then why weren't the words he spoke his own words? It is simply because the word being made flesh means something completely different than the pagan idea that a god-person named "Word" was incarnated.

If we really "hear" Jesus, we find that his explanation of himself isn't an explanation of an incarnated deity (as in paganism), but rather, is the thoroughly biblical concept of "agency." We can see a classic description of agency at work in the very words of Jesus himself: "The words... *I speak **not** from myself*; but the Father who lives in me" (John 14:10). This is agency. Jesus just defined himself as an agent of the Father, and, at the same time, absolutely refuted that he was claiming to be the person of the Father.

Agency (Hebrew *shaliah*) is a biblical concept that I never heard of in all my years as a Oneness Pentecostal. It is shameful that it isn't taught in Incarnationist camps, because it clears up so much confusion about what Jesus explained! It is amazing how clear Jesus' words become in the light of the OT teaching of agency!

We can see that the concept is entirely biblical if we look at one of the prime examples of "agency" at work: the scene of Moses at the burning bush.

> I am the God of your father, the God of Abraham, the God of Isaac, and the God of Jacob. (Exodus 3:6)

Most Incarnationists conclude that this was literally God Himself speaking to Moses. But is that true? Is that what the Bible actually teaches? We find the answer by backing up a few more verses and reading the setting of the narrative:

> <u>The angel</u> of Yahweh <u>appeared</u> to him in a flame of fire out of the midst of a bush. He looked, and behold, the bush burned with fire, and the bush was not consumed." (Exodus 3:2)

This tells us so clearly that God didn't, Himself, literally talk to Moses; rather, it was actually God's angel, His *messenger,* that appeared and spoke to Moses as a faithful agent of God's exact words! In fact, we even have Stephen explaining this very thing to us in the NT:

> When forty years were fulfilled, *an angel* of the Lord *appeared* to him in the wilderness of Mount Sinai, in a flame of fire in a bush. (Acts 7:30)

> This Moses, whom they refused, saying, "Who made you a ruler and a judge?"—God has sent him as both a ruler and a deliverer by the hand of *the angel who appeared* to him in the bush. (Acts 7:35)

So you see, when Moses spoke to God, he actually only spoke directly with the angel of the Lord. But the profound thing is that the angel of the Lord, as God's agent, acted and spoke precisely as if he were God Himself! Chances are, if you are Oneness like I was, you were taught that Moses was literally speaking to God. But that is not the case, according to Exodus 3:2 and Stephen's Spirit-inspired preaching in Acts 7:30, 35.

Now let's look at how the Jewish law of agency captures and describes in detail how things work with God's messengers:

> AGENT (Heb. *shaliah*): The main point of the Jewish law of agency is expressed in the dictum, "a person's agent is regarded as the person himself" (Ned. 72b; Kidd. 41b). Therefore any act committed by a duly appointed agent is regarded as having been committed by the principle, who therefore bears full responsibility for it with consequent complete absence of liability on the part of the agent... The agent is regarded as acting in his principle's interest and not to his detriment...[1]

This is how Jesus comes to be confused with God Himself: Onenessians and Trinitarians interpret his ministry through the lenses of pagan incarnation. They aren't using the OT schoolmaster to bring them to Christ. If they did view him through the OT schoolmaster, they would see that Jesus was acting as an agent of God the Father, not as an incarnation of God.[2]

Let's look at another clear example and explanation of agency. One of the favorite proof texts of Onenessians comes from Zechariah:

---

[1] R. J. Zwi Werblowsky and G. Wigoder, editors, *The Encyclopedia of the Jewish Religion* (New York: Adama Books, 1986), 15.

[2] For further study on the biblical concept of agency/shaliah, a good place to start would be this introduction: http://www.21stcr.org/multimedia-2012/1-articles/re-shaliah-introduction_law_of_agency.html.

> The word of Yahweh concerning Israel... They will look to me whom they have pierced; and they shall mourn for him, as one mourns for his only son, and will grieve bitterly for him, as one grieves for his firstborn. (Zechariah 12:1, 10)

This verse, taken out of context, initially appears to support the idea that Messiah would be an incarnation of the person of God Himself. But again, that is only when the Bible isn't consulted for context and explanation. In fact, in context, this passage prophesies explicitly that Messiah would be an agent of God, and not God Himself. We find clarification by simply backing up a couple of verses:

> In that day Yahweh will defend the inhabitants of Jerusalem... and the house of <u>David will be like God, like the angel</u> of Yahweh before them. (Zechariah 12:8)

There we have it: the Bible actually explains to us in prophecy that God's Son, whom we have seen was born of the house of David and was David's heir, would be "like God," thus not actually God but acting as God's agent, "like the angel of Yahweh" who acted as an agent (shaliah) of God and spoke in God's place; that is, both of them acting with God as their principle.

This is how pagan doctrines (like incarnation) are superimposed upon, and end up replacing in some people's minds, scriptural doctrines (like agency). This is how people end up adopting or assuming pagan concepts (as in Acts 14:11) rather than biblical explanations.

When we choose to interpret John the way Jesus taught us, we find that the words Jesus spoke were not his words; they were simply the words that God gave and commanded Jesus to speak. These words were with God, and these words were God, and then the Son came and spoke and lived God's words as God's agent! It is in this way that "the word was made flesh." Jesus became an embodiment of God's words, just as a book embodies the words of the author, but a book is not an incarnation of the author.

Again, the concept that God was incarnate was never stated in the Bible. That idea can only be reached by imposing later thoughts upon the text. But when we interpret by letting the Bible explain itself, as Jesus taught us, the false idea of *incarnation* completely disappears from the Bible.

There are then two ways to "interpret" John 1:14: through the pagan viewpoint, which allows that gods/God do/did indeed personally come to earth in the form of men (which the Bible never, ever clearly describes Jesus as being); *or, by removing the pagan-shaded lenses and viewing this passage from the OT point of view.*

When we view John's words through a Jewish viewpoint, it clears things up immediately and makes the whole passage very clear, simple, and understandable... and it also refutes both Trinitarianism and Onenessianism:

> In the beginning was the plan, and the plan was with God, and the plan was God... The plan became flesh, and lived among us. We saw his glory, such glory as of the one and only Son of the Father, full of grace and truth. (John 1:1, 14, for use of "plan" see below)

Britannica defines the Greek word *logos,* used above in John, as, "word, reason, *or plan.*"[3] There is a world of difference between God being made flesh and his plan being made flesh. Onenessians typically agree with interpreting *logos* (word) as "plan"; for example, "In Greek usage, *logos* can mean the expression *or plan* as it exists in the mind of the proclaimer... "[4]

To say the plan was made flesh simply means that God's plan was made a reality in our natural world. This is a literal interpretation; it is not jumping to a conclusion. A plan being made flesh is like saying an architect's plan has become a reality when the actual building is finished. In such cases, the builders don't take the paper on which the plans were drawn and transform it into a building. Rather, they gather the needed raw materials (steel, wood, and the like) and use them to actually craft the building. Nevertheless, when the building

---

[3] https://www.britannica.com/topic/logos.

[4] David Bernard, *The Oneness of God*, 60.

is done the architect can say, "My plans have been made physical reality." In light of the Jewish understanding of "word," this is all that John clearly said and likely meant when he stated, "And the plan/word was made flesh." That is because God's plan became a very particular and definite type of physical reality: the Messiah of God's foreknowledge became a flesh and blood human being just like the rest of us.

Now let's take a brief look at what John meant when he said, "And the plan/word was with God and the plan/word was God." It is obvious that John didn't simply say "and the word was a second deific person in the godhead, and he joined himself to human flesh." Well, neither did he simply say that the word was God. He said, "the word was *with* God *and* was God."

So John was telling us something different in his first chapter. In no way was he saying that God and His word are exact synonyms. Nevertheless, God was all about His plan and His plan was all about God. We know architects in the world who make their living at that trade. Even when they take their work home with them, they generally have a life outside of their "job." They have their family and recreation and you get the idea. That's not the case with God. God is totally wrapped up in His plan, and His expressed plan (*logos*) reveals everything that God felt was critical for us to know, and this plan was made into a human so we could see it! If that is "jumping to conclusions," then try finding a Scripture that negates what was just written here.

But while you're looking, consider the magnitude of what John said if he meant it to be interpreted in light of paganism; namely, that God had been *made* flesh just like pagans believe happens! It would have been as big a Christological explosion as the change from monotheism to a trinity. Remember, up until right around the time John wrote his gospel, *Christianity was still a sect within Judaism*. The sheer magnitude of these two doctrines (Trinity and God-became-man) alone would have ousted early Christianity completely out of Judaism. But the fact is, *Jews didn't reject the God of the earliest Christians any more than they rejected the idea of the Messiah.* The first Christians were preaching the same Messiah that was foretold by the prophets of the Jewish Bible. Most Jews had only rejected *Jesus himself as personally being that Messiah*! They rejected Jesus' message as being in opposition to their man-made traditions, but they did not reject *the Jewish idea of a Messiah*. So what a complete turnaround for the later Christians to build up pagan-influenced, man-made traditions about the Messiah and then reject what the Messiah was from a Jewish standpoint in order to adopt pagan views instead!

So God's *"logos"* was both God's architectural plan and God's self-expression. But *that doesn't mean that the material on which the plans were conceived in the mind of God was also to be the raw material by which the plan would be made into reality.* Let's look at it from another angle. If John had said, "In the beginning was love, and love was with God and love was God... and love was made flesh," would we interpret that as meaning that God was made flesh? No, because we understand that love describes an attitude, not a substance, and every time anyone loves does not mean those persons who are in love are incarnations of God. To say "love" is made flesh is simply a way of saying that love has been manifested through something or someone in our observable world, and that is what Jesus the Anointed One is! Jesus said as much when he said, "He who has seen me has seen the Father... I speak *not from myself*; but the Father who lives in me... " (John 14:9–10). Onenessians read right over the part where Jesus said he didn't speak from himself, and turn Jesus' words completely around to mean the opposite of what he explained. This is a clear case of confirmation bias on the part of Onenessians. Yet Jesus' words, which are right there in black and white in our Bibles, state: "I speak *not* from *myself*." Jesus himself thus refutes and rejects Onenessianism. If Jesus wasn't a Trinitarian, should we be? No. If Jesus wasn't Oneness, should we be? Again, no.

What the OT Schoolmaster Teaches Us

The Bible tells us clearly, explicitly, consistently and emphatically that the raw material that God used to make Jesus was the seed of Eve, Abraham, and David. This is what we are saying when we say that the law is the schoolmaster to bring us to Christ. In the OT and the NT, the raw material that the Son of God is "made out of" is spelled out. And using such Scriptures is the key to rightly, biblically interpreting and understanding what John said in John 1:1, 14. Let's look at some passages that describe what the Messiah was to be. These passages lay out God's plan, His word, which was made into fleshly human reality upon the birth of Jesus:

> When your days are fulfilled, and you shall sleep with your fathers, *I will set up <u>your seed after you, who shall proceed out of your bowels</u>, and I will establish his kingdom*. He shall build a house *for my name*, and I will establish the throne of his kingdom forever. <u>*I will be his father, and he shall be my son*</u>... Your house and your kingdom shall be made sure for ever before you: your throne shall be established forever. (2 Samuel 7:12–16)

> [Moses said] YHWH your God will raise up to you a prophet *from the midst of you, <u>of your brothers, like me</u>*; to him you shall listen; according to all that you desired of YHWH your God in Horeb in the day of the assembly, saying, Let me not hear again the voice of YHWH my God, neither let me see this great fire any more, that I not die. <u>YHWH said</u> to me, They have well said that which they have spoken. I will raise them up a prophet *from among their brothers, <u>like you</u>*; and I will put my words in his mouth, and he shall speak to them all that I shall command him. It shall happen, that whoever will not listen to my words which he shall speak in my name, I will require it of him. (Deuteronomy 18:15–19)

Such OT Schoolmaster verses as these clearly show that the Messiah was always part of God's plan, but not that the Messiah was to be God Himself. These passages clearly teach us that the Messiah would be made out of one substance; as the genetic offspring of King David, he would be made just as human as Moses and his Israelite brothers were. This was God's plan from the very beginning.

But this plan (or "word," Greek *logos*) wasn't merely some external building or non-living shell that was only "animated" as long as the glory of God abode in it, such as the "figure of Christ" that the temple in the OT was. Nor was he, being God's very word, completely unrelated to God. As these Scriptures plainly declare, this word made flesh was God's plan for God's revelation of Himself made through a complete and *entire human being distinct from the person of God* Himself. This whole human has become the temple of God! This human being had absolutely every faculty of humanity that you and I possess, including our strengths and weaknesses, abilities and limitations. That means he necessarily had a human heart, mind, body, soul, and spirit. It also means he had to have had a human—that is, a completely human, and only human—self-awareness. For this man was made like his brothers, that means you and I, *in all things*. This is what Hebrews 2:14–18 explicitly teaches: by obligation, he was *made* like *us* in *all* things.

> Since then the children have shared in flesh and blood, he also himself in like manner *partook of the same*... Therefore *he was obligated in all things to be made like his brothers*, that he might become a merciful and faithful high priest in things pertaining to God, to make atonement for the sins of the people... (Hebrews 2:14–18)

This verse clearly disallows Christ as a God-man hybrid by clearly defining him as being made in all things like his brothers. This verse simply reiterated the description that God gave to Moses, namely that the Messiah would be like his brothers. Onenessians deny God's clear definition of messiahship in order to justify adopting a pagan view of incarnation. There are no such corresponding passages where Jesus is clearly explained to be a God-man hybrid. It wasn't a God-man hybrid that came to save us, so the God-man hybrid doctrine must be rejected as contrary to salvation because it is contradicted by the aforementioned clearly stated passage.

When we remove the dark shades of paganism, we are left with two foundational, biblical truths that ought to "color" or inform all of our "views" of God and His Anointed One. This is what we see through those biblical glasses:

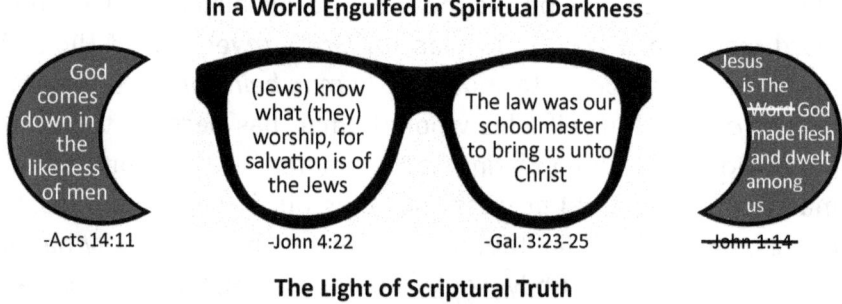

The Light of Scriptural Truth
Is a REVELATION Indeed!

This is our "revelation"! This graphic shows how our biblical revelation has moved the false, pagan views of Christ out of our field of vision!

Now we confess *"Jesus is the Christ—the Anointed One, the Son of God"* (Matthew 16:16; Mark 8:29; John 11:27). We are able to say we believe every word of this foundational, apostolic confession without any pagan, philosophic, or gnostic influences upon what any of those words mean, either individually or collectively.

Summary: The intent in these studies is to show what can be discovered simply by reading what is plainly stated in the Scriptures and confirmed by applying these simple, basic, biblical methods of interpreting the Bible. And yes, the answer is profoundly different than what is influenced by extrabiblical ideas!

CHAPTER FOUR

Biblical Arithmetic:
Don't Add To or Take Away From God's Word

What do we need to add to God's word to find truth?

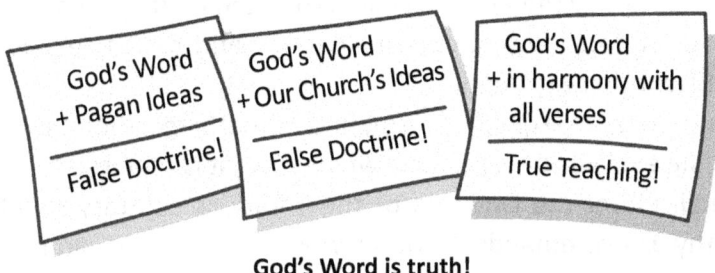

God's Word is truth!

> *¹⁸I testify to everyone who hears the words of the prophecy of this book, if anyone adds to them, may God add to him the plagues which are written in this book. ¹⁹If anyone takes away from the words of the book of this prophecy, may God take away his part from the tree of life, and out of the holy city, which are written in this book. (Revelation 22:18–19)*

This passage, and others, states the concept for our next rule.

Rule #3: The third rule is simply to "teach no other doctrine" (1 Timothy 1:3).

This is the "arithmetic" step in "reading, writing, and arithmetic." The third rule simply means, don't add to or take away from what the Bible says and Jesus and the apostles taught. This rule shouldn't be at all hard to accept or understand or difficult to adhere to by any sincere Christian.

The word "doctrine," in the passage above simply means "that which can be taught." The root word for teach (*didasko* G#1321) includes the meaning, "to explain or expound".[1]

To "explain" means "to make (an idea, situation, or problem) clear to someone by describing it in more detail or revealing relevant facts or ideas."[2]

To "expound" means "to present and explain (a theory or idea) systematically and in detail."

So, 1 Timothy (*heterodidaskaleó*, G#2085) literally means *not* to, "explain in detail any other explanation" and *not* to "expound in detail any other expounding."

Therefore, to explain or expound something other than what the Bible explains or expounds, which is what is required to explain in detail either the Oneness or the Trinity, is contrary to what 1 Timothy 1:3 commands. In other words, you simply can't explain or expound the particular, distinctive principles of either the Oneness or Trinity theories in detail without going against 1 Timothy 1:3! You can't quote Scriptures explaining that God is one essence in three persons, just as you can't quote Scriptures that explain in detail how Jesus is God the Father incarnate. These types of distinctions have to be presumed and read back into the Scriptures.

To claim otherwise, that the Oneness or Trinity are explained or expounded in detail in the Bible, when they are not, is thus also to commit what the Bible calls "handling the word of God deceitfully" (3 Corinthians 4:2). That means a person must ultimately sacrifice their integrity to teach either Oneness or the Trinity.

This also means that the True Son of God doctrine (i.e., that Jesus is a male human approved of God) is the only Christology that is not contrary to biblical commands to preach (to openly and clearly proclaim) and/or teach (to explain and expound in detail) because the particular, distinctive principles of this teaching are precisely what the Bible does explain and expound on, quite thoroughly and consistently, in detail in the Bible.

---

[1] http://biblehub.com/greek/1321.htm.

[2] https://www.oxforddictionaries.com.

Here's another Scripture that presents this simple truth in a different way:

> All Scripture is given by inspiration of God, and is profitable for doctrine, for reproof, for correction, for instruction in righteousness, that the man of God may be complete, *thoroughly equipped for every good work*. (2 Timothy 3:16–17; NKJV)

To be "thoroughly equipped" expresses the idea that we don't need to add to the Bible's teachings. Everything that is *good* is already provided in the Scriptures. This is why the apostle could say to teach no other doctrines. It is interesting how people claim to believe this but then find excuses why their pet doctrines aren't clearly stated in the Bible.

Now note Peter's phrase, "the present truth," in the following:

> Therefore I will not be negligent to remind you of these things, though you know them, and are *established in the present truth*... Knowing that the putting off of my tent comes swiftly... I will make every effort that you may always be able to remember things after my departure. (2 Peter 1:12–15)

There is a good reason Peter described the truth the apostles delivered as a "present truth" that he wanted to establish for future generations. One of his biggest concerns was that others would come and revise it, change it, and even pervert it. Think of truth as a rock that is unchangeable. How much sense would there be in creating a field of study called "the history of the unchanging rock"? If nothing had been done to change the rock, there would be no sense in creating a "history of the rock for the last 2,000 years," right? That's because the rock simply would have stayed the same throughout that time period. It may be interesting to consider the history that happened *around* that rock or *what happened to or was done to* that rock, but not directly about that unchangeable rock. The solid, unmovable, unchangeable rock of truth the apostles laid some 2,000 years ago was meant to be the same solid, unmovable, unchangeable rock of today. This is the only way that what was a present truth in Peter's day would still be a present truth today.

What the apostles intended is not the case with "The History of Christian Doctrine," which is a very interesting and involved study indeed. When historians talk about the "History of Christian Doctrine," they are really talking about the historic record of the big and small changes that have been made over the years to the original teachings that the apostles left us in their writings.

When gnostic and philosophic theologians of the second and third centuries started adding and taking things away from what the Scriptures said and the apostles taught, they moved away from that rock of "present truth" that Peter was talking about. That is, they started revising basic Christian teachings into ideas the apostles would never have recognized. If American Indians of 500 years ago, who were familiar with Mount Rushmore in their day, were blindfolded and set in front of Mount Rushmore today, would they recognize it right away? It's not likely, even though they might recognize some similarities to what it once looked like. Likewise, if the apostles were to rise from the dead and listen to the theologians of the 3rd and 4th centuries and beyond, up until today, would they recognize what is being taught as the same teachings they had left behind, or would it look all carved up to them, like Mount Rushmore would to our Indians? Undoubtedly the latter. In fact, if many of the ideas that are floating around Christianity these days are true, then our time-traveling apostles would have to become students of these later teachers to understand what they say, rather than the other way around!

If the Bible already thoroughly provides us with every *good* work, why would Christians want to change the truth? The answer, unfortunately, is because they actually believe they can improve it. Why do people Photoshop models? It's because they think they can improve upon the image. It's like saying that the old rock is ugly: let's chisel here and there and take away what we need to make it into a shape like a statue of our heroes; then we can paint on a face and some clothes... there, now, isn't that ole rock now a thing of beauty since we've redone it? In reality, that would only be the case if you didn't think it was a thing of beauty and perfection before you started messing with it!

Theologians tend to do this with the Scriptures. They believe that they somehow know what the Bible "really" means or was "trying to say" but that they could improve the message by putting it better in their own words. The problem with that is, as the saying goes, don't fix what's not broken. The truth as handed down from the apostles in our Bibles is and was not broken—quite the contrary! Those who attempt to *fix it* are really trying to *change it*. The very desire to change or supplement the Bible is evidence they are not satisfied that it says what they think it should say; therefore, they feel the need to "correct" it until it does. Of course, no one can actually improve it by changing it. Any change is really an adding to or a taking away from. This is what Peter was concerned about. Onenessians understand this concept very clearly when it is directed at the Trinity, but they have an impossible task in attempting to hold their Oneness position to the same standard.

The apostle Paul clearly said that he left behind for us the whole counsel of God. He refers to Ezekiel's exhortation (Ezek. 33:8) to speak to the wicked lest their blood be on his hands, and said:

> [26]I am clean from the blood of all men, [27]for *I didn't shrink from declaring to you the whole counsel of God*... [29]For I know that after my departure, vicious wolves will enter in among you, not sparing the flock... [32]Now, brothers, I entrust you to God, *and to the word of His grace*, which is able to build up, and to give you the inheritance among all those who are sanctified. (Acts 20:26–32)

We can see from the words of these apostles that they believed what they had written was thorough. And they were concerned that false teachers would come later and pervert their words. This means that what latecomers view as improving the Bible, would look to the apostles like perversions of the truths they had delivered. We agree with the apostles, which is what being apostolic really means.

Let's look at how the scriptural truth of not adding to or taking away can be shown through simple math. Below we have a simple numeric subtraction problem on the left and a similar word problem on the right. On the left we have three passages of Scripture; if we take away two, the difference is one. On the right, we have the three Scriptures we're talking about (Luke 1:30–31, Rev. 19:10 and 22:9). If we take away two, we are left with one. In this case we are left with the one that says, effectively, "Mary will conceive Jesus." If we take away the Scriptures that teach us not to worship at the feet of those who are our brothers, meaning our equals, then we are left with a high view of Mary but no constraints on what this could mean. It would be like we had the promise that we wouldn't dash our feet without the limitation not to tempt the Lord God. Here's how it looks mathematically:

3	Luke 1:30-31 Mary...will conceive...Jesus with Rev. 19:10, 22:9
- 2	- Rev. 19:10 & 22:9 See you do it not
1	Mary, mother of Jesus

This is how Catholics interpret the "Mary as mother of Jesus" statements and then read more into them than is meant: by taking away other biblical Scriptures that are there to help explain what is meant. Non-Catholics understand what we mean when we say that Catholics view the phrase "Mary, mother of Jesus" in a completely different way than the rest of us. Of course, Catholics will say they don't really "worship" Mary like they do God; they just "venerate" her as the mother of God. But the point is,

Jesus is the only human being who has been exalted by God above Christians (Hebrews 1:9). In this way, Catholics have added the unbiblical notion of venerating Mary and have negated the passages that teach not to do so.

Now let's look at the way addition works.

	1		Mary mother of Jesus
+	1	+	pagan worship of goddesses
	2		Mariolatry/veneration of Mary

The historical truth is that nowhere in the Scriptures do the apostles ever teach in words or by example to give any kind of veneration or prayers to dead saints such as Mary. However, this idea *is* found in paganism and certainly derives from it. So Catholics have allowed themselves to be influenced by pagan forms of religion. This is "adding to" the Scriptures. Of course Catholics deny that they do this. They claim that Scriptures like Luke 1:30–31 give them justification for their conclusions; and that is our point. So do Trinitarians. Ultimately, so do Onenessians, by denying they have added the pagan idea of incarnation, which they adopted from Trinitarians, who adopted it from paganism. This "addition" and "subtraction" is the reason behind showing these as "math problems."

Simple math shows what happens in adding to and subtracting from scriptural truth. As we've done with our previous rules, let's first see how our graphic for this rule shows how Trinitarians fell off the tracks.

First, I will explain the "word problem," then show it in the graphic. The high points of the Trinity's development went like this: Christianity began with a very Jewish Messiah (Christ) and his Jewish apostles who believed in the Shema; namely, "the Lord our

"I AM NOT ALONE"

God is one Lord." Just like all other Jews, they believed that meant that God was personally one. The Gnostic Christians and early Philosopher/Christians decided for themselves that the Jews *did not know* what Jews worshiped, so they *subtracted* or redefined Jesus' words in John 4:24. This created a void, a big question mark, so the early Trinitarians *added* the pagan idea that a deity had come down to earth in the form of a man *and added* the gnostic inventions of both the Trinity *and* the Dual Natures in the person of Christ *and* the idea of "persons" in the godhead (which Gregory of Nyssa admitted came from Greek philosophy). This left the early Trinitarians, at the beginning of the third century, with a doctrine known as *Subordinationism,* wherein the Son was viewed as inferior to the Father. Along came Origen, who invented (*added*) the concept of "eternal generation," and from then on all the raw material for full-blown Nicene (coequal/coeternal) Trinitarianism was ripe for the councils of Nicaea and Chalcedon and so forth to codify the new teaching and make it the *new* "present truth," which supplanted the old "present truth" that the apostles had been preaching.

And all the Onenessians say "amen," that's what the Trinitarians did. At the same time, most if not all of the Trinitarians become defensive and present all manner of vile accusations against the author, as if I've made all this up and as if it isn't easily found through study. These steps are actually admitted by many of their own scholars!

Now then, let's see how our Trinitarian theory math problem looks in graphic, mathematical notation. Just the main points here; details and references will be added in later chapters. The intended way of reading these charts is left to right (equation to explanation) and then down to next row. And yes, it is complicated—in order to demonstrate that this doctrine is clearly not the simplicity of Christ!

SECTION ONE - RULES FOR INTERPRETING

	Equation		Explanation
	The Lord our God is One (Luke 12:29)	<->	Start with this biblical foundational truth
-	We know what we worship (John 4:24)	<->	Subtract Jesus' limiting words on interpretations
=	The Lord our God is...? ~~One~~ ~~(Luke 12:29)~~	<->	You remain with a gray area as to what God is
+	(Pagan) gods come down in the likeness of men	<->	Add the pagan idea of incarnations of deities
+	Gnostic Trinity (early-mid 2nd century)	<->	Add the gnostic invention of a Trinity
+	Gnostic Dual Natures	<->	Add the gnostic invention of dual natures in Christ
+	Neoplatonic "persons" (Numenius 2nd century)	<->	Add the pagan idea of "persons"
=	Justin, Tertullian, and Arius' Subordinationist Trinitarianism	<->	You come up with an early form of the Trinity
+	Origen's eternal Son doctrine (3rd century)	<->	Add Origen's invention of eternal persons
=	Nicene Trinitarianism	<->	You have arrived at three coequal/coeternal persons in the Godhead

This is what the Bible calls "adding to" and "taking away from" the Scriptures. This complex formula is not the simplicity of Christ, but it does accurately list the high points of the evolution of the Trinity doctrine. It is in this way that the Trinitarians landed on a teaching that is mathematically shown to be different than the sum total of the doctrine on God that the apostles left for us. This shows how dishonest it is for Trinitarians to claim that the Trinity is merely a way of explaining what Christians always believed.

To the contrary, we uphold that what the apostles left for us thoroughly equips us with everything we need in matters of doctrine, correction, and righteousness, as it says in 2 Timothy 3:16–17 quoted above. Paul also wrote:

> ⁶I marvel that you are so quickly deserting him who called you in the grace of Christ to a *different 'good news'*; ⁷and *there isn't another 'good news.'* Only there are some who trouble you, and *want to pervert the Good News of Christ.* ⁸But even though we, or an angel from heaven, should preach to you any 'good news' other than that which we preached to you, let him be cursed. ⁹As we have said before, so I now say again: if any man preaches to you any 'good news' other than that which you received, let him be cursed. ¹⁰For am I now seeking the favor of men, or of God? Or am I striving to please men? For if I were still pleasing men, I wouldn't be a servant of Christ. ¹¹But I make known to you, brothers, concerning the Good News which was preached by me, that it is not according to man. ¹²For neither did I receive it from man, nor was I taught it, but it came to me through revelation of Jesus Christ. (Galatians 1:6–12)

Paul adamantly warned against anyone preaching (or declaring) a different good news or a different Christ than that which the apostles preached. You see, by saying there isn't another good news, Paul is saying that changing the teachings of the Bible doesn't make it better. It doesn't even make it good; it makes it a perversion! Not only was Paul afraid that the gospel would be perverted, but he also was explicitly concerned that "another Jesus" would be introduced in place of the one *they preached*:

> I fear, lest... your minds may be corrupted from the simplicity that is in Christ. For if he who comes preaches *another Jesus whom we have not preached*, or if you receive a different spirit which you have not received, *or a different gospel* which you have not accepted—you may well put up with it! (2 Corinthians 11:3–4; NKJV)

It is practically certain that every Oneness teacher who has ever addressed the Trinity doctrine understands, at least in concept, about not perverting or changing the gospel or preaching another

Jesus. And it is likely that any Oneness teacher with even a limited knowledge of history would agree with our estimation of how the Trinitarians developed their "another Jesus" whom the apostles never preached.

But through much study and simply "hearing" the Scriptures, some of us have come to realize that the Oneness position isn't really that different, fundamentally, from Trinitarianism especially *in regard to its method* of arriving at its understanding of the Christ. In fact, *it was derived by the same methods of interpretation* and indeed *often from the same sources* as those of Trinitarians; namely, pagan *and antichristian* theories. Onenessians just came up with a slightly different "math word problem" than Trinitarians.

This time, let's first look at the Oneness model through our mathematical "word problem" graphic, and then we'll explain it.

	Equation		Explanation
	The Lord our God is One (Luke 12:29)	<->	Start with this biblical foundational truth
-	I am not alone (John 8:16 & 16:32, etc.)	<->	Subtract Jesus' clear explanation
-	OT was schoolmaster bringing us unto Christ (Gal. 3:23-25)	<->	Subtract Paul's limiting words on interpretations
=	God ~~Word~~ became flesh (John 1:14)	<->	You remain with a gray area about Christ, so you start redefining what the Bible says and means
+	(Pagan) Gods come down in likeness of men	<->	Add the pagan idea of incarnations of deities
+	Gnostic Dual Natures	<->	Add the Gnostic invention of dual natures in Christ
=	Monarchianism of Praxeas, Noetus, and Sabellius	<->	Your new "present truth" is called Modalistic Monarchianism, known today as Oneness

This complex formula is the way that modalistic monarchianism evolved. Historically, the first modalistic monarchians (Onenessians) were actually Praxeas, Noetus, and Sabellius (all from late 2nd to early 3rd century). These were the first theologians to actually formulate (*add*) the Oneness creed that says, "Jesus is an incarnation of the very person of God the Father" (which is still, as indicated in Acts 14:11, based on the pagan doctrine of "gods coming to earth in the likeness of men"). This was also a *subtraction* of Jesus' words that *he was not alone*. This step happened well after Gnosticism had polluted Christianity with its doctrines of the incarnation of a literal preexistent deific being, dual natures, and a trinity of persons in the godhead. So the early Onenessians (then known as Monarchians) also *added* those extrabiblical teachings.

When theologians such as Tertullian were putting forth the gnostic idea of a literal preexistent son who was begotten before all of creation and a second person in the godhead, the Monarchians rejected that part of the influence of Gnosticism, but then some or many of them kept the ideas of dual nature and the incarnation of God. In contrast to the Trinitarians, Onenessians simply reasoned, "if" Jesus is God, then instead of Christ being a second person, he must be the one God the Father himself. In this they weren't all that much different than Tertullian, who also didn't adopt the gnostic view of Christ intact but revised it just enough to make it more acceptable.

In our last chapter, we raised the issue of gods coming down in the likeness of men as originating in pagan mythology. Now we have observed that the doctrine of dual natures was an invention of antichristian Gnostics and was totally repugnant to the early apostolic Christians. We will briefly demonstrate that point here, and we'll address it more fully later in Chapter Twelve. Irenaeus, who preceded Tertullian by a generation, stated this:

> The Gospel, therefore, *knew no other son of man but him who was of Mary*, who also suffered; and *no Christ who flew away from Jesus before the passion*; but... <u>blasphemous systems which divide the Lord</u>... say... <u>that he was formed of two different substances</u>. For this reason also he has thus testified to us in his Epistle: "Little children, it is the last time; and as ye have heard that Antichrist doth come, now have many antichrists appeared..." (Irenaeus, *Against Heresies*, Book 3, Chapter 16, par. 5)

Let these words sink in: *"blasphemous systems...divide the Lord... saying that he was formed of two different substances."* You have just read where the idea of the dual natures in Christ came from: the antichristian Gnostics. Nowhere in the Bible will you read where it describes Christ as personally made of two natures. To the contrary, the historical truth is that the early Christians sharply rejected the "two substance" or "two nature" doctrine as *an antichristian invention*.

Since the Bible does not preach (openly declare) or teach (by expounding in detail) the idea that Christ is personally formed of two natures, adopting this idea is to go against the biblical rules of interpretation being recognized here.

This is an extremely important truth: without the *antichristian "dual natures" doctrine*, both Trinitarianism and Onenessianism *completely fall apart*. That is simply because of the absolute abundance of Scriptures clearly describing Jesus as a human, personally separate and distinct from his God and Father. Just as with the concepts of incarnation and the Trinity, you won't find either the words "dual nature" or the concept clearly explained or described anywhere in the Bible. Again, just like the Trinity, it is a jumping to conclusions. It is not a Jewish view of the Messiah, and it is clearly adding to and taking away from the Messiah as he is clearly described in the Scriptures.

Onenessians are right to criticize Trinitarians for adopting the idea of three persons in the godhead from pagans. Why then don't they realize that Gnostics invented their precious "dual natures" doctrine? How can anyone believe that the Gnostics, the (antichristians of the Bible, according to Irenaeus), had a better way of explaining Jesus' human relationship to deity than the one explained in detail in the Bible?

Let us quote again:

> Since then the children have shared in flesh and blood, he also himself in like manner partook *of the same...Therefore he was obligated in all things to be made like his brothers*, that he might become a merciful and faithful high priest in things pertaining to God, to make atonement for the sins of the people... (Hebrews 2:14–18)

We will have much more to say on this topic; in fact, it is one of the main issues that will be covered in this book from many different angles. But let us just state for now that adopting the antichristian doctrine of dual natures in Christ will be shown to be an insurmountable problem for both Trinitarians and Onenessians. Any Christian who wishes to be true to the NT Scriptures and the words of Christ needs to seriously consider the evidence we are prepared to disclose. If you can't go to the Scriptures and show where it clearly and explicitly teaches that Christ is personally made of two natures, then you can be certain that you are adding to the Bible a teaching that was *invented by antichristians*, and you are redefining—that is, taking away from—what the Bible does say Christ is.

Both the Trinity and Oneness are refined forms of Gnosticism. Both are thus "Neo-Gnosticism."

We know that, unfortunately, many people, even when faced with these truths, will still cling to the idea that their personal "revelations," their jumped-to conclusions, their man-made traditions, somehow trump what the Scriptures clearly teach. This is why Trinitarians cling tenaciously to the Trinity even though it is clearly refuted in many ever-so-clearly stated Scriptures. Such was the same attitude the original *antichristians* had. That is why they called themselves "Gnostics." The word *gnosis* refers to "knowledge." *The Gnostics claimed they had a special knowledge* of their destiny in God, and they also claimed a specially revealed insight into the hidden truths of the Scriptures. When you think about it, that's what the first deception in the Garden of Eden was about: tricking people to look for a deeper meaning by reading between the lines of what God's word actually says. That is also what Onenessians are doing when they claim that the Oneness is a "revelation," even though it isn't called such in the Scriptures and even though, as with the Trinity, when the Scriptures are allowed to speak for themselves they clearly describe something completely different than either the Trinity or Modalism.

It isn't being supposed that this book will be able to sway anyone who thinks they have *a special revelation* that trumps God's word in the Scriptures or gives them an ability to see truths beyond what God's word actually explains and describes. Rather, this is being written for the sake of those who are willing to "try the spirits," as the word of God teaches (1 John 4:1), and who are interested in hearing what the Scriptures actually say. This book is written because "it is already time for you to awaken out of sleep, for salvation is now nearer to us than when we first believed" (Romans 13:11).

It is high time to awaken God's people to a <u>*purely*</u> biblical view of Christ. Unfortunately, this view is one that the majority of self-professing Christians have moved away from. It seems ironic that the Christ that the Bible clearly explains is a view of Christ that most of today's Christianity considers a heresy! All that is being proclaimed here is that we need to get back to a view of Christ that isn't polluted by worldly philosophy, pagan mythology, or antichristian theories. In other words, we need to get back to the Christ as the apostles actually preached him to be:

> ...Jesus of Nazareth, <u>*a man approved by God*</u> to you by mighty works and wonders and signs which God did by him... (Acts 2:22)

Summary: Up to this point a summary has been given of what is going to be covered in this book. All of these issues and topics will be covered in more depth, precept upon precept, line upon line. But the desire here was to bring the reader, by this point, to: a) an understanding of these opposing methods of interpretation, b) a clear, open, and straightforward presentation of the substance of *what this book will be advocating and what will be renounced*, c) the unbiblical and ungodly sources of the alternatives being contended against, and finally, d) the gravity of falling for false views of

Christ and God. Of course the main purpose of the book is in turning things around and showing just how much more glorious God's message of hope toward fallen humanity is, and can be seen to be, when viewed through the knowledge of the true and biblical Christ, God's prototype for humankind.

We will begin to restore this correct view by next going back to the schoolmaster, the OT, to hear its lessons for us on who and what the Messiah is as he is meant to be understood. Once we understand what the terms meant from the OT Schoolmaster, we can start interpreting the NT through the proper lens—the scriptural words and testimonies of Jesus Christ himself and his apostles.

SECTION TWO

Jewish Prophecies:
The True Foundations of Messiah

> ⁵:¹²*For when by reason of the time you ought to be teachers, you again need to have someone teach you the rudiments of the first principles of the oracles of God.* You have come to need milk, and not solid food. ¹³For everyone who lives on milk is not experienced in the word of righteousness, for he is a baby. ¹⁴But solid food is for those who are full grown, who by reason of use have their senses exercised to discern good and evil.
>
> ⁶:¹Therefore leaving the doctrine of the first principles of Christ, let us press on to perfection—*not laying again a foundation* of repentance from dead works, of faith toward God, ²of the teaching of baptisms, of laying on of hands, of resurrection of the dead, and of eternal judgment. ³This will we do, if God permits. (Hebrews 5:12–6:3)

The foundational passage for this section teaches us to adhere to the first principles of the word of God. It seems that a lot of people, both Trinitarians and Onenessians, believe that the foundational "first principles" that this passage is referring to are those of their denominational affiliation, or the traditions they've been taught from their pastors or in their seminaries. Nothing could be further from the truth if those traditions stray from the faith once delivered to the saints.

Instead of just assuming that everyone knows the first principles of the oracles of God, we're going to lay them out as plain as day so any reader can see whether we are merely showing what the Scripture teaches or whether, conversely, we are adding our own opinions and conclusions.

This section is particularly important for demonstrating some basic biblical principles. Certainly, right along with Onenessians, we know that Trinitarians need to learn the foremost rudiment of all of the first principles of the Hebrew Bible: God is one. Yet, perhaps surprisingly, that is also true of the Onenessian view of Christ: saying that God is one means not only that He is one person, but that He is also, as He has always been, one in nature or essence.

And again, these are lessons we also had to relearn and be retaught. Our assertions aren't meant to be personal attacks any more than Onenessians intend when they try to show the errors of Trinitarianism. Sometimes truth just needs to be taught, whether or not a recipient decides to become defensive or to not give the messenger the time of day. We hope better of our Onenessian neighbors. We feel very confident that those who have a sincere love for the truth and are willing to try the spirits, and reason together with us, will be able to see just how, where, and why the Onenessian viewpoint simply isn't the biblical view of the Christ the apostles preached.

In order for us to teach the truth, it is critical that we stand on the firm foundation of biblical concepts of the Messiah. What we intend to demonstrate in this section is that foundation, and just how far Onenessians and Trinitarians have strayed from it.

CHAPTER FIVE

Seed of Eve, Abraham, and David

"Seed" or "Offspring" means "descended from..."

Adam and Eve begat Seth...
Seth begat Enos...
Enos begat Cainan... etc...

Abraham begat Isaac...
Isaac begat Jacob...
Jacob begat Judah...

Boaz begat Obed...
Obed begat Jesse...
Jesse begat David...etc...

Luke 3 & Mattew 1

> Surely the Lord YHWH will do nothing, unless he reveals his secret to his servants the prophets. (Amos 3:7)

It is safe to say that most Christians realize that the idea of a Messiah (a Hebrew word), which we call "Christ" (from the Greek translation of the Hebrew word), is *a Jewish concept*. That isn't to say there weren't types of "Christs" in other cultures and religions. It is to say that the true, *biblical* Christ is not one of those others. We believe in and are contending for belief in *the Messiah that was prophesied throughout the Jewish OT Scriptures and has been made known in the* Christian *NT* Scriptures.

As our opening verse tells us, we believe that God told the OT prophets exactly what He planned to do. We believe *it also means that God would not clearly say He was going to do one thing and then do something completely different.*

The biblical descriptions of the Messiah go all the way back to God's first promise of a savior. (This is known by many scholars as the principle of "First Mention," where the first mention of a topic usually establishes its usage and understanding in subsequent mentions of the same idea.) God made that first messianic prophecy in judgment against the serpent for deceiving Eve and causing sin to enter the world. Simply put, *nothing beyond the human offspring of Eve* was stated or implied in that first messianic promise. Moreover, this basic, foundational truth did not change throughout the OT:

> YHWH God said to the serpent, "Because you have done this, cursed are you above all livestock... I will put enmity *between you and the woman, and between your offspring and her offspring*. He will bruise *his* head, and you will bruise *his* heel." (Genesis 3:14–15)

This passage is as first principle as one can get on the subject of the Messiah. As we can see, God called the offspring of the woman "he," and this particular "he" was *all that God says* would be needed to ultimately bruise, or crush, the head of the serpent. Furthermore and most importantly, God our Father speaks of the woman's male offspring in a third person pronoun (*he*, not *I*), showing quite clearly that *He, God, was speaking of a different individual from Himself.* Thus, the idea that the Messiah would be an incarnation of God our Father Himself is ruled out here in the same way that Genesis 1:27 rules out that God was implying He was a Trinity in verse 26.

Even the word *offspring* is contrary to human traditions regarding Christ: the very word means he would be a descendant, *genetically downstream* from Eve. The unbiblical idea that the Messiah would be recreated with a pre-fall human nature is actually disproven by this word "offspring."

This concise yet complete description of the future Messiah is a very important first principle because it proves that the opposite idea is not what is prophesied in the Scriptures. Rather, the opposite idea can be seen to be pagan in origin. For example, we have the following pagan philosopher explaining his view of the requirements of a pagan savior...

...it seems to me that, as the body (by itself naturally) tends to become dispersed, *it would need a savior that was a divinity.*[1]

Numenius is well known among Oneness theologians because of Charles Biggs. Biggs pointed out something that Onenessians are known to use against the Trinitarian position. Biggs wrote, "... *Numenius... boasts that he has gone back to the fountain head*, to Plato, Socrates and Pythagoras, *to the ancient traditions... and has restored to the schools the forgotten doctrine of Three Gods.*"[2]

Thus, the idea of a savior being a deity *"only"* is *pagan in origin*, just as much as the Trinity itself is, and both are contrary to the OT prophecies. In other words, God consistently said He would do one thing (i.e., save humanity through the offspring of Eve), yet many people believe He actually did something completely different (i.e., save humanity by incarnating Himself in human form).

The NT clearly spells out the same idea we read in God's first mention of a savior, and which is seen throughout the OT:

> [21]For since death came by man, the resurrection of the dead also came by man. [22]For as in Adam all die, so also in Christ all will be made alive. (1 Corinthians 15:21–22)

> [12]Therefore, as sin entered into the world through one man, and death through sin; and so death passed to all men, because all sinned... [15]...For if by the trespass of the one the many died, much more did the grace of God, and the gift by the grace *of the one man, Jesus Christ*, abound to the many... [16]The gift is not as through one who sinned: for the judgment came by one to condemnation, but the free

---

[1] Numenius, *The Neoplatonic Writings of Numenius,* collected and translated from the Greek by Kenneth Guthrie (Lawrence, KS: Selene Books, 1987), 8.

[2] Charles Bigg, *Christian Platonists of Alexandria,* (1886; rpt. Kessinger Publishing, 2003), 249–252.

gift came of many trespasses to justification...¹⁸So then as through one trespass, all men were condemned; *even so through one act of righteousness, all men were justified to life.* ¹⁹For as through the one man's disobedience many were made sinners, even so *through the obedience of the one will many be made righteous.* (Romans 5:12–19)

Here we clearly see that the false, pagan idea that Jesus "had to be God in order to save us" is *clearly refuted* by the plain wording of Romans 5:12–19. The key here is that *something else is clearly spelled out*. This passage teaches that, just as Adam sinned and passed death onto mankind, likewise the Messiah had to be a man in order to *reverse Adam's disobedience* and redeem us *through obedience*.

This passage says nothing about the Messiah needing to be a hybrid God-man in order to meet what is actually a man-made requirement to be both God and man; nor does any other Scripture. Finally, it would simply be nonsensical, and certainly extrabiblical, to claim that *God had to be obedient to himself* in order to reverse the human Adam's transgression! And yet that's what both Trinitarians and Onenessians subtly want us to believe. No Scripture teaches or explains in detail such a doctrine. So, they want us to believe that pagans had a better idea, a better explanation, of what our savior should be made of than what God's words in the Bible describe! We think that kind of thinking is both absurd and faithless, because faith comes from hearing the word of God!

Now all this isn't to say that God would not be involved in man's salvation. And this is where many get tripped up, because God does declare Himself as humanity's Savior and Redeemer. But the question is in what way does the Bible *explain* all of this? What is obvious in the Bible from beginning to end is that *it is God's power and plan, and no one else's.* And that includes Jesus Christ, as we see in his own words:

> Jesus therefore said to them, "When you have lifted up the Son of Man, then you will know that I am he, and *I do nothing of myself, but as my Father taught me, I say these things.*" (John 8:28)

Here we see that Jesus disagrees with anyone claiming that Jesus was the person of the Father. He also disagrees that he is personally God, because he says *he can do nothing of himself*. He didn't say he couldn't do anything of his human nature; there is no such talk or wording in the whole Bible! You never hear the Father say such things, for with God all things are possible.

> Jesus therefore answered them, "*My teaching* is not mine, *but his who* sent me." (John 7:16)

Even his teaching wasn't his! Jesus was explicitly *not alone and was not acting on his own*. In fact, he did nothing of himself. Rather, he gave all credit to God and away from himself. *God plans and speaks, and man hears, believes, and acts on God's direction, and this truth extends to Christ being himself a man!* Christians ought to understand this concept completely. They certainly understand it when it applies to themselves. It is just as Paul said, "I worked more than all of them; *yet not I*, but the grace of God which was with me" (1 Corinthians 15:10; see also Galatians 2:20). This was also the pattern of Christ's ("I do nothing of myself") life, and it is the same formula found in righteous people throughout the Bible (Hebrews 11:8–11).

The OT taught throughout that Christ would be *made entirely from Abraham and David according to the flesh*. NT Scripture sums up the following OT biblical verses like this, "For verily he took not on him the nature of angels; but *he took on him the seed of Abraham*" (Hebrews 2:16, KJV).

> For all the land which you see, I will give *to you, and to your offspring* forever. (Genesis 13:15–16)

> I will *give* to you, and *to your seed after you*, the land where you are traveling, all the land of Canaan, for an everlasting possession. I will be their God. (Genesis 17:8)

> Behold, the word of YHWH came to him, saying, *"This man will not be your heir, but he who will come forth out of your own body will be your heir."* (Genesis 15:4–5; see also Genesis 28:13, 35:12)

> Now the promises were spoken to Abraham and to his seed. He doesn't say, "To seeds," as of many, but as of one, "To your seed," which is Christ. (Galatians 3:16)

As we can see, the OT prophecies concerning the *nature* of Christ are consistent. Although the first three verses do not refer only to the Messiah, Galatians 3:16 does, and it limits the Messiah to being the offspring of Abraham. More specifically, the Messiah is to be the offspring of Eve, Abraham, and David. "Offspring" necessarily means *genetically descended from*, and therefore just as clearly and specifically, *not* a re-creation of a purer humanity *upstream* from his ancestors. In fact, *no* prophecy claimed that the Messiah would be a recreation made of *untainted* humanity. Such an idea is a total man-made fabrication! In fact, the very idea of a "sin-nature" is foreign to Jewish thought, but it certainly exists in pagan philosophical thought, where it is called *dualism*. Why then do some Christians believe that the OT isn't as good a schoolmaster as pagan philosophy is? It can only be because they aren't really as interested in hearing the Scriptures as they are in using the Scriptures to justify pagan ideas that make more sense to them...and they just don't admit they are pagan ideas.

Furthermore, *no* prophecy of the Jewish Scriptures state that Christ would be an incarnation of God. In fact, the NT faithfully restates these OT truths in many ways. One such NT passage makes it very clear and specific that Jesus was made *in all things just like you and I* are:

Since then the children have shared in flesh and blood, he also himself in like manner *partook of the same*, that through death he might bring to nothing him who had the power of death, that is, the devil, and might deliver all of them who through fear of death were all their lifetime subject to bondage. For most assuredly, *not to angels does he give help, but he gives help to* the seed of Abraham. Therefore *he was obligated in all things to be made like his brothers, that he might become* a merciful and faithful high priest in things pertaining to God, to make atonement for the sins of the people. For in that *he himself* has suffered being tempted, he is able to help those who are tempted. (Hebrews 2:14–18)

All flesh is not the same flesh, but *there is one flesh of men*, another flesh of animals... (1 Corinthians 15:39)

Not only was Jesus made in all things like us, but furthermore, there is only one type of flesh "of" humanity. That means if Jesus came in a *different* flesh from all other humans, he would have been a different kind of creature from us. If he was different than us, then he didn't come to save us. Hebrews 2:14–18 makes it abundantly clear that *Christ couldn't be any different than us* because it is us that he came to save! Thus, the NT Scriptures reiterate the OT truth that the Messiah was to be made from the seed, or offspring, of David:

Concerning His Son Jesus Christ our Lord, which *was made of the seed of David according to the flesh*... (Romans 1:3, KJV)

My relatives according to the flesh... Are Israelites... *From whom is Christ as concerning the flesh*... (Romans 9:3–5)

Remember that *Jesus Christ of the seed of David* was raised from the dead according to my gospel. (2 Timothy 2:8, KJV/NKJV)

> For there is one God, and *one mediator* between God and men, *the man* Christ Jesus. (1 Timothy 2:5, WEB, KJV, NKJV)

As we close this chapter, consider again our opening verse. Notice that the foundational truth of God's promise regarding Eve's offspring did not change genetically or mathematically over time. God *grounded* His people in the concept by expounding on the idea, progressing from Eve's seed, to further being Abraham's seed as a great blessing, to being David's seed that would build a house for the name of the Lord. But never once did God say through the prophets anything to the effect of, "and furthermore it will be I myself who will incarnate myself into that promised offspring so that I myself will become the Messiah." Just as there is no such language describing the Trinity in the OT, there is no such language describing this Oneness conclusion either. The Messiah of the OT would be born of the seed of Eve, Abraham, and David.

Jumping to Conclusions versus "It is Written": The idea that the Messiah would be made of the seed of Eve, Abraham, and David, and would thereby be their offspring according to the flesh, is consistently taught in both Testaments. It would definitely be jumping to conclusions to determine that God was "trying to say" that He would incarnate Himself as the Messiah.

The OT Schoolmaster: The idea that Christ would be human is the only description the OT gives of the Messiah. The idea that humans need a savior that is *only* deific is of pagan origin.

Teach No Other Doctrine: It is clearly written in 1 Corinthians 15:21–23 that since death came by man, the resurrection of the dead also comes through a man. The idea that humans need a savior, who would reverse the sinfulness of man, who is personally deific is a pagan, philosophical teaching that is not stated in the Scripture and should thus be discarded and rejected.

CHAPTER SIX

The Son of David is The Son of God

In this chapter we want to establish the OT Schoolmaster's meaning of the phrases "Son of God" and "Son of David." When we let the OT Scriptures inform our thoughts, as we should, we find that both these terms simply refer, in idiomatic ways, to the biblical truth that Jesus was a man who was the offspring of David. We will also show that Jesus was not God incarnate; rather, he had to first be perfected here on earth before attaining to his ultimate status of perfection.

Let's begin by examining the term "Son of God" and what it means and doesn't mean. Although the *plural* phrase "sons of God" is used early in the Bible, the singular term "Son of God," as far as the Messiah is concerned, has its roots in God's promise to King David. Here again is the foundational passage:

> ⁸Now therefore thus shall you tell my servant David, Thus says YHWH... ¹²*When your days are fulfilled*, and you shall sleep with your fathers, *I will set up your seed after you, who* shall proceed *out of your bowels*, and I will establish his kingdom. ¹³*He shall build a house for my name*, and I will establish the throne of his kingdom *forever*. ¹⁴*I will be his father, and he shall be my son*: *if he commit iniquity*, I will chasten him with the rod of men, and with the stripes of the children of men; ¹⁵but *my loving kindness shall not depart from him*, as I took it from Saul, whom I put away before you. ¹⁶*Your house and your kingdom shall be made sure for ever before you: your throne shall be established forever*. ¹⁷According to all these words, and according to all this vision, so did Nathan speak to David. (2 Samuel 7:8–17)

Note that God explicitly said that David's son would be God's Son: "I will be *his* Father, and *he* shall be my son." This, coupled with other Scriptures like it, is the biblical source for calling the Messiah *the Son of God*. It is explicitly because God Himself said that David's son would be His, God's Son. Thus "Son of God" and "Son of David" are *synonymous* terms for all practical purposes.

Most importantly, this is God's definition of His Son. This is God's testimony through the prophet Nathan as recorded by Samuel! In other words, God's definition in the Scriptures is true, and those of Trinitarians and Onenessians are simply man-made lies against God's sworn oath!

Note also that God is speaking in the future tense. This future son of David's, who was to be the Son of God, was not yet in existence. Now note that this promise was considered by the apostles of our Lord to be one of the most solemn of oaths:

> Brothers, I may tell you freely of the patriarch David, that he both died and was buried, and his tomb is with us to this day. Therefore, being a prophet, and knowing that *God had sworn with an oath to him that of the fruit of his body*,

according to the flesh, he would raise up the Christ to sit on his throne. (Acts 2:29–30)

The Trinitarians have concluded that "the Son of God" is a code phrase for the second person in their Trinity theory. The Onenessians have concluded that "the Son of God" is a code phrase for the deity of the person of God in Jesus. Both are totally without biblical support (at least that is until they jump to conclusions). However, the idea that "the Son of God" is a biblical "code phrase" for the Son born of the seed from the bodily issue of King David, whom God would make His own son, is *clearly defined as such and reiterated in many clear passages of Scriptures.*

Now let's take a brief look at some of the opportunities that Trinitarians and Onenessians take for jumping to their conclusions. Let's begin by considering the following Psalm as the OT prophets understood it:

> Your *divine throne* is everlasting; your royal scepter is a scepter of equity. You have loved righteousness and hate wickedness; rightly has God, *your God*, chosen to anoint you with oil of gladness over all *your peers*. (Psalms 45:7–8 in Jewish Scriptures, 6–7 in Christian Scriptures)

Although later Christians attempt to reinterpret this Psalm differently, in Hebrews 1:8, above, is the way David would have understood it. *This Psalm was originally written as God speaking to and about King David.* Today's theologians seem to conveniently forget this little truth. Certainly David *did not take his sworn oath from God to mean that he himself was God* or that his son or future sons would be God. This is how false interpretations attempt to read into such passages *what they never would have meant to the OT prophets who wrote them*. Note the internal witness to what we are saying: "rightly has God, your God, chosen to anoint you... " So the one about whom this was written had a God above him and was anointed above his peers. The peers of course are the rest of us humans, if not David's Israelite brothers in particular!

No legitimate Jew ever thought that Psalms 45:7–8 should be interpreted to mean that David was YHWH-God Himself. Why then do Trinitarians and Onenessians interpret it in such a way? Answer: because they interpret it through the lenses of pagan ideas about incarnated deities, rather than through the OT Schoolmaster! For evidence of the meaning of the verse in question, there is another passage of Scripture that helps inform our understanding of what Psalms 45:7–8 would have meant to the ancient Jews:

> Then *Solomon sat on the throne of YHWH as king* instead of David his father, and prospered; and all Israel obeyed him. (1 Chronicles 29:23, JPS)

Solomon sat on the throne of God! This is how the people of the Old Covenant understood the concept in Psalms 45:7–8: not that the Messiah would be an incarnation of God the Father, but that *a human son of David would sit on God's throne*. This interpretation is not jumping to conclusions, but rather it is doing what Jesus demonstrated by looking for another passage that provides more clarity.

Now let's consider the overall context of the Messiah as a *Son of David*. David wanted to build a house for God made of stone and wood. That is the one that Solomon built, known as Solomon's temple. But the temple that God had in mind was actually to be the very people of God. They would be called by God's name, and God would be housed in their hearts. In this way, Jesus is ultimately the Son of David who would build the house that God was talking about. This is why the Book of Hebrews says that Jesus is the builder of the house. As you read this passage keep in mind God's words to David *that David's son would build the house*. In other words, keep in mind the biblical code phrase for the Son of God, instead of viewing the passage through the lenses of the traditions of men.

> [1]Therefore, holy brothers, partakers of a heavenly calling, consider the apostle and High Priest of our confession, Jesus; [2]*who was faithful to Him who appointed him, as also*

was Moses in all his house. ³*For he has been counted worthy of more glory than Moses,* inasmuch as he *who built the house has more honor than the house.* ⁴For every house is built by someone; but He who built all things is God. ⁵*Moses* indeed was faithful in all his house *as a servant,* for a testimony of those things which were afterward to be spoken, ⁶*but Christ is faithful as a Son over his house; whose house we are, if we hold fast* our confidence and the glorying of our hope *firm to the end.* (Hebrews 3:1–6)

According to verse 1, the subject of the passage is Jesus. The two distinct "him" pronouns in verse 2 show that he is personally distinct from God who appointed him. Jesus was faithful as a son (in contrast to Moses, who was faithful as a servant), and Jesus was therefore, as verse 3 says, "counted worthy" of more glory and honor than Moses. This all demonstrates clearly that *Jesus was not inherently worthy by deific substance or personality.* Rather, it says *he had to prove himself through faith*; thus, Jesus was *"faithful to Him who appointed him."* The house that Jesus builds, which is the topic here, is not the whole world or all of mankind—that is what God built. The house that Jesus is building is limited to the household of the saints—us—in whom God is "templed" if we hold firm to the end.

Unfortunately, views such as Oneness destroy the wonderful truth of what this passage is telling us. Keep in mind that Onenessians ultimately dispose of the flesh of Jesus; but here, that flesh, that human person, is exalted for his faithful obedience to the Father. In Oneness terms, that would be like you or me exalting our bodies for getting up and going to work to provide for our needs. It is simply nonsense to contend that God had to be obedient to Himself to be counted worthy of glory.

The fact that Jesus had to *prove* himself faithful to God the Father has further witness in the NT. For example:

And Jesus *increased* in wisdom and stature, and *in favor with God* and men. (Luke 2:52)

This passage begs the question, how could "God" possibly *increase* in favor with Himself? The very word "increased" used in this passage proves to be very insightful. It originated as a navigational metaphor that means, "to drive forward by means of blows." "Increased."[1]

This verse is saying that Jesus fulfilled the part of the prophecy wherein God had said, "*I will be his father, and he shall be my son: if he commit iniquity, I will chasten him with the rod of men, and with the stripes of the children of men*; but *my loving kindness shall not depart from him.*" You may recall, the Scripture says, "... *if you are without discipline*, of which all have been made partakers, *then are you illegitimate*, and not sons" (Hebrews 12:8). This is a truth about sons that cannot ring true with the pagan idea that Christ is God Himself incarnate in the flesh rather than God's Son born of the seed of David his father according to the flesh.

While Trinitarians and Onenessians conclude by assumption that Jesus was perfect because he was God incarnate, the Bible explains his perfection a different way by explaining it as something that he had to attain, and it even explains how he had to attain it:

> [10]For it became him, for whom are all things, and through whom are all things, in bringing many children to glory, to make the author of their salvation *perfect through sufferings*. [11]For both he who sanctifies and those who are sanctified are all from one, for which cause he is not ashamed to call them brothers, [12]saying, "I will declare your name to my brothers. In the midst of the congregation I will sing your praise." [13]Again, "I will put my trust in him." Again, "Behold, here am I and the children whom God has given me." (Hebrews 2:10–13)

He was made perfect through sufferings. Is that true of God? Of course not! So then, in saying that Jesus was faithful, and thereby

---

[1] *Exegetical Dictionary of the New Testament* (Location: Eerdmans, 1990), Biblesoft, 2006.

counted worthy, the passage in Hebrews alludes to what is said in Psalms 45:7: "You have loved righteousness, and hated wickedness. <u>Therefore</u> God, your God, has anointed you with the oil of gladness <u>above your fellows</u> (or peers)." It is in this context that God designates, exalts, and anoints Jesus above all his fellow human beings.

Perhaps Jesus had this verse in mind when he said, "I am ascending to my Father and to your Father, to my God and your God" (John 20:17). What we can say with certainty is that this set of passages has *nothing to do with an incarnation of the person of God* and *everything to do with God's sworn oath* to David regarding the Son that would proceed out of David's issue. And we do know that God kept his promise to David and that because of Jesus' faithful obedience he has been exalted above the rest of his fellows, peers, and brothers; namely, us.

We know this because, in proclaiming this Jesus on the day of Pentecost, Peter said:

> Let all the house of Israel therefore *know assuredly* that God has *made him both Lord* and Christ, this Jesus whom you crucified. (Acts 2:36)

Jesus was made Lord. Think about what that means. Was God "made" God or Lord? Of course not. We teach and believe in the Jesus whom the apostles preached; that is the one who was made both Lord and Messiah, the one who was born of the offspring/seed of David.

Jumping to Conclusions versus "It is Written": The idea that a future son of David's would be God's Son is not jumping to conclusions; it is stated in many Scriptures. The idea that David's son would be an incarnation of God Himself is never clearly stated in Scriptures and can only be arrived at by jumping to conclusions.

The OT Schoolmaster: The idea that a future son of David's would be God's Son (thus, the Son of God) is clearly and consistently taught in the OT. In Matthew 26:63, the high priest insisted that

Jesus tell him if he was "the anointed one, the Son of God." This shows that the high priest understood the title "Son of God" to mean the "Anointed One," or "Messiah," and is strong evidence that Jews did not expect their Messiah to be an incarnation of their God the Father.

> But Jesus held his peace. The high priest answered him, 'I adjure you by the living God, that you tell us whether you are the Christ, the Son of God.' (Matthew 26:63)

Teach No Other Doctrine: The idea that the Son of God, the Son of David, would be none other than God Himself made into a human has no basis in OT prophecies or theology. In fact, quite the opposite was the basis of Nathanael's confession of right belief in Christ! For Nathanael, the title "Son of God" was another way of saying that Jesus was the King of Israel.

> Nathanael answered him, "Rabbi, *you are the Son of God! You are King of Israel!*" Jesus answered him, "Because I told you, 'I saw you underneath the fig tree,' do you believe?" (John 1:49–50)

CHAPTER SEVEN
Son of Man

God is not a man, that he should lie, *Neither the son of man*, that he should repent: Has he said, and will he not do it? Or has he spoken, and will he not make it good? (Numbers 23:19)

Let your hand be on *the man of your right hand*, On *the son of man whom you made strong for yourself.* (Psalms 80:17)

"God is not... the son of man!" Did you catch that? Rather, the son of man is someone whom God *makes* and *uses* as His own right hand. That's what the Bible says. In this chapter, we will look at the phrase "son of man" and see what it means biblically, in contrast to the way Trinitarians and Onenessians typically view it. In the OT, the phrase "son of man" is used 108 times.[1] In every single one of them, it means just what it says, *male offspring of mortal humanity*.

This is clearly the bulk of scriptural witness to the truth that "Son of Man" is an idiomatic phrase for a human being. This phrase is used unclearly only once, in a way that causes some mistakenly to believe that it is really just a code word for the unbiblical phrase "God the Son." Here is the passage:

> I saw in the night visions, and behold, there came with the clouds of the sky *one like a son of man*, and he came even to the ancient of days, and *they brought him near before him*. (Daniel 7:13)

Three things are stated here that a lot of people seem to overlook. First, the one like the son of man is being *given* a kingdom. In other words, the authority of the kingdom is *not* inherent to his person as it is with God. This is perfectly in line with the OT basis of Jesus' claim in the NT that all authority in heaven and earth had been *given to him* and that he could do nothing of himself. Second, the passage interprets for us who this person is, as we'll show below. And third, Daniel himself is called "son of man" in the same book (Daniel 8:17). Surely we aren't to believe Daniel was the person of God Himself because he is called "son of man."

Let's take a look at the key verses...

> [13] I saw in the night visions, and behold, there came with the clouds of the sky *one like a son of man*, and he came even to the ancient of days, and *they brought him near before him*.

---

[1] The 108 instances of son of man in the OT are: Numbers 23:19; Job 25:6, 35:8; Psalms 8:4, 80:17, 144:3, 146:3; Isaiah 51:12, 56:2; Jeremiah 49:18, 33, 50:40, 51:43; Ezekiel 2:1, 3, 6, 8; 3:1, 3, 4, 10, 17, 25; 4:1, 16; 5:1; 6:2; 7:2; 8:5, 6, 8, 12, 15, 17; 11:2, 4, 15; 12:2, 3, 9, 18, 22, 27; 13:2, 17; 14:3, 13; 15:2; 16:2; 17:2; 20:3, 4, 27, 46; 21:2, 6, 9, 12, 14, 19, 28; 22:2, 18, 24; 23:2, 36; 24:2, 16, 25; 25:2; 26:2; 27:2; 28:2, 12, 21; 29:2, 18; 30:2, 21; 31:2; 32:2, 18; 33:2, 7, 10, 12, 24, 30; 34:2; 35:2; 36:1, 17; 37:3, 9, 11, 16; 38:2, 14; 39:1, 17; 40:4; 43:7, 10, 18; 44:5; 47:6; and Daniel 7:13, 8:17.

> ¹⁴ There *was given him dominion, and glory, and a kingdom,* that all the peoples, nations, and languages should serve him: his dominion is an everlasting dominion, which shall not pass away, and his kingdom that which shall not be destroyed. ¹⁵As for me, Daniel, my spirit was grieved in the midst of my body, and the visions of my head troubled me. ¹⁶I came near to one of those who stood by, *and asked him the truth concerning all this. So he told me, and made me know the interpretation* of the things.
>
> ¹⁷"These great animals, which are four, are four kings, who shall arise out of the earth.¹⁸ But *the saints of the Most High shall receive the kingdom*, and possess the kingdom forever, even forever and ever." (Daniel 7:13–18)
>
> ²¹I saw, and the same horn made war with the saints, and prevailed against them; ²² until the ancient of days came, and *judgment was given to the saints of the Most High*, and the time came that the saints possessed the kingdom. (Daniel 7:21–22)
>
> ²⁶But the judgment shall be set, and they shall take away his dominion, to consume and to destroy it to the end. ²⁷*The kingdom and the dominion, and the greatness of the kingdoms under the whole sky, shall be given to the people of the saints of the Most High*: his kingdom is an everlasting kingdom, and all dominions shall serve and obey him. (Daniel 7:26–27)

The interpretation of the identity of the one "like the son of man" is given to Daniel three times: in verses 18, 22, and 27: *the saints of the Most High!* Not many people are willing to accept it, though. We, however, have plenty of "it is written again" type Scriptures to help us see this great and marvelous truth.

To begin with, this scene has a very close parallel passage in Revelation. Note in particular the outcome of the scene:

¹I saw, in the right hand of him who sat on the throne, a book written inside and outside, sealed shut with seven seals. ²I saw a mighty angel proclaiming with a loud voice, "Who is worthy to open the book, and to break its seals?" ³No one in heaven above, or on the earth, or under the earth, was able to open the book, or to look in it. ⁴And I wept much, because no one was found worthy to open the book, or to look in it.

⁵One of the elders said to me, "Don't weep. Behold, *the Lion who is of the tribe of Judah, the Root of David*, has overcome; he who opens the book and its seven seals."

⁶I saw in the midst of the throne and of the four living creatures, and in the midst of the elders, *a Lamb standing, as though it had been slain*, having seven horns, and seven eyes, which are the seven Spirits of God, sent out into all the earth. ⁷*Then he came, and he took it out of the right hand of him who sat on the throne.*

⁸Now when he had taken the book, the four living creatures and the twenty-four elders fell down before the Lamb, each one having a harp, and golden bowls full of incense, which are the prayers of the saints. ⁹They sang a new song, saying, "You are worthy to take the book, And to open its seals: For you were killed, And bought us for God with your blood, Out of every tribe, language, people, and nation, ¹⁰*And made them kings and priests to our God, And they reign on earth.*"

¹¹I saw, and I heard something like a voice of many angels around the throne, the living creatures, and the elders; and the number of them was ten thousands of ten thousands, and thousands of thousands; ¹²saying with a loud voice, "Worthy is the Lamb who has been killed *to receive the power, wealth, wisdom, strength, honor, glory, and blessing!*" (Revelation 5:1–12)

The interpretation is incredibly simple and clear. Jesus Christ, the Lamb who has been slain, has not only redeemed his people, but he has also secured for himself and them a kingdom in which they will reign as kings and priests along with him. And furthermore, it is at this time that the Lamb receives the power of the kingdom, wealth, wisdom, strength, honor, glory, and blessing!

We may ask, why then is the "one like the son of man" seen as a single person in Daniel's vision? The answer is a truth that is clearly spelled out for us in the Scriptures:

> [12]For *as the body is one, and has many members*, and all the members of the body, being many, are *one body; so also is Christ.* [13]For in one Spirit we were all baptized into one body, whether Jews or Greeks, whether bond or free; and were all given to drink into one Spirit. [14]For the body is not one member, but many... [18]But now God has set the members, each one of them, in the body, just as he desired. [19]If they were all one member, where would the body be? [20]But *now they are many members, but one body.*
> (1 Corinthians 12:12–20)

It is clearly stated that there are many persons in one body in Christ. Does that make us incarnations of the Trinitarian person of "God the Son," or incarnations of God the Father as in Onenessianism? No, a thousand times no. And it is just as unreasonable for Trinitarians and Onenessians to conclude that because Christ operates as the body of God that he must be an incarnation of the person of God. If that is so, then he is not the firstborn of many brothers; rather, he is a pagan form of an incarnation of a deity.

Now let's read a few other passages that add to our understanding of what is meant in calling Jesus "the Son of Man":

> So also it is written, "The first man, Adam, became a living soul." *The last Adam became* a life-giving spirit. However *that which is spiritual isn't first, but that which is natural, then that which is spiritual.* The first man is of the earth, made of dust. The second man is the Lord from heaven. (1 Corinthians 15:45–47)

> He is the head of the body, the assembly, who is *the beginning, the firstborn* from the dead; that in all things he might have the preeminence. (Colossians 1:18)

> We know that all things work together for good for those who love God, to those who are called according to his purpose. For whom he foreknew, he also predestined to *be conformed to the image of his Son, that he might be the firstborn among many brothers.* (Romans 8:28–29)

Through these Scriptures we can see that God "worked it out" so that the ultimate offspring of humanity (or "Son of Man") is and was to become the ultimate firstborn among many brothers in the kingdom of the resurrected ones, that he might attain reconciliation for all unto God "in one body." This is clearly stated in Scripture:

> [13]But now in Christ Jesus you who once were far off are made near in the blood of Christ. [14]For he is our peace, *who made both one*, and broke down the middle wall of partition, [15]having abolished in the flesh the hostility, the law of commandments contained in ordinances, *that he might create in himself one new man of the two*, making peace; [16]and might reconcile them *both in one body to God* through the cross, having killed the hostility thereby. (Ephesians 2:13–16)

Thus, the NT certainly echoes the theme found in Daniel 7, that one man/one body is given dominion, and which the passage goes on to interpret as the "saints of the Most High" being given a kingdom and dominion:

> [10]For it became him, for whom are all things, and through whom are all things, *in bringing many children to glory*, to make *the author of their salvation* perfect through sufferings. [11]For both he who sanctifies and those who are sanctified are all from one, for which cause *he is not ashamed to call them brothers*, [12]saying, "I will declare your name to my

brothers. In the midst of the congregation I will sing your praise." ¹³Again, "I will put my trust in him." Again, "*Behold, here am I and the children whom God has given me.*" ¹⁴Since then the children have shared in flesh and blood, *he also himself in like manner partook of the same*, that through death he might bring to nothing him who had the power of death, that is, the devil, ¹⁵*and might deliver all of them* who through fear of death were all their lifetime subject to bondage. ¹⁶For most assuredly, not to angels does he give help, but he gives help to the seed of Abraham. ¹⁷Therefore he was obligated in all things to be made like his brothers... (Hebrews 2:10–17)

This is God's plan, and Jesus is God's ultimate original prototype. Jesus is the head of *the* body, the assembly, and the "one body" that is "like the son of man" (that is, the *body* of Christ made up entirely of human beings) he will bring before God, the true Ancient of Days, where all the saints, the brothers of the Lord Jesus, will receive crowns as kings and priests to reign as heirs with Christ.

So then, all the authority that God has "given" Jesus and which we see displayed in and through Jesus beginning with the testimony of the apostles and continuing to this day, is exactly what God has planned for each of us once we come into our promise, at which time we will rule and reign with Christ and, ultimately, to a time when, "God is all in all."

Summary: The truth that the phrase "son of man" means *a human being* is well and thoroughly established throughout the Bible. The one passage in Daniel 7:13 that discusses "one like a son of man" refers to the coming day when Christ, the firstborn among many brothers, will bring all of his fellow saints together *as one body* before the throne of God to be crowned as kings and priests along with Jesus Christ when he comes into his kingdom. There is no legitimate reason to interpret the phrase "son of man" as a code word indicating that Christ is an incarnation of God, or some other preexistent spiritual being. Rather, such a false interpretation hides the ultimate plan of God, which is the hope and promise that God extends to people who will repent to dead works and turn to God.

Jumping to Conclusions versus "It is written": The man-made idea that the title "son of man" signifies the deity of Christ based on Daniel 7:13 is a jumping to conclusions. The "it is written again" Scriptures that refute that assumption are Daniel 7:18, 22, 27; Revelation 5:1–12; 1 Corinthians 12:12–20, Colossians 1:18, Romans 8:28–29; Ephesians 2:13–16 and Numbers 23:19, all quoted above, and include all the 108 passages that are listed above wherein "son of man" refers exclusively to human beings.

The OT Schoolmaster: The idea that God the Father would make Himself a "son of man" was simply never taught in the OT, but rather was clearly refuted in Numbers 23:19.

Teach No Other Doctrine: Since the apostles never taught that "son of man" was a mystic "code word" for deity, or the fleshly body of the personality of God Himself, such ideas should be rejected as adding to and taking away from the word of God.

CHAPTER EIGHT

A Man Like Unto Moses and His Brothers

A Man Like Moses

¹⁵YHWH your God will raise up to you a prophet *from the midst of you, of your brothers, like me*; to him you shall listen; ¹⁶according to all that you desired of YHWH your God in Horeb in the day of the assembly, saying, Let me not hear again the voice of YHWH my God, neither let me see this great fire any more, that I not die. ¹⁷YHWH said to me, They have well said that which they have spoken. ¹⁸*I will raise them up a prophet from among their brothers, like you; and I will put my words in his mouth*, and he shall speak to them all that I shall command him. ¹⁹It shall happen, that whoever will not listen to my words which he shall speak in my name, I will require it of him. (Deuteronomy 18:15–19)

Here is yet another very clear prophesy that describes and explains details about the promised Jewish Messiah.

Notice that this prophecy was given in answer to a corporate prayer to YHWH from His people. In response to their prayer that they not hear again the direct voice of God, God decreed that they had spoken well, and from then on they would hear from Him indirectly through a man like them. But look closely at what God explicitly said. The prophet that God would raise up would be, first, *like Moses*, and second, *would be from among them and like them*, the Israelites. Was Moses a hybrid God-man? Were any of the Israelite children with Moses hybrid God-men? Were any of the prophets that rose up after Moses God-man hybrids? Of course they were not. God described the Messiah to them in very precise terms: he would be as human as they were. But most importantly, we should ask, did the NT apostles apply this prophecy directly to Jesus? Why yes, they most emphatically did.

The following quote is the second recorded preaching of the gospel after the day of Pentecost. In this instance, Peter adds to our understanding of Christ. Instead of pointing to Jesus as David's offspring, he established Jesus as the prophet of whom Moses had spoken. Peter began his preaching by contrasting and distinguishing the God of the Jews from the man whom God calls His servant. Nowhere in Peter's preaching of the gospel did he tell the Jews "this Jesus is a hybrid God-man..." There was simply no such "incarnation of God" language in Peter's preaching of Christ, either here or anywhere else in the Book of Acts.

> [13]*The God of* Abraham, Isaac, and Jacob, the God of our fathers, *has glorified His Servant Jesus*, whom you delivered up, and denied... [14]But you denied the Holy and Righteous One, and asked for a murderer to be granted to you, [15]and killed the Prince of life, whom God raised from the dead, to which we are witnesses. [16]*By faith in his name* has his name made this man strong, whom you see and know. *Yes, the faith which is through him* has given him this perfect soundness in the presence of you all.
> [17]Now, brothers, I know that you did this in ignorance, as did also your rulers. [18]But *the things which God announced by the mouth of all His prophets, that Christ should suffer, He thus fulfilled.* [19]Repent therefore... [22]*For Moses indeed*

> said to the fathers, "The Lord God will raise up a prophet for you from among your brothers, like me. You shall listen to him in all things whatever he says to you. ²³It will be, that every soul that will not listen to that prophet will be utterly destroyed from among the people."... ²⁶God, having raised up His servant, Jesus, sent him to you first, to bless you, in turning away everyone of you from your wickedness. (Acts 3:13–26)

Jesus was God's servant, a man like Moses. This is what the apostles preached him to be. Similarly, the martyr Stephen, just as Peter had, also preached that Christ was a man like Moses:

> ³⁷This is that Moses, who said to the children of Israel, 'The Lord our God will raise up a prophet for you from among your brothers, like me... (Acts 7:37)

But we will cover Stephen's preaching when we get to him in our examination of Acts. The verse is just being mentioned here as confirmation that Peter wasn't alone in applying Moses' prophecy to Jesus. These verses testify that God *raised Jesus up from among the people*, and he was like Moses. Peter also reiterated the prophecy that anyone who doesn't listen to Jesus will be destroyed from among the people. Jesus is never stated in the Bible to be God incarnate. But here, in Peter's words, we have a simple and clear explanation of Jesus' authority over all. It is simply because God raised him up from among the people and glorified him.

Also noteworthy is that Peter didn't even call Jesus "God's Son." In the first sentence, Peter called Jesus "God's *servant*." This word is *pais* in the Greek. It is Strong's number 3816, meaning: "a boy (as often beaten with impunity), or... a child; specifically, a slave or servant (especially a minister to a king; and by eminence to God)."

In this way, Peter preached the one (Jesus) whom God glorified as being distinct from God (the God of their fathers) who glorified him. For Peter, the one being glorified was clearly not inherently the God of their fathers. Peter was not preaching a Trinitarian or

Onenessian version of Jesus, but rather was preaching the only Jesus that saves. People who preach a different Jesus than this are really saying they don't believe Peter's message, which is the true message that Jesus himself gave Peter to deliver to us!

There is another very important point in the above passages. God told Moses, "I will put *my words in his* mouth" (Deuteronomy 18:18). This is similar to Moses and Peter saying, "You shall listen to him in all things whatever he says to you." Let's look at Jesus' own pertinent words:

> The word which you hear *isn't mine*, but the Father's *who* sent me. (John 14:24)

> He who sent me is true; and the things which I heard from him, these I say to the world. (John 8:26)

> For *I spoke not from myself*, but the Father who sent me, *he gave me a commandment, what I should say, and what I should speak*. I know that his commandment is eternal life. The things therefore which I speak, even as the Father has said to me, so I speak. (John 12:49–50)

> Now they have known that *all things whatever you have given me are from you*, for *the words which you have given me I have given to them*, and they received them, and knew for sure that I came forth from you, and they have believed that you sent me. (John 17:7–8)

It doesn't seem as though Jesus could be clearer or more consistent: the words he spoke weren't his words. This was such an important theme that even John the Baptist, Jesus' forerunner, said the very same thing: "For *he whom God has sent speaks the words of God; for [because] God gives* the Spirit without measure. The Father loves the Son, and has *given all* things into his hand" (John 3:34–35).

Clearly, Jesus, Peter, and even John the Baptist all identify Jesus in terms personally distinct from God. Jesus wasn't God, rather, he was given and spoke the words God had given him. In words and testimonies such as these, we can see that Jesus truly was a fulfillment of the OT prophecies. Of course, this is just a small sample. The important theme, which all of these Scriptures reiterate, is that God gave Jesus the words to speak. These passages do not say that Jesus spoke from his human nature at one point and from his deific nature at other times. Those who say Jesus spoke as God in one instance and as man in another make these Scriptures void through their traditions that they deliver.

Peter made another very important point about Jesus in Acts 3 (above). In verse 18 he said that God fulfilled *everything spoken beforehand by the Hebrew prophets*. The most important prophecy for our salvation has to do with the suffering of *this* Jesus.

There is no denying that the Jewish Scriptures prophesied the suffering *servant* of YHWH. This theme goes all the way back to the time when God said that the serpent would crush his (Messiah's) heel but he (Messiah) would crush the serpent's head.

Isaiah prophesied that the Messiah would be cut off from the land of the living, which is to say, he would experience death for the transgressions (sins) of God's people. Isaiah's prophecy improved our understanding of what Christ would do and be, but it did not in any manner contradict or change the prophecy given in Genesis about Eve's offspring.

> ³*A Man of sorrows...* he was wounded for our transgressions, He was bruised for our iniquities...
> ⁵And by his stripes we are healed...
> ⁶And *[Yahweh] has laid on him* the iniquity of us all...
> ¹⁰Yet it pleased [Yahweh] to bruise him; *He has put him* to grief. When *You make his* soul an offering for sin...
> ¹¹*My righteous Servant* shall justify many, For he shall bear their iniquities.
> ¹²*Therefore* I will divide him a portion with the great, And he shall divide the spoil with the strong, *because* he poured out

his soul unto death, And he was numbered with the transgressors, And he bore the sin of many, And made intercession for the transgressors. (Isaiah 53:4–12; NKJV)

This Scripture says that Christ would be a man of sorrows. Peter preached that Jesus fulfilled this prophecy and all that the prophets said about suffering. This is a man suffering. God may suffer vicariously through us because He feels our pain and what we are going through, including His only begotten son. But this passage is very clear in stating that it is God's servant who will actually bear the burden of the suffering he would be subjected to for our salvation and healing.

This Messiah was fully human. This Messiah stood in very clear personal distinction from the God who "put him to grief" and "made his soul an offering for sin." No prophecy foretold, explained, or described that Messiah would receive his personality from the "God-side" of his being. No prophecy foretold that only Christ's human nature would suffer, but his deific nature was God, making him a personal incarnation of God Himself. There simply is no such talk in the entire Bible, let alone in any of the prophecies concerning Jesus. Therefore, if Jesus was the theorized, hybrid, dual-natured God-man, as many try to make him today, then he simply is not the Messiah prophesied in the Jewish Scriptures.

Jumping to Conclusions versus "It is written": The Bible passage at the beginning of this chapter couldn't be clearer: [15]"YHWH your God will raise up to you a prophet *from the midst of you, of your brothers, like me*; to him you shall listen... [17]YHWH said to me... [18]*I will raise them up a prophet from among their brothers, like you; and I will put my words in his mouth*" (Deuteronomy 18:15–19). This is not jumping to conclusions; it is what the Bible clearly and plainly teaches us. On the other hand, to claim that Jesus is more than this man like the rest of us, is to jump to conclusions.

The OT Schoolmaster: ³"*A Man of sorrows...* ¹¹*My righteous Servant shall justify many, For he shall bear their iniquities.* ¹²*Therefore I will divide him a portion with the great, And he shall divide the spoil with the strong, Because he poured out his soul unto death, And he was numbered with the transgressors, And he bore the sin of many, And made intercession for the transgressors*" (Isaiah 53:4–12; NKJV). The OT teaches us to believe that Christ was God's servant whom God sent.

Teach No Other Doctrine: You will never read in the Bible that Jesus is *clearly and unmistakably* taught or preached to be inherently God, or that he is God incarnate, or that he is "100% God and 100% man." Rather, in Peter's words in Acts 3:13–26, we have a simple and clear explanation of Jesus' authority over all. It is simply because God raised him up from among the people and glorified him.

CHAPTER NINE

The Messiah = The Anointed One

"He has anointed me"
Luke 4:18

¹⁸"The Spirit of the Lord is on me, Because *he has anointed me to preach* good news to the poor. *He has sent me to heal* the brokenhearted, To proclaim release to the captives, Recovering of sight to the blind, To deliver those who are crushed, ¹⁹And to proclaim the acceptable year of the Lord." ²⁰He closed the book [of Isaiah], gave it back to the attendant, and sat down. The eyes of all in the synagogue were fastened on him. ²¹He began to tell them, *"Today, this Scripture has been fulfilled in your hearing."* (Luke 4:18–21)

Jesus indicated here that he was anointed by God to preach, heal, set captives free, restore sight to the blind, bring deliverance, and more. We have come to believe this proclamation is literal. Furthermore, we believe that interpreting this otherwise would not be taking Jesus at his word.

In this chapter we intend to reestablish the OT Schoolmaster's meaning and definition of the term "Messiah", which literally means "*Anointed One.*" The Hebrew word for Messiah (*mashiyach*) and the Greek word for Christ (*christos*) are completely synonymous words. In both cases, Hebrew and Greek, the root words (Heb. *mashach* and Gr. *Chrio*) literally mean "to anoint with oil." However, when these words are "transliterated" into our English Bibles as "Christ," they lose the simplicity and clarity of the meaning. To illustrate this point, consider the following phrases:

1. Jesus the Anointed One
2. Jesus Christ

The first phrase describes something specific even to us English readers. The second phrase is more ambiguous in English and allows us to attach whatever meaning our tradition would like.

So then, in the original languages, the word *clearly described the one who is "given" authority, which stands in stark contrast to God who gave him that authority. This is how using* the word "Christ," instead of "anointed," obscures the real meaning, and truth, behind the title. It is when the clear meaning is obscured that another meaning can be interjected in its place. Thus, we want to restore the original meaning by looking to the usage of the word in the Bible.

In the first instance of the word *mashach* in Genesis 31:13, God reminded Jacob of the stones that he had poured oil over. These were the stones that Jacob had used for a pillow the night he received his famous dream of "Jacob's ladder" in Genesis 28:11–22. The next time the word was used, in Exodus 28:41, God instructed Moses to consecrate and sanctify the sons of Aaron into the priesthood by pouring oil over their heads.

So the first thing we need to understand about being "anointed" is that it meant something specific. Calling Jesus "Christ" wasn't like calling him "Jesus Smith" or "Jesus Jones." Attaching the title of "Messiah" to Jesus was to attach a title that described an anointing done to him by God. Yet there is so much more to keep in mind about what this title means and represents from a biblical standpoint. The point is that quite often those who use the title of "Christ" for Jesus don't even really believe in what the title actually represents.

To continue, let's look at some passages about anointing that were first announced in the OT and then realized in the NT:

> You have loved righteousness, and hated wickedness. Therefore *God, your God, has anointed you* with the oil of gladness *above your fellows*. (Psalms 45:7 and Hebrews 1:9)

> The Spirit of the Lord YHWH is on me; *because YHWH has anointed me* to preach good news to the humble; *he has sent me* to bind up the broken-hearted, to proclaim liberty to the captives, and the opening of the prison to those who are bound. (Isaiah 61:1 and Luke 4:18; see also Acts 4:24–27 and 10:38; Psalms 2:2)

The first passage referred to King David, who was anointed by God. Hebrews 1:9 considered this same passage to be a prophesy about God's Son, Jesus Christ. In other words, however much it applied to King David, it would also apply to Jesus.

Similarly, the passage in Isaiah originally applied to Isaiah, but it was also a prophecy about Jesus Christ. Jesus Christ quoted Isaiah 61:1 in Luke 4:18 and claimed the prophecy applied to him. In this way, Jesus described himself by using a great economy of words. First, by using the word "anointed," he defined his relationship to God in understandable terms. He was saying that this verse which originally applied to Isaiah, also applied to him: just as Isaiah was anointed and sent by God (and thus was not God), in like manner Jesus was anointed by God. In addition, by referring to God as "Him"—in distinct contrast to "me"—he has indicated in the plainest terms that he is "personally" distinct from the one who anointed him. Thus, Jesus described himself in terms that are neither Trinitarian, nor Onenessian, nor with reference to a pagan incarnation of deity, but in a way that is thoroughly Jewish and completely in line with the Jewish prophecies of Messiah.

This is why it is so important to keep in mind that "Messiah," "Christ," and "Anointed One" all mean exactly the same thing. Let's break out the dictionary to make the point as clear as possible. Vine's dictionary provides a good definition of what it means to be "anointed" in the Bible.

> The sacred use of oil was *for anointing things or persons in consecrating them to God*... Anointing was a symbol of the *qualifications divinely imparted* in the consecration of persons *for the discharge of their office*, whether *prophets* (1 Kings 19:16...); *priests* (Leviticus 4:3...), or *kings* (1 Samuel 10:1)... David was anointed three times in connection with his kingship, first, prospectively, 1 Samuel 16:13; then as king over Judah, 2 Samuel 2:4; then over all Israel, 5:3. "The Lord's anointed" was the phrase used to designate the king chosen by God (1 Samuel 12:3, Lamentations 4:20). Christ is twice so designated, as the Messiah (Psalms 2:2; Daniel 9:25, 26...)...[1]

The verb for "*Messiah*" in the OT means "to be anointed" (*mishchah*, Strong's H#4888). It comes from the root word *anoint* (*mashach*, Strong's H#4886). The word has the following definition in Strong's Bible Dictionary: "unction (the act); by implication, *a consecratory gift*." This latter notion of a gift very clearly and specifically means that something has been *granted or given* to the one being anointed. For example, Jacob's pillow rocks didn't anoint themselves. Nor did the sons of Aaron anoint themselves when they were anointed by Moses. Thus, when Jesus Christ said, "*All authority has been given to me* in heaven and on earth..." (Matthew 28:18), *this is precisely what he was referring to*: the OT concept of being the anointed one and having authority *gifted* to him by God.

Now notice how the NT describes, very clearly, what this anointing means, and clearly states the same thing the OT taught us about being anointed:

---

[1] W. E. Vine, *Vine's Expository Dictionary of Old and New Testament Words* (Old Tappan, NJ: Fleming H. Revell, 1981), 18.

> [4]*Nobody takes this honor on himself*, but he is called by God, *just like Aaron was.* [5]*So also Christ didn't glorify himself* to be made a high priest, but *it was he who said to him,* "You are my Son. Today I have become your father." [6]As he says also in another place, "You are a priest forever..." (Hebrews 5:4–6)

The whole point of being anointed is that it is an *"official"* act of someone *giving or bestowing* honor or power *on someone else*. It is absolutely *NOT something one takes on himself*. And ever so clearly, the Bible says, *"so also Christ."* If words and language mean anything at all, then this passage is a clear, "it is written again" Scripture that *completely refutes the Onenessian jumped-to conclusion* that God the Father made Himself into the Messiah. If God anointed Himself, then by the very description given of being anointed, even He is disqualified! God is not the author of confusion and does not go against His own word!

This realization is particularly applicable to the Oneness view, which claims that the person of Jesus' deity anointed Jesus' impersonal humanity. This is how we know the Oneness position is not true: because Hebrews 5:5 explicitly said *"so also is Christ"*! Can it be said that Aaron's spiritual nature anointed his impersonal human flesh? No! Therefore, the claim that Jesus' deific nature anointed His own human fleshly nature is not just a poor interpretation, but rather is actually contrary to the Bible and its description of what it means to be anointed.

The kind of dishonesty that Onenessians perform with the word of God is hardly different than the hocus-pocus games of Trinitarians. Trinitarians claim they believe in one God, even though they believe that each of the three persons in the godhead is equally and fully God in his own right; in any real sense, that makes three Gods. Onenessians claim they believe Jesus the Son is distinct from God the Father, all the while claiming they are both personally the same. In either case you simply can't have it both ways. What both of these groups need to do is abandon their man-made traditions and follow what the Bible clearly, expressly, and consistently describes:

Jesus Christ is a man, approved, anointed, and sent by God—which means he is not God but represents God, and that is what gives him the authority he used!

Those attempting to prove Jesus is God incarnate usually jump to Hebrews 5:6 (above) to argue that Jesus was eternal because he was made a priest after the order of Melchizedek. Friends, that is jumping to conclusions, exactly after the manner in which the devil interprets the Bible. Although it *is said of Melchizedek* that he was without father and without mother (Hebrews 7:3), *this fact isn't true of Jesus. "For it is evident that our Lord has sprung out of Judah"* (Hebrews 7:14). That is to say, *we know from which tribe Jesus came*. This shows us that types and analogies only go so far. Such theorists hide the real truth, and that truth is spelled out in Scripture. It does not need to be assumed or interjected or made up by any man. Rather than list the biblically stated conclusions, we've underlined them below so you can read them in context:

> ⁵They indeed of the sons of Levi who receive the priest's office have a commandment to take tithes of the people according to the law, that is, of their brothers... ⁶but <u>he whose genealogy is not counted from them</u> has taken tithes of Abraham, and has blessed him who has the promises... ¹¹Now if there was perfection through the Levitical priesthood... what further <u>need was there *for another priest to arise*</u> after the order of Melchizedek, and <u>*not be called after the order of Aaron*</u>? ¹²For <u>*the priesthood being changed*</u>, there is <u>*of necessity a change made also in the law*</u>. ¹³For he of whom these things are said <u>*belongs to another tribe*</u>, from which no one has officiated at the altar. ¹⁴For <u>*it is evident that our Lord has sprung out of Judah*</u>, about <u>which tribe Moses spoke nothing concerning priesthood</u>. (Hebrews 7:5–14)

Verse 14 clearly says, "Our Lord has sprung out of Judah," so it should be obvious that, unlike Melchizedek, we do know Christ's genealogy. Those who try to make Jesus a preexistent God or other literal, preexistent being based on the analogy of Melchizedek are jumping to false conclusions. Scripture never teaches that. Those who try to say Melchizedek actually was Christ are preaching "another Christ" than the one the apostles preached.

Let's return to the OT to learn more about anointing, in this case of the kings, beginning with Saul. Here we have God speaking to Samuel the prophet:

> Tomorrow about this time I will send you a man out of the land of Benjamin, and *you shall anoint him* to be prince over my people Israel; and he shall save my people out of the hand of the Philistines: for I have looked on my people, because their cry is come to me. (1 Samuel 9:16)

> Then Samuel took the vial of oil, and poured it on his head, and kissed him, and said, Isn't it that *YHWH has anointed you to be* prince *over his inheritance*? (1 Samuel 10:1)

Note carefully what the purpose of the anointing of a king means: that the one anointed has been set over God's inheritance! After King Saul fell out of favor with God for his disobedience, He sought out a suitable replacement and chose one in David, the son of Jesse:

> ²Samuel said, How can I go? If Saul hear it, he will kill me. YHWH said, Take a heifer with you, and say, I am come to sacrifice to YHWH. ³Call Jesse to the sacrifice, and I will show you what you shall do: and *you shall anoint to me him whom I name to you.* (1 Samuel 16:2–3)

> ¹¹Samuel said to Jesse... Send and get him [the youngest]... ¹²[Jesse] sent, and brought him in...YHWH said, Arise, *anoint him*; for this is he. ¹³Then Samuel took the horn of oil, and *anointed him* in the midst of his brothers: and the Spirit of YHWH came mightily on David from that day forward. So Samuel rose up, and went to Ramah. (1 Samuel 16:11–13)

What is it that we learn from these Scriptures about being anointed? For one, David didn't take the honor of being king of Israel upon himself. He didn't overthrow some previous kingdom and thereby obtain the authority by force. Nor did he inherit it through his lineage as if he were inherently a king by birthright! Rather, he was called out and anointed by God into the ministry that God had chosen for him. This is the kingdom that Jesus ultimately inherited from David, but even then Jesus still had to be anointed by God in order to have it given to him by God.

Now notice how consistent the words of Peter are on the Day of Pentecost regarding this exact same theme:

> ²²Men of Israel, hear these words! Jesus of Nazareth, *a man approved by God* to you by mighty works and wonders and signs which God did by him in the midst of you, even as you yourselves know, ²³him, being delivered up by the determined counsel *and foreknowledge of God*, you have taken by the hand of lawless men, crucified and killed... ³⁶Let all the house of Israel therefore know assuredly that *God has made him both Lord [King] and Christ [the Anointed One], this Jesus [a man approved by God]* whom you crucified. (Acts 2:22–23, 36)

This Jesus was a man who was *made* Lord and Christ in the same manner by which David was made a king. Keep in mind that God was not "made" God or Lord by anyone, but Jesus, God's Son, was! Not another Jesus, this Jesus, the one that is and was a man approved by God and who, by that fact, is distinct from the person of God. There is no reason to give something to someone (like God) who already has those things (i.e., Exodus 19:5; Job 41:11). God imparted the offices of prophet, priest, king, and anointed one (messiah) upon this Jesus. That was the plain truth that Peter told the Jews to accept and believe for their salvation. And that is what Jesus testified of himself.

What does all this teach us about the title of "Christ"? Very simply, to say that Jesus is "Christ" is to say it was given to him to be the anointed one (messiah). To say Jesus is "Christ" is to say he was not inherently anointed, but that *God had to give an anointing to him. The definition of anointing includes the qualification that no one, including and particularly Christ, takes this upon himself,* but rather is called by God just as Aaron was:

YES!!!
"He has anointed me"
Luke 4:18

NO!!!
"Nobody takes this honor on himself... Christ didn't glorify himself"
Hebrews 5:4-5

⁴*Nobody takes this honor on himself,* but he is called by God, just like Aaron was. ⁵*So also Christ didn't glorify himself* to be made a high priest, but *it was he who said to him,* "You are my Son. Today I have become your father." ⁶As he says also in another place, "You are a priest forever..." (Hebrews 5:4–6)

Those who say that Christ was made of dual natures deny the truth that is simply stated in this passage! That is, they are against (anti) the definition of Christ; therefore, they are, as the Bible correctly identifies them: "*anti*-christ-ians."

Thus, to call Jesus "Christ" is, technically, to absolutely deny that he is inherently God, because if he were God, if he were the very person of God who incarnated Himself as a man, he would need nothing added or given to Him, and *he would be disqualified of the title of Christ since an anointed one is one who does not take this honor upon one's self!* Those who believe that Jesus is a dual-natured God-man hybrid (as both Trinitarians and Onenessians believe) should *stop calling him by the title "Christ,"* because the thoughts are actually contradictory and mutually exclusive!

When Onenessians and Trinitarians call Jesus by the title "Christ," they are, literally and technically, denouncing their own doctrines by that word. These folks need to make up their minds: either Jesus truly is "Christ" ("the Anointed One"), or he is God incarnate. If Jesus is Christ, as the Bible says, then Jesus is a man who was anointed by God and did not take this honor unto himself, just like Aaron didn't and just like David didn't, or anyone else that was ever anointed by God.

In the beginning of this section we quoted Hebrews 5:12–6:3, which in part says, [12]"...when... you ought to be teachers, *you again need to have someone teach you the rudiments of the first principles of the oracles of God...* [6:1]"Therefore leaving the doctrine of the first principles of Christ, let us press on to perfection—*not laying again a foundation...*" (Hebrews 5:12–6:3)

The natural tendency when we are being corrected is to become defensive, which often includes shooting the messenger. That isn't the commanded biblical way to respond, which is to search the Scriptures whether these things be so. We are confident that we have provided enough biblical basis, in these last five chapters particularly, to show Onenessians that they haven't been holding onto the first principles of the oracles of God but have gone ahead and laid a different foundation that the apostles never laid.

Jumping to Conclusions versus "It is Written": The very title of Christ, the Anointed One, is one of the rudimentary principles that is taught in the word of God. Its biblical meaning throughout the OT and NT refutes both the Onenessian and the Trinitarian theories claiming that Jesus is inherently God, for it is written:

> [4]*Nobody takes this honor on himself*, but he is called by God, just like Aaron was. [5]*So also Christ didn't glorify himself* to be made a high priest, *but it was he who said to him*, "You are my Son. Today I have become your father." [6]As he says also in another place, "You are a priest forever..." (Hebrews 5:4–6)

The OT Schoolmaster: The idea that to be the Messiah, or Christ, means to have received *a consecratory gift* is well established throughout the OT.

Teach no other doctrine: The idea that Jesus is inherently God is contradicted by the very truth that he is called "The Anointed One" (Christ). It is a biblically stated truth, by the biblical definition of what it means to be "anointed" as Aaron was, that Jesus did not take this honor upon himself but was given this honor by God.

CHAPTER TEN
Isaiah 9:6: His Name Shall be Called

Why was God's name bestowed on people, places, and things in the Old Testament?

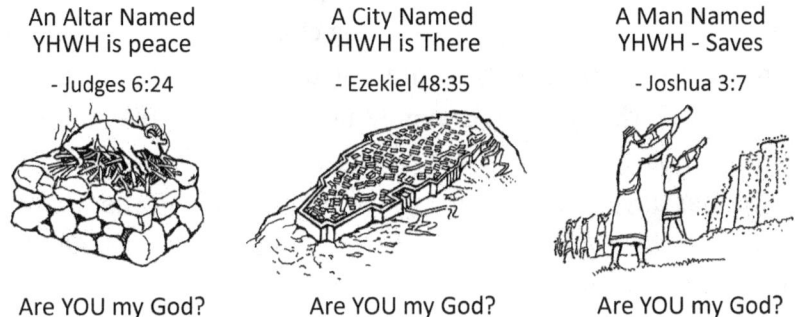

An Altar Named YHWH is peace	A City Named YHWH is There	A Man Named YHWH - Saves
- Judges 6:24	- Ezekiel 48:35	- Joshua 3:7
Are YOU my God?	Are YOU my God?	Are YOU my God?

Was it because whatever God's name was bestowed upon was God Himself? No, it was to commemorate God's characteristics!

> ⁶For a child has been born to us, a son has been given to us. And authority has settled on his shoulders. He has been named 'The mighty God is planning grace; The Eternal Father, a peaceable ruler' ⁷In token of abundant authority and of peace without limit upon David's throne and kingdom, that it may be firmly established in justice and equity now and evermore. The zeal of the Lord of Hosts shall bring this to pass. (*Tanakh*; Isaiah 9:6–7 Christian Bibles, 9:5–6 Hebrew Bibles)

In this chapter we are going to address the common Onenessian notion that Isaiah 9:6 proves that Jesus is God incarnate.

This passage teaches us a powerful lesson in cultural differences and will help us see how easy it is to impose our own ideas upon other cultures. And that is, overall and in general, what Trinitarians and Onenessians end up doing to the Hebrew prophecies regarding the Messiah.

I have a Latino friend whose first name is Jesus (pronounced "heh-SOOS"). Naming children "Jesus" is culturally acceptable among Latinos but is pretty much taboo among Anglos. The reason Latinos name their sons "Jesus" is out of a deep respect for, and commemoration of the Lord Jesus Christ. Of course Anglos, for their part, seem to find this somewhat pretentious or arrogant.

Does a cultural bias against naming children "Jesus" mean that Latinos who do so actually fit the Anglo bias and are pretentious in doing so? The answer is simply no. The Anglo bias does not mean Latinos are guilty of Anglo biases. Now let's get to our real point, *does anyone believe my friend was named "Jesus" because his parents believed him to be an incarnation of Jesus Christ of Nazareth?* I certainly hope not, because nothing could be further from the truth.

And yet, that is precisely what a lot of Christians, both Trinitarians and Onenessians, do with Isaiah 9:6, *without any regard* for the Jewish culture behind the passage! *Based on their cultural bias and nothing else*, such Christians presume that if Jesus was given a form of God's name, then that could only be undeniable evidence that he is God Himself incarnate. In reality, that idea is simply ridiculous when examined from the perspective of the OT. It would be just as ridiculous as accusing my friend's parents of believing their son was Jesus reincarnated because they named him "Jesus."

God's Name Bestowed in Commemoration

One of the things we learn from the OT Schoolmaster is God's compound names, such as *YHWH-Shammah, YHWH-Jireh, YHWH-Shalom, YHWH-Nissi*. But how many Oneness Pentecostals know that we learned these names because these names were given to places and altars? For example:

> ...And *the name of the city* from that day shall be, YHWH is there [*YHWH-shammah*]. (Ezekiel 48:35)

> ...Abraham called *the name of that place* YHWH Will Provide [*YHWH-Jireh*]. (Genesis 22:14)

> Then Gideon built *an altar* there to YHWH, *and called it* YHWH is Peace. (Judges 6:24)

> Moses built *an altar*, and called *the name of it* YHWH our Banner [*YHWH-Nissi*]. (Exodus 17:15)

Are these altars and places that were called by God's name actually God incarnate? If not, why not, if calling something by the names or titles of God is absolute proof that doing so is to be understood as identifying God Himself? People who have enough sense to realize these cities and altars aren't God just because God's name was bestowed on them should have the sense to realize that calling men by God's name doesn't make them God either!

The truth is simply that these titles of YHWH were given in commemoration of some specified aspect of YHWH. Take for example "YHWH-Jireh," which means "my provider." Since Onenessians insist that proper names of God are to be understood as only applying to God Himself, then are we to believe this place was YHWH? And whenever Israelites wanted to receive a sacrifice provided by God, that was the place they would return to? The idea is ridiculous, is it not? Well then, that is exactly how ridiculous it is to impose our bias on how and what it signifies when something or someone was given God's name. This is how Onenessians are seen to be unbiblical, in the way they understand how God's names are used when bestowed upon persons or things other than God Himself.

Actually, YHWH was being commemorated by Abraham at the place where God provided a lamb for a sacrifice instead of Isaac. It is just that simple and uncomplicated.

As we've mentioned, God's name was not only bestowed upon places. Let's look at some of the names of the prophets and see what they tell us:

- Joshua (YHWH + yasha) = YHWH-saved.
- Elijah (El + Yah) = My God is Yah.
- Elisha = God is salvation.
- Jeremiah = YHWH lifts up
- Joel = YHWH is his God
- Micah (Micaiah) = Who is like Yah(weh)
- Zecharia = Yah(weh) is renowned
- Hezekiah = Yah(weh) strengthens

As we can see, it was fairly common practice in Judaism to name humans with the name of YHWH in combined (concatenated) Theophoric names. And those names often bore some significance to the role or message of these prophets. But certainly no one is claiming that these prophets were God incarnate because they bore and came in God's name! Yet because the Messiah was called by God's name, Onenessians believe he should be identified as God Himself. That would only be true if it were taught by the OT Schoolmaster. As it is, this is only one of the traditions of men that attempts to make the word of God of no effect.

Here's a question: If Jesus is proved to be God by his given name, what then do we do with the fact that in the Hebrew language *Joshua was given the exact same name as "Jesus" ("Yehoshua")?* Was then Joshua the son of Nun also, by that same reasoning, God Himself incarnate? Of course not. So then why are Onenessians so adamant that Isaiah could only possibly mean that Jesus is the everlasting Father? This is just faulty reasoning caused by *imposing our culture* on the Bible and then claiming that Scripture supports our bias, when it says no such thing. It is actually *that attitude* that *is* pretentious and arrogant.

The Mighty Men are Not the Mighty God

Why were men called "Elohim" in the Old Testament?
Old Testament - "Mighty Men"
- Ezekiel 32:21

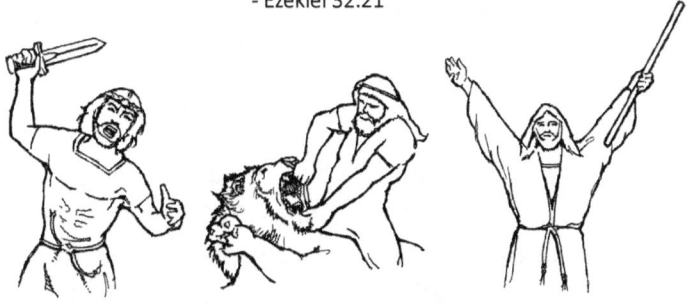

Are YOU my God?
Was it because men were actually Gods?
No, it's because the word for Elohim (for God)
was not only used for YHWH God

Another relevant fact is that the phrase "mighty god" in Isaiah 9:6 has been applied to humans. For example:

> The strong ['eeleey] among the mighty [gibowriym] shall speak to him out of the midst of Sheol with those who help him: they are gone down, they lie still, even the uncircumcised, slain by the sword. (Ezekiel 32:21)

Although this passage is in the plural, it is otherwise the same exact phrase found in Isaiah 9:6, where the KJV translates it as "the mighty God" (though the Hebrew lacks the definite article "the"). If we use the same rule for interpreting as those who believe this can only mean the Messiah is God Almighty, then these ancient ones also were each "the mighty God," which we know is not true. It is the translation method that is false, not the words of Ezekiel 32:21. This passage, then, is reminiscent of the following passage:

> [34]Jesus answered them, "Isn't it written in your law, '*I said, you are gods?*' [35]If *He called them gods*, to whom the word of God came (*and the Scripture can't be broken*), [36]do you

say of him whom the Father sanctified and sent into the world, 'You blaspheme,' *because I said, 'I am the Son of God?'* ³⁷If I don't do the works of my Father, don't believe me. ³⁸But if I do them, though you don't believe me, believe the works; that you may *know and believe that the Father is in me*, and I in the Father." (John 10:34–38)

The Hebrew word that is translated above as God comes from the word *el*, or *elohim* in the plural. The simple fact is, God called men in Scripture by the name *el* or *elohim not* because they are the Almighty God, but because the word simply means that they are powerful or mighty (whether their might came directly from God Himself or not). This truth is spelled out in the following lexicon of Biblical Hebrew and in the passages to which it refers:

OT:410 'el (ale) 1. *applied to men of might and rank*... mighty one of the nations Ezekiel 31:11 (of Nebuchadnezzar)... mighty men Job 41:17... mighty heroes Ezekiel 32:21... Ezekiel 17:13; 2 Kings 24:15... Exodus 15:15.[1]

¹⁰Therefore thus said the Lord YHWH: Because you are exalted in stature, and he has set his top among the thick boughs, and his heart is lifted up in his height; ¹¹I will even deliver him *into the hand of the mighty one [el]* of the nations; he shall surely deal with him; I have driven him out for his wickedness. (Ezekiel 31:10)

When he raises himself up, the *mighty [elim]* are afraid. They retreat before his thrashing. (Job 41:25)

As we can see by both the dictionary definition of "el" and by its usage in the Scriptures, the word "el" means "mighty" and can apply to God or to men. It is not used exclusively of YHWH God.

---

[1] Brown-Driver-Briggs, *Hebrew and English Lexicon*, Unabridged, Electronic Database; Biblesoft: 2006.

The Everlasting Father

God...GAVE to him the name
- Philippians 2:9-11

One of Onenessians' favorite OT proof texts is the occurrence of the phrase "everlasting father" in Isaiah 9:6. For Onenessians this is a prophetic announcement that the Son himself will literally be the "everlasting father." Thus they use it as a proof text for their doctrine that Jesus is an incarnation of the person of Father.

Although there are many difficulties with their conclusion, there is at least one huge problem with that assumption: Jesus is never clearly and unambiguously called the Father, and the Father is never, ever called Jesus anywhere in the Bible, but particularly in the NT where we would expect it to be found.

To the contrary, as we've been demonstrating, Jesus always held himself personally distinct from the Father. For instance when he said, "I am ascending to my Father and to your Father, to my God and your God" (John 20:17). Or when he said, "...I am not alone, but I am with the Father who sent me" (John 8:16). Or when he taught us to pray, saying, "Pray like this: *'Our* Father in heaven...'" (Matthew 6:9).

Not only Jesus, but the apostles also, always kept the Father personally distinct from Jesus, the Son. For example:

> [27]For, "He put all things in subjection under his feet." But when he says, "All things are put in subjection," *it is evident that he is excepted who subjected all things to him.* [28]When all things have been subjected to him, then the Son will also himself be subjected to him who subjected all things to him, that God may be all in all. (1 Corinthians 15:27–28)

> Grace, mercy, and peace will be with us, from God the Father, and from the Lord Jesus Christ, *the Son of the Father, in truth and love.* (1 John 1:3)

We can very clearly see that God's name, in concatenated forms, is and has been bestowed upon people, places, and things in commemoration of God. Meanwhile, absolutely no evidence shows that doing so identifies those persons, places, and things as God. It thus becomes clear that the biblical precedent is simply to give such names in commemoration of particular aspects of God.

For Onenessians to adamantly claim otherwise, as they do, simply puts the onus, the responsibility of providing the evidence, back on them. Any honest seeker of truth will soon find that calling Jesus by the name "Father" is just as lacking in the Scripture as those calling God a Trinity.

The very fact that Onenessians can only interpret like the devil and Trinitarians do in order to come to their conclusions is proof they aren't handling the word of God in an honest manner.

Furthermore, the Onenessian practice of calling Jesus "the Father" is as unbiblical and unapostolic as the Trinitarian practice of calling Jesus "God the Son." Although they come to different results, both groups use the same false, devilish methods to reach their conclusions.

Isaiah 9:6 from Hebrew and Apostolic Views

Let's look again at Isaiah 9:6 with the Jewish background we've provided in mind. Here is how the passage looks in its original setting, with the name transliterated and all the other words translated:

> For a child is born unto us, a son is given unto us; and the government is upon his shoulder; and his name is called Pele-joez-el-gibbor-Avi-ad-sar-shalom. (Isaiah 9:6(5) 1917)[2]

As we can see, in Hebrew it appears as just one long name. If the OT prophets were given YHWH's name combined with one other characteristic of God's, this son seems to outdo them all by having many characteristics of God contained in his name. But *that still doesn't mean that any legitimate Jew ever interpreted* this passage to mean that *this* son was to be an incarnation of YHWH. That idea is still far, far from their understanding. Such an idea not only was never spelled out in the OT, but it was also contraindicated, as we have seen in the previous chapters of this section.

Furthermore, it isn't even true that the Jews understood this to be one long name for this son.

Here is another way that Jewish translators have expressed the passage:

> For a child has been born to us, a son given to us, and the authority is upon his shoulder, and the wondrous adviser, the mighty God, the everlasting Father, *called his name*, "the prince of peace." (Isaiah 9:6[5])[3]

---

[2] JPS Electronic Edition, Larry Nelson, accessed 2/22/2015, http://www.breslov.com/bible/Isaiah9.htm#6. Note that the Hebrew numbering is slightly different than the Christian; thus, it is v.5 in JPS.

[3] The Complete Tanach with Rashi's Commentary, trans. The Book of Isaiah Volume 1, ed. Rabbi A. J. Rosenberg (Judaica Press, 1982), accessed 2/22/2015 from http://www.chabad.org/library/bible_cdo/aid/15940.

So here is another issue to deal with. It isn't clear from the Hebrew text that the full name-string is applied to the child. To the contrary, as interpreted here, it could name the one who provided the name for the child (which would make the child's name "the prince of peace," not the "everlasting Father").

And yet another significant fact is that *no* NT writer *ever* quoted any part of Isaiah 9:6 as referring to Jesus Christ. However, the verse following Isaiah 9:6 is referred to in Luke 1:33. In this instance the angel is telling Mary what the identity of her miraculously born son was to be:

> He will be great, and will be called the Son of the Most High. The Lord God will *give him the throne of his father, David,* and he will reign over the house of Jacob forever. *There will be no end to his Kingdom.* (Luke 1:32–33; see also Isaiah 9:7)

Here we have an angel's description of Jesus that fits very well with Isaiah 9:7. But anyone taking the time to read Isaiah 9:7 will notice no personal pronoun in the pronouncement besides the one used for David. It actually goes like this: "Of the increase of *the* government and peace there shall be no end upon *the throne of David and upon his kingdom* and to establish it with judgment and with justice from henceforth even forever... The zeal of YHWH of hosts will perform this." (Isaiah 9:7(6), ITB).[4] Thus, this prophecy is simply about restoring the throne of King David *to the rightful son and heir of David*, and lends no support to the assumption this son would be an incarnation of God.

When we examine the internal evidence based on what Isaiah actually wrote, we realize it is YHWH who is going to give this son of David to us, who will give this son his name, and who will establish

---

[4] Interlinear Transliterated Bible, 2006 by Biblesoft. See also Young's Literal Translation, Holman Christian Standard Bible, and the Complete Jewish Bible, which are included within the referenced software. The following translations have "his" in italics, indicating that it did not exist in the texts they were translating: KJV, NKJV, NASV, NASB, and others.

this son's government and the peace it will bring. So, we have God giving another individual, the Messiah, his name, which is not the same as saying that the Messiah is God. The Bible concurs that Jesus' name did *not* mean he was God simply because the name was not his inherently, but was gifted to him:

> I will declare your name to my brothers. In the midst of the assembly, I will praise you. (Psalm 22:22)

> I have come in my Father's name, and you don't receive me. If another comes in his own name, you will receive him. (John 5:43)

> I revealed your name to the people whom you have given me out of the world. They were yours, and you have given them to me. They have kept your word. (John 17:6)

> I made known to them your name, and will make it known; that the love with which you loved me may be in them, and I in them. (John 17:26)

So, Jesus himself testified that his name wasn't his own name but rather the Father's name and was bestowed upon him by his Father. Jesus' words refute the Onenessian contention that Jesus' given name is proof he is God. The problem then is that Onenessians simply refuse to interpret Isaiah 9:6 through the OT as our schoolmaster. In order to come to their unbiblical conclusion, they must ignore the fact that names of God were applied to places and people other than God.

Note in particular *the angel's explicit words* in Luke 1:32–33. The angel referred to Christ when saying he would be "*called* the Son of the Most High" and then explicitly said that the Most High would *give him* the throne "<u>of his father</u>, David." The person of God would not need to be given a throne He already owned by inherent right. When Moses asked God to reveal His name, God didn't say, "I have given Myself the Name YHWH, that is my name..." So Jesus was given a throne in the same way he was given his name. Such explicit wording rules out that this son is an incarnation of God by what it clearly states.

Even if it could be proven that the name referred to in Isaiah 9:6 was Jesus' concatenated name, Scripture is very clear that he was "*given*" his name:

> Therefore God also highly exalted him, and *gave to him the name* which is above every name; that at the name of Jesus every knee should bow, of those in heaven, those on earth, and those under the earth, and that every tongue should confess that Jesus Christ is Lord, to the glory of God the Father. (Philippians 2:9–11)

Thus, according to the Scriptures and Jesus himself, his name was not undeniable evidence, let alone even a slight clue leading in that direction, that he is the God who gave him the name. So the Oneness conclusion is nothing but pure conjeccture based on jumping to conclusions!

Biblically speaking, this son, Jesus *Christ* (the Anointed One), was simply to be the fulfillment of God's sworn oath to David. Thus Jesus *Christ* was declared to be neither more nor less than a fulfillment of both Isaiah 9:7 and 2 Samuel 7:12–16:

> When your days are fulfilled, and you shall sleep with your fathers, I will set up your seed after you, who shall proceed out of your bowels, and I will establish his kingdom. He shall build a house for my name, and I will establish the throne of his kingdom forever. *I will be his father, and he shall be my son*: if he commit iniquity, I will chasten him with the rod of men, and with the stripes of the children of men; but my loving kindness shall not depart from him, as I took it from Saul, whom I put away before you. Your house and your kingdom shall be made sure for ever before you: your throne shall be established forever. (2 Samuel 7:12–16)

This is who Jesus is and was and always was supposed to be: God's Son, not God Himself. No prophesy anywhere in the OT Scriptures said that the Messiah would be an incarnation of the God of Abraham, Isaac, and Jacob. The method that people use to come to that conclusion is no different than the method Trinitarians use to try to "prove" the OT declared the Trinity. In either case, the method used is reading into the text by interpretation what it never actually states. The idea that Jesus Christ is an incarnation of God Himself (as in Onenessianism) or an eternal, coequal "God the Son" (as in Trinitarianism), is a case of reading a cultural bias and/or preconceived, man-made idea *back into the texts*, but it simply is not there, was never understood that way by the ancients, and is clearly refuted when other Scriptures are brought to bear on the subject.

So what does Isaiah 9:6–7 actually mean? Based on the way God's name was given to places and people, the bestowing of God's name and characteristics was a way of honoring God for those specific characteristics. That this son honors many characteristics of God shows the basis of Jesus' statement that "all that the Father has are mine." Jesus doesn't represent certain aspects of God, but does represent many of them, and certainly all of God's moral characteristics. The characteristics of God that Jesus denied possessing were those such as, "I can of my own self do nothing," whereas "with God all things are possible." Furthermore, the Son, by definition of the word "son" itself, was born in the process of time, whereas the Father actually always existed. Above all, Jesus was seen, and handled, but God is a Spirit.

The wording of the prophecy shows that it is actually still in the future: "Of the increase of his government and of peace there shall be no end, on the throne of David, and on his kingdom, to establish it, and to uphold it with justice and with righteousness from that time on, even forever" (Isaiah 9:7). It is for the time when Jesus returns and establishes the Davidic kingdom on earth and extends it to eternity. That it says, "The zeal of YHWH of Armies will perform this" (Isaiah 9:7) speaks to the truth that, as in all things, even with Jesus, it is God who is actually the one doing the "works." This verse said the same thing Jesus did in clearly giving the Father Himself credit for everything that Jesus did.

> I know that His commandment is eternal life. The things therefore which I speak, even *as the Father has said to me, so I speak.* (John 12:50)

> The words that I tell you, *I speak not from myself*; but the Father who lives in me does His works. (John 14:10)

If Jesus didn't think himself to be God, why should we? Jesus said all power and authority was given to him, and that is what the title Christ means, and what we are to believe about Jesus.

Isaiah's Prophecies of Messiah

YHWH's Righteous Servant
- Isaiah 53:11

A few final points need to be addressed relating to Isaiah's understanding of the prophecy he gave, and how Jesus understood and applied Isaiah's prophecies.

When we read through the Book of Isaiah, we find a number of prophecies regarding the Messiah that were fulfilled in Jesus' first coming (i.e., Isaiah 7:14–16; 9:1–2, 7; 11:1–5, 10; 40:3–5; 50:6;

52:13–14; 53:1–12 and 61:1–2). In none of these prophecies does Isaiah ever explain or predict that the Son he spoke of would be an incarnation of YHWH. Instead, Isaiah described him in ways that could only distinguish him from God in terms of personality.

For example:
- 7:14–16 The Messiah would be born of a virgin and have to learn how to refuse evil and choose the good (with Luke 1:26–31 and Hebrews 5:8–9).
- 8:18 The Messiah would be given children from YHWH (with Hebrews 2:3 and John 10:28–29).
- 11:1–5 The Messiah would spring from David's father, Jesse, and have the Spirit of God rest on him, including the spirits of "knowledge and fear of YHWH."
- 50:6–7 Speaking in the Messiah's place, Isaiah says, "I gave my back to the strikers...for YHWH will help me," showing that the Messiah would trust in YHWH.
- 52:13–14 The Messiah is called the servant of YHWH and will be exalted, but he will also be marred.
- 53:2 The Messiah grew up before YHWH ("he grew up before him").
- 53:6 YHWH laid on him the iniquity of us all.
- 53:10 It pleased YHWH to bruise him.
- 53:11 He is called YHWH's righteous servant.
- 53:12 YHWH will "divide him a portion with the great, and he shall divide the spoil with the strong."

It would be misleading and downright strange if Isaiah had heard God tell him that the Messiah would be an incarnation of YHWH but then keep speaking about him as if he were a different person than YHWH. Actually, what is strange and misleading is imposing upon Isaiah's words meanings that had to come from pagan views of incarnated deities rather than from the biblical record.

When God presented himself to Moses (through the angel, vs. 3) at the burning bush in Exodus 3, He told Moses exactly who He was, what His name was, why He was calling out to Moses, and what He had planned. When Jesus presented himself to Israel to begin his public ministry, what did he proclaim of himself? Did he claim that he was YHWH incarnate in fulfillment of Isaiah 9:6? No he did not. Although he did quote Isaiah, not once did he or any apostle claim Jesus was a fulfillment of Isaiah 9:6. In declaring who he was and what he was about to do, Jesus quoted the following from Isaiah 61:

> [18]"The Spirit of the Lord is on me, because *he has anointed me* to preach good news to the poor. *He has sent me* to heal the brokenhearted, to proclaim release to the captives, recovering of sight to the blind, to deliver those who are crushed, [19]And to proclaim the acceptable year of the Lord." [20]He closed the book [of Isaiah], gave it back to the attendant, and sat down. The eyes of all in the synagogue were fastened on him. [21]He began to tell them, "Today, this Scripture has been fulfilled in your hearing." (Luke 4:18–21)

Here, Jesus was given the whole scroll of Isaiah and had to unroll it to near the back. He had to have passed right by 9:6. He chose instead to declare his ministry by presenting himself as both personally distinct from God who sent him and having been anointed by God. We recall that to be anointed was something no one took upon himself.

Instead of taking Jesus at his word, the Onenessian position is to claim that he was 100% God and 100% man. Onenessians often describe this condition by saying that "God robed Himself in flesh" to make Himself known. Jesus made a similar analogy when he said:

> Beware of false prophets, who come to you in sheep's clothing, but inwardly are ravening wolves. (Matthew 7:15)

Jesus' point is that those who robe themselves in clothing that hides and disguises their true identity are really just masquerading in order to deceive. The problem with the theory of the "100% God/100% man" idea is twofold. First, God cannot lie; and second, God cannot be tempted. Jesus claimed to be anointed by God and spoke of God in the third person, which would be a lie if he himself were indeed God. For the second point, as we see in the comparison to wolves in sheep's clothing, wearing outer clothes doesn't change the inner personality. If Jesus were "God robed in flesh," as people assume, then He certainly couldn't have been tempted by sin like the Bible says of him (a topic we will return to when we cover the Synoptic Gospels).

Jumping to Conclusions versus "It is Written": To attempt to use Isaiah 9:6 as a "proof text" of Christ's deity seems to be a clear case of jumping to conclusions, since it means imposing an interpretation that is not clear in the text itself or in the culture of Judaism. It was never quoted this way by the apostles, and even according to Jesus himself, his name was given to him and thus was not proof of an inherent divine nature or deity.

The Bible does interpret for us what it means for Jesus to "come in the name of the Lord," which is to come in the same way that David's kingdom came in the name of the Lord, for it is written:

> Those who went in front, and those who followed, cried out, "Hosanna! Blessed is he who comes in the name of the Lord! Blessed is *the kingdom of our father David that is coming in the name of the Lord*! Hosanna in the highest!" (Mark 11:9–10)

So then, to understand how David "came in the name of the Lord" is to understand how Jesus came in the name of the Lord. That is, it means to be sent and anointed by God into the office and position that was ordained by God.

Since Jesus is the true witness, we must listen to him rather than the theories of men, especially when those theories are never stated in the Scriptures and when something to the contrary is consistently presented as the truth. No Scriptures teach that Jesus is an incarnation of YHWH, but hundreds of Scriptures explain and show that he is quite personally distinct from his God and our God, who is also his Father and our Father.

The OT Schoolmaster: The OT does not teach that being given a name containing Yah or YHWH makes that person God incarnate. To the contrary, it does contain many examples of people who had concatenated (linked together) names containing Yah or YHWH, just like Jesus' name, but no one ever assumed they were incarnations of God. What the OT Schoolmaster teaches us through many examples is that bestowing God's name upon some person, place, or thing is done to commemorate something about God and should not be taken to mean that the person, place, or thing is the person of God.

Teach No Other Doctrine: The idea that the "name" given in Isaiah 9:6 referred specifically to Jesus Christ is not explicitly taught in the Bible and was never applied or said to mean such by anyone in the Bible. It is therefore entirely an interpretation that was added after the time of the apostles.

In Closing, Section Two

In this section we have sought to restore certain basic, fundamental "first principles of the oracles of God" by looking at the Hebrew prophesies of Christ from several prominent biblical angles. In each one of these areas the Hebrew Messiah is understood to be a man, foreknown of God since before all of creation, descended from the lineage of David, whom God would claim as His Son. The Hebrews had no understanding of a Trinity of persons in the godhead, let alone that one of those persons would incarnate into humanity and become their Messiah. Onenessians quite often use this same truth against Trinitarians; however, the same holds equally true against the methodology they use to arrive at the Oneness doctrine. No OT prophecies taught or proclaimed that YHWH, God of the Israelites would incarnate Himself into a man. That doesn't stop Onenessians from imposing and interjecting their man-made ideas into the texts by jumping to conclusions in the same way as the Trinitarians they counter.

What we see in the Bible is that the idea of incarnated gods is quite prominent in pagan religions, as is attested in Acts 14:11. Since the apostles preached that they believed all things that were written in the law and the prophets, and they proclaimed Jesus to be the fulfillment of the Hebrew prophecies concerning the Messiah, then in order to believe in the true Christ, we need to follow the apostles in their convictions and their preaching. Onenessians claim themselves to be "apostolic," primarily because they correctly baptize in Jesus' name, they believe in one God, and they reject the Trinity (which the apostles never taught). But to be truly apostolic, we also need to *teach and preach the same Jesus that the apostles actually believed in for salvation and preached and described*, not only in Acts 2, but throughout the Book of Acts!

In our next section we will address the main contrasting worldviews that seem to be prominent in swaying people's understandings away from biblical ideas and toward pagan positions with the intention of turning things around for truth.

SECTION THREE

PAGAN AND ANTICHRISTIAN/GNOSTIC VIEWS IN CONTRAST TO THE WAY OF CHRIST

CHAPTER ELEVEN

A Question of Coincidence, or Influence of Pagan Views?

A Case of Robbery by Exchange!
Don't let anyone rob "you"...

After his philosophy and not after Christ!
Colossians 2:8

Be careful that you don't let anyone rob you through his philosophy and vain deceit, after the tradition of men, after the elements of the world, and not after Christ. (Colossians 2:8)

²⁹For I know that after my departure, vicious wolves will enter in among you, not sparing the flock. ³⁰Men will arise from among your own selves, speaking perverse things, to draw away the disciples after them... ³²Now, brothers, I entrust you to God, and to the word of his grace, which is able to build up, and to give you the inheritance among all those who are sanctified. (Acts 20:29–32)

In the last section our goal was to restore the biblical meanings of several basic, core terms, such as "Son of God," "Son of Man," and "The Anointed One" (or "Christ"). When these terms are correctly understood in their biblical context and meaning, it is easy to recognize when false imitations are being introduced. As Christians, we have many Scriptures warning us to beware of and reject false teachers and counterfeit gospels. The verses above are just a small sample. Since we are called to "worship" in "spirit and in truth," it is critical to rightly discern between truth and error.

The intent in this section is to show the exact methods and a few of the actual sources that have been used to corrupt these concepts away from simple, biblical meanings. We will start by showing how the Trinitarians adopted extrabiblical sources, and then show how Onenessians apply the same false methods to come up with their ideas.

This chapter will show that the earliest Christians did not believe in a Trinity at all, and that it truly was a later invention and development. Subsequent chapters in this section will show how the Onenessians followed the examples, and even adopted some of the extrabiblical teachings, of the Trinitarians in formulating their unique view.

Most Onenessians are aware that the Trinity owes its doctrine to pagan views and concepts. Onenessians are typically against adopting pagan concepts by which to view God. Most Onenessians realize that adopting pagan doctrines doesn't make those concepts "Christian"; it just makes those Christians who adopt paganism into idolaters. What most Onenessians aren't aware of is just how dependent the Oneness doctrine is upon many of those same pagan concepts, just not the obvious one of three gods.

We must forewarn you that this chapter, by the nature of its subject matter, will be much deeper and more complex than previous chapters. That is because the biblical Jesus is simple, whereas the unbiblical Jesus is complex and complicated. This chapter, by exposing the very complicated nature of both Trinitarianism and Onenessianism, will demonstrate how their positions complicate an otherwise very simple truth: the Son of God doctrine.

The issue we want to address now is *"coincidences* vs. *influences."* For example, Trinitarians have long been accused of being *influenced by* and *adopting* a form of polytheism (many-god-ism) from pagan cultures. A typical Trinitarian response is that any similarity is merely *coincidental*. So we want to show enough of the evidence to convince any discerning soul that pagan influence upon the Trinity is a valid charge and that we can rule out their claim of mere coincidence. (This isn't intended to be a thorough piece against the Trinity. For that, see the author's 2nd Edition of *"God is One and Christ is All: Biblical Truth Against the Trinity."*)

In this first chapter of this section we will show the nuts and bolts of *the exact method* Trinitarians use to justify resorting to pagan "categories of thought" in their attempt to "prove" the Trinity is biblical. This method is one that Jesus himself clearly defined. He called it "setting aside the commandment of God, and holding tightly to the tradition of men" (Mark 7:8).

> ³...Why do you also disobey the commandment of God because of your tradition?... ⁷You hypocrites! Well did Isaiah prophesy of you, saying, ⁸"These people draw near to me with their mouth, And honor me with their lips; But their heart is far from me. ⁹And in vain do they worship me, Teaching as doctrine rules made by men." (Matthew 15:3–9)

Together with Onenessians, we know the Trinity originated in the ancient triads of the pagan gods. These triads evolved into distinct persons during the period of the Neoplatonists and antichristian Gnostics during the first and second centuries of our era. This idea was soundly repudiated by Irenaeus in the mid- to late-second century. Then Tertullian and his contemporaries directly adopted the ideas from the antichristian Gnostic Valentinus.

Robbery by Exchange!

| The Biblical View | | The Philosophical Trinity |

אֱלֹהֵינוּ, יְהוָה אֶחָד.

"Our God, the Lord is one"
Deuteronomy 6:4

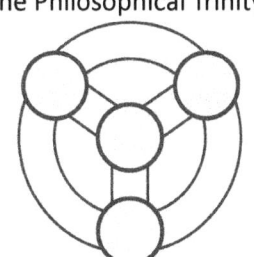

Following, in the words of one Trinitarian author (Carl Brumbach) quoting another (A. H. Strong), is one of the ways they attempt to justify the development of the Trinity. This quote provides us with a good example of the subtle errors of interpretation that Trinitarians make. He is writing defensively in response to an accusation that the Trinity was a fourth century invention, along with other novelties such as Mariolatry, infallibility of the Pope, purgatory, and so forth.

> Tertullian, who wrote during the early years of the church (190–211), is generally credited with being the first to use the term Trinity. It is obvious that the term predated the Roman Catholic era... *It <u>must be admitted</u> that the doctrine of the Trinity was <u>developed</u> during the centuries in which the Romanesque errors were being introduced and developed. This, however, does not necessitate the belief that it is of Romanist origin...* Please observe that I do not state that the doctrine of the Trinity was *introduced* during these post-apostolic years. *It... "was implicitly held* by the apostles and other NT writers in their declaration with regard to the Father, Son and Holy Ghost, even though <u>they did not formulate it</u> as a precise doctrine. *They held it, as it were, in solution; only time, reflection, and the shock of controversy and opposition caused it to crystallize into definite and dogmatic form."* It should be understood that the men who sat in the various councils and <u>forged</u> the creeds adopted there *were only attempting to place in theological terminology that which they believed to be biblical teaching.*[1]

On the surface this all may sound fairly reasonable, but as we are about to show, this "explanation" has all the characteristics of the

---

[1] Carl Brumbach, *God in Three Persons: A Trinitarian Answer to the Oneness or 'Jesus Only' Doctrine Concerning the Godhead and Water Baptism* (Cleveland, TN: Pathway Press, 1998), 20–21. He is quoting A. H. Strong, *Systematic Theology*, p. 304.

devil's method of interpreting the Bible. Notice how he admits that the apostles did not "formulate [the Trinity] as a precise doctrine." That is an admission that the apostles did not *openly proclaim (preach)* what Trinitarians believe. So the Trinity was developed directly against the NT command to preach no other Jesus!

Next we're going to show how our circles of discernment (from Chapter Two) expose, in a practical way, the Trinitarian dogma as a teaching that, undeniably, can only be found *through the left-handed circle* approach of biblical interpretation. Unfortunately, *the Trinity is not the simplicity of Christ*, so we will have to wade into some of the ugly depths of its complexity in order to suitably address it. As we will show with graphics, Trinitarians are not without their own falsely applied proof texts! But what will become clear is how dependent the Trinity is on stretching the gray-area verses beyond their original intent.

The next part of the quote from our Trinitarian author is:

> Tertullian... is *generally* credited with being the first to use the term Trinity. It is obvious that the term predated the Roman Catholic era... It must be admitted that the doctrine of the Trinity was developed during the centuries in which the Romanesque errors were being introduced...This... does not necessitate the belief that it is of Romanist origin...[2]

This statement is full of half-truths that attempt to hide the real issues. First, it is true that Tertullian held an earlier *version* of a Trinitarian position, but *it was definitely not the same one as was developed later* (thus, a half-truth). It is also correct that early forms of the Trinity doctrine predated Constantine and the Council of Nicaea by more than a hundred years. So it is actually only half true that non-Trinitarians are creating a straw-man argument when they accuse the Trinity of being *"invented"* in the fourth century at the Council of Nicaea. The subtlety of error lies in the fact that there is a huge difference between something being "invented" and some-

---

[2] Brumbach, ibid.

thing being "developed." It would be like saying, "man has had *cell phones for decades*, because the telegraph was invented long ago"! The fact is that the Trinity of the fourth century developed far beyond what theologians such as Tertullian would have recognized. Tertullian was in fact *far* from being a Nicene ("coequal/coeternal") Trinitarian.

However, that still isn't the root of the matter. There is yet another truth that is being dodged and covered up: *Tertullian wasn't the first to say "Trinity"*. This means *it is very misleading* to claim that "Tertullian is generally credited with being the first to use the term Trinity." *The truth is that the antichristian Gnostics were the first Trinitarians, and they were also the ones who actually first used the word Trinity. And it was directly from the antichristian Gnostics that Tertullian, by his own confession, adopted the core idea of the Trinity: the emanation of one god from another*. In other words, the above Trinitarian, though trying very hard to make his defense appear to be technically accurate, attempts to convey some very misleading and thus *totally deceptive* information. In particular, he hides the actual origin of the word and concept of the Trinity. Furthermore, while it is accurate that certain forms of a Trinity existed before the fourth century, it is far, far from the truth to state or imply that the Trinitarian views of the fourth century originated in early apostolic Christianity, or that they were *ever* held by any Trinitarians at all before the fourth century. And that is the real issue! Sadly, Christians need to be on guard for these types of deceptive theological smokescreens!

The acclaimed historian of Christian dogma, Adolf von Harnack,[3] referred to and agreed with historian Charles Bigg (mentioned earlier), that *the antichristian Gnostics were the first to use the word "Trinity."* Harnack pointed out that the Gnostics were also the first to speak of the persons as being "of one substance" (*homoousios*). This was before Nicaea, and before Tertullian. It means that Nicene Trinitarianism owes its main technical terms of *trias* (Trinity) and *homoousios* (one substance/essence) to the antichristian Gnostics.

---

[3] see http://www.ccel.org/ccel/harnack.

Robbery by Exchange!

Father   Mother   Son

Biblical Son made of Flesh
- 1 John 4:2

Gnostic son made of substance of the Father - Light from Light doctrine

Here is what Harnack has to say:

> The Gnostic terminologies within the Æon speculations *were partly reproduced* among the Catholic theologians of the third century; *most important is it that the Gnostics have already made use of the concept '**homoousios**'*; see Iren., I. 5. I,... I.5.4,... I.5.5...In all these cases the word means 'of one substance.'...*Other terms* also which have acquired great significance in the Church since the days of Origen (e.g., *agénnetos*) *are found among the Gnostics*... Bigg. (1. c. p. 58, note 3) calls attention to the appearance of **trias** in Excerpt. ex. Theodotus § 80, perhaps the earliest passage.[4]

The Greek word *trias* is the equivalent to the English word *trinity* and the Latin word *trinitas* (that Tertullian used). The word Trinity did not originate with Tertullian, but with the antichristian Gnostics! This alone ought to alert any sensible Christian that the Trinity was not an apostolic teaching, but originated as an antichristian teaching!

---

[4] Adolf von Harnack, *History of Dogma* (Grand Rapids, MI: Christian Classics Ethereal Library, 2005), I, 259: "The Attempts Of The Gnostics To Create An Apostolic Dogmatic, And A Christian Theology; Or, The Acute Secularising Of Christianity," § 3, footnote 357.

A current historian, Christopher Stead, agrees that the word *homoousios* (meaning "of the same substance," an essential component of Nicene Trinitarian dogma) originated with the Gnostics. That is, *it is an antichristian invention!* This is the origin of the Trinitarian idea that God is three persons in "one substance" (*homoousios*).

> The word *homoousios*, usually translated 'consubstantial' or 'coessential', appears to have been *introduced by Gnostic Christians* of the second century... It originally meant, 'having the same substance', ousia...It thus means roughly, 'made of the same... kind of stuff.'[5]

Furthermore, Tertullian even admitted that he was teaching a revised form of the same Gnosticism that the infamous Gnostic Valentinus had been teaching. In fact, Tertullian also admitted that he was *introducing* a doctrine—the emanation [prolation] of one god out of another—just as Valentinus did!

> ...*I am introducing*...one thing out of another, *as Valentinus does*...wherein we declare that the Son is a prolation from the Father, without being separated from him. For God sent forth the Word, as the Paraclete also declares, just as the root puts forth the tree, and the fountain the river, and the sun the ray. For these are...*emanations, of the substances from which they proceed*.[6]

Emanations of substances, without separation from the parent, are not the same as a birth of a son or daughter where an umbilical is severed. Thus, Tertullian, under the influence of antichristians, just redefined God's "son" in an antichristian fashion. This same unbiblical gnostic redefinition has tainted the Trinity doctrine to this day.

---

[5] Christopher Stead, *Divine Substance* (Oxford: Oxford University Press, 1977), 190.
[6] Tertullian, *Against Praxeus*, Chapter 8.

This is how Tertullian, one of the earlier Trinitarians, introduced into the supposedly non-Gnostic assembly, the Valentinian Gnostic idea of a projection of one god-being out from another god-being, without separating him from the first god-being. Tertullian's pregnant little statement about "emanations of substances" is actually *the signature mark of antichristianism that John warned us about in saying it is an antichristian spirit that doesn't confess Christ coming in the flesh.*

Trinitarians, such as Brumbach, whom we are currently examining, want you to believe that the Nicenes were only formalizing what earlier Christians always believed. The problem with that claim is that the earliest apostolic Christians expressly did not believe in a Trinity at all, and the earliest Trinitarians (such as Gnostics, and Tertullian after them) believed in the Trinity in a form that later Trinitarians would condemn as absolute, intolerable heresy!

So how do we know that earlier Christians "expressly" did not believe in the Trinity? Irenaeus is a great source of information. He predated Tertullian by a generation, and he has always been considered to hold (for the most part) right teachings, both in his day and since. Note what Irenaeus said in the following quotation. He was speaking of antichristian Gnostics, and he wrote quite clearly against the idea of a production of one god out of another at all, from any angle or perspective!

> They affirm (that this emission took place) *just as a ray proceeds from the sun*, then, as the subjacent air which receives the ray must have had an existence prior to it, so (by such reasoning) they will indicate that there was something in existence, into which the intelligence of God was sent forth, capable of containing it, and more ancient than itself.[7]

---

[7] Irenaeus, *Against Heresies*, Book 2, Chapter 13, par. 4–6.

Here Irenaeus shows us that Tertullian's later "ray from the sun" idea also originated with the antichristian Gnostics. This antichristian view and expression eventually made it into the creeds that were formulated by Trinitarians in the fourth century. The creeds of Trinitarianism are forever tainted with this antichristian understanding.

This passage of Irenaeus also exposes the farce of Gnosticism and Trinitarianism. It is, according to Irenaeus, ridiculous to emit a God-being into nothing, especially since it never left its original place. He is effectively describing the same hoax as the eternally begotten son of Trinitarianism, only he was writing before the so-called "orthodox" Christians adopted the "emanation" idea from the Gnostics (and thus became 'Trinitarians').

Irenaeus also addressed and opposed the exact view the Nicene Trinitarians eventually "developed." He went on to say, "If, again, they affirm that that (intelligence) was *not sent forth beyond* the Father, *but within the Father Himself*, then, in the first place, *it becomes superfluous to say that it was sent forth at all.*"

This is an accusation that points directly at the Trinity dogma. This is absolute proof that the earlier apostolic, non-Gnostic Christians were not Trinitarians, and *for today's Trinitarians to say that later Trinitarians just crystallized what was always believed is a blatant lie!* What Irenaeus did was to *totally denounce the concept* that the word "Trinity" is a label of. But Irenaeus has done us a greater service than using an ambiguous label; he has precisely described the belief of the antichristian Gnostics, who first introduced the belief of one god being begotten from another god. This was a real and serious heresy according to Irenaeus!

Trinitarians, just as some Gnostics, don't believe the Son was sent forth *beyond* the Father, but was *within* the godhead before creation. We quoted Tertullian a bit earlier, who said this exact thing: "The Son is a *prolation* from the Father, *without being separated from him*." According to Tertullian, the Trinitarian Word wasn't born *out of* the Father *into something else*. Irenaeus says that such thinking makes the relationship between the Father and his begotten son, superfluous—meaningless and valueless. Therefore, just as in antichristian Gnosticism, there was no point, purpose, or result in the begetting of the Son in the Trinitarian godhead. And that is exactly what the Trinitarian eternal begetting of the Son is. The Trinitarian "eternal son" is as eternally superfluous as the Gnostic one is according to early Christians like Irenaeus. And that is because the Trinity is just a refined continuation of the Gnosticism adopted by Tertullian.

These statements by Irenaeus prove that he didn't believe in *any* generation of the Son of God before creation, let alone the "eternal generation" doctrine of later Trinitarians introduced by Origen. And just as importantly, such quotes prove that the Trinitarians of the fourth century were not simply "crystallizing" what Trinitarians had "always believed." They were modifying it because it really didn't make sense. In other words, they had to cover up the first lies with more fabrications.

Which leads us to ask, where did the Gnostics get this idea of multiple persons in the godhead? Answer—it is a concept that was also being taught by the pagan philosopher Numenius. It is in philosophy that we find the real source of the Trinity's idea of "persons" in the godhead.

In this next quote, you will see *the Trinitarian source for speaking of God in materialistic terms.* You will also see *the source for the "light from light" doctrine of Trinitarianism's Nicene Creed.* And that source is *pagan philosophy*, as is spelled out by the philosopher Numenius:

> But as the second (Divinity) is double, he himself produces the Idea of himself, and the World, inasmuch as *his nature is that of a Creator*, although he himself remains intelligible... *The First God may not undertake creation, and therefore the First God must be considered as the Father of the Creating Divinity...* When, however, *the Divine is communicated, and passed over from the one to the other*, it does not leave the Giver while being of service to the Receiver; *not only does the Giver not lose anything* thereby, but he gains this further advantage, the memory of his giving (or generosity).

This beautiful process occurs with knowledge, by which the Receiver profits, as well as the Giver. This can be seen *when one candle receives light from another by mere touch*; the fire was not taken away from the other, but its component Matter was kindled by the fire of the other.[8]

As is quite obvious, this is certainly *not the simplicity of Christ* that the apostle warned us not to be moved from. However, *this is the pagan philosophical source of "persons" in the godhead*. This is where the concept of the Trinity actually came from: pagan philosophy. But you don't have to take our word for it; one of the main defenders of the Nicene Trinity admitted they got the idea of "persons" in the godhead from Greek philosophy:

> ...The mystery [meaning the Trinity]... is *separate as to personality yet is not divided as to subject matter. For, in personality, the Spirit is one thing and the Word another*, and yet again that from which the Word and Spirit is [i.e., the Father is], another [person]. But... the one First Cause is not split and cut up into differing Godships, *neither does the statement harmonize with the Jewish dogma, but the truth passes in the mean between these two* [Greek and Jewish] conceptions, <u>destroying each heresy</u>, and yet *accepting what is useful to it from each*. The <u>Jewish dogma is de-</u>

---

[8] As quoted in *The Neoplatonic Writings of Numenius*, trans. Kenneth Guthrie (Lawrence, KS: Selene Books, [1917], rpt. 1987), 26–30.

stroyed by the acceptance of the Word, and by the belief in the Spirit; *while the polytheistic error of the Greek school is made to vanish by the unity of the Nature...* While yet again, of the Jewish conception, *let* the unity of the Nature *stand*; and *of the [pagan/Greek] Hellenistic, only the distinction as to persons...*[9]

Here we have one of the champions of Trinitarianism openly admitting that they had destroyed Jewish monotheism. This is how the Trinity dogma destroys the Jewish view of God. When a man-made idol is worshiped in the place of God, it is called idolatry. That is what Gregory has created: an idol. Such a blatant rejection of the Jew's understanding of what God is, as we see here, is exactly the opposite of the position held by Jesus when he said, "we worship that which we know" in John 4:22.

Just by its complexity we can see the similarity the Trinity has with philosophy, which is also certainly not the simplicity of Christ. The main point is that Gregory of Nyssa said that the concept of the "persons" in the Trinitarian godhead came from pagan philosophy: *"accepting what is useful from each... of the Hellenistic... the distinction as to persons..."* That is a confession that they got the concept of *persons in the godhead* from pagan, Greek, Hellenistic philosophy! So once again, no, the Trinitarians were not merely crystallizing what earlier Christians always believed. In actuality, they were *purposely* interpreting the Bible through their philosophic lenses and imposing those ideas on biblical expressions, thereby replacing biblical truth with a source that is outside of the "faith once delivered to the saints."

By adopting the pagan idea that the Son was an "emanation of the substance of the Father" (as the sun emanates a ray), the Trinitarians *enabled themselves to openly deny that the actual son was made of flesh* and made of his mother, Mary. This is according to explicit statements from Athanasius, the champion of Nicene Trinitarianism:

---

[9] Gregory of Nyssa, *The Great Catechism*, 1, 3.

...nor, as man from man, has the Son been begotten... 'Son is nothing else than what is generated from the Father.[10]

...We are driven to say that what is from the essence of the Father, and proper to him, is entirely the Son... that which is begotten is neither affection nor division of that blessed essence. Hence it is not incredible that God should have a Son, the *Offspring of his own essence*; nor do we imply affection or division of God's essence, when we speak of 'Son' and 'Offspring'; but rather, as acknowledging the genuine, and true, and Only-begotten of God, so we believe.[11]

Considering what John wrote in his epistles about people who deny Christ coming in the flesh, this admission that the Trinitarian son is of no other essence than that of the Father ought to be a shocking revelation indeed! But instead, Trinitarians are all too willing to be duped into accepting this antichristian view!

Robbery by Exchange!

Father   Mother   Son
Biblical Son of Flesh
- 1 John 4:2

Trinitarian son is made of **no other substance** than that of the Father

This is how Trinitarianism denies that Jesus Christ has come in the flesh. They do so by claiming belief in a son who is of *no other substance* than deific substance. *That means flesh is excluded.* John

---

[10] Athanasius, *Four Discourses Against the Arians*, Discourse 1, Chapter 5, par. 14.

[11] Athanasius, *Four Discourses Against the Arians*, Discourse 1, Chapter 5, par. 16.

told us that to deny that Jesus came in the flesh (that is, was made of flesh) is to be antichrist. Trinitarianism explicitly rejects the *biblical* one and only begotten Son of God, who is the one that God swore to David would be the offspring of David. From this point, any claim that Trinitarians believe in a human son should be regarded as lip service.

That's because, when Trinitarians say they believe in the Son, they aren't necessarily saying they believe in the Son who was made of a woman, made under the law. They are saying the Son they actually confess only appeared to be human, temporarily. While inwardly and consciously, in their view, he always remained "God" being made of no other substance than that of God.

In assuming that "son" can only mean an offspring of a father's essence, Trinitarians are guilty of forgetting how often the Bible uses figures of speech. For example, in Genesis 4:20 we are told "Jabal... was the father of those who dwell in tents and have livestock," and then in verse 21 we are told "Jubal... was the father of all who handle the harp and pipe." Think how foolish someone would appear if they were to claim that these verses absolutely prove that only people who are the genetic offspring of Jabal dwell in tents and have livestock, and only those who are descendants of Jubal play musical instruments. This is a case of demanding the literal when the intention was figurative.

Another clear example of this particular idiom is found in Romans 4:11, which says that Abraham "received the sign of circumcision, a seal of the righteousness of the faith which he had while he was in uncircumcision, *that he might be the father of all those who believe*, though they be in uncircumcision, that righteousness might also be accounted to them." Are we to take this literally, that only those who are the biological offspring of Abraham will ever have faith? No, obviously not; in fact the following verse explains that Abraham was "the father of circumcision *to those who also walk in the steps of that faith* of our father Abraham, which he had in uncircumcision" (Romans 4:12). It is in just such a way that the Bible explains that the word *father* can be used for the first person to set an example which other people follow.

In John 8 we have yet another clear example explaining this very principle:

> ³⁸I say the things which I have seen with my Father; and you also do the things which you have seen with your father. ³⁹They answered him, "Our father is Abraham." Jesus said to them, "If you were *Abraham's children, you would do the works of Abraham*. ⁴⁰But now you seek to kill me, a man who has told you the truth, which I heard from God. Abraham didn't do this. ⁴¹You do the works of your father." They said to him, "We were not born of sexual immorality. We have one Father, God." ⁴²Therefore Jesus said to them, "If God were your father, you would love me, for I came out and have come from God. For I haven't come of myself, but he sent me. ⁴³Why don't you understand my speech? Because you can't hear my word. ⁴⁴You are of your father, the devil, and you want to do the desires of your father. He was a murderer from the beginning, and doesn't stand in the truth, because there is no truth in him. When he speaks a lie, he speaks on his own; for he is a liar, and the father of it." (John 8:38–44)

Think about this: did Jesus just claim that these Jews had seen the devil? Well, that's what Jesus said, but that isn't what he literally meant. It is ironic that people will say Jesus must be God because he claims to have seen the Father, but they have no problem seeing that these Jews didn't literally have to have seen the devil for Jesus to claim they had. Yet Jesus said they saw their father, the devil, in the same way he had seen and thereby followed his father. This is how Jesus explains the manner in which God is his Father. Out of all human-kind, only Jesus can make this claim: that he alone has unwaveringly said and done the things shown and taught to him by the Father. That is what God foresaw and what God foreordained regarding His son.

Jesus went on to explain that if they were Abraham's children in truth (meaning in a way that truly fits the figurative speech describing Abraham as their example), then they would have done the works of Abraham. That is, they would have followed in Abraham's example. Yet they kept insisting, belligerently, on a literal, natural interpretation. This is what Trinitarians do when they claim Jesus had to be an offspring of the Father's essence to truly be the Son of God. But that isn't what the Bible explains. What the Bible explains is that those who are led by the Spirit of God are the sons of God:

> [14]For as many as are led by the Spirit of God, these are children of God. [15]For you didn't receive the spirit of bondage again to fear, but you received the Spirit of adoption, by whom we cry, "Abba! Father!" [16]The Spirit himself testifies with our spirit that we are children of God. (Romans 8:14–16)

> Beloved, now we are children [sons] of God, and it is not yet revealed what we will be. But we know that, when he is revealed, we will be like him; for we will see him just as he is. (1 John 3:2)

> [14]Do all things without murmurings and disputes, [15]that you may become blameless and harmless, children [sons] of God without blemish in the midst of a crooked and perverse generation, among whom you are seen as lights in the world. (Philippians 2:14–15)

We are sons of God by our actions, not by our essence. Now look how silly it sounds to insist that being a son of God necessarily means being the offspring of God's essence. If that is the case, then none of us have any hope of ever being God's children. Fortunately, that isn't the case, and those who deny it are simply mistaken because they insist on interpreting everything carnally rather than really hearing what the Bible explains. And so it is with their view of Jesus as the Son of God. Rather than hearing the scripture where God promised David that his offspring would be God's Son, they insist on an unbiblical, pagan, gnostic view that Jesus could only be the Son of God if he is indeed an offspring of God's very essence. This is what the gnostic "light-from-light" doctrine is really all about: exchanging the biblical Son of God for the antichristian abomination.

Athanasius Said, If The Son Isn't Deific Substance Then There is No Trinity

As if all of this weren't enough to expose the Trinity as neo-Gnostic heresy, Athanasius himself tells us *that if the Son is made of flesh, then there can be no Trinity doctrine*. He declares that if the Son is made of anything else but the "Father's essence" (which necessarily excludes his mother Mary's essence), then there is not and never was a Trinity. He can be so candid because he is writing against the Arians, who do believe in a Trinity but a different type of Trinity than Athanasius believes in. The circumstance doesn't change the fact that Athanasius bluntly stated: if the Son was made of humanity, in the process of time, then the Trinity is no Trinity because these concepts are incompatible.

> ... And further, *if the Son is not proper offspring of the Father's essence, but of nothing has come to be, then of nothing the Triad consists*, and once there was not a Triad, but a Monad; and a Triad once with deficiency, and then complete; deficient, before the Son was originated, complete when he had come to be; and henceforth a thing originated is reckoned with the Creator, and what once was not has divine worship and glory with him who was ever.[12]

With these words Athanasius rejected the biblical, prophetic promise of a human savior. The son didn't "come of nothing," the son "came of Mary." Athanasius absolutely denied the scriptural human son, born and made of the seed of Eve, Abraham, and David, ac-

---

[12] Athanasius, *Four Discourses Against the Arians*, Chapter 6, par. 17.

cording to the flesh. He denied the Son that God Himself said He would be a Father to in a future tense. Athanasius stated that if the Son the Bible describes is true, then there is no such thing as a Trinity. Athanasius further denied the true humanity of the Son in the following statement:

> ...*Things originate, being from nothing*, and not being before their origination, because, in truth, they come to be after not being, have a nature which is changeable; but the Son, being from the Father, and *proper to his essence*, is unchangeable and unalterable as the Father Himself.[13]

All things that are created originated from nothing, including the entire human race. According to Athanasius, Jesus could not be a member of the human race and also their deific savior. This is why he had to envision Jesus as emanated from "no other than" the father's essence or substance. This is why they adopted the pagan "light from light" doctrine. Because, they reasoned, if Jesus was truly God, then he couldn't be partially God (and the Father couldn't be partially God either by sharing His deity with the Son). Thus they created two gods, with the understanding that those two retained "one substance" and therefore (they supposed) weren't polytheistic deities. The pagan and Gnostic "light from light" doctrine enabled Athanasius and his ilk to think like this.

---

[13] Athanasius, *Four Discourses Against the Arians*, Discourse 1, Chapter 10, par. 36.

If you will notice, in the "light from light" graphic, there are now two flames; that is how they made God into two and three Gods. This illustrates their reasoning that, since it is the same substance, they were still retaining the concept of "one God" that the Bible demands. That was the big issue in the debates in the fourth century: Arians believed the Son was made of a "similar" substance, but the Athanasians insisted the Son had to be the exact same substance if he were truly to be fully God. However, they were all just deceiving themselves. There is no Scripture explaining any of this, and it was in fact an idea that came to them straight from paganism.

Athanasius was also just restating Gnostic doctrine. The Gnostics taught that the Son took nothing from the woman who bore him, but passed through her without being changed. The Scriptures described the Son completely differently than the Gnostics and their Trinitarian descendants. The Bible (Hebrews 2:14–18) says that the Son had to be made like his brothers in all things, so that he could be our advocate. The Bible also says that the Son learned obedience by, and was perfected through, suffering. In other words, contrary to Athanasius, the Son did have to undergo a change in order to be perfected. The son the Bible describes is a different son than Trinitarians believe in.

> He... though he was a Son, yet learned obedience by the things which he suffered. Having been made perfect, he became to all of those who obey him the author of eternal salvation. (Hebrews 5:7–9)

The Trinitarians made this passage into a lie by saying the Son's humanity added nothing. If the Son did not change, then he was simply not made flesh. He could have remained in heaven and not have gone through all the suffering he did. But the truth is the opposite of the Gnostic and Trinitarian position. In truth, the Son was purely human in his essence, or substance. The Bible says the Son was born of the seed of David according to the flesh and manifested (made known) the attitudes of God through that humanity.

Biblically, the Messiah's substance was human, and that same humanity revealed the character and personality of God.

This is what we mean by addressing coincidences versus influence. By no means is the Trinity simply coincidental to pagan triads; rather, Trinitarians purposely adopted their Trinity from paganism because they were heavily influenced by pagan philosophy.

But most importantly, recall that Gregory admitted that the Trinitarian view *does not harmonize with the Jewish belief in one God; in fact, the Trinity destroyed it*. It isn't just an issue of coincidence or influence; it is a matter of the Trinity doctrine negating the true doctrine of the one God of the Bible! The rejection of the God of the Jews is simply a fact of the Trinity doctrine. They try to hide this inconvenient truth by claiming that the Jews didn't understand who they worshiped, but that is contrary to what Jesus said.

> Ye worship ye know not what: *we know what we worship*: for salvation is of the Jews. (John 4:22, KJV)

Trinitarians are more concerned with justifying and defending their man-made tradition than they are in hearing, receiving, and being conformed by the truth of Jesus' words!

"I AM NOT ALONE"

A Case of Robbery by Exchange!
Don't let anyone rob "you"

God is a Spirit
- John 4:24

The spirit of Yahweh
will rest on him:
The spirit of wisdom
and understanding,
The spirit of counsel
and might,
The spirit of knowledge
and of the fear Yahweh...

- Isaiah 11:2

A spirit has attitudinal
attributes and is not made
of any kind of "substance."

Aristotle

"The fountainhead of
Substance Metaphysics...
From whom the fathers
inherited the concepts...
of their "**substance**"
formulations."
- W.P. Alston

Trinity: Three persons
in one "**substance**"
(homoousios).

After his Philosophy and not after Christ!
Colossians 2:8

Don't think for a minute that Gregory was alone in admitting that the concept of the Trinity comes from pagan philosophy. This next quoted author is in the middle of explaining his view that modern theologians should use twentieth century logic to help make the Trinity less mysterious. In doing so, note his admission about the source of the *concepts* of "three persons in one substance":

> Rather than presenting at this point some formulations from the Fathers, *I will first go back to the fountainhead of substance metaphysics, Aristotle, from whom* the Fathers inherited the concepts in terms of which they set out their substantialist formulations.[14]

---

[14] William P. Alston, "Substance and the Trinity," in *The Trinity: An Interdisciplinary Symposium on the Trinity*, eds. Stephen T. Davis, Daniel Kendall, and Gerald O'Collins (Oxford: Oxford University Press, 1999), 180.

Here we see that Trinitarians do admit that the "fathers" of the Trinity *did inherit concepts* (not just words) *from the substance metaphysics of the pagan philosopher Aristotle*. This is a contemporary admission that the actual source of the Trinity is pagan philosophy. Truly an exchange was made with the acceptance of the Trinity: the pagan view was adopted and the biblical view was rejected. What is the Trinity, then, but going after the gods round about them? This is precisely what Paul warned against when he said not to be spoiled by philosophy after the rudiments of the world (Colossians 2:8, 20). Paul also explicitly said that he taught things through words that the Holy Spirit teaches, in contrast to the words of men (1 Corinthians 2:13). Trinitarians reverse the way Paul taught and have adopted philosophy, with only very slight modifications, in order to view, explain, and understand God as a Trinity. This position is the exact opposite of using the OT as the schoolmaster to bring us to Christ.

Now let's look at the proof, from his own words, that Tertullian did not believe in the Nicene version of the Trinity.

> Because God is in like manner a Father, and He is also a Judge; but He *has not always been Father* and Judge, merely on the ground of His having always been God. *For He could not have been the Father previous to the Son*, nor a Judge previous to sin. *There was*, however, *a time when neither* sin *existed* with Him, nor *the Son*; the former of which was to constitute the Lord a Judge, *and the latter a Father*. ("Tertullian, *Against Hermogenes* 3.18").

What Tertullian just described is *absolutely repugnant to post-Nicene*, coequalist, coeternalist *Trinitarians*; in fact, this is the major reason why they had the battles in the fourth century in which the Council of Nicaea played such a huge role. This absolutely proves that the Trinitarians of the fourth century were not at all just crystallizing what earlier Trinitarians had always believed, making our Trinitarian author a liar, plain and simple. It was roughly a century after Tertullian that this exact belief caused the Nicene Trinitarians to "develop" their one-substance, coequal, coeternal doctrine of the Trinity. Briefly, the bishop of Alexandria and his disciple Athanasius argued that if the Son were truly God, then there could not have been a time when he was not. And yet, that is exactly what earlier Trinitarians such as Tertullian believed. But earlier Christians than Tertullian, such as Irenaeus, didn't believe in a pre-human birthing of Christ at all (with the exceptions of the antichristian Gnostics)!

The Trinity
Crafted on the Workbench...
of Post-biblical Theologians

Here, then, is a summary of how the Trinity evolved: The antichristian Gnostics were the first to attempt harmonizing Christianity with certain teachings from paganism, both philosophy and mysticism. Some of those teachings were the Trinity and the idea of one God birthing another God before the rest of creation. These Gnostics harmfully influenced a lot of nominal Christians. *At one time Valentinus was one of the men being considered for the bishopric of the city of Rome.* Fortunately, he lost the vote, but that shows how much influence he had and indicates there were quite a number of Gnostics. Irenaeus is credited with being one of the main contributors in exposing the errors of the antichristian Gnostics. However, Gnostic teachings had already crept in and begun their corruptive influence on many. Tertullian was among those who were corrupted with some of Gnosticism's ideas, and he repackaged some of those ideas (such as the projection of one God out of another) into a form of the Trinity in such a way as to make them seem reasonable. Tertullian's form of the Trinity has been called Subordinationism, which refers to his belief that the Son was not eternal and was not coequal with the Father but instead was subordinate. Other theologians also did a lot of damage by purposely merging Christian thought with pagan philosophy. Among these were Justin Martyr, Clement of Alexandria, Origen, and many others. These Philosopher-Christians are the ones the Trinitarians call their Church "Fathers" (even though they lived hundreds of years after the apostles). It was Origen (who lived around 184–254) who first taught the doctrine of *eternal* generation of the Son. This was the doctrine that led to the full-blown Nicene Trinity (coequal/coeternal persons) being developed. Arius actually maintained the older Subordinationist Trinitarianism, and Alexander and Athanasius, who came after and were thus disciples of Origen's *eternally* begotten doctrine, believed they were championing the ancient position. But both the Arians and the Nicenes were wrong; neither of their positions was the faith once delivered. All forms of Trinitarianism used words and concepts adopted from pagan philosophy and antichristian Gnosticism. All the Trinitarian "Fathers" of the fourth century accomplished was to have *hammered out a new way* of understanding and talking about God so that the Father, Son, and Holy Spirit could all be coequal in deific authority and coeternal in existence, and thus the full-blown Trinity was formed. That dogma was then thrust upon the Christian world through the secular, legal authority of the Roman Emperors.

Did you note that I said, "hammered out"? It is quite true. Trinitarians even admit it. Look at this:

> The formula 'one ousia in three hypostaseis' was *crafted on the workbench of theologians*... In standard Greek, and in Christian theological usage for much of the fourth century, the words ousia and hypostasis were synonyms. The history

of the formula is the history of the growth of a distinction in meaning between them, and the fact that the Cappadocians had to struggle to explain the distinction shows that it was anything but obvious.[15]

This is yet another Trinitarian confession. The doctrine of the Trinity was *"crafted on the workbench of theologians."* This is a confession that says, in simpler words, they made it. They went to their workshop, and—with a hammer and chisel—they hammered out their god. If you can imagine such a scene in OT days, with the theologians literally sitting down at their workbenches and hammering out the gods they would worship, then you will have grasped just how idolatrous the Trinity doctrine really is. And they admit it. Did you ever wonder, in reading the OT, how the idolaters could be so open about what they were doing? Well here it is in a Christian setting. In fact, the Trinitarian I first quoted made the same confession, although it is, perhaps, a bit more "veiled," when he wrote: "...It should be understood that the men who sat in the various councils... *forged the creeds* adopted there..." This is what spiritual idolatry looks like.

In light of these historic facts, let's now return to the quote from our Trinitarian author, Brumbach, and show how his words fit the pattern of the left-handed circle method. He said,

> *The Trinity was developed...* It was *'implicitly held* by the apostles and other NT writers in their declaration with regard to the Father, Son and Holy Ghost, even though they did not formulate it as a precise doctrine. *They held it, as it were, in solution*; only time, reflection, and the shock of controversy and opposition caused it to crystallize into definite and dogmatic form.' (A.H. Strong)... It should be understood that the men... [who] forged the creeds... were only

---

[15] Joseph T. Lienhard, "Ousia and Hypostasis: The Cappadocian Settlement and the Theology of 'One Hypostasis'," in *The Trinity: An Interdisciplinary Symposium on the Trinity*, 103.

attempting to place in theological terminology that which they believed to be biblical teaching.[16]

This whole defense would belong in the left-most segment of the left circle if we could fit it all in. Alas, we'll have to abbreviate it. For his "proof text," of course, he is referring to such Scriptures as Matthew 28:19 and the like. Now notice in particular his words, "it was implicitly held" and "they held it, as it were, in solution." These are his "plausibility" statements that allow him to believe that his jumped-to conclusion is within the circle of biblical conformity. This is his way of drawing the left-hand circle around his conclusion and his proof texts, to try to contain them each as parts of one whole. Now, if all we had were such Trinitarian-like verses, that might be true. If the devil had quoted Psalm 91 to Jesus and there were no commandment not to tempt the Lord, then it might be true that Jesus could have jumped off the pinnacle and expected to come out unscathed in accordance with God's promise. The problem is, there are "it is written again" Scriptures that constrain, and thus absolutely negate, the jumped-to conclusions of the author quoted above.

For that, in the far right segment of the right circle, we have two sets of biblical commandments. The first set contains the commandment that we are to "teach no other doctrine" (1 Timothy 1:3). Doctrine simply means that which can be taught. *Biblical* doctrines are teachings, therefore, that are *not* hidden wisdom (unlike Gnostic wisdom or "implied" teachings), because these teachings are written for all to see. Rather, doctrine is by definition thoughts and ideas that can be taught to others. Everything the apostles taught can be found in the Scriptures. This is what 2 Timothy 3:15–17 clearly says:

> From infancy, you have known the sacred writings which are able to make you wise for salvation through faith, which is in Christ Jesus. Every writing inspired by God is profitable

---

[16] Brumbach, 20–21.

for teaching, for reproof, for correction, and for instruction which is in righteousness, that the man of God may be complete, thoroughly equipped for every good work. (2 Timothy 3:15–17)

Now we're ready to examine Brumbach's statement within our circles of discernment:

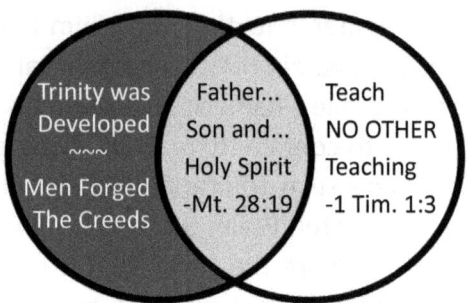

The mere mention in Scriptures of the Father, Son, and Holy Spirit is a long, long way from the Scriptures clearly teaching, let alone intending, that there are three coequal, coeternal persons in the godhead, or that the term "one God" means "one nature" and not "one personal individual." This should be as clear and evident as the truth that just because God promised he would charge his angels to keep you, doesn't mean you can conclude that it will be okay to tempt God. Anyone who is truly honest with the Scriptures ought to be able to recognize each of these simple truths.

The second set of Scriptures *explicitly warns against being spoiled by pagan philosophy.*

> Now this I say that no one may delude you with persuasiveness of speech... *As therefore you received Christ Jesus, the Lord, walk in him,* rooted and built up in him, and established in the faith, *even as you were taught*, abounding in it in thanksgiving. Be careful that you don't let anyone rob [KJV= *spoil*] you through (the) philosophy and vain deceit, after the tradition of men, after the elements of the world,

and not after Christ. For in him all the fullness of the Godhead dwells bodily... (Colossians 2:4–9)

Take note of what one Bible dictionary says about the word variously translated as rob (WEB), cheat (NKJV), or spoil (KJV) in this verse. It means, "of the carrying off of truth into the slavery of error"![17] In other words, those who allow themselves to be persuaded by philosophy have allowed themselves to be robbed of the truth. Is it any wonder, then, that those who have been "spoiled" by philosophy can't seem to "see" the truth?

The apostle admonishes Christians to adhere to what has already been taught and established regarding the faith of Christ and God. It is noteworthy that philosophy is specified as an area of concern. Such Scriptures seem to be of little interest to Trinitarians, who easily belittle them in one way or another. So we can diagram their position in this way:

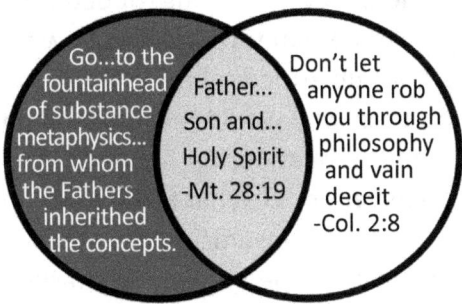

Somehow, Trinitarians ignore the commandment not to be "carried off into slavery" by philosophy. Instead, they find it *important to look to philosophy* because that is where they can find the concepts and words with which to explain what they believe about God. They certainly can't find the concepts or words in the Bible to explain the Trinity in the way they want the Trinity to be believed.

---

[17] *Exegetical Dictionary of the New Testament* (Grand Rapids, MI: Eerdmans, 1990.

Again, this is what Jesus called "setting aside the commandment of God, and holding *tightly* to the tradition of men" (Mark 7:8). The apostles taught that the Scriptures are profitable for teaching and that they thoroughly furnish us all good works. Why then do people who call themselves Christians hold on so "tightly" to their extrabiblical traditions? Did our Lord Jesus Christ not make himself very, very clear that man-made traditions can ruin truth? Could it be because people think that they are doing God a service? Is that what the Pharisees thought they were doing? Or were they just being obstinate against the possibility of losing their coveted position as leaders and experts on God's word? Either way, one thing is clear, not yielding to the whole counsel of God, but laying aside part of God's word to overemphasize another to the point of negating God's word, was obviously the attitude of the devil and is not acceptable behavior for Christians.

In addition to presenting the positive behaviors we are to walk in, the Scriptures also denounce evil works, and one of those works denounced in the Bible, clearly, is being robbed through philosophy. Would Christians take up adultery to learn how to show Christian love? Would they take up armed robbery in order to learn Christian hospitality? If not, then why would they take up pagan philosophy in order to describe the relationship between God and Christ in a way that Scripture never does? What the Trinitarians are really saying is that the Scriptures are insufficient for teaching doctrines. Are we exaggerating? Not one little bit! One Trinitarian put it this way:

> ...The church, in developing the doctrine of the Trinity, *had recourse to certain thought forms already present in the philosophical* and religious environment, in order that, *with the help of these*, it might give its own faith clear *intellectual expression*... As far as the New Testament is concerned, *one does not find in it an actual doctrine of the Trinity. This does not mean very much, however,* for generally speaking the New Testament is less intent upon setting forth certain doctrines than it is upon proclaiming the kingdom of God...

> At the same time, however, there are in the New Testament the *rudiments of a concept* of God that was *susceptible of further development* and clarification, along doctrinal lines...[18]

Recall that Paul said not to be moved away from the Jesus they preached, which meant the one the apostles openly proclaimed and declared. Yet Trinitarians admit they had to go to pagan religions for help with words and concepts with which to "express" what they believe. This is how they openly reject the Jesus whom the apostles preached: by redefining him in pagan terms and concepts.

This statement also exposes the Trinitarian attitude toward the Scriptures as far as the doctrine of the godhead: it "does not mean very much" to them that the Trinity isn't taught in the Scriptures. Isn't this just another way of saying the Scriptures are insufficient for them? Since what they want to see is not in the Scriptures, they take this as permission to reinterpret Scripture until it fits their fancy. That is the real reason it took them so long to "develop" the doctrine: they were trying to get all the puzzle pieces to fit! They didn't fit very easily, so they got out their hammers and pounded and chiseled until they seemed to fit in!

In other words, what we are calling "gray areas" of Scripture, they call "rudiments of a concept... susceptible of further development."

In the bigger picture, this writer is really just playing a shell game. He or she only maintains that doctrine doesn't mean much when it comes to the doctrine of the Trinity. Yet the Trinity is apparently the only teaching that the author doesn't require to be spelled out in the Bible. For all other teachings, biblical doctrines are vitally important to this (presumably) very same author:

---

[18] http://www.bible.ca/trinity/trinity-pagan.htm, accessed 8/10/2017.

> In the Bible, the doctrine of Christ includes his virgin birth, his miracles, his death, burial and resurrection, and ascension to the right hand of God. However, there are other things that are important which are in the doctrine of Christ. They include his *church, worship, repentance, baptism, the Holy Spirit, the Lord's Supper, right living, and his second coming* as well as others...
> Yes.—doctrine is important, especially if it is the doctrine of Christ as revealed in the Bible.[19]

We wholeheartedly agree that doctrine is important, especially if it is the doctrine of Christ that is revealed in the Bible! That's the point of this book! But do you see how this writer contradicts himself? Now he is saying that doctrine revealed in the Bible *is* important, especially regarding the doctrine of Christ, but *doctrine didn't mean very much* when he spoke *in reference to the Trinity*! Shouldn't that be a clear indication that the apostles, at the very least, didn't put any emphasis on the Trinity? Are we really to believe that such a monumental change to Jewish Monotheism blew through their theological belfries without so much as a curtain being rustled? Are we simply to swallow the idea, without so much as a gag, that after all these centuries of God telling His people He is one and alone, and not to go after the gods round about them, now we're to believe that pagan philosophy is the best place to go to find among those very same forbidden heathen the words, terms, "concepts," and "thought forms" to express what God hid from His chosen people? No, much rather, it is highly likely that this is exactly the type of "leaven of the Pharisees" that Jesus warned us against, which he also went on to liken to swallowing camels and straining at gnats! All we can say is somebody must be wearing some powerfully tinted dark glasses if they really can't see the bright light of this scriptural truth: *don't be robbed by philosophy!*

Let's try to put these two opposite views from the same writer

---

[19] Is Doctrine Important?, accessed 8/10/2017, http://www.bible.ca/d-doctrine-important.htm.

in perspective with the other teachings he claims are important. Imagine this same author saying that we shouldn't be concerned if the Bible doesn't teach those other truths either. Here is what that might look like:

> *In developing the doctrines* of Christ's virgin birth, or his death, burial and resurrection, the church had *recourse to certain thought forms already present in the philosophical* and religious *environment*, in order that, with the help of these, it might give its own faith clear intellectual expression.

If the Bible didn't teach these doctrines, but pagan philosophers did, and we practiced what those pagan philosophers did instead of what the Bible taught, would we be legitimate in calling ourselves "Biblical Christians?" Or would we be "pagan philosophers?" Apparently for Trinitarians, all the other things that are spelled out in the Bible are important teachings, but the fact that the Trinity isn't spelled out in the Bible isn't important, and only the teaching about "what God is" in the Scriptures doesn't mean much.

We beg to differ. The problem isn't just that the Trinity isn't in the Bible, but that a) the Bible does spell out quite clearly, consistently, and constantly a truth that is the polar opposite of the Trinity, and b) the elements of the Trinity are and were spelled out in pagan philosophy! That is the real reason why Trinitarians had to resort to pagan words and concepts to describe their view. The Trinity isn't merely "coincidentally" like pagan triads. The Trinity is an outright adoption of them.

For us, what God is and what Christ's true relationship to God is, are actually even more important than the other biblical teachings on the "church, worship, repentance, baptism, the Holy Spirit, the Lord's Supper, right living, and his second coming as well as others." That's because *the truth of who Christ is in relationship to the Father is what makes these other teachings important and even possible!* These other things are not what makes anyone a Christian without knowing who and what God and His Christ truly are! After all this is why the first commandment is the first commandment!

Robbery by Exchange

Before wrapping up our look at the Trinity in this chapter, there is one additional area that shows just how disobedient the Trinitarians are to the Scriptures. We will let our Trinitarian author, and those that he quotes, spell out their position in that area:

> The Hebrews employed the plural form of the name of God in the sense of the singular. *They never understood this to indicate anything but absolute unity: they had no idea of plurality of persons* in the Godhead. The plural was used by them, in this as in other cases, intensively. Elohim means simply, 'the supreme God.'[20]

If you recall the words of Gregory of Nyssa, quoted earlier in this chapter, he said that the development of *the Trinity did not harmonize with Jewish monotheism,* and, through the formulation of the Trinity, the Jewish heresy had been destroyed: "neither does the statement [i.e., Trinitarian confession] harmonize with the Jewish dogma, but the truth passes in the mean between these two [pagan and Jewish] conceptions, *destroying each heresy,* and yet accepting what is useful to it from each. The Jewish dogma is destroyed by the acceptance of the Word." Not only did Gregory of Nyssa claim that Jewish monotheism had been destroyed, but he actually called it a heresy equal to pagan polytheism! This is simply outrageous, and anyone who holds Jesus Christ dear ought to

---

[20] Brumbach, 37–38.

be appalled at this kind of talk. Why? Because, as was pointed out earlier and bears repeating, here's what the Lord Jesus Christ said about the matter: "Ye worship ye know not what: *we know what we worship*: for salvation is of the *Jews*" (John 4:22, KJV).

When Jesus said *"we,"* he purposely, unmistakably, and unalterably associated himself with the Jewish *understanding* of their monotheistic God. Jesus didn't even refer in this case to the Scriptures, oh no. He was talking *only* about the truth that *the Jews knew* what they worshiped. Thus, Jesus spoke explicitly against any view that claims the Jews did not understand what they worshiped. There is simply no getting around this extremely clear and simple declaration of the Lord Jesus Christ's! Jesus said, in Luke 6:46, "Why do you call me, 'Lord, Lord,' and don't do the things which I say?" Mark 9:6 and Luke 9:35 recorded how God the Father spoke from heaven, saying, "this is my beloved son, hear him."

Are the testimonies of the Father and son enough proof for somebody to decide to really hear Jesus? Is someone ready to accept that maybe the doctrines of pagan philosophers and antichristian Gnostic theologians don't really provide better words and concepts for describing a bigger and better understanding of "what" God is than Jesus Christ himself clearly testified to? Is someone ready to admit that the early Trinitarians were wrong for calling exactly what Jesus believed "a heresy" and thus relegating it to the same level of rubbish as pagan polytheism as to destroy it? How much more wrong would the early Trinitarians have to be before people who say they "love the Lord Jesus Christ" realize they can't believe both the Trinity and Jesus at the same time? Was Jesus wrong for criticizing the developing of traditions and teachings of men (Matthew 15 and Mark 7) when he should have known all along that is exactly what it was going to take to define, declare, and defend a doctrine as huge and important as Trinitarians believe the Trinity is, but that Jesus and his apostles never spelled out?

Are we exaggerating a bit here? Well, let's consider what Moses had to say about that which the Apostles reiterated. Let's let them tell us, and then let the reader decide:

For Moses indeed said to the fathers, 'The Lord God will raise up a prophet for you from among your brothers, like me. You shall *listen to him in all things* whatever he says to you. It will be, that *every soul that will not listen to that prophet will be utterly destroyed* from among the people.' (Acts 3:22–23)

I don't know how you read this verse, but it sure seems to be clear that there is no salvation if we do not listen to Jesus in *all* things. It seems very hard to believe that anyone would try to make a case that being utterly destroyed from among the people is equal to salvation. But then again, the serpent taught Eve to believe eating the forbidden fruit would be a good thing, so it's possible someone will try. We certainly wouldn't recommend anyone risking his or her soul over it.

Having made our case in words, now let's look at how this idea of the Trinitarians graphically fits in our circles of discernment:

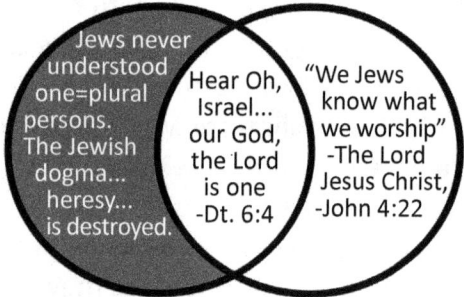

The simple truth is that the position of the Trinitarians is opposite to that of Jesus. Are we to believe that Jesus was mistaken? Or that he could learn something about the multiple persons in the godhead from the Trinitarians? That is what Trinitarians imply.

You may have noticed we've removed the gray area from the graphic. It seemed to border on blasphemy to think or even imply that the first and greatest of all commandments of both the Old and New Testaments, as attested by none other than our Lord, King, and Master, Jesus Christ, is or could somehow be viewed as a "gray area!" Oh no, dear reader, it is not a gray area! It is only by a sleight of hand that Trinitarians even try to make it appear "gray" in the first place—so they can reinterpret it!

To anyone for whom the commandments are "not grievous," the first commandment of all is *more plain, clear, and straightforward than any other sentence of words in any given language on earth...* that is, except when viewed through the darkened lenses of man's traditions, philosophies, and rudiments of the world. This is precisely what the apostle meant when he warned us not to be robbed by philosophy and vain deceit. The first commandment is not a gray area...

> [11]For this commandment which I command you this day, *it is not too hard for you, neither is it far off.* [12]It is not in heaven, that you should say, Who shall go up for us to heaven, and bring it to us, and make us to hear it, that we may do it? [13]Neither is it beyond the sea, that you should say, Who shall go over the sea for us, and bring it to us, and make us to hear it, that we may do it? [14]*But the word is very near to you, in your mouth, and in your heart, that you may do it.* [15]Behold, I have set before you this day life and good, and death and evil; [16]in that I command you this day to love YHWH your God, to walk in *his* ways, and to keep *his* commandments and *his* statutes and *his* ordinances, that you may live... [17]But *if your heart turn away, and you will not hear*, but shall be drawn away, and worship other gods, and serve them; [18]I denounce to you this day, that you shall surely perish...[19]I call heaven and earth to witness against you this day, that I have set before you life and death, the blessing and the curse: therefore choose life, that you may live, you and your seed; [20]to love YHWH your God, to obey *his* voice, and to cleave to *him*; for *he* is your life. (Deuteronomy 30:11–20)

It sounds pretty clear that God and Moses felt the commandments of God were pretty clear. How much more so the very first and most important one?

What our circles of discernment have shown is that Trinitarians have effectively negated and made of no effect certain very real biblical concepts... and commandments! This they did by moving those qualifying, "it is written again," biblically stated truths *outside of the circle of their understanding and belief system*. This is what our circles show: that the Trinitarians laid aside certain commandments of God in order to take up their man-made idol to worship. In doing so, they have effectively moved those, and many, many other Scriptures right out of their reckoning...

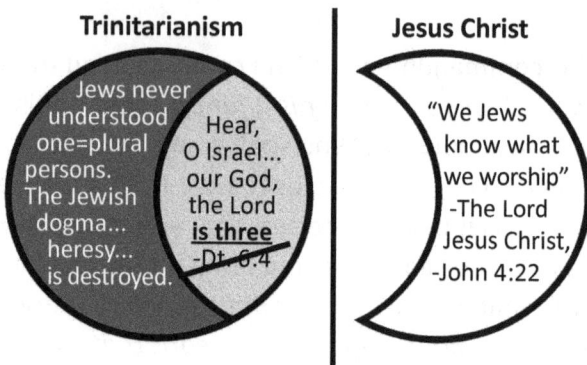

As this graphic demonstrates, by rejecting and distancing themselves from Jesus' words on the right, Trinitarians have effectively set themselves apart from Jesus' form of worship, which employs every word of God. Obviously, laying aside some verses of Scripture to keep jumped-to conclusions based on other verses is not a "Christ-like" attitude; it is by nature, therefore, non-Christian.

If you have ever wondered what the word "sect" (Gr. *hairesis*) in the Bible means (or "heresy," which is derived from the same Greek word), here we have it graphically described. Sects are those that *sect-ion* themselves off from certain truths in the Word of God, only to emphasize others *beyond their originally intended scope so as to make them untruths*. Trinitarianism makes Jesus' words into just such an untruth.

We will have more to say about the Trinity as we proceed through this book. But remember, the scope of this book isn't primarily intended for addressing the Trinity, but rather, for presenting the true

Christ in contrast to Onenessianism. Thus far, we have put forward our position against the Trinity primarily for the purpose of finding common ground with Onenessians. We expect that Onenessians will completely agree with us in the way we have shown how unbiblical and disobedient Trinitarianism is. Now here's the kicker: we are going to use the same methods to address Onenessian jumped-to, unbiblical conclusions, and thereby show that Onenessians stoop to the same false methods as the Trinitarians they disagree with. If they agree with the techniques we've used so far against our common rival, they should recognize how legitimate and appropriate it is to use those same techniques to examine their own beliefs. Likewise, if we can show that Onenessians use the same false methods of adopting extrabiblical and even antichristian ideas as the Trinitarians, then they should also be able to see that their Oneness doctrine is no more scriptural than is the Trinity.

Robbery by Exchange

Bible:
Christ is
Come in
The Flesh

Gnostic:
Christ is
Come in Deific
Substance

Our goal in the following chapters will be, as before, to reestablish the simplicity of the biblical Jesus and to expose exactly how unscriptural teachings have been imposed on biblical ones and caused the truth to be hidden from view and understanding. This attention is most necessary regarding the following three groups of opposite topics:

- Foreknowledge vs. Preexistence
- Made of the Seed of David vs. Dual Natures
- Man approved by God vs. God come down in the likeness of men

Each of the first items in the list is biblical and refutes Onenessianism (and Trinitarianism). Each of the opposing ideas is of pagan origin and contrary to the biblical ones, but has been adopted by Onenessianism in order to "describe" the Onenessian viewpoint. That is, they are *not* mere coincidences because a) the Bible does not spell them out (expressly), and b) we can see the point in history when these ideas were adopted into Christianity. They were thus not "truths" contained in the apostle's "faith once delivered."

In other words, just as with those who support the Trinity doctrine, those who believe in Onenessianism, after they have seen the evidence we are about to share, to be honest and biblical, should concede that paganism and antichristian Gnosticism have provided better definitions, expressions, and statements of their belief system than their Bibles. And that is why, just as with Trinitarianism, Onenessianism has been left with no other option than to adopt pagan and antichristian perspectives in order to express their view.

More on the Gnostic Trinity

The following modern quote asserts that the Gnostics were pioneers in developing the Trinity. In particular, the writer refers to various early second century Gnostics represented in Irenaeus' writing, *Against Heresies* (I, 29–30). These Gnostics were the ones, this writer argues, who "profoundly influenced Valentinianism," which Gnostics also, in turn, as we've briefly shown, influenced Tertullian, who in turn influenced Trinitarianism, which in turn influenced modalistic monarchianism, which is the same as Onenessianism today:

> ...About... the two related myths of Irenaeus *Adv. Haer.* 1.29 and 30... their ideas profoundly influenced Valentinianism... ...These Christian *Gnostics... constructed a myth of primal Father, Mother and Son* as an alternative myth of origins to Genesis... *these Gnostics*, along with those of (Irenaeus') 1.30, *may with justice be seen as the pioneers in developing an understanding of God as triadic or Trinitarian... both develop alternative Trinitarian schemes...* The system in 1.29...

> develops a triad of Father, Mother and Son, splitting the Mother into a higher and lower Sophia (wisdom), that latter of whom it identifies with the Holy Spirit.
> The system in 1.30, on the other hand... can best be interpreted as an attempt to develop a triad of (male) Father, (male/female) Son and (female) Spirit, generating Christ as the Only-Begotten Son... Whereas the system of 1.29 identifies Christ as *the Son within the Trinity, the system of 1.30 has Christ outside of the Trinity, ascending to it.*
> *This reference to emanation indicates another major characteristic of the underlying Gnostic myth... the pervading influence of Platonic/Pythagorean ideas,* hinted at in Basilides, even more obvious in Valentinus. *All three share, according to Irenaeus' account, a concern with the ineffable, nameless, unoriginate Father, his self-revelation by a process of emanations, of which the first or supreme male is Nous and a later is Logos.*[21]

This same author reiterates that the Gnostics derived their method of interpretation from pagan philosophy, which implies philosophy's forms and ideas.

> Indeed it could be suggested that the Gnostics were among the first Christians to be influenced by Platonism... To detect a (later) Platonization is slightly misleading: the Gnostics were Platonists from the first! They developed their Platonism in dialogue with the evolving Platonic tradition, perhaps even anticipating Neoplatonism in some respects.[22]

Gnosticism and Neoplatonism were developing at the same time in the second century. Neoplatonists like Numenius may have gotten the idea to assign personality to the platonic *logos* in dialogue, or in

---

[21] Alastair H. B. Logan, *Gnostic Truth and Christian Heresy* (Peabody, MA: Hendrickson, 1996), 29, 32–33.
[22] Ibid., 34.

conversation, with Gnostics. That doesn't mean they were entirely in agreement. It just means they were selectively picking up certain of each other's points as they contended with each other.

This insight adds significantly to the drama of Gregory of Nyssa's confession that Trinitarians got their "thought forms" for the idea of "persons" in the godhead from Hellenist philosophers. What this author is saying is, those "Hellenist Philosophers" were, more precisely, the antichristian Gnostics who were "Platonists from the first," just as they were always Trinitarians. The source of Trinitarianism (as contrasted with actual pagan tri-theism) is actually antichristian Gnosticism.

The Bottom line is this:

> But evil men and impostors will grow worse and worse, deceiving and being deceived. (2 Timothy 3:13)

The Trinity doctrine is one of those doctrines made worse and worse. Trinitarians feel as if they have just gotten better and more sophisticated in explaining the Trinity. In fact, they have just been perfecting their craft of robbing the truth through their philosophy and vain deceit.

CHAPTER TWELVE
Made of the Seed of David vs. Dual Natures

The Apostle's Good News

"Teach No Other Doctrine!"

> ...Jesus Christ... was made of the seed of David according to the flesh. (Romans 1:3, KJV)

> ...blasphemous systems... divide the Lord... saying that he was formed of two different substances. For this reason also he has thus testified to us in his Epistle: "Little children, it is the last time; and as ye have heard that Antichrist doth come, now have many *antichrists* appeared..."[1]

What we want to show in this chapter is extremely simple. On one hand, the Scriptures are very clear and consistent that Christ was made of the seed of David according to the flesh. On the other hand, early Christians like Irenaeus called the "Dual Nature" doctrine "blasphemous" and "antichristian."

The first quote provided above encapsulates the simplicity of Jesus. The second quote encapsulates and refutes the opposite view. If you can see the difference between those two quotes, then you've grasped the point here. The rest of this chapter will be spent

---

[1] Irenaeus, *Against Heresies,* Book 3, Chapter 16, par. 5.

covering the details and exposing the magnitude of influence of antichristianity, the actual inventors of the dual-nature doctrine.

Onenessians love to call themselves "apostolic" because they deem themselves to be closer to apostolic Christianity than other Christians. But is this label entirely accurate? Consider this question as you read this chapter: just how "apostle-like" would it be to embrace and teach what the apostles called "*antichristian*" doctrines?

The apostles said they used great plainness of speech (2 Corinthians 3:12). Some versions interpret this as great boldness of speech. Either way, there would be no sense whatsoever for them to hide what they were saying about the Son of God in "code words" that mean exactly the opposite of what has been spelled out throughout the Bible. Ignoring these truths is how the Trinitarians ended up with the Trinity.

Like the Trinitarians, Onenessians use "code words" that mean something entirely different than what the Bible means when using those same phrases. That is what we are going to show in this chapter: the Onenessians *deceive* people into believing that Father and son are "code words" for Christ's dual natures of deity and flesh rather than referring to specific *types of relationships between separate individual personalities as they clearly and consistently indicate in all literature, biblical or otherwise.*

In our last chapter we wrote, "the antichristian Gnostics were the first Trinitarians... And it was directly from the antichristian Gnostics that Tertullian... adopted the idea of the Trinity." The truth we are going to show in this chapter is that this is also true about the source of the "dual nature" doctrine. Like the Trinity, Tertullian also adopted this doctrine from the antichristian Gnostics and made it acceptable to those who otherwise wouldn't consider themselves Gnostics.

Let's first ground our position in the Scriptures. The following passages clearly and consistently teach one truth: that Jesus Christ was made of the seed of David according to the flesh and was made like us in all things. This should be as simple and as cut and dried as anything that ever was. It is almost as clear as the first commandment!

> Concerning His Son, *who was born of the seed of David according to the flesh*, who was *declared to be* the Son of God with power, according to the Spirit of holiness, *by the resurrection from the dead, Jesus Christ our Lord*, through whom we received grace and apostleship, for obedience of faith among all the nations, for his name's sake. (Romans 1:3–5)

> My relatives *according to the flesh*... Are Israelites... *From whom is Christ as concerning the flesh*... (Romans 9:3–5)

> Remember that *Jesus Christ of the seed of David* was raised from the dead according to my gospel. (2 Timothy 2:8, KJV/NKJV)

This concept of Jesus being the offspring of David comes from *God's sworn oath* to David:

> Therefore, being a prophet, and knowing that *God had sworn with an oath to him that of the fruit of his body, according to the flesh*, he would raise up the Christ to sit on his throne, he foreseeing this spoke about the resurrection of the Christ. (Acts 2:30–31)

Why would people want to believe their man-made definitions and doctrines trump God's sworn oath? This oath was originally captured in this passage:

> ⁸...Thus says YHWH [to David]... ¹²When your days are fulfilled, and you shall sleep with your fathers, *I will set up your seed after you, who* shall proceed *out of your bowels*, and I will establish *his kingdom*. ¹³*He shall build a house for my name*, and I will establish the throne of his kingdom *forever*. ¹⁴*I will be his father, and he shall be my son*. (2 Samuel 7:8–14)

This isn't deep. It isn't mysterious. It isn't shrouded in unfathomable mystery. It is a simply stated truth in the Bible. And it is emphasized by the fact that it is one of the few places in the Bible where God (who cannot lie in any way) swore with an oath that it would come to pass. And yet, even still, some people have a hard time believing God's sworn oath without adding to it or diminishing from it. These verses are simply explaining the truth.

The Bible even clearly explains how Christ was made:

> But when *the fulness of <u>the time</u> was come*, God sent forth his Son, <u>*made of a woman*</u>, made under the law. (Galatians 4:4)

Notice carefully that this verse doesn't say that only Christ's *flesh* was "*made of*" a woman, it says God's Son was *made of* a woman. "Made of" is two words, and means literally "to become of" a woman. In Genesis 2:7 we are told, "God formed man of the dust of the ground." Most Christians have no problem accepting this on faith since it is what God's word declares. Next we find in Genesis 2:21 that God made woman out of one of Adam's ribs. Again, most Christians believe this on faith because it is written in God's word. But then we come to Jesus, whom the Bible says was "made of a woman," and now, people hesitate. But that is exactly what happened. God's word says that God's Son has been "made of a woman." That's the simple, biblical, and yet amazing truth.

Notice also that *this son was born at a certain point in time*, and that moment in time was when he was made of a woman. This refutes all Trinitarian ideas (both Arian and Athanasian) of an eternal or pre-human existence of the Son of God.

Next we look at a passage that has caused a lot of confusion. Later we will show exactly where that confusion originated. For now, let's look at what it says.

> The book of the generation [genesis=beginning] of Jesus Christ, the Son of David, the Son of Abraham... (Matthew 1:1)

Matthew is using *genesis* here as a Greek rendering of the Biblical Hebrew used when listing genealogies in the Bible (the "begats"). It means "beginning" or "origin" in the sense of family descent. So Matthew has deliberately patterned his wording on that used in the Hebrew Bible. That means, according to Matthew, Jesus didn't begin before this. The word for beginning used here means "source, origin, a book of one's lineage, i.e. in which his ancestry or progeny are enumerated, used of birth, nativity... "[2] Then Matthew goes on to describe Christ's miraculous birth from his mother Mary:

> [16]Jacob became the father of Joseph, the husband *of Mary, from whom* was born Jesus, *who is called The Anointed One.* [17]So all the *generations* [source/nativity] from Abraham to David are fourteen generations; from David to the exile to Babylon fourteen *generations*; and from the carrying away to Babylon to the Christ, fourteen generations. [18]Now *the birth of Jesus Christ* was like this; for after his mother, Mary, was engaged to Joseph, before they came together, she was found pregnant by the Holy Spirit. (Matthew 1:16–18)

First, recall the two words from Galatians 4:4 above: "made of" a woman. Next, note that Matthew does not likewise say that Christ was "made of" the Holy Spirit, only that Christ was in Mary's womb "by" the Holy Spirit. This is *a huge difference* because of the use or lack of one word. That one word designates what this son was "made from." The Holy Spirit *made this happen* just as God said He would when He told David, "*I will set up your seed after you*" (2 Samuel 7:12, above). So in perfect agreement with this, *Matthew does not say that the Son was "made of" the Holy Spirit in the way he is said to be "made of" a woman.* Matthew did not spend all that time recounting Jesus' genealogy, his nativity, his source, and then when he got to verse 18 say, "Oh, and by the way *he is also 'made*

---

[2] ("NT:1078" Thayer's Greek Lexicon, PC Study Bible formatted Electronic Database, 2006 by Biblesoft).

of' the Holy Spirit." No, he was merely mentioning that it was the Holy Spirit that made this happen, which is what we know as his miraculous virgin birth. Matthew 1:18 does not negate all the other clear Scriptures in the Bible, such as the ones we've just read, no matter how many people try to read that into the passage. God did not "renege" on His sworn oath that the Messiah, His son, would be born of the seed (or offspring) of David! The Bible doesn't explain it any further than this other than to say Jesus was "made of a woman." That tells us that God made Jesus out of the woman in the same way He made Adam out of dust and Eve out of Adam.

Let's take a look at the meaning of the word *genesis* as used in the Book of Matthew.

> NT:1078 1. Genesis is found 5 times in the NT, *in the sense of birth* (Matthew 1:18; Luke 1:14), *genealogy* (Matthew 1:1), *and source, root* (James 1:23; 3:6).
> 2. In secular Greek, esp. in Plato, genesis is attested *in the sense of origin and beginning,* in contrast to *fqora* (dissolution); and *in the sense of becoming, in contrast to ousia (being)* and what has come into being, or creation (*kosmos*). It is also used in temporal contexts *for lineage and descent.* In the latter sense *it is used genealogically*; i.e., every god, every hero looked proudly to his descent...
> 3. Matthew 1:1, in dependence on the language of Genesis 5:1, speaks of the "book of the genealogy" (or *history of the origin) of Jesus Christ* and proceeds from David and Abraham...[3]

In other words, by using the word *genesis* for Christ's birth, Matthew was clearly disallowing *that Jesus is an incarnation* of a previously existing deity. The word "incarnation" isn't in the Bible, nor is the meaning of "incarnation" spelled out anywhere in the Bible. What is the difference in these two words? Well, everyone alive today can point to a day when they were "born," but how many of us call

---

[3] Cited from the *Exegetical Dictionary of the New Testament* (Location: Eerdmans, 1990.

our birthday our "incarnation" day? According to the Bible, Jesus had a birth, not an incarnation. Matthew was talking about Jesus Christ's actual, literal beginning and his genealogy by which he was brought into being. Luke's telling of the story adds some additional insight into the way Jesus' birth was understood. Keep in mind that even though this book was written from the viewpoint of the time of Jesus' life, it was actually penned many years after the apostles had received the Holy Spirit and had been walking in the full truth.

> [31] Behold, you will conceive in your womb, and bring forth a son, and will call his name 'Jesus.' [32] He will be great, and *will be called* the Son of the Most High. The Lord *God will give him the throne of his father*, David. (Luke 1:31–32)

This passage makes clear that Jesus would *actually be the Son of David*, but would be "*called*" the Son of the Most High (God), and God would "*give*" him the throne of his father, David. No talk of Jesus being an incarnation of God here, just evidence that *Jesus is the fulfillment of God's plan* for the Messiah to be declared His own son, just as He had sworn.

This passage confirms all that we've read so far and adds more detail to emphasize Christ's humanity:

> [14] Since then the children have shared in flesh and blood, he also himself in like manner *partook of the same*, that through death he might bring to nothing him who had the power of death, that is, the devil, [15] and might deliver all of them who through fear of death were all their lifetime subject to bondage. [16] For most assuredly, not to angels does he give help, but he gives help to the seed of Abraham. [17] Therefore *he was obligated in all things to be made like his brothers*, that he might become a merciful and faithful high priest in things pertaining to God, to make atonement for the sins of the people. [18] For in that he himself has suffered being tempted, he is able to help those who are tempted. (Hebrews 2:14–18)

He was *obligated* to be made like us in *all* things. Not in some things, as some would have it; not somewhat like us, as many suppose. How many of us are made up of 100% deity and 100% humanity? No one. If Christ was made out of deity at all, in his personality or anything, then he was not made like us in all things. It's that simple, and anything else is jumping to conclusions. This Scripture even explains to us *why* this is so. Jesus had to be the same flesh as us in order to save us.

As we've seen so far, this biblical truth was spelled out and described quite clearly, consistently, and thoroughly. However, *the antichristian Gnostics came up with another idea, which is called the "Dual Natures of Christ" doctrine.*

We will get back to that in a moment, but first, let us prepare by reviewing what John, speaking in response to the antichristian Gnostics, said about Christ's flesh. As you read these, recall our second quote at the beginning of this chapter, where Irenaeus identified those "blasphemous systems" that divide the Lord into two substances as being of the spirit of "antichrist." Recall that Irenaeus said these next verses were written to testify against the "two natures" doctrine of the antichristians:

> ...Many deceivers... don't confess that Jesus Christ came in *the flesh*. This is the deceiver and the Antichrist.
> (2 John 7)

> ...Every spirit who doesn't confess that Jesus Christ has come in *the flesh* is not of God, and this is the spirit of the antichrist... (1 John 4:2–3)

Note that John didn't say Jesus came in "a" flesh, but rather in "the" flesh. In this way we know that John obviously agreed with Paul that *there is only one type of human flesh*:

> All flesh is not the same flesh, *but there is one flesh of men*, another flesh of animals... (1 Corinthians 15:39)

There simply are not two or more types of human flesh. What does this mean? It just means that if Jesus came in a different flesh, or different type of humanity than that of the rest of us, *then he was a different kind of creature than us*. And if he was a different kind of creature than us, then he is not eligible to be the high priest for us, according to Hebrews 2:17. And *if anyone says that he is of a different humanity than us, John calls this the spirit of antichrist*.

Now let's read what Jesus said about being born human:

> ⁶That which is *born of the flesh is flesh*. That which is born of the Spirit is spirit. ⁷Don't marvel that I said to you, You must be born anew. (John 3:6–7)

Jesus was confirming an obvious truth: that which is born of the flesh is flesh. Consider that in connection with what John said, that those who don't confess "Jesus Christ has come in the flesh" are of the spirit of antichrist. Therefore, to deny that Jesus was made of the one flesh of man when he was born of Mary would be to make both Jesus and John out to be untrue. Thus, the dual nature doctrine of Gnostics is precisely the antichristian spirit, or attitude, that John was warning us against! This also explains why Jesus had to be baptized and receive the Spirit of God just like the rest of us: he also was born of the flesh!

Even Jesus himself, though he kept the law and never committed sin, also had to walk by faith, and through faith receive the born-again-of-the-Spirit experience. Why? Because it is written:

> ...A *man is not justified by the works of the law but through the faith* of Jesus Christ, even we believed in Christ Jesus, that we might be justified by faith in Christ, and not by the works of the law, because *no flesh will be justified by the works of the law.* (Galatians 2:16)

> ²⁰Because *by the works of the law, no flesh will be justified in his sight*. For through the law comes the knowledge of sin. ²¹But now apart from the law, a righteousness of God has

been revealed, being testified by the law and the prophets; ²²even *the righteousness of God through faith* in Jesus Christ to all and on all those who believe. For there is no distinction. (Romans 3:20–22)

No flesh, apart from faith, is justified in the sight of God. This also applies to Jesus, who John says came in the flesh. If we don't want to be "against Christ," we'll believe it! That means the opposite is also true: those who want to make Christ the man into a spiritual being do so because they don't truly believe that Jesus came in the flesh. Instead, they have a spirit of antichrist, because that is exactly what the antichristians did: redefine Christ to be something personally extra-human.

These verses speak of having faith in Christ, but we can only have faith in Christ because Christ first displayed faith to God, and it is that faith we are to emulate:

> ¹Therefore, holy brothers, partakers of a heavenly calling, consider the Apostle and High Priest of our confession, Jesus; ²*who was faithful to him who appointed him*, as also was Moses in all his house. (Hebrews 3:1–2)

Therefore, Jesus could say he gave us an example (John 13:15), and this is also why he submitted himself to John's baptism, saying "Allow it now, for this is the fitting way for **us** to fulfill all righteousness" (Matthew 3:15). By explicitly using the word "us" (Greek *hemin*), Jesus declared that he was just as responsible to submit faithfully to God's will as the rest of us. That is, he had to come to God by faith, just as the rest of us are commanded to do, and faith is hope, and hope that is seen is not hope. If Jesus were in any way God, then his faith would have been nothing more than a sham!

All this helps us understand that when the Bible uses the word "flesh," it isn't merely talking about a "human nature" that God somehow "robed himself in," as in Trinitarianism and Onenessianism. Instead, it is saying that Jesus Christ came solely and completely as a flesh and blood human being, even as he said:

> See my hands and my feet, that it is truly me. Touch me and see, for a spirit doesn't have flesh and bones, as you see that I have. (Luke 24:39)

This is all biblically stated truth. These Scriptures teach us clearly and straightforwardly about the flesh, the humanity, of Jesus Christ, *and that is the simplicity of Christ we are not to be moved from.* In quoting these Scriptures, we have added no man-made teachings, nor any decisions made in councils hundreds of years after the apostles walked the earth. We haven't had to reach into pagan philosophy or Gnostic inventions for words and concepts. With the exception of some dictionary definitions of words the Bible uses, we've just let the Scriptures speak.

On the other hand, *there are absolutely no Scriptures in the entire Bible that state, teach, explain, or even imply that the person of Christ himself was made of or consisted of two natures or substances.*

So then, having laid the biblical foundation, we will now see how Christians moved away from the biblical ("Born of the seed/offspring of David") Christ.

Recall from Chapter Nine that the term "Christ" is the English equivalent of "Anointed One" and specifically means that something has been granted or given to the one being anointed. That being the case, *the phrase "antichrist" literally means to be against the idea of an Anointed Man as our savior!*

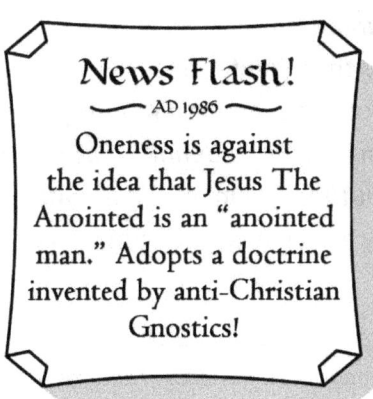

News Flash!
— AD 1986 —
Oneness is against the idea that Jesus The Anointed is an "anointed man." Adopts a doctrine invented by anti-Christian Gnostics!

The critical point to keep in mind is simply that Jesus' title "Christ" is descriptive of the manner in which he received his calling and office. As Jesus said, "*All* authority *has been given to me* in heaven and on earth..." (Matthew 28:18–19). This is why it is important to understand that to be "antichristian" is to be *against* the idea that Jesus was a man to whom God *gave all authority*. It's just that simple. When we read the term "antichrist" in the Bible, we should reinterpret it in our minds to mean "against-the-anointed-one."

So just how big of a deal is this? Well, notice what prominent Oneness writer David Bernard wrote on the subject:

> It is *necessary* to distinguish clearly between the deity and the humanity of Christ... *Jesus was both God and man* at the same time...*Jesus was* fully God, *not merely an anointed man*...[4]

In other words, the Oneness confession of belief, as stated above, is expressly *against the idea of Jesus being* "*merely an anointed man*" who, as such, *was given all authority* by God. Thus, according to David Bernard, and any Onenessians who agree with him, it is "necessary" to interpret Jesus through the antichristian doctrine of dual natures! This is how people unwittingly confess to being against the anointed one (antichristian) simply by adding that Jesus was also the very God who anointed him. This idea totally negates the very meaning of being *anointed*!

In the same way that Trinitarians claim they believe in one God but then redefine "one" to mean that multiple persons are that one God, so Onenessians *merely redefine what it means to be a human who was given all authority*. Onenessians who hold such beliefs are actually saying they are against the anointed one *in the same exact*

---

[4] David Bernard, *Symposium on Oneness Pentecostalism 1986*, (Saint Louis: Word Aflame Press, 1986), 126.

way as the original Gnostics were: by claiming that Christ was an incarnated deity made of two natures, deific and flesh, and thus "not merely an anointed man."

This is what we learned from Irenaeus. So let's recall Irenaeus' words again. We quoted him briefly above, but now let's read what he says in context and note particularly how he uses the Scriptures to make his case *against* the "dual natures" doctrine of the antichristians.

> Therefore did the Lord also say to his disciples... "Thus it is written, and thus it behoved Christ to suffer, and to rise again from the dead, and that repentance for the remission of sins be preached in his name among all nations." Now this is *he who was born of Mary; for he says:* "The Son of man must suffer many things, and be rejected, and crucified, and on the third day rise again." The Gospel, therefore, *knew no other son of man but him who was of Mary*, who also suffered; and no Christ who flew away from Jesus before the passion; but him who was born it knew as Jesus Christ the Son of God, and that this same suffered and rose again, as John, the disciple of the Lord, verifies, saying: "But *these are written, that* ye might believe that Jesus is the Anointed One, the Son of God, and that believing ye might have eternal life in his name," –foreseeing *these blasphemous systems which divide the Lord*, as far as lies in their power, *saying that he was formed of two different substances. For this reason also he has thus testified to us* in his Epistle: "Little children, it is the last time; and as ye have heard that Antichrist doth come, now have *many antichrists appeared*..."[5]

---

[5] Irenaeus, *Against Heresies,* Book 3, Chapter 16, par. 5.

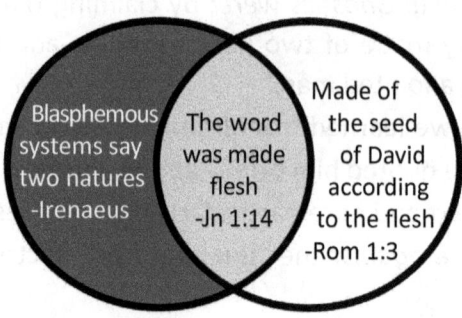

In Irenaeus' time it was *"blasphemous systems..."* that *"divide[d] the Lord... saying that he was formed of two different substances."* As with the Trinity, talk of two natures or two substances is not found anywhere in Scripture. The first ones to talk like this were the Gnostics. And with that thought, keep in mind that this disciple of John's disciple Polycarp testifies to us that *it was "for this reason," that of the blasphemous dual nature doctrine itself, that John wrote against the antichristian Gnostics!*

This, again, is something I used to teach and believe, but it was in ignorance, as I'm sure it is with many well-meaning Onenessians. But now that the light of truth is being shed on the origin of the "dual natures" idea, it puts the onus back on Onenessians either to quote the Scripture that actually says Christ was made of two natures, or to search the Scriptures to see if the things being presented here are so.

Now, let's read what Irenaeus wrote against *the Gnostic idea that Christ was made of a different humanity* than the rest of us:

> Those, therefore, who *allege that he took nothing from the virgin* do greatly err... For *if He did not receive the substance of flesh from a human being,* He neither was made man nor the Son of man; and *if He was not made what we were,* He did no great thing in what He suffered and endured...
> The Apostle Paul, moreover, in the Epistle to the Galatians, declares plainly, "God sent His Son, *made of a woman."* (Gal. iv. 4) And again, in that to the Romans, he says, "Concerning

> His Son, who was made of the seed of David according to the flesh... Jesus the Anointed One our Lord." [Rom i. 3, 4]... Superfluous, too, in that case [of the Gnostic invention] is His descent into Mary; for why did He come down into her if He were to take nothing of her?..."[6]

According to Irenaeus, the early Christians understood that Christ was made human because *he got the substance of his humanity from a human being*. That means that the true, early, apostolic Christians did *not* believe that the Son got his humanity from God, which is something antichristians had also been saying. The early Christians did not believe that Christ was made of any kind of deific flesh or deific seed; rather, *he was made from a woman*, just as the Bible clearly and emphatically states.

These words pertain to all the Scriptures we quoted above that teach very clearly that Jesus was made of the seed (in Greek, the *sperma*), or offspring, of Eve, Abraham, and David! In the early years of Christianity, only the antichristians believed that Jesus received deific seed as part of his human makeup. This in itself is another major refutation of both Trinitarianism and Onenessianism!

Let's see which side Bernard has taken on this additional issue of whether Jesus inherited his humanity from and through Mary as the Bible teaches, or was created of a different humanity than the rest of us, as Irenaeus spoke against the antichristians.

> God *started the human race all over again with Christ*, so He might yet have the perfect humanity He originally intended when He created Adam...To fulfill this role, *Christ came with an innocent, perfect humanity like Adam had in the beginning*.[7]

---

[6] Irenaeus, *Against Heresies*, Book 3, Chapter 22, par. 1–3, Ante-Nicene Fathers, Vol. 1 (Buffalo, NY: Christian Literature Publishing Co., 1885), 454–455.

[7] David Bernard, *Symposium on Oneness Pentecostalism*, 125.

There you have it: Bernard's doctrine is against the Scriptures and in support of antichristian concepts. According to the Bible, *Christ was the (genetic/genesis) offspring* of Eve, Abraham, and David. Yet according to Bernard and the Onenessians who agree with him, Christ did not receive his humanity from David through Mary, but *rather was made of recreated humanity resembling Adam before the fall*. Where is the Scripture for that? Does Bernard's opinion trump all the Scriptures that we quoted above, including God's sworn oath? If Oneness opinion trumps Scripture, then why are these Onenessians so adamant that they only teach what the Bible says? Let's see if our circles of discernment can help shed any light on this.

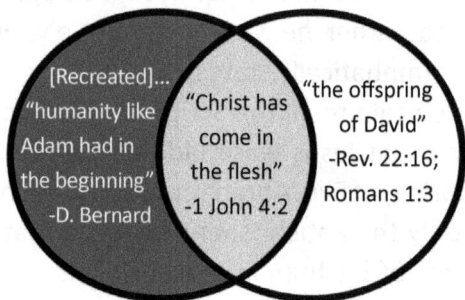

According to Bernard, Jesus was made with "an innocent, perfect humanity like Adam had in the beginning." How can that be if he was explicitly the *offspring* of David and was made of the seed of David according to the flesh? Would Bernard claim that David also had that "innocent, perfect humanity like Adam had in the beginning"? Of course not, because he already told us he believes God started the human race all over again with Christ.

So how is it that the "dual-nature" doctrine and the "recreated human nature" doctrine have now become the prominent doctrines of both Trinitarianism and Onenessianism? Answer: They have both been "spoiled" by philosophy, just as the apostle warned!

Let's back up a moment and show how the idea of adopting Gnostic teachings evolved. We've already quoted Irenaeus enough to know that he identified these as false positions originating with the Gnostics. Now let's look at how these ideas were adopted and expressed by Tertullian. Here's what he wrote:

...I am introducing some *"probohl"* that is to say, some pro-lation of one thing out of another, as Valentinus does when he sets forth eon from eon, one after another... This will be the prolation... wherein we declare that the Son is a pro-lation from the Father, without being separated from Him. For God sent forth the Word... *just as the root puts forth the tree, and the fountain the river, and the sun the ray.* For these are *"probohls"* or *emanations*, of the substances from which they *proceed*. I should not hesitate, indeed, to *call the tree the son or offspring of the root*, and the river of the fountain, and the ray of the sun; because every original source is a parent, and everything which issues from the origin is an offspring. Much more is (this true of) the Word of God, who has actually received as His own peculiar designation the name of Son. But still the tree is not severed from the root, nor the river from the fountain, nor the ray from the sun; nor, indeed, is the Word separated from God. Following, therefore, the form of these analogies, *I confess that I call God and His Word-the Father and His Son-two*.[8]

This is the way in which Tertullian redefined the words *father* and *son* as they applied to God and Jesus. The problem is, a "son" is not the same thing as a "root," a "river," or a "ray."

Here is a graphic of the normal meaning of a father and son (with mom added in since Jesus was, after all, made of a woman named Mary).

Father   Mother   Son

---

[8] Tertullian, *Against Praxeas*, Chapter VIII.

That's pretty simple, right? This is the normal and obvious meaning of the terms father, mother, and son. This is so simple I believe a three-year-old could comprehend it.

Now let's compare the graphic above with Valentinus and Tertullian's redefinitions of the Father and son. In addition, we have added the pagan "light from light" doctrine, which we introduced in Chapter Eleven:

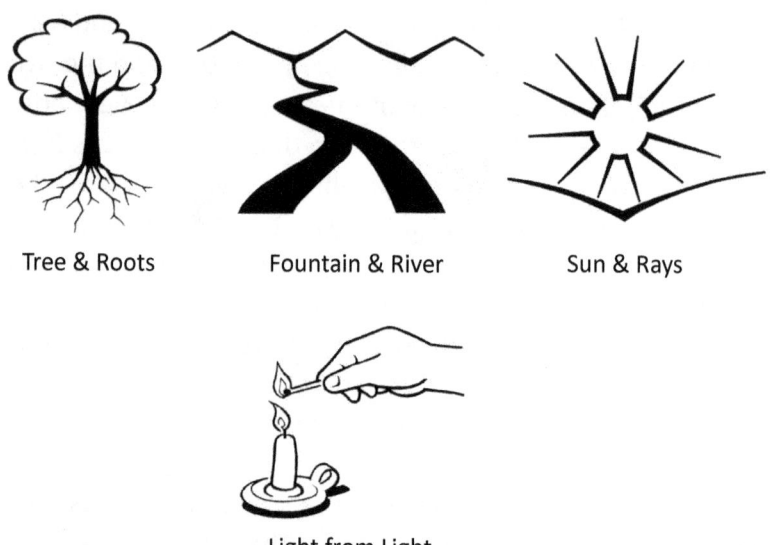

Tree & Roots   Fountain & River   Sun & Rays

Light from Light

We can clearly see the difference in ideas. In the four graphics above, there is no *absolute, personal separation*. The emanation of one god out of another is not a "birth." *In a human birth, there is an umbilical cord that is severed. In the first three emanations, there is no such severing of one individual from another. In the fourth, an identical substance is duplicated without any subtraction from the first.* Biologically, in a human birth, the new child has its own DNA from conception, and the umbilical is merely a conduit for providing the baby with nutrients, etc. None of this is so in the pagan light-from-light doctrine. So Trinitarians don't really believe in a father and son in the true meanings of the words; they believe in emanations, or extensions of one "god-substance" between the "persons" they "call" "Father," "Son," and "Holy Spirit."

So what about the "light from light" doctrine? In our graphic there is a separation, but the problem is that in that analogy, the Son of God is still the same substance, or essence, of the Father. That makes the "light from light" doctrine entirely antichristian because *it claims that Christ was not "of any other essence than that of the father."* In other words, he couldn't have been flesh if he was only made of the same essence as the Father. John tells us that is antichrist. Even human children have their own unique DNA. The Trinitarian son is made of the exact same essence as the Father, which is what makes them "coequal" according to that theory.

These graphics demonstrate the major hurdle that the antichristian individuals had in supplanting the biblical view of Christ with the pagan view of an incarnation of deity. They demanded a deific savior, while the Bible declares a human savior. The idea of "three gods" isn't the only concept that links the Trinity to pagan philosophy; rather, practically everything else about their descriptions of God's Son does also.

On the other hand, Onenessians believe they are immune to such accusations of pagan influence. So, while we're using graphics, let's look at a graphic image of the Oneness view:

Oneness Father and Son

This image fits the Oneness view for the following reasons: a) there is only one personality, in their view, and the Father and son are accurately portrayed as that one person; b) as with the Trinitarian emanations, there is no severing of an umbilical cord and beginning of a whole new personality that necessarily exists in a true father/son relationship; c) the Son alone is made of dual natures and, in their view, God "dwelling in" Christ means that Christ is the person of God Himself; and d) the Son has no personality; in fact, according to Bernard, Christ would be an empty, lifeless shell of humanity if not for the Spirit of the Father in him:

> Without the Spirit of God there would have been *only a lifeless human, not the living Christ*. Only in these terms can we describe and distinguish the humanity and deity in Jesus...[9]

Descriptions such as this make the graphic above entirely fitting for Oneness. Just as with a puppet in the puppet master's hand, in the graphic it is only the Spirit of God that gives life, personality, and animation to an otherwise lifeless son. This view negates hundreds and hundreds of clearly stated Scriptures to the contrary.

In the Oneness View

"God has made him...

...both Lord and Christ, this Jesus" (Acts 2:36)

---

[9] David K. Bernard, *Symposium on Oneness Pentecostalism*, 130.

These graphics show that Modalism is the same antichristian rejection of Christ as the Trinity is, due to the simple fact that the personality of the Son in both cases is, supposedly, God. The antichristian "dual-nature" invention and the pagan idea of "gods coming to earth in the form of man" tie these together as equally rooted in Gnosticism.

Many people who claim to be "Christian" today (such as Trinitarians and Onenessians) *unknowingly show themselves to be antichristian by the simple fact that they are adherents of the same "two-substances" or "dual natures" teaching that the Gnostics invented.* Many adopt these ideas from Gnosticism without even being aware of it, because they've been wrongly taught this is what Christians have always believed! But that is simply not true.

We are not ignorant of other ways of explaining the "ontological hypostatic union" by Onenessians other than David Bernard. But the point is the same: absolutely none of them can merely go the Bible and quote the place where it simply explains their personal theory any more than Mr. Bernard can. That is one of the tragedies of the Oneness position: watching them grope for words that aren't in their Bibles by which to explain their beliefs, and ultimately looking to pagan philosophy for the words and concepts they can finally be satisfied with. That is what idolatry is. Remember the golden calf that Aaron made? They called it YHWH, but the conception was purely pagan. It is the same with the method used to arrive at the Oneness doctrine, just a different era, and a different medium, and a different conclusion.

How the Gnostic Source of the "Dual Natures" Doctrine was Made Acceptable

We've shown previously that Tertullian got his idea of one god projected out of another god from the antichristian named Valentinus. And we saw earlier that Tertullian is usually credited with being the first to use the word Trinity, when in fact the Gnostics used that term before him. Well, now we are seeing that it was this same Tertullian who is often "credited" (wrongly) with being the first to tackle the issue of the two natures!

One historian (J. N. D. Kelly) has this to say about Tertullian's introduction of the "two substance" doctrine:

> *Tertullian's Christology was its grasp of the two natures in Christ*; to use the term which he preferred, *the Saviour was composed of 'two substances'... If Jesus Christ, then, consists of 'two substances'... Tertullian has the distinction of being the first theologian frankly to tackle this issue...* he sums up: 'We observe a twofold condition, *not confused but conjoined*, Jesus, in one Person *at once God and man'... If it is said that Christ suffered and died, the reference is to*

> *the human substance. God does not suffer; the Christ-spirit cannot even have 'suffered with' (compassus) the flesh, as the modalists like to plead...*[10]

You may not have caught the theological cover-up here. This is how *they hide the fact* that the Trinity originated in antichristian Gnosticism. Somehow, Tertullian "has the distinction of being the *first* theologian frankly to tackle this issue." For whatever reason, this historian has overlooked the facts of history. Antichristians had been teaching the doctrine of *two natures* well before Tertullian did. In fact, as we have already pointed out, Irenaeus, also before Tertullian, had quite effectively "tackled" the issue. But, unlike Tertullian, Irenaeus had spoken *against* the idea, calling it blasphemous! What else should an antichristian view be called if not blasphemous?

This is another example of what we mean by influence and not coincidence. It is not a coincidence that the antichristians also taught the "dual natures" doctrine of both Trinitarians and Onenessians, because we have Irenaeus testifying that it was repugnant to Apostolic Christians before Tertullian.

News Flash! — AD 1986 — Oneness leader D. Bernard reveals that Onenessians got their Dual Nature doctrine from the Trinitarian council of Chalcedon (just like the one at Nicaea), and not the Bible!

---

[10] J. N. D. Kelly, *Early Christian Doctrines* (San Francisco: HarperCollins, 1978 rev.), 150–152.

Do you remember the Trinitarian author from the last chapter who wanted us to believe that the reason the Trinity wasn't spelled out in the Bible is because the apostles didn't set out so much to teach doctrine? But we know the truth is that *something different is taught* in the Bible. Here we have that same attitude repeated with Onenessians, a smokescreen to try and explain why their man-made teaching isn't in the Bible:

> Actually Oneness believers *do not look to the creeds for doctrine but to Scriptures alone*. While *we can find important truths both in the Council of Chalcedon and in Nestorianism*, neither is adequate. Therefore we should avoid the nonbiblical, trinitarian language of the traditional creeds...[11]

That initially sounds credible. But the question is, *why, if Oneness believers look to Scriptures alone would they need any other source for help in defining their beliefs*? If Bernard really believes what he says, shouldn't he also reject the "dual nature" doctrine? On closer examination, his statement is *exactly* like statements from Trinitarians saying they didn't get their Trinity from pagan philosophy, yet they then admit *they do use philosophy to supply the words and concepts to explain it*! That is what being double-minded is. To clarify the situation, here are some definitions of the beliefs Bernard is referring to:

> *The Council of Chalcedon*... attempted to resolve the issue of how to express the concept of Christ as being both fully human and fully divine.[12]

> *Nestorianism* is a Christological doctrine that emphasizes the disunion between the human and divine natures of Jesus.[13]

---

[11] David Bernard, *Symposium on Oneness Pentecostalism*, 144.

[12] *Council of Chalcedon*, accessed 1/26/2017, http://www.newworldencyclopedia.org/entry/Council_of_Chalcedon.

[13] *Nestorianism*, accessed 1/2/017, https://en.wikipedia.org/wiki/Nestorianism.

In other words, by referring to Chalcedon and Nestorianism, Bernard is admitting, though in subtly concealed, complex, technical, "ecclesiastical-speak," that Onenessians *have been able to "find important truths" about "Christ... being fully human and fully divine" from those Trinitarian councils that defined and adopted the "dual nature" doctrines from the antichristians*! That is, Bernard has just admitted to us that Onenessians got the idea of their "dual nature" doctrine directly from the Trinitarians, who got it directly by way of Tertullian from the antichristian Gnostics.

So then his claim that they look to Scriptures alone for doctrine *is as empty and false and misleading as the same claim from the Trinitarians* that they don't look to pagans for their doctrine of the Trinity!

All one should have to do to refute Onenessianism is to ask the simple question, where does the Bible explain that Christ is made of dual natures? Or we might ask it this way: Why is an antichristian teaching preferable to the teachings of disciples just two generations removed from John, disciples who considered the "dual nature" doctrine blasphemous and even claimed that was the very reason John took up the task to write against "antichristians"?

Of course, Bernard is not alone. Many, if not most, Onenessians can be quoted as advocating the antichristian doctrine of "dual natures." For example:

> ...*He was God and He was man... He had a dual nature*. He was absolutely flesh but He was absolutely God. He was absolutely the Father; He was absolutely the Son. He's altogether the Father and the Son...[14]

> It is important to remember that because of the incarnation of God—the Spirit of God dwelling in human flesh—*Jesus had two completely different natures: divine and human*... I Timothy 3:16 shows that the mystery of godliness is con-

---

[14] Anthony Mangun, "Jesus the Man," *The Dual Natures of Christ* (DVD, 2006), Disc 5, track 5 at 0:00–0:24.

cerned with the two natures of Jesus and what He did as the divine Messiah. It is a mystery because we as human beings cannot absolutely comprehend how Jesus could have two natures that would make him both fully God and fully man.[15]

Any valid *incarnational* theology *must maintain that God is man, that it is God who is man*, and that it is man whom God really is... Maintaining all three maxims requires that God's incarnational becoming be of a certain sort. First, *the union of the divine and human natures must be ontological*, not merely functional...The only grounds upon which God can be said to *be* man, and the man He became can be said to *be* God, is if the union is ontological in nature."[16]

I wonder if any of these Onenessians are aware that the idea of the "dual natures" of Christ originated with the antichristians. Or how will they react once this fact is made known to them? Will they continue to hold onto this teaching that was once called heresy by the early apostolic-taught Christians? Time will tell.

This is the Antichrist, He Who Denies the Father and the Son

²¹I have not written to you because you don't know the truth, but because you know it, and because no lie is of the truth. ²²Who is the liar but he who denies that Jesus is the Anointed One? *This is the Antichrist, he who denies the*

---

[15] R. Brent Graves, *The God of Two Testaments* (Hazelwood, MO: Word Aflame Press, 2000), 67–68.

[16] Jason Dulle, "Avoiding the Achilles Heels of Trinitarianism, modalistic monarchianism, and Nestorianism: The Acknowledgement and Proper Placement of the Distinction Between Father and Son;" http://www.onenesspentecostal.com/ugstsymposium.htm.

Father and the Son. ²³Whoever denies the Son, the same doesn't have the Father. He who confesses the Son has the Father also. (1 John 2:21–23)

Let's take a closer look at what this verse is saying. John says it is against the Anointed One (antichristian) to deny the Father and the Son. If we are to take these two words at face value based on the abundant and consistent and inflexible biblical usages, we would view these words as meaning this:

> **Father** is from the Greek word *pater*, and carries with it the idea of one personality who begets another individual or personality, or who precedes another, or who teaches and instructs another, or of God who has ultimately begotten us all as distinct individuals and personalities from Himself. "Jesus said, 'I am ascending to <u>*my Father and your Father*</u>, to my God and your God'" (John 20:17). According to Jesus, we are sons to God *in the exact same context in which he is a son to God.*

> **Son** is from the Greek word *huion,* which "in most cases... is used to refer to *descendants* in the literal *or figurative* sense."[17]

In the KJV Bible, as per a word search in Biblesoft's One Touch software, and using a wild card to catch possible variant endings, there are some 3,597 occurrences of the word "son" and 1,718 occurrences of the word "father." Even so, *never once* is the word "son" used or defined as a son to one's self, nor is "father" used as a father to one's self. Each word is exclusively used for distinguishing separate personalities. That is, *they are both terms that describe a certain, specific type of relationship between two individuals.* Those relationships do have some range of meaning, but that range is finite and fixed. A father is always and without exception prior and/

---

[17] NT:5207 from *Exegetical Dictionary of the New Testament.*

or superior in either time or authority in relation to another individual or group of individuals, and a son is always either morally inferior or afterward in time, being in some way produced by an act of a prior, separate individual, such as a father, mother, or mentor.

Thus, to change the definitions of these words to something different than what the Bible uses them to mean is to disbelieve in the concept the apostle was referring to when using those particular words. Thus, those who believe that Jesus was not a personally distinct son from the Father actually are the very ones John was writing against in 1 John 2:21–23!

So then what is the Oneness view of 1 John 2:21–23? To answer that, let us look at what Anthony Mangun, Pastor of The Pentecostals of Alexandria, LA, teaches:

> We believe in separate offices of God or manifestations of God the Father in the Son... The reason I believe in that is because I don't want to be antichrist...
>
>> "1 John 2:22 Who is the liar but he who denies that Jesus is the Christ? This is the Antichrist, he who denies the Father and the Son."
>
> You can't deny the Father and the Son but what you've got to proclaim is both of them are one. Father is Spirit, Son is flesh... We acknowledge the Father and the Son but we believe they are in Jesus Christ... It means you believe there was a Spirit that was God the Father that got in the flesh and came to this earth and that flesh was his Son and that he lived and he died and he was buried and he rose again... As Father in the OT, as Son in Matthew, Mark, Luke and John, as Holy Ghost in Acts through Revelation. That's where we are today, we now have the Holy Ghost inside of us that is the third manifestation of Almighty God...
>
>> "1 John 2:23 Whoever denies the Son, the same doesn't have the Father. He who confesses the Son has the Father also."...

Why is this? Because Jesus and the Father are one. He said if you deny Jesus you deny the Father also...[18]

Before addressing these statements, I want to give the reader a little background. I attended Anthony Mangun's church in Alexandria, Louisiana, from 2000 to 2004. While I was there I was always very impressed by Brother Anthony, and I was also very supportive of him, and indeed still consider myself to have been blessed to be part of that congregation. However, no matter how much I may like or respect anyone personally, the question needs to be asked: Is that enough to overlook when an antichristian teaching regarding Christ is being put forth as the correct way to view Christ? Do I owe loyalty to someone who would preach an antichristian doctrine and expect us to believe it as truth?

The bottom line is that a Christian's ultimate loyalty must be, first, foremost, and always to the true, biblical One God and His Christ, no matter whom it may offend. This is what being a truly One God person means! Anthony Mangun himself, several times in these teachings, asked the congregation to prove him wrong if they could. He also said this:

> I have felt it *necessary to let you know what error is and from whence it comes*. Because the truth stands; whether I believe it, whether you believe it, whether no one believes it, truth is still truth. If that is a beige color, whatever color that is, I can sit here and believe it is black all I want to. And I can convince you that wall is black. But the truth is, it's not black, it is beige. Truth is truth and no one can change truth.[19]

---

[18] Anthony Mangun, "God in Christ," *The Dual Natures of Christ*, (DVD, 2006), Disc 4, track 1 at about 37:00–41:00.

[19] Ibid., Disc 4, track 1 at about 4:20.

Likewise, I have felt it necessary to show what an error the "dual nature" doctrine is and from whence it comes. So also, I owe it to Anthony Mangun and all my Oneness friends and acquaintances to help them come out of error into the marvelous light of truth that sets free.

Now, imagine my surprise when, sometime after moving away from Alexandria, about the same time I was discovering the true origin of the doctrine of dual natures, lo and behold, brother Anthony put out a series of teachings named that very thing, "The Dual Natures of Christ." Anthony Mangun's most essential problem is not that someone may or may not prove him wrong. His essential problem is that he has yet to prove himself right by the Bible!

Now let's look at our graphic illustration of a father, mother, and son again, as compared to the Oneness view:

Father   Mother   Son   Oneness Father & Son

What jumps out at you is that, compared to the "son of the father in truth" view on the left, Mangun has changed the meaning of father and son into a different meaning. This he has done in the same manner in which he said you can call "beige" "black" all you want, but that doesn't change it. The same is true with the words father and son. You can point to a puppet all day long and call it a son, and the puppet master its father, but that doesn't change the definitions of father and son. That doesn't mean you actually believe in a father and son. It means you have deceived yourself into believing an untruth, a lie! Onenessianism does not have The Father and The Son in truth; they only have a father and son to the extent they can redefine the words to mean something that they don't mean!

Now compare these with the Trinitarian view of two persons in one nature, or essence.

What Onenessianism does is very much like the method that Trinitarians use. By redefining them, the Onenessians change the biblically separate persons into "natures" in one individual person. What Trinitarians do is change the one God into distinct persons having the same nature, or essence, and then claim they still believe in one God. But neither of these views is spelled out in Scripture, and both of these views absolutely negate what the Bible describes, which is the graphic of a father with a son who was made of a woman!

The Oneness graphic also shows us that we don't have to rely only on Irenaeus to prove that *the "dual nature" doctrine is antichrist* (literally *against the doctrine of the Anointed One)*. John had defined "antichrist" as being in *denial of the Father and the Son*. By *redefining* father and son to mean something *different than those words mean*, including the fact that they *always* refer to separate, personal individuals in specific relationship to each other, Mangun has *quite effectively denied the true father and the true son by denying their true meanings and redefining them as something else and then supplanting the real father and son with something that means something akin to a puppet master and a puppet.*

Contrary to Mangun's interpretations, the real reason that you can't have the father without the son is very simply because having a son or daughter is what makes a man a father! It is just like the fact that no man is a husband until he has a wife. On the other hand, you can have spirit without flesh (i.e., angels), and you can have flesh without spirit (i.e., a dead body), just as (to use Mangun's analogy) you can have beige without black all you want. Black isn't dependent on beige to exist, nor is beige dependent on black (though perhaps some may disagree). But that isn't true with father and son. A father without a son is simply a man, and no son has ever been born who didn't have a father. So you see these relationships of fathers and sons are totally *dependent on each other hierarchically, and that is the difference between the truth and Mangun's substituted man-made definitions!*

I realize many Onenessians would call Jesus "Father," but how many of them would say to him, "Jesus, my Son"? This helps emphasize the distinction in these titles. The idea would be blasphemous even to Onenessians to call Jesus their son! Thus, these relationships *are dependent upon each other in a very specific manner.* Though I'm a son, I'm not a son to everyone. I'm a father also, but I'm not everyone's father. The terms are relative and dependent upon each other, and they have meaning that inherently includes a personal distinction between the two.

But so far, we still have just scratched the surface! Above all, we need to keep in mind that the relationship between a father and a son is, first and foremost, a moral one with moral values. Biblically, sons and fathers simply cannot be the same person; nor can they be coequal, because, by moral decree from God, children are to honor their fathers and mothers:

> Honor your father and your mother, that your days may be prolonged in the land which the LORD your God gives you. (Exodus 20:12)

²"Honor your father and mother," which is the first commandment with a promise: ³"that it may be well with you, and you may live long on the earth." (Ephesians 6:2)

One of Jesus' prime examples against the Pharisees who made God's commandments void, was through their practice of redefining, and resultantly negating, the moral values of the relationship between children and their parents:

> ⁶He answered them, "Well did Isaiah prophesy of you hypocrites, as it is written, 'This people honors me with their lips, *but their heart is far from me.* ⁷But *in vain do they worship me, teaching as doctrines the commandments of men.*' ⁸For you set aside the commandment of God, and hold tightly to the tradition of men—the washing of pitchers and cups, and you do many other such things." ⁹He said to them, "Full well do you reject the commandment of God, that you may keep your tradition. ¹⁰For Moses said, 'Honor your father and your mother;' and, 'He who speaks evil of father or mother, let him be put to death.' ¹¹But you say, 'If a man tells his father or his mother, 'Whatever profit you might have received from me is Corban, that is to say, given to God;' ¹²then you no longer allow him to do anything for his father or his mother, ¹³*making void the word of God by your tradition*, which you have handed down. You do many things like this." (Mark 7:6–13)

These Pharisees made void the word of God by redefining the moral roles of children and parents. Incarnationists do the same thing when they redefine the roles of father and son between God as Father and Jesus as His Son. In doing so, they aren't committing anything significantly different than those who redefine marital roles, which are also relationships that have moral values associated with them (e.g., Mathew 19:4; Romans 1:27; 1 Corinthians 5:1).

It is staggering to think of all the ramifications that are changed and corrupted from their original meaning by redefining the terms father and son as Onenessians especially do, but Trinitarians also do in their own way. With one stroke of redefinition, suddenly what the Bible so carefully and consistently defined has been transformed at their making into something different.

In the Incarnationist (Oneness, Trinity and Arian) model:
- It wasn't really the Father's "only begotten Son" ("made of a woman" as defined in the Bible) that the Father gave in John 3:16, but something different.
- It wasn't really God's "Son" who was born of Mary, and given the throne of David (Luke 1:32), but something else entirely.
- It wasn't really God's "Son" that God sent (John 4:14) into the world, not to condemn the world, but that the world through him would be saved, as we are taught to believe in John 3:17.
- It wasn't really a "Son" that God was speaking to in Matthew 17:5, when the voice out of the cloud said, "This is my beloved Son, in whom I am well pleased. Listen to him."
- It wasn't really a "Son" that Stephen saw at the right hand of God in Acts 7:56.
- It wasn't really the very "Son of God" that the demons were afraid of in verses like Mark 5:7.
- It wasn't really for God's "Son" that a marriage was planned and arranged by God, as Jesus taught in Matthew 22:2.
- It wasn't really God's "Son" by whose death we have been reconciled to God, nor was it by that same "Son's" life that we are saved, as we are taught in Romans 5:10.
- It isn't really a "Son" that we are to believe in to escape the condemnation of the world, as John 3:18 tells us.
- It isn't really a "Son" that we are to acknowledge in order that God remains in us, as is written in 1 John 4:15.
- It isn't really a "Son" we are to believe on, as it says in 1 John 5:5, that we may overcome the world, but some other undefined *thing*, defined by man, that we are to believe in and confess instead.
- It isn't really a "Son" that sets you free, as Jesus claimed in John 8:36.

How long would we need to go on with this list in order to make the case ironclad that Jesus is truly the "Son OF God" and not an incarnation of the Father or some emulation of the Father's essence, which would change, pervert, and corrupt the bulk of the Scriptures that clearly define what it means, biblically, for Jesus to be the true Son of God?

Why, then, do some Christians feel inclined to redefine relationships to suit their whims and pet doctrines? The answer is given above: "This people honors me with their lips, but *their heart is far from me*" (Mark 7:6). So, according to this passage, changing God's word is an outward symptom of a heart that inwardly rejects the truth of God's word. This is why homosexuals justify gay marriages, it is why Trinitarians justify negating the first commandment to keep their Trinity, and it is why Onenessians redefine the relationship of Father and Son from God and Jesus and cling to their dual nature doctrine instead.

By their fruits you will know them, Jesus said in Matthew 77:20. That is why by the fruits of our lips we confess that Jesus is the Anointed One, the Son of God (Matthew 16:16, 26:63–64; John 20:31; and so on)! And that is why true, biblical Christians are just as appalled at the Trinity and Onenessian redefinitions of The Father and The Son as they are at professing Christians redefining marriage.

The question really comes down to, what is God's actual intent in the words of the Bible? It is wrongheaded to ask instead, "What can be concluded by reading into God's words what it may seem to imply, but doesn't clearly say?" There are no scriptures simply stating that a marriage between people of the same gender is as legitimate as a marriage between a man and a woman. No same-sex marriage has ever naturally produced offspring. This alone proves its inequality with heterosexual relationships, which form the basic building blocks of society. If everyone were homosexual, then in just one generation the whole human species would become extinct. Thus, the Bible never condones or even clearly defines in a positive light, a homosexual marriage. However, the Bible does clearly and consistently teach marriage between a man and a woman. For example:

> [4]He answered, "Haven't you read that he who made them from the beginning made them male and female, [5]and said, 'For this cause a man shall leave his father and mother, and shall join to his wife; and the two shall become one flesh?' [6]So that they are no more two, but one flesh. What therefore God has joined together, don't let man tear apart." (Matthew 19:4–6)

Just as there are no scriptures clearly affirming gay marriage, there are also no scriptures that clearly explain or describe that the Son is an incarnation of the Father (in the Oneness sense) or that God is three persons (in the Trinitarian sense). If any of these viewpoints (homosexual marriages, Oneness, or Trinity), is biblically acceptable, why doesn't the Bible clearly proclaim it and then expound on it in detail? It is simply because none of them are what the Bible intended to portray, declare, or teach! To the contrary, the Bible DOES clearly teach and expound the details of the opposites of these conclusions: heterosexual marriages, and The Son of God doctrine! All those false, man-made relationships, therefore, have at least the following things in common: they lay aside the commandments of God in order to replace them with traditions and doctrines of men, making the word of God—in the area of the biblically defined moral relationships of each—null and void.

To be clear, Christians don't have anything personal against gay people or gay marriages. The issue is solely what God's word says about it. Beyond the propagation of our species, the real issue is that it annihilates the typology of the bride of Christ, in relation to Christ as her bridegroom. Marriage, Paul says, is a great mystery that teaches us about Christ and his ecclesia by way of typology:

> [28]Even so ought husbands also to love their own wives as their own bodies. He who loves his own wife loves himself. [29]For no man ever hated his own flesh; but nourishes and cherishes it, even as the Lord also does the assembly; [30]because we are members of his body, of his flesh and bones. [31]"For this cause a man will leave his father and mother, and

> will be joined to his wife. The two will become one flesh."
> ³²This mystery is great, but I speak concerning Christ and of the assembly. (Ephesians 5:28–32)

This passage clearly teaches us that the marriage between a man and a woman represents the truth; namely, that the body of Christian believers under Christ is not morally or hierarchically "coequal" with Christ. He is our king and lord and corporate bridegroom. The reason that Christians don't accept homosexual marriages as biblically viable is simply because that would be to confuse the role distinctions between Christ and the corporate body of believers. That is what a God-ordained marriage between a man and a woman represents (which isn't to say a God-ordained marriage doesn't also have validity in its own right).

Here is one of the best verses for teaching us that the moral values existing between God the Father and His Son, Jesus Christ, are similar to the moral values existing between husbands and wives, and between believers and Christ:

> But I would have you know that the head of every man is Christ, and the head of the woman is the man, and the head of Christ is God. (1 Corinthians 11:3)

This verse proves quite conclusively that Christ is not the person of the Father, any more than wives are the same person of their husbands, or any more than all the people who make up the body of Christ are the person of Christ! The verse also proves quite conclusively that there are both moral values and hierarchical roles among each of these three sets of individuals, and furthermore, that those roles and values have been ordained and established by God. Because it is God who has ordained and defined them, they are not to be redefined by man!

Both Trinitarianism and Onenessianism demolish these roles and their moral values by redefining the relationship between the Father and Son in the same way that homosexual marriage demolishes the roles of true husbands and wives. This explains why believers in the true Son of God doctrine cannot accept false views of Jesus as the true Son of God, any more than most Christians can accept homosexual unions as biblically viable, true marriages.

Since the presence of specific moral values is necessary for understanding the true Son of God, we would expect to find the Bible teaching and explaining in detail those moral values that exist between God the Father and Jesus His Son; and in fact, we do:

> [8]Now therefore thus shall you tell my servant David, Thus says YHWH... [12]...*I will set up your seed after you, who* shall proceed *out of your bowels...* [14]*I will be his father, and he shall be my son*: *if he commit iniquity*, I will chasten him with the rod of men, and with the stripes of the children of men... (2 Samuel 7:8–14)

> [49] He said to them, "Why were you looking for me? Didn't you know that I must be in my Father's house?"... [52]And Jesus increased in wisdom and stature, and in favor with God and men. (Luke 2:49–52)

> [8]Though he was a Son, yet learned obedience by the things which he suffered. [9]Having been made perfect, he became to all of those who obey him the author of eternal salvation. (Hebrews 5:8–9)

> For it became him, for whom are all things, and through whom are all things, in bringing many children to glory, to make the author of their salvation perfect through sufferings. (Hebrews 2:10)

> [8]But *if you are without discipline*, of which all have been made partakers, *then are you illegitimate*, and *not children*. [9]Furthermore, we had the fathers of our flesh to chasten

us, and we paid them respect. Shall we not much rather be in subjection to the Father of spirits, and live? [10]For they indeed, for a few days, punished us as seemed good to them; but he for our profit, that we may be partakers of his holiness. (Hebrews 12:8–10)

Where both Trinitarians and Onenessians have failed to find details of their views of the relationship between The Father and The Son explained in Scripture, the Son of God position has not failed to deliver. These verses very clearly and specifically define Jesus' relationship to the Father in matters of moral value and significance. If these moral values did not apply to Jesus, then he would have been illegitimate, and not a child or Son.

When you change the roles of father and son, you negate and annihilate what those relationships truly signify. That is why Onenessians and Trinitarians have changed their definitions: they don't believe in, and apparently don't *want* to believe in, the true Son of God that is spelled out in the Bible, any more than gays *want* to believe in the biblical definitions and biblical moral values of marriage that are spelled out in the Bible.

By tampering with the moral values that help describe God's true Son, and by negating Jesus' moral relationship in subjection to God as Father, Incarnationists have made their versions of Jesus into an "illegitimate" being, something that is NOT a son!

Now let's compare how Onenessians use the exact same manner of interpretation that Pharisees used in making the word of God of none effect:

> [10]For Moses said, 'Honor your father and your mother;'... [11]But you say, 'If a man tells his father or his mother, 'Whatever profit you might have received from me is Corban, that is to say, given to God;' [12]then you no longer allow him to do anything for his father or his mother. (Mark 7:6–13)

> "You can't deny the Father and the Son, but what you've got to proclaim is both of them are one. Father is Spirit, Son is flesh... As Father in the OT, as Son in Matthew, Mark, Luke, and John..." Anthony Mangun[20]

This type of redefining of the moral roles of fathers and sons is what Jesus clearly called: "[13]*making void the word of God by your tradition*, which you have handed down. You do many things like this" (Mark 7:6–13).

To the contrary of the misguided extrabiblical definitions that Onenessianism and Trinitarianism introduce, there is seemingly no end to definitions and discussions of Jesus as God's Son and God as Jesus' Father in the Bible!

The graphics provided above make the relationships crystal clear. John said it is antichrist not to believe in the Father and in the Son. So, which one of the graphics truthfully illustrates a father and son relationship? The obvious answer is that the relationship of a father, mother, and son represents a true father and son. The graphic representing the Oneness attitude, is a perversion of a true father and son relationship. Thus Onenessians do not have "The Father and The Son" because they have redefined the true ones away, and inserted impostors in their places. Likewise, the Trinitarian view of

---

[20] Anthony Mangun, "God in Christ," The Dual Natures of Christ, (DVD, 2006), Disc 4, track 1 at about 37:00–41:00.

emulation of substance is also a perversion of a true father and son relationship, as previously shown. Ironically, Trinitarians claim to believe in a true Father and Son relationship by making the Son an emanation of the Father's essence, but then they redefine the emanation to be something that never did apply to any fathers or sons!

Interestingly, Mangun made a very good point against Trinitarians. He said *they didn't have the authority or the anointing to change what the Bible said*. Who then gave Onenessians the authority and the anointing to change and thereby negate the biblical meaning of the relationship between a father and son in the case of God and Jesus the Anointed? Or perhaps some Oneness theologian would like to show us, w*here in the thousands of occurrences of the words "son" and "father" in the Bible was anyone said to be a father to themselves or a son to themselves?*

This illustrates why we must keep in mind that words are labels that represent concepts. If this were not the case, our words would be meaningless and thus useless for communicating. The Bible says as much:

> [8]For if the trumpet gave an uncertain sound, who would prepare himself for war? [9]So also you, unless you uttered by the tongue *words easy to understand*, how would it be known what is spoken? For you would be speaking into the air.
> (1 Corinthians 14:8–9)

It is critical to maintain the accurate meaning of words, particularly in the word of God and especially when it is trying to keep people from the error of antichristianity! A better way for Mangun to distance himself from the antichristian position would be to reject their "incarnation of deity" doctrine and their novel "dual nature" doctrine!

Let's look at some of the Apostle John's writings to discern whether we can see for ourselves if Jesus agrees with the Onenessian interpretation, or whether he writes as if the titles Father and son pertain to two distinct and separate personalities.

> ³⁰*I can of myself do nothing.* As I hear, I judge, and my judgment is righteous; because *I don't seek my own will,* but the will of *my Father who* sent me. ³¹*If I testify about myself,* my witness is not valid. ³²It is *another who* testifies about me. I know that the testimony which he testifies about me is true. ³³You have sent to *John, and he has testified* to the truth... ³⁶But the testimony which I have is greater than that of John, for the works which the Father gave me to accomplish, the very works that I do, testify about me, that the Father has sent me. ³⁷*The Father himself, who sent me, has testified about me. You have neither heard his voice at any time, nor seen his form.* (John 5:30–37)

Jesus is not God because he can do nothing of himself! That is his explanation of himself! In John 5:30–37 Jesus couldn't be clearer. He spoke of "myself" in distinction to the person of John the Baptist. No one I know believes John the Baptist was an incarnation of God. The point is, it is in this same *context*, that of personal distinctions, and using the same personal pronouns, that Jesus first established who he was and then distinguished himself from the "who" of the Father. He even went on to state that his audience had neither heard the Father's voice nor seen His form at any time. Thus, those who claim that Jesus was an incarnation of God, or was the very person of God the Father in bodily form, make Jesus a complete liar or utter deceiver in this passage. That is to say, they aren't willing to hear all the words of God *or* Jesus, only the ones that fit their preconception; any others they simply reinterpret to mean what they don't say.

The Son of the Father in Truth

> Grace, mercy, and peace will be with us, from God the Father, and from the Lord Jesus Christ, *the Son of the Father, in truth* and love. (2 John 3)

This verse calls Jesus "the Son of the Father *in truth.*" As mentioned earlier, there are about 1,718 occurrences of the word *father* and about 3,597 occurrences of the word *son* in the Bible, and not one of them refers to anyone who is a father or son to themselves. But there is so much more to understand about what truly defines this "son of the Father in truth."

So, in this subchapter, we're going to continue showing how the Bible defines the sonship of Jesus Christ. Often people assume that Jesus is spoken of as a Son of God in the manner of human fathers and sons (for example, as if Christ were naturally an offspring of God's essence), but this isn't the case, as we shall see.

The first thing to keep in mind is that to be "true" means to be "biblical," for "your word is truth" (John 17:17) means that what the Bible spells out is what is true. And what it spells out is that one of David's offspring would be "declared" to be God's Son. These next verses spell out this "truth":

> ¹²When your days are fulfilled, and you shall sleep with your fathers, I will set up *your seed* after you, who shall proceed *out of your bowels*, and I will establish his kingdom. ¹³He shall build a house for my name, and I will establish the throne of his kingdom forever. ¹⁴*I will be his father, and he shall be my son*: if he commit iniquity, I will chasten him with the rod of men, and with the stripes of the children of men... ¹⁶Your house and your kingdom shall be made sure for ever before you: your throne shall be established forever. (2 Samuel 7:12–16)

> ³For I could wish that I myself were accursed from Christ for my brothers' sake, my relatives according to the flesh, ⁴who are Israelites; whose is the adoption, the glory, the covenants, the giving of the law, the service, and the promises; ⁵of whom are the fathers, and from whom is Christ as concerning the flesh. (Romans 9:3–5)

In the first passage, God Himself says that David's offspring would be His Son. This is so important, because *this is God's definition of His own son. God knows what he is talking about*, and *God is true*.

The passage from Romans reiterates this truth by saying it in another way: "Israelites... are the fathers... *from whom* is Christ as concerning the flesh." This verse is essential because it defines Christ's genealogy in a different way than is often presumed to be taught in John 1. While John 1 may *appear* to say "God was made flesh," in truth all John said is that God's "word" was made flesh. Now, in Romans 9:3–5, we have the "it is written again" passage that explains to us that *"the Israelites... are the fathers... from whom is Christ... concerning the flesh."* Which is the opposite of the idea behind the conclusion that "God was made flesh" as if the Son were made of some deific substance.

Then Galatians further explains the "substance" of which the Son was "made": "But when the fullness of the time was come, God sent forth His Son, *made of a woman*, made under the law" (Galatians 4:4, KJV). These verses tell us that Jesus was made out of Mary, who was an offspring of David, and in this way, Israelites are the "fathers" of Jesus as concerning the flesh.

This truth, that Jesus is actually the son of Israelites (ultimately via Mary) in terms of "genealogy" (Matthew 1:1) is so immutable, that God swore to it with an oath to David:

> Yahweh has *sworn* to David in truth. He will not turn from it: "I will set *the fruit of your body* on your throne." (Psalms 132:11)

> [30]Therefore, being a prophet, and knowing that God had *sworn with an oath* to him that *of the fruit of his body, according to the flesh, he would raise up the Christ* to sit on his throne, [31]he foreseeing this spoke about the resurrection of the Christ, that neither was his soul left in Hades, nor did his flesh see decay. [32]This Jesus God raised up, to which we all are witnesses. (Acts 2:30–32)

God was very clear in His *sworn oath* to David: David's offspring, would be, future tense, God's Son. The apostles preached this promise was fulfilled when God raised up Jesus. In quoting Psalms

16:10, Peter was pointing out to the Jews that one of the promises made by God was that the true Son of David would not suffer the corruption of his flesh in the grave. This was certainly not true of David, or Solomon, or any other descendent of David. Only Jesus of Nazareth has had that promise from God fulfilled upon him.

This explains precisely why one of the main points Paul makes is that, in raising Jesus from the dead, God fulfilled his promise to the fathers through David. Neither Peter, nor Paul, nor any other biblical writer explained that event in any way other than God raising Jesus. This was not God raising Himself from the dead; this was God raising David's offspring from the dead:

> [32]We bring you *good news* of the promise made to the fathers, [33]that *God has fulfilled* the same to us, their children, *in that he raised up Jesus*. As it is also written in the second psalm, "You are my Son. *Today I have become your father.*" [34]Concerning that he raised him up from the dead, now no more to return to corruption, he has spoken thus: "I will give you the holy and sure blessings of David." [35]Therefore he says also in another psalm, "You will not allow your Holy One to see decay." [36]For David, after he had in his own generation served the counsel of God, fell asleep, and was laid with his fathers, and saw decay. [37]But he whom God raised up saw no decay. [38]Be it known to you therefore, brothers, that *through this man is proclaimed to you remission of sins*, [39]and by him everyone who believes is justified from all things, from which you could not be justified by the law of Moses. [40]Beware therefore, lest that come on you which is spoken in the prophets: [41]"Behold, you scoffers, and wonder, and perish; For I work a work in your days, A work which you will in no way believe, if one declares it to you." (Acts 13:32–41).

Furthermore, for Paul, it was David's son that was born of the seed of David, and it was that very same whom God raised from the dead:

> ¹Paul, a servant of Jesus Christ, called to be an apostle, set apart for the Good News of God, ²which he promised before through his prophets in the holy Scriptures, ³concerning his Son, who was born of the seed of David according to the flesh, ⁴who was *declared to be the Son of God* with power, according to the Spirit of holiness, *by the resurrection from the dead*, Jesus Christ our Lord. (Romans 1:1–4)

Scriptures such as these help us understand what it means for Jesus, *biblically*, to be "the Son of the Father in truth." As we can see, there is a wealth of biblical data waiting to inform us if we would just listen and believe; yet nowhere does the Bible reveal such details in a Onenessian or a Trinitarian sense.

It is through such passages, and others like them, that we are taught that being a "son," in the case of the Messiah, doesn't have anything biblically to do with him being "emulated" from the "essence" of God's "nature" in the manner that we humans are conceived and born. There are no such Scriptures, but an abundance of Scriptures do explain the Son otherwise.

There is an interesting truth about Christ's actual humanity spelled out in 1 Corinthians 15, specifically in explaining the nuts and bolts of the resurrection:

> ³⁵But someone will say, "How are the dead raised?" and, "With what kind of body do they come?" ³⁶You foolish one, that which you yourself sow is not made alive unless it dies. ³⁷That which you sow, *you don't sow the body that will be*, but a bare grain, maybe of wheat, or of *some other kind*... ⁴²So also is the resurrection of the dead. *It is sown in corruption; it is raised in incorruption.* ⁴³It is sown in dishonor; it is raised in glory. It is sown in weakness; it is raised in power. ⁴⁴It is *sown a natural body; it is raised a spiritual body*. There is a natural body and there is also a spiritual body. ⁴⁵*So also it is written*, "The first man, Adam, became a living soul."

> *The last Adam became a life-giving spirit.* ⁴⁶However that which is spiritual isn't first, but *that which is natural, then that which is spiritual.* (1 Corinthians 15:35–46)

This passage explains to us that Jesus wasn't raised with the same "body" that was put in the tomb. He was changed at the moment of his resurrection. Paul stated that Christ became a life-giving spirit at his resurrection. This explains why the uniquely Christian baptism, or infilling, of the Holy Spirit was not available until after Christ's death, burial, and resurrection. (See also Hebrews 9:8–9 and 10:1–14.) Paul's statement that "the last Adam became a life-giving spirit" was about the one who was raised from the dead, not about the God who raised him. The one who was raised, Jesus Christ, was *made* a life-giving spirit in a manner very similar to the way Adam was made a living soul.

What these scriptures, then, do not say is that Christ was God beforehand, or that he somehow became the Son of God at his resurrection. A careful reading of all the texts on the topic simply doesn't support such ideas. It is foundational Christianity to understand that Jesus was David's son all along, and that it was as David's son (in the sense of offspring and heir) that Jesus was God's Son all along.

Jesus was the Son of God in God's plan and foreknowledge before the world was even created, and it was through, or in view of and because of, God's Son, who was born in Bethlehem, that God made the world:

> ¹God, having in the past spoken to the fathers through the prophets at many times and in various ways, ²has at the end of these days spoken to us by his Son, whom he appointed heir of all things, through whom also he made the worlds. (Hebrews 1:1–2)

Jesus was proclaimed to be the Son of God at, and even because of, his birth:

> ³¹"Behold, you will conceive in your womb, and bring forth a son, and will call his name Jesus. ³²He... will be called the Son of the Most High... " ³⁵The angel answered her, "The Holy Spirit will come on you, and the power of the Most High will overshadow you. Therefore also the holy one who is born from you will be called the Son of God." (Luke 1:31–35)

When he was 12 years old, Jesus proclaimed God as his Father:

> He said to them, "Why were you looking for me? Didn't you know that I must be in my Father's house?" (Luke 2:49)

Thus, Jesus affirmed that he understood himself, even at a very young age, to be the Son of God, not that he was God or would someday come to be God's Son.

Furthermore, we know that Jesus was declared to be God's Son by the heavenly voice that was heard at his baptism (Matthew 3:16–17; Mark 1:11; and Luke 3:22). We also know that the apostles confessed him to be the Messiah, *the Son of God* (Matthew 14:33 and 16:15), during his earthly ministry. Then we have John 3:16, the most quoted and translated verse in the whole Bible, declaring to us that Jesus was God's Son even at the moment in time when he died to be the propitiation for sins for the whole world (Isaiah 53:12; Romans 3:25; 1 John 2:2 and 4:10):

> ¹⁶For God so loved the world, that *he gave his one and only Son*, that whoever believes in him should not perish, but have eternal life. ¹⁷For God didn't send his Son into the world to judge the world, but that the world should be saved through him. ¹⁸He who believes in him is not judged. He who doesn't believe has been judged already, because he has not believed in the name of the one and only Son of God. (John 3:16–18)

> In this is love, not that we loved God, but that he loved us, *and sent his Son* as the atoning sacrifice for our sins. (1 John 4:10; see also Romans 3:25 and 1 John 2:2)

SECTION THREE - VIEWS IN CONTRAST TO THE WAY OF CHRIST

No Scripture clearly teaches otherwise. The idea that God incarnated Himself in order to die for our sins is an idea that is totally foreign to the teachings of the Bible. To change the Son into an incarnation of the Father in any manner is to change this most fundamental of all principles of Christianity, that God sent His Son, Jesus:

> Jesus answered them, "This is the work of God, that you believe in him whom he has sent." (John 6:29)

> [42]Therefore Jesus said to them, "If God were your father, you would love me, for *I came out and have come from God. For I haven't come of myself, but he sent me.* [43] Why don't you understand my speech? Because you can't hear my word." (John 8:42-43)

> [1]Jesus said these things, and lifting up his eyes to heaven, he said, 'Father, the time has come. *Glorify your Son, that your Son* may also glorify you; [2]*even as you gave him authority over all flesh, he will give eternal life to all whom you have given him.* [3]This is eternal life, that they should know *you, the only true God,* and *him whom you sent, Jesus Christ.* (John 17:1–3)

> As you sent me into the world, even so I have sent them into the world. (John 17:18)

> [21]that they may all be one; even as you, Father, are in me, and I in you, that they also may be one in us; that the world may *believe that you sent me.* [22]The glory which you have given me, I have given to them; that they may be one, even as we are one; [23]I in them, and you in me, that they may be perfected into one; *that the world may know that you sent me,* and loved them, even as you loved me. (John 17:21–23)

It is in the context of God's one and only begotten and anointed son, and only in that context, that Jesus was born, lived, suffered on the cross for our sins, and was resurrected, and will continue forever. Moreover, it is only through belief in this teaching that we can be saved!

These Scriptures we've been looking at all help describe what it means for Jesus to be, as John wrote, "the Son of the Father in truth."

So John is saying that Jesus is the Son of the Father in the biblically *true* meaning of what God swore his son would be. Thus, the titles of father and son clearly refer to two distinct personalities (the man who was first sent and later resurrected and the God who sent him and later resurrected him) and are not to be taken in the *false, untrue* meaning of the man-made "blasphemous system" that redefines the Father and son as dual natures in one personality.

> ⁹Whoever transgresses and doesn't remain in the teaching of the Anointed One, doesn't have God. *He who remains in the teaching, the same has both the Father and the Son.* ¹⁰If anyone comes to you, and doesn't bring this teaching, *don't receive him* into your house, *and don't welcome him,* ¹¹for he who welcomes him participates in his *evil works.* (2 John 9–11)

This verse has very similar wording to 1 John 2:22–23 and reemphasizes just how we should "treat" those who deny the true doctrine of Father and son. The verse says nothing to negate the understanding that father means father relationally and son means son relationally. So the directive is actually against the novel Oneness interpretation that redefines the meanings of the words father and son.

> That which we have seen and heard we declare to you, that you also may have fellowship with us. Yes, and our fellowship is with the Father, and with his Son, Jesus Christ. (1 John 1:3)

> But if we walk in the light, as he is in the light, we have fellowship with one another, and the blood of Jesus Christ, his Son, cleanses us from all sin. (1 John 1:5–7)

In these passages, John once again referred to the Father and His Son without making any mention of them being two natures of the person of Jesus the Anointed One. So John wrote expecting us to believe that the normal definitions of father and son were to apply to God and His Son, not as two natures of one person, but as two distinct personalities.

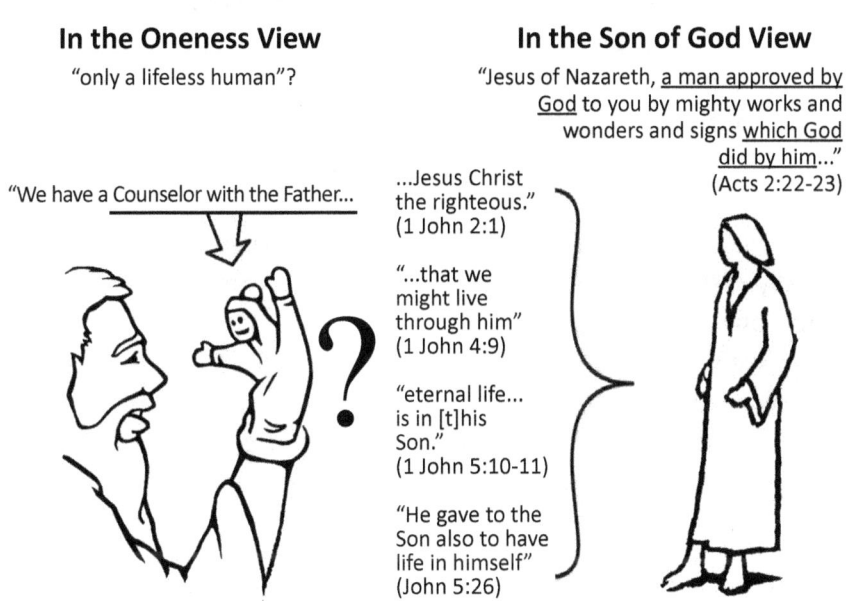

The above graphic conveys how ridiculous Modalism is in comparison to what the Scriptures say that God did through Christ. We begin with this Scripture:

> My little children, I write these things to you so that you may not sin. If anyone sins, *we have a Counselor with the Father, Jesus Christ, the righteous*. (1 John 2:1)

John is not talking about an impersonal "human nature," as in the Oneness view. Jesus the Anointed One is our Counselor to and with another personal entity (the Father) on our behalf.

> ⁹By this was God's love revealed in us, *that God has sent his one and only Son* into the world that we might *live through him*. ¹⁰In this is love, not that we loved God, but that he loved us, *and sent his Son* as the atoning sacrifice for our sins. ¹¹Beloved, if God loved us in this way, we also ought to love one another. ¹²*No one has seen God at any time.* If we love one another, God remains in us, and his love has been perfected in us. ¹³By this we know that we remain in him and he in us, because he has given us of his Spirit. ¹⁴We have seen and *testify that the Father has sent the Son* as the Savior of the world. ¹⁵Whoever confesses that *Jesus is the Son of God*, God remains in him, and he in God. (1 John 4:9–15)

Once again we have a passage that speaks of the Son as being personally distinct from the Father. It is in this context that Jesus is God's only son.

As we've seen above, Oneness ministers like Mangun and Bernard want us to believe that "son" is some type of a code word for the impersonal "flesh" of Jesus Christ. But 1 John 4 refutes that idea. Let's look at how ridiculous it would be if we were to assume that "son" is synonymous with "impersonal flesh":

> ⁹By this was God's love revealed in us, *that God has sent his one and only [impersonal flesh]* into the world that we might *live through [the impersonal flesh]*. ¹⁰In this is love, not that we loved God, but that he loved us, *and sent his [impersonal flesh]* as the atoning sacrifice for our sins. ¹¹Beloved, if God loved us in this way, we also ought to love one another. ¹²*No one has seen God at any time.* If we love one another, God remains in us, and his love has been perfected in us. ¹³By this we know that we remain in him and he in us,

> because he has given us of his Spirit. ¹⁴We have seen and
> testify that the Father has sent the [impersonal flesh] as the
> Savior of the world. ¹⁵Whoever confesses that *Jesus is the
> [impersonal flesh] of God*, God remains in him, and he in
> God. (1 John 4:9–15)

As should be obvious, what we've inserted in brackets isn't what John was saying, nor is it said like this anywhere else in the Bible. Rather, it is quite obvious that "flesh" is not synonymous with "son." To the contrary, son and father are used by John in the well-known, and understood relationship between two distinct and separate personalities. Accordingly, to claim that "son" is in some manner a code word for the impersonal flesh of God's personality is simply a lie.

Now, any Onenessian who realizes that John *is* referring to a human person in contradistinction to the God-the-Father person, has arrived at the Son of God doctrine as opposed to the Onenessian position. The position that Christ is a complete human person in his own right, distinct from his Father, is not the Oneness position. That's because, as Bernard stated above, according to the Oneness position, without the Spirit of God in him, Jesus would have been lifeless flesh! So Onenessians believe that there is only one personality in Jesus—God the Father (who makes himself known through the impersonal flesh). Although they don't typically use the word "impersonal" when saying Christ is the "flesh," that is their smokescreen, which is being exposed in this work! When they say "flesh," they mean an impersonal, lifeless flesh. Were they to say the opposite, that the Son has a personally human heart, mind, body, soul, and human spirit entirely distinct from the personal Spirit/Father, they would no longer be truly "Oneness." That is because the core ideas of Onenessianism are that Jesus was an incarnation of the very person of God the Father and that he was conscious of being so. These are teachings the Bible never states.

> Who is he who overcomes the world, but he who believes
> that *Jesus is the Son* of God? (1 John 5:5)

Here then is a real issue. Overcoming the world is something special, something defined, and something that not everyone does. Specifically then, overcoming the world means believing that Jesus is the Son of God. It doesn't say that overcoming the world is to come to understand or to gain an extrabiblical *revelation* that son means the impersonal human-nature half of a dual-natured individual.

Thus, to adopt the Gnostic, antichristian idea of a "dual nature" is the reverse: it is to be overcome by the world!

> [10]He who *believes in the Son of God* has the testimony in himself. *He who doesn't believe God has made him a liar, because he has not believed in the testimony that God has given concerning his Son.* [11]*The testimony is this, that God gave to us eternal life, and this life is in his Son.* [12]He who has the Son has the life. *He who doesn't have God's Son doesn't have the life.* (1 John 5:10–12)

If you read this passage as a Onenessian, you would think it means that "God gave to us eternal life, and this life is in his impersonal flesh." That is simply not what John said! And to imply that is what John meant in saying "flesh" is to tell a lie against John and the Scriptures of God that John penned. A lifeless Christ with God as his puppet master is simply not a true view of the biblical Son of God. Therefore, people who believe the "dual nature" doctrine make God out to be a liar; that is what John just said.

So then, Onenessians have committed a great travesty in attempting to redefine the word "son" to mean God's "impersonal flesh." The Bible is actually very clear that impersonal flesh is not alive apart from the spirit within that animates it. So James writes, "... the body apart from the spirit is dead, even so faith apart from works is dead" (James 2:26). And again, note what Jesus said in John 5:

> [26]For as the Father has life in himself, even so he gave to the [*impersonal flesh*] also to have life in himself. [27]He also gave him authority to execute judgment, because he is a [*impersonal flesh*] of man. (John 5:26–27)

No, again it doesn't fit. Jesus actually said these things in regard to himself as the Son, not as an impersonal flesh, as has been inserted to make the point. The word "son" is simply not synonymous with "flesh." Using the Onenessian's own code words (i.e., son = impersonal flesh, and father = personal spirit) shows that the Scriptures utterly refute their position.

The doctrine of "dual natures" in the individual personality of Jesus Christ was never, ever described or spelled out in the Scriptures. Yet, the teaching of Christ having two natures was one of the main doctrines by which antichristian Gnostic teachings replaced the biblical teaching of the Jewish Messiah.

By latching onto this deviation from apostolic teaching, whether knowingly or unknowingly, both Trinitarians and Onenessians have changed their foundation from the OT Schoolmaster and replaced it with a pagan form of Christ. The biblical teaching is that Jesus the Anointed One was born of the seed of David according to the flesh, a man approved of God, born by miraculous birth, but made of Mary, and who was *obligated to be made in all things like us, his brothers*. That is the biblical Jesus.

> Trust in YHWH with all your heart, And don't lean on your own understanding. (Proverbs 3:5)

Jumping to Conclusions versus "It is Written": It is an antichristian doctrine to claim that "son" means the impersonal flesh and "father" refers to the personal spirit in two halves of a dual-natured Christ. In fact, Irenaeus said this teaching in particular was why John wrote against the antichristian Gnostics. So this doctrine isn't just jumping to conclusions; it is also adopting Gnostic—that is, antichristian teaching. As Onenessians themselves have stated, their Christ is "not just an anointed man," which is exactly opposite of asserting what the title Christ signifies. They are thus anti-christians. Onenessians, like Trinitarians, are also Neo-Gnostics.

The OT Schoolmaster: If we are going to be true to Paul's admonition to use the OT as the schoolmaster to bring us to Christ, then we simply must accept the fact that the OT only describes and envisions a human Christ whom God declared to be His Son, not a hybrid God-man, and not an incarnation of a preexistent deity. The very word Messiah, from the OT, means an individual who has been anointed (officially authorized) by divine command, and thus does not ever refer to God Himself. No Jew ever conceived of Messiah as an incarnation of God, and no Scripture ever explained or clearly prophesied that the Messiah would be an incarnation of God. Therefore, we must conclude that the concept of Christ as an "incarnation" comes entirely from extrabiblical, pagan sources.

> Most Jews... conceived [of] the Messiah as a man. We may indeed go a step further and say that no Jew at bottom imagined him otherwise; for even those who attached ideas of preexistence to him, and gave the Messiah a supernatural background, *never advanced to speculations about assumption of the flesh, incarnation, two natures and the like. They only transferred in a specific manner to the Messiah the old idea of pre-terrestrial existence with God*, universally current among the Jews. *Before the creation of the world the Messiah was hidden with God, and, when the time is fulfilled, he makes his appearance...* Nowhere do we find in Jewish writings a conception which advances beyond the notion that the Messiah is the man who is with God in heaven; and who will make his appearance at his own time.[21]

---

[21] Adolf von Harnack, *History of Dogma*, Vol. I, Appendix I.

Teach No Other Doctrine: The "dual nature" doctrine of Onenessians and Trinitarians, which was first invented by the antichristian Gnostics, is definitely an adding to and taking away from a scriptural view of Christ.

> But when the fulness of the time was come, God sent forth his Son, made of a woman, made under the law. (Galatians 4:4, KJV)

CHAPTER THIRTEEN

"Alone" or "Not Alone" vs. Dual Natures

YHWH of Armies, the God of Israel, who is enthroned among the cherubim, *you* are the God, even *you alone*, of all the kingdoms of the earth. *You* have made heaven and earth. (Isaiah 37:16)

Thus saith the LORD, thy redeemer, and he that formed thee from the womb, I am the LORD that maketh all things; that stretcheth forth the heavens *alone*; that spreadeth abroad the earth by *myself*. (Isaiah 44:24, KJV)

...*I am not alone*, but I am with the Father who sent me. – Jesus Christ of Nazareth (John 8:16)

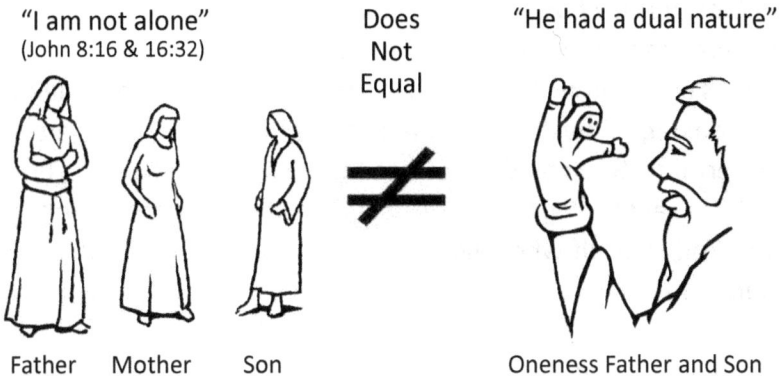

Consider how simple the statements are in the two Isaiah passages above. They use two simple words that everyone knows and understands: *alone* and *myself*. From the Jewish, Onenessian, and

"I AM NOT ALONE"

our point of view, Trinitarians seem to want to either *ignore or redefine these words*. Instead of accepting the plain meaning in these verses, Trinitarians assert that God eternally existed as three "persons," or individuals, within "one godhead," and for them these verses must mean that the *overall* "godhead" was alone, but not so with "the Father, the Son, and the Holy Spirit" *within* the godhead. This is why we accuse the Trinitarians of redefining the words "myself" and "alone" as meaning something nonsensical, along the lines of, *"he was not alone because he always had themselves."* They try to tell skeptics not to be concerned that this appears nonsensical, because, as they explain it, it is a mystery that *"God has to reveal to you."* They also claim that three being one isn't a contradiction, because God is above human reasoning. However, the apostle referred to this as handling the word of God deceitfully (2 Corinthians 4:2).

Now consider in contrast Jesus' words, *"I am not alone."* Everything that we just said about the way Trinitarians interpret the OT passages is true about the way Onenessians reinterpret these words of Christ himself to mean his dual natures.

It is the Bible that describes what we are to understand about God. The fact remains that God described Himself as one in the Bible. The fact remains that He says He is alone in the Bible. *The very fact that He has said these things means that He believes we can understand these things.* It isn't our place to say that what He means is completely different than what He said, and then claim He was speaking in mysteries! If men can say, "God is three persons," then certainly God could formulate those same exact words, but He didn't. He said the opposite. He said I am alone and by myself! And it was God Himself who said that He has witnesses who know and understand Him!

> You are my witnesses, says YHWH, and [you are] my servant whom I have chosen; that you may *know* and *believe* me, *and understand* that *I am he*: before me there was no God formed, neither shall there be after me. (Isaiah 43:10)

The reason Trinitarians view the "alone" and "by myself" declarations of God as meaning the opposite of what they say is because they view such passages through the darkened lenses of pagan mythology, philosophy, and even antichristian Gnosticism!

And once again, just as Trinitarians reject what the Scriptures plainly say, and interpret them to mean something the Scriptures don't say, the Onenessians also do the same, interpreting the "I am ***not*** alone" statements of Jesus to mean something different than what was written.

It is ironic that Onenessians *absolutely refuse to accept the very clear phrase that Jesus is "not alone"* in exactly the same way that they rightly contend against Trinitarians for rejecting the very clear statements that *God is "alone."*

If you can see in the above quotes that personal "whos" are being referred to, not impersonal natures, then you've grasped the simplicity of Jesus we wish Christians to return to.

Of course, it may be too simplistic for some who are steeped in their traditions to the contrary. So let's take some time to review a sampling of the many Scriptures explaining that Jesus is not alone.

> Even if I do judge, my judgment is true, for *I am not alone*, but I am with the Father who sent me. (John 8:16)

> He who sent me is with me. The Father *has not left me alone*, for I always do the things that are pleasing to him. (John 8:29)

> Behold, the time is coming, yes... that you will be scattered... and you will leave me alone. Yet *I am not alone*, because the Father is with me. (John 16:32)

According to Jesus, he and his God, who is the Father, are personally distinct. Through the third passage above we can see that *they are personally distinct from each other in the same way that Jesus was personally distinct from the disciples* (who would soon all forsake him for a short time).

Now watch how Jesus used the personal pronouns in the following verse:

> Jesus said to her, 'Don't touch *me*, for *I* haven't yet ascended to *my* Father; but go to *my* brothers, and tell them, "*I* am ascending to *my* Father and *your* Father, to *my* God and *your* God." (John 20:17)

God the Father is Jesus' God and Father in the exact same way, and in the exact same context, in which the Father is our God and Father. This couldn't be any clearer.

Even when Jesus spoke in parables, those parables illustrated the truth; they didn't hide the truth by teaching a completely opposite concept. Jesus didn't try to teach the color black by painting a word picture of white. No, his parables were true, if only hidden by teaching with examples rather than being straightforward. The only way to teach that Jesus meant "natures" when he was talking about separate and distinct personal "selves" is to add to the word of God and to jump to conclusions in the way the devil interprets the Bible. But it is also to negate what Jesus did say. It is just that simple.

Now that we have established that Jesus was *not alone*, and we can see clearly the context in which he was not alone, we are able to remove our darkened antichristian (against-the-anointed-one) glasses and read what was plainly written. The following passages make it quite clear that Jesus was, yet again, speaking in context of *personalities*, not mere "natures." In light of these passages, Onenessians have no more evidence that Jesus and the Father are *uni*-personal than the Trinitarians have that they are *multi*-personal within the godhead. In fact, there are hundreds of verses that speak directly against the Onenessian theory. Now let's consider Jesus' words and see if this is what he is saying.

> [17]"It's also written in your law that *the testimony of two people is valid.* [18]*I am one <u>who</u> testifies about <u>myself</u>, and the Father <u>who</u> sent me testifies about <u>me</u>.*" [19]They said

therefore to him, "Where is your Father?" Jesus answered, "You know neither me, nor my Father. If you knew me, you would know my Father also." ²⁰Jesus spoke these words in the treasury, as he taught in the temple. Yet no one arrested him, because his hour had not yet come. ²¹Jesus said therefore again to them, "I am going away, and you will seek me, and you will die in your sins. Where I go, you can't come." ²²The Jews therefore said, "Will he kill himself, that he says, 'Where I am going, you can't come?'"
²³He said to them, "You are from beneath. I am from above. You are of this world. I am not of this world. ²⁴I said therefore to you that you will die in your sins; for unless you believe that I am he, you will die in your sins." ²⁵*They said therefore to him, "Who are you?"* Jesus said to them, "Just what I have been saying to you from the beginning. ²⁶I have many things to speak and to judge concerning you. However *he who* sent *me* is true; and the things which *I heard from him*, these I say to the world." ²⁷They didn't understand that he spoke to them about the Father. ²⁸Jesus therefore said to them, "When you have lifted up *the Son of Man*, then you will know that I am he, and *I do nothing of myself*, but as my Father taught me, I say these things." (John 8:17–28)

Recall how Trinitarians ignore the context of Genesis 1:26–27 and zero in on the "let us make man" phrase while ignoring the words of verse 27? The Onenessians use that same selective interpretation tactic as Trinitarians do when they interpret John 8. They ignore the context and jump to verses 24 and 28 so as to put meanings into Jesus' words that he did not say, and that are contradicted by the context and details of what he actually did say! That's because their Gnostic-tinted glasses cause them not to be able to see "two people" so that they automatically reinterpret that phrase to mean "two natures," even though that is not what Jesus said, here or anywhere else!

Notice all the personal pronouns Jesus used to distinguish himself from the person of the Father. Next notice verse 28, where Jesus explicitly states that his self is a different self than the Father's: "I do *nothing* of *myself*, but as my Father taught me, I say these things." These are very clear. Finally, notice that Jesus said, "Just what I have been saying to you from the beginning." In other words, Onenessians don't seem to hear Jesus' words stating that he was in a continual dialog with these other people. He expected them to keep in mind what he had already said. And what he had already stated is what Onenessians must ignore or denigrate or redefine in order to force-fit their opinions upon the texts of this passage.

Notice what Jesus had said to them in John 5, just three chapters earlier:

> [19]Jesus therefore answered them, "Most assuredly, I tell you, *the Son can do nothing of himself*, but what *he* sees the Father doing. For whatever things *he* does, these *the Son* also does likewise. [20]For the Father has affection for the Son, and shows *him* all things that *he himself* does. *He will show him* greater works than these, that you may marvel. [21]For as the Father raises the dead and gives them life, even so the Son also gives life to whom he desires. [22]For the Father judges no one, but *he has given all* judgment to the Son, [23]that all may honor the Son, even as they honor the Father. He who doesn't honor the Son doesn't honor the Father *who sent him*.
> [24]Most assuredly I tell you, he who hears my word, and *believes him who sent me*, has eternal life, and doesn't come into judgment, but has passed out of death into life. [25]Most assuredly, I tell you, the hour comes, and now is, when the dead will hear the Son of God's voice; and those who hear will live. [26]For as the Father has life in himself, *even so he gave to the Son* also to have life in himself. [27]*He also gave him* authority to execute judgment, *because he is a son of man*. [28]Don't marvel at this, for the hour comes, in which all that are in the tombs will hear his voice, [29]and will come out; those who have done good, to the resurrection of life; and those who have done evil, to the resurrection of judg-

ment. ³⁰*I can of myself do nothing. As I hear, I judge, and my judgment is righteous; because I don't seek my own will*, but the will of *my Father who* sent me.
³¹*If I testify about myself,* my witness is not valid. ³²It is *another who* testifies about me. I know that the testimony which *he testifies about me* is true. ³³You have sent to John, and he has testified to the truth. ³⁴But the testimony which I receive is not from man. However, I say these things that you may be saved. ³⁵He was the burning and shining lamp, and you were willing to rejoice for a while in his light. ³⁶But the testimony which I have is greater than that of John, for the works which *the Father* gave *me* to accomplish, the very works that I do, testify about me, that the Father has sent me. ³⁷The *Father himself, who sent me,* has testified about me. *You have neither heard his voice at any time, nor seen his form.*" (John 5:19–37)

This passage causes a real dilemma for Onenessianism. In this passage Jesus clearly and thoroughly described himself as personally distinct from his Father. There are no such verses in the Bible that say Jesus is an incarnation of the Father, or that he is made of dual natures of humanity and deity. Modalism rejects these clear, emphatic descriptions, just as Trinitarians reject biblical descriptions of God. If Modalism is true, then Jesus was lying. Remember how in John 16:32, Jesus established the identities of the personal pronouns by including the disciples? Thus, in context, the natural reading is that Jesus was just as personally distinct from the Father as he and his disciples were to each other and the Father. Well, in the above passage Jesus did the same thing. But here he used John the Baptist to help reveal the subject identities. Notice his topic was the testimony of two people, which he clearly stated to mean personalities, not natures. He used the example of John as one witness and the Father as another witness. Now unless someone wants to claim that John was another one of Jesus' natures, then we have it from Jesus that he and his Father are as personally distinct from each other as John the Baptist was to them, or else Jesus' testimony is not true!

Indwelling Does Not Mean Identity

One of the big problems with the Onenessian viewpoint is that "indwelling" does not equal "identity." This is very similar to what Trinitarians do. When Trinitarians read about the Son of God in distinction to the Father (take, for example, Jesus praying "not my will"), it is understood by them as one God-Personality speaking to another God-Personality rather than as clear evidence of the human Christ in distinction from the personality of the one God. Similarly, when Onenessians see the "indwelling" of God in Christ, somehow for them it means "incarnation," even though they know very well that when saints are indwelled by God's Spirit that does not make them incarnations. The word "indwelling" simply does not mean or signify "identity"! How many of us would say that our soul *indwells* our body? No, we are by definition "soul and body," we don't indwell ourselves!

Let's consider what happened when man was first created:

> YHWH God formed man from the dust of the ground, and breathed into his nostrils the breath of life; and man became a living soul. (Genesis 2:7)

This is the source of our understanding that man does not indwell his body; man is himself complete only as long as he is composed of body and soul as one unit. This is the biblical view. To speak otherwise, as if a man's soul or spirit could exist apart from his body, is totally of pagan philosophical origin. [See the next chapter for discussion of spirit beings coming to earth as humans.]

Let's look at some passages that help us see clearly what indwelling means biblically.

> And if the Spirit of Him who did raise up Jesus out of the dead doth *dwell in you*, He who did raise up the Christ out of the dead shall quicken also your dying bodies, through *His Spirit dwelling in you*. (Romans 8:11, YLT)

> Don't you know that you are a temple of God, and that
> *God's Spirit <u>lives</u> in you*? (1 Corinthians 3:16)
>
> Or don't you know that your body is a temple of *the Holy Spirit which is in you*, which *you have from* God? You are not your own. (1 Corinthians 6:19)
>
> The good thing committed guard thou through the Holy Spirit that is dwelling in us. (2 Timothy 1:14, YLT)

Unless someone wants to believe that Christians, who are indwelt by the Spirit of God, become one and the selfsame person with the person of God the Father, then these passages thoroughly disprove the idea that indwelling equates to identity or incarnation of the one who indwells another. When Paul the apostle was struck down by a brilliant light, he asked the Lord, "Who are you?" and Jesus replied, "I am Jesus whom you are persecuting." Does that mean that the saints that Paul had been persecuting were all themselves little incarnations of the person of Jesus? Of course not! Rather, they were certainly in a real sense "members of his body." But being members of the body of Christ does not make us incarnations of Christ, and it does not cause us to relinquish our own personalities. And the Scripture is very clear that God is the head of Christ, just as Christ is the head of us. That certainly doesn't make us all the person of God the Father, but it does explain God's language regarding the members of His body in Christ.

> [12]For as the body is one, and has many members, and all the members of the body, being many, are one body; so also is Christ. [13]For in one Spirit we were all baptized into one body, whether Jews or Greeks, whether bond or free; and were all given to drink into one Spirit. [14]For the body is not one member, but many. (1 Corinthians 12:12–14)

> But I would have you know that the head of every man is Christ, and the head of the woman is the man, and the head of Christ is God. (1 Corinthians 11:3)

So there we have the truth of the matter: God is the head of Jesus *in the same way that Christ is the head of the ekklesia, which is in the same way that a man is the head of the woman in marriage.* Certainly no one believes that a woman is therefore without her own personality and becomes an incarnation of the person of her husband when they say their wedding vows! And yet that is exactly how unbiblical it is for Onenessians to claim that Christ is an incarnation of the person of God because he is indwelled by the Father.

The very fact that Jesus was *indwelt by* the Spirit of God proves he wasn't a personal incarnation of God.

CHAPTER FOURTEEN

A Man Approved of God vs. Gods Come Down in the Likeness of Men

Biblical:
"a man approved of God"

Not Biblical:
"gods come down in the likeness of men"

Men of Israel, hear these words! Jesus of Nazareth, *a man approved by God* to you by mighty works and wonders and signs which God did by him in the midst of you, even as you yourselves know. (Acts 2:22)

And when the people saw what Paul had done, they lifted up their voices, saying in the speech of Lycaonia, *The gods are come down to us in the likeness of men*. (Acts 14:11)

One of the major lessons to be learned about Trinitarians is the way they have adopted pagan philosophical concepts to describe and define their view of God. By doing so, they have allowed themselves to be spoiled by philosophy, against the apostle's warning. Of course, they don't seem to see it that way. It's as if they were looking at the Scriptures through a lens that turned everything upside down and backwards, making it nearly impossible for them to see things any other way!

Look at the following graphic showing how lenses have a way of flip-flopping physical images:

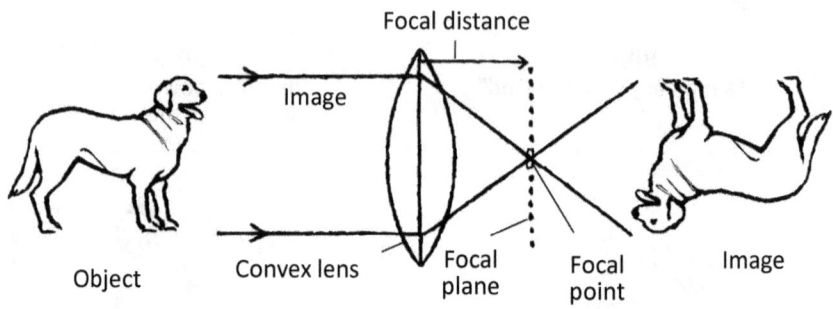

It is almost bizarre how Trinitarians can look at the same Bible the rest of us are reading and come up with an image that is completely opposite (upside down and backwards) from the Jewish view while lining up so closely to pagan Neoplatonism and antichristian-Gnostic views. It isn't rational, because it is a spiritual blindness. This is what happens when we are spoiled by philosophy and look through the lens of paganism: it becomes almost impossible to see things right-side-up! But look at the refracted image. The problem isn't that the image is out of focus; it's that the focus displays a reversed image from what is really there. It *appears* that all the features and elements are intact. That appears to be what makes it hard for them to accept that their vision is askew. We say that the dog has a leg, and they say, "check, our dog has a leg too." We say the dog's mouth is open, and they say, "check, our dog's mouth is open too." We say our dog's feet are on the ground, and they say, "that's no big deal, we are still looking at a dog, and our dog is just as (biblically) viable as yours." You see, that's where it gets touchy... when you start getting into the real specifics and making sure everything lines up scripturally, *rather than* just accepting man's preconceived image, no matter how spoiled by philosophy it may be in justifying why and how such an image could be equally as valid as anyone else's.

The problem is not limited to Trinitarians. The same phenomenon has afflicted the vision of the Onenessians. In fact, the core Oneness doctrines causing them to see the image the way they do came from the exact same sources in paganism and Neoplatonism! Helping Onenessians become aware of this fact is where we turn our attention next.

Notice again the two Scriptures we've chosen to head this chapter. If you can see that what the apostles preached is the truth, and that it is a pagan view to believe that god(s) come down in the likeness of men, then we've basically made our point. But not everyone believes it can be that simple. They still see any similarities as coincidental or a pagan theft of the idea from the truth. Everything else in this chapter is meant to explain just how true the apostle's words were, and just how unbiblical the pagan view is.

In fact, the two views are just exactly the type of mirror-imaged views that our graphic shows. They both talk about man and God. One view is from the Jewish apostles preaching the Anointed One they believed in and wanted others to believe in, and the other was the pagan view that was so completely unacceptable to the apostles that when they heard of it they rent their clothes in disgust! Let's take a look at the story:

> [11]When the multitude saw what Paul had done, they lifted up their voice, saying in the language of Lycaonia, '*The gods have come down to us in the likeness of men!*' [12]They called Barnabas "Jupiter," and Paul "Mercury," because he was the chief speaker. [13]The priest of Jupiter, whose temple was in front of their city, brought oxen and garlands to the gates, and *would have made a sacrifice along with the multitudes.* [14]But when the apostles, Barnabas and Paul, heard of it, they tore their clothes, and sprang into the multitude, crying out, [15]"Men, why are you doing these things? We also are men of like passions with you, and bring you good news, that you should turn from these vain things to the living God, who made the sky and the earth and the sea, and all that is in them..." (Acts 14:11–15)

Clearly, the apostles were thoroughly appalled at the pagan doctrine of gods coming down to earth in the form of men. Anyone should be able to see that what the apostles declared in Acts 2 was, "Jesus of Nazareth, *a man approved by God* to you by mighty works and wonders and signs *which God did by him.*" This stated truth is diametrically opposite to the pagan idea of gods coming to earth in the likeness of men. The latter is upside down and backwards from the truth. We don't have to spell out this fact—the apostles have already done that! The problem comes when people aren't as repulsed by pagan concepts as much as the apostles were. What Onenessians need to learn is to be just as repulsed by the pagan (non-Jewish) doctrine of "gods come to earth in the form of man" as they are of the pagan doctrine of three gods from which the Trinity developed and evolved.

So let's take a closer look at the topic of gods coming to earth in the likeness of men.

It is well known among historians that *the idea of gods appearing on earth as humans is a thoroughly pagan idea.* One writer, in referring to the above passage, explains the backdrop to the pagan-inspired conclusion regarding Paul and Barnabus in Acts 14:

> Ovid records a famous myth that serves as the likely backdrop to this incident. According to this story, *Zeus and Hermes come to earth disguised as humans*, and go to a thousand homes looking for shelter... Thus, when the people of Lystra behold Paul's power to work miracles, they assume the gods have come down to them in human form...[1]

In another place, Paul had been accidentally bitten by a venomous snake. At first the local inhabitants thought that Paul was being

---

[1] Kyle R. Hughes, "THE GOSPEL FOR PAGANS: PAUL AND BARNABAS IN LYSTRA" accessed 1/26/2017, http://taarcheia.files.wordpress.com/2012/08/exegesis-of-acts-14-8-20.pdf.

judged by God for being a murderer or some such. But when they saw that he was not affected, they changed their minds and said he was a god!

> ³But when Paul had gathered a bundle of sticks and laid them on the fire, a viper came out because of the heat, and fastened on his hand... ⁶ But they expected that he would have swollen or fallen down dead suddenly, but when they watched for a long time and saw nothing bad happen to him, they changed their minds, and said that he was a god. (Acts 28:3–6)

This confirms how thoroughly pagan it is, and how naturally it comes to such a way of thinking, to view miracle workers as gods! Those who claim it is the Bible that leads them to believe Jesus is God are just displaying a more refined form of the same type of attitude. A more careful study of the word of God does not confirm that such natural reactions are true to what the Scriptures teach. Rather, that idea comes from a superficial examination of the Scriptures. Then, once they get this idea in their heads, they read the Scriptures in such a way as to confirm their preconceived bias, rather than really hearing what the Scriptures explain.

This attitude of superficiality was also shown against our Lord. In John 7:52, Nicodemus had attempted a small defense of Jesus, but the Pharisees, the religious leaders of the day, claimed that no prophet was to come out of Galilee, and thus dissuaded themselves from looking into Jesus further. If they had taken the time to search out the truth, they would have found that Jesus was actually born in Bethlehem, not Galilee. This is how superficiality causes people to resist hearing the truth.

The very fact that Paul, in Acts 14, reacted to the pagan view negatively and found nothing positive in it to use as a teaching opportunity is very important. This fact shows that, in Paul's view, this was an idea that was totally pagan and bore no resemblance to Christ. Otherwise it would have been totally out of character for Paul not to have built on the idea at the point where the pagans left off. Paul clearly told us in 1 Corinthians about his method of reaching souls:

> [20]To the Jews I became as a Jew, that I might gain Jews; to those who are under the law, as under the law, that I might gain those who are under the law; [21]to those who are without law, as without law (not being without law toward God, but under law toward Christ), *that I might win those who are without law.* [22]To the weak I became as weak, that I might gain the weak. *I have become all things to all men, that I may by all means save some...* (1 Corinthians 9:19–22)

Paul didn't mean he was willing to be deceptive. Notice how he qualified his words by saying he remained under the law to Christ (which would necessarily keep him from lying or being deceptive). He was simply saying that he was willing to find common ground and even to go as far as to meet others in their traditions, as long as it didn't cause him to sin against Christ. We can see how Paul applied this method on the occasion when he came across certain philosophers in the city of Athens, and he took on the role of an orator such as they were...

> [22]Paul stood in the middle of the Areopagus, and said, "You men of Athens, I perceive that you are very religious in all things. [23]For as I passed along, and observed the objects of your worship, I found also an altar with this inscription: 'TO AN UNKNOWN GOD.' *What therefore you worship in ignorance, this I announce to you.* [24]The God who made the world and all things in it, he, being Lord of heaven and earth, *doesn't dwell in temples made with hands,* [25]neither is he served by men's hands, as though he needed anything, seeing he himself gives to all life and breath, and all things. [26]*He made from one blood every nation of men* to dwell on

> all the surface of the earth, having determined appointed seasons, and the boundaries of their dwellings, *[27]that they should seek the Lord, if perhaps they might reach out for him and find him, though he is not far from each one of us. [28]'For in him we live, and move, and have our being.' As some of your own poets have said, 'For we are also his offspring.' [29]Being then the offspring of God, we ought not to think that the Divine Nature is like gold, or silver, or stone, engraved by art and design of man. [30]The times of ignorance therefore God overlooked. But now he commands that all people everywhere should repent, [31]because he has appointed a day in which he will judge the world in righteousness by the man whom he has ordained; of which he has given assurance to all men, in that he has raised him from the dead."* (Acts 17:22–31)

This, then, was Paul's method of operation (*modus operandi*): he would take a common starting point and build on that thought. Note the contrast between his response here and his earlier response in Acts 14:11, where he was nothing but appalled! Paul could have been just as concerned in this context at these philosophers, because in both the Jewish and Christian religions God is able to be known (e.g., Jeremiah 24:7; 1 Corinthians 2:6–13; and Hebrews 8:11). But instead, in this instance, he took the opportunity to introduce the God that they worshiped in ignorance. Thus, he found a common ground and built on it.

The difference in Acts 14:11 was that there was apparently no common ground upon which Paul felt he could preach Christ. Apparently nothing was further from his mind than the idea that maybe Christ was the true or better manifestation of the pagan idea of "gods come down to earth in the likeness of men." But that isn't to say that he didn't find some common ground by which to preach to them.

But that common ground wasn't deity; rather, it was their common humanity. Paul said, "Sirs, why do ye these things? *We also are men of like passions with you*, and preach unto you that ye should turn from these vanities unto the living God..." (Acts 14:11–15). Interestingly, Paul did not use this opportunity to even bring up Christ; at least not in the account we are given in the Bible.

However, the point is, Jesus the Anointed One, was also very much as Paul claimed, a "man of like passions with you." That is what the following Scriptures clearly teach:

> [14]Since then the children have *shared in flesh and blood, he also himself in like manner partook of the same*, that through death he might bring to nothing him who had the power of death, that is, the devil, [15] and might deliver all of them who through fear of death were all their lifetime subject to bondage. [16]For most assuredly, not to angels does he give help, but he gives help to the seed of Abraham. [17]Therefore he was obligated in all things to be made like his brothers, that he might become a merciful and faithful high priest in things pertaining to God, to make atonement for the sins of the people. [18]For *in that he himself has suffered being tempted, he is able to help those who are tempted*. (Hebrews 2:14–18)

> [14]Having then a great high priest, who has passed through the heavens, Jesus, the Son of God, let us hold tightly to our confession. [15]For we *don't* have a high priest who *can't* be touched with the *feeling of our infirmities*, but one *who has been in all points* tempted like we are, yet without sin. (Hebrews 4:14–15)

If we remove the double negatives in the last sentence, we see the message is that we have a high priest *who was touched with the feeling of our infirmities* and *was tempted in all points like we are*. The difference is that whereas we have all succumbed to sin, he did not.

Now look again at the contrasting view of the apostles on the day of Pentecost: "Jesus of Nazareth, *a man approved by God* to you by mighty works and *wonders and signs which God did by him* in the midst of you, even as you yourselves know" (Acts 2:22).

Three things are evident here: a) Jesus was a man approved of God, clearly distinguished from God; b) God did wonders and signs "by him" clearly distinguishing two individuals (not mere "natures"); and c) this was something they already knew.

This Jesus they were preaching was thoroughly Jewish. These Jews did not in any way "know" that Jesus was "God Himself come in the likeness of men," as many theologians (Onenessian and Trinitarian) want you to believe he was. What the apostle said these Jews knew was that Jesus was a man approved of God. It was those words that encouraged them to repent and turn toward Christ.

These then are the two images represented by our graphic. One is right-side up, and that is what the apostles preached; the other is upside down and backwards, and that pagan view is what the apostles opposed. Jesus the Anointed One fits within the human side of Paul's argument: *"We also are men of like passions with you"* in complete opposition to the pagan idea of *"gods have come down to us in the likeness of men."*

The following passage warns us about mixing paganism with our Christianity. It also mentions the roles of fathers and sons and sheds even more light on the distinctions between God the Father and His human sons.

> ¹⁴Don't be unequally yoked with unbelievers, for what fellowship have righteousness and iniquity? *Or what communion has light with darkness?* ¹⁵*What agreement has Christ with Belial?* Or what portion has a believer with an unbeliever? ¹⁶*What agreement has a temple of God with idols?* For *you are a temple of the living God.* Even as God said, 'I will dwell in them, and walk in them; and I will be their God, and they will be my people.' ¹⁷Therefore, "Come out from among them, And be separate,' says the Lord, 'Touch no unclean thing. I will receive you. ¹⁸*I will be to you a Father. You will be to me sons and daughters,'* says the Lord Almighty.' ⁷:¹ Having therefore these promises, beloved, let us cleanse ourselves from all defilement of flesh and spirit, perfecting holiness in the fear of God. (2 Corinthians 6:14–7:1)

This passage very clearly separated between what is pagan and what, biblically, is godly. The Bible very clearly stated that the idea of "gods come down in the likeness of men" was pagan in origin. This passage also indicates that if and when we come out of such paganism, God will receive us and make us His sons and daughters.

In the last chapter we covered the truth that "indwelling" does not equal "identity." In other words, to be "indwelt by God" explicitly means that He remains a distinct and separate personality from ourselves. This passage above reiterates that idea.

Very clearly, verses 16 through 18 establish the biblical truth that being indwelt by God is practically synonymous with being sons and daughters of God. This is true both of us and of Jesus the Anointed One, God's one and only, truly unique son. This is the true biblical position that other views of Christ, particularly as an incarnation of gods after the pagan view, nullify and make of no effect.

The Bible presents Jesus as having been full of the Holy Spirit. He spoke of himself as a temple, just as we are to be temples of God. These ideas clearly indicate that Jesus truly was and is a man of like passions.

CHAPTER FIFTEEN

A Man Approved of God
The "Therefore... Because" Passages

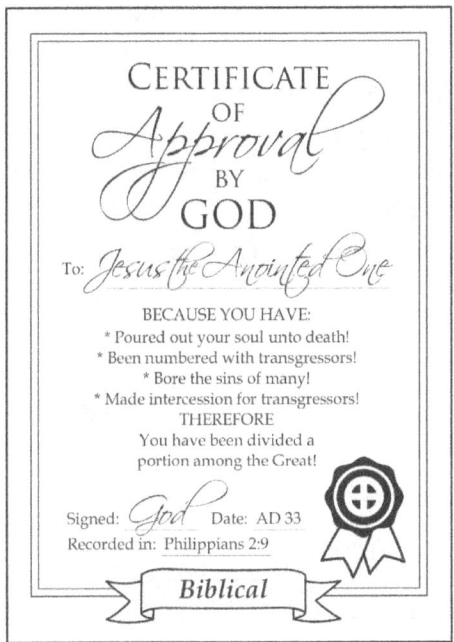

³A Man of sorrows... ⁵he was wounded for our transgressions, He was bruised for our iniquities... ¹¹My righteous Servant shall justify many, For he shall bear their iniquities. ¹²***Therefore*** I will divide him a portion with the great, And he shall divide the spoil with the strong, ***Because*** *he poured out his soul unto death*, *And he was numbered with the transgressors, And he bore the sin of many, And made intercession for the transgressors.* (Isaiah 53:3, 5, 11–12; NKJV)

Our focus in this chapter is the biblically stated reason *why* Christ was anointed, which is clearly indicated by the words "because" and "therefore" in the passage cited above. (It will become clear that the point being made in this chapter is similar to our earlier comparison of "alone" and "not alone.") We can state at the outset the reason is clearly <u>not</u> because he is an incarnation of a deific personality. That is a jumped-to conclusion of Trinitarians and Onenessians. The biblically stated reason refutes both those extrabiblical conclusions.

In verse 12, above, Isaiah gave no less than four reasons why the Messiah would be counted "great" and "strong." Not one of these reasons had to do with him being an incarnation of God. The reasons provided were: **1)** his death; **2)** his being "numbered with the transgressors" (that is, he was made in all things like his brethren, as described in Hebrews 2:17–18); **3)** his having borne the sins of many; and **4)** his having "made intercession for the transgressors."

But these reasons are just the beginning of our "because and therefore" type of Scriptures. The following twin passages provide two more reasons why Jesus was anointed above the rest of us, his brothers:

> *You have loved* righteousness, and hated wickedness. *Therefore* God, *your* God, *has anointed you* with the oil of gladness *above your fellows*. (Psalm 45:7)

> *You have loved* righteousness, and hated iniquity; *Therefore* God, *your* God, *has anointed you* with the oil of gladness *above your fellows*. (Hebrews 1:6–9)

Jesus loved righteousness and hated wickedness, *and those are two more reasons why God anointed him* above the rest of us.

Recall what we established previously about personal pronouns. These passages begin with the personal pronoun "you." They are thus not talking about YHWH's mythical, unbiblical "human nature" being exalted by his supposed "deific nature" for loving righteousness and hating iniquity. No, these are speaking personally, much like Jesus used distinctions of persons in John 8:17. These verses finish by saying that the subject ("you") person is exalted above other persons ("your fellows"), whom we know as Christ's brother-followers.

Anyone who rejects the truth clearly stated in these passages minimizes what Jesus Christ accomplished as a human *person*. Men have made up the idea that he was God acting as a man, but they have absolutely no Scriptures that say so. If it were true, the Bible would have explained in detail his being so, but instead it clearly and consistently describes in detail something different. If Jesus was the *person of God* in any manner, then he simply did not accomplish these things as a human being. That is the ugly truth behind the Trinitarian and Onenessian theories and any other theory that assigns deific *personality* to Jesus the Anointed. In effect, they are implying that he "cheated," because there is no way that God Himself could ever have really been tempted the way we are. They give lip service to believing in Jesus' humanity, when they claim he is "also" God, just as Trinitarians give lip service to believing that God is one, when they remain adamant He is three. God being tempted while pretending to be a man is just such religious nonsense! Jesus was exalted by God because he overcame! That is the powerful truth these Incarnationists are belittling and denying, whether they realize or admit it or not! By making Jesus into God, they have attempted to cloak their sins, for who could truly accomplish what Jesus did if indeed he were God incarnate? This false notion is what these "therefore... because" Scriptures are effective in neutralizing, but only for those who are truly willing to hear the word of God!

Here is yet another "therefore" type passage in which Jesus tells us the reason why God his Father and our Father did not leave him alone:

> He who sent me is with me. The Father hasn't left me alone, *for* [because, since] I always do the things that are pleasing to Him. (John 8:29)

Again we see a *clear and specific reason given* for a result between two distinct personal pronouns. This isn't the person of God's human nature speaking to *his* deific nature; this is between two personal individuals. Because personality number two (Christ Jesus) always does the things that are pleasing to personality number one

(God the Father), personality number one (God) does not leave number two (Christ) alone. Clearly the Bible establishes two *personalities* (not mere natures) who are *not alone*. Which one of us would say that "*I am not alone because* I always do the things that are *pleasing to my brain*"? Putting it this way shows how unreasonable, even nonsensical, the Onenessian conclusion is.

This next passage explains the exact reason that Jesus was given a name above all names. Once again, it wasn't because he "was God"; rather, *it was because he was obedient to the one who commanded him*:

> *Have this in your mind*, which was also in Christ Jesus, who, *existing in the form of God*, didn't consider it robbery to be equal with God, but emptied himself, taking the form of a servant, being made in the likeness of men. And being found in human form, *he humbled himself, becoming obedient* to death, yes, the death of the cross. *Therefore* God also highly exalted him, *and gave to him the name* which is above every name; that at the name of Jesus every knee should bow, of those in heaven, those on earth, and those under the earth, and that every tongue should confess that Jesus Christ is Lord, to the glory of God the Father. *So then, my beloved*, even as you have always obeyed, not only in my presence, but now much more in my absence, *work out your own salvation* with fear and trembling. (Philippians 2:5–12)

This passage is often misunderstood, but if we use other Scriptures that talk about the same topic, we can gain a better understanding. For example:

> **Therefore** the Father loves me, **because** I lay down my life, that I may take it again. No one takes it away from me, but I lay it down by myself. I have power to lay it down, and I have power to take it again. *I received this commandment* from my Father. (John 10:17–18)

When we compare and interpret these two passages together, it should be hard to miss the true meaning. The first thing to note in Philippians is that *it begins and ends with how we are to think* and how *we* are to put those thoughts into action. Certainly *we* aren't supposed to think that *we* eternally preexisted and temporarily submitted ourselves to be made human so that we could show how submissive we can be to our deific nature. But that is basically what it means if viewed through the lenses of Trinitarians and Onenessians.

The next thing it says in Philippians is that Christ existed "in the form of God," which refers to the truth that he is the second Adam, who was also made in the form, or image, of God. Adam was told the purpose of mankind was to have dominion over the earth and subdue it. Philippians goes on to state exactly how Jesus overcame Adam's failure: by his obedience even unto death. And if we are confused about what this all means, we have Jesus' own explanation that the Father loves him because he lays down his life. The real clincher is that Jesus said he received this as a commandment from his Father. This shows that Jesus neither was the Father (as in the Onenessian theory), nor was he "coequal" with the Father (as in the Trinitarian theory).

Along these same lines, and totally in harmony with what we've just seen established by the Scriptures, the Book of Hebrews provides yet another "because... therefore" passage.

> ¹Therefore, holy brothers, partakers of a heavenly calling, consider the apostle and High Priest of our confession, Jesus; ²*who* [personal pronoun] was faithful to *Him* [personal pronoun] who appointed *him*, as also was Moses in all his house. ³For *he has been counted worthy* of more glory than Moses, inasmuch as he who built the house has more honor than the house. ⁴For every house is built by someone; but He who built all things is God. ⁵Moses indeed was faithful in all his house as a servant, for a testimony of those things which were afterward to be spoken, ⁶but *Christ is faithful as*

a Son over his house; whose house we are, if we hold fast our confidence and the glorying of our hope firm to the end. (Hebrews 3:1–6)

Jesus was faithful to another, his Father, who *is* God, and Jesus was therefore, as verse 3 says, "counted worthy" of more glory and honor than Moses. The point this passage was making is that he (Jesus) had to be faithful to Him (God the Father) who appointed him (Jesus). This demonstrates that Jesus was not inherently worthy by "deific substance" (as in Trinitarianism), nor was he an incarnation of the Father (as in Modalism). Rather, it says he had to prove himself through faith; thus, Jesus was *"faithful to Him who appointed him."* These personal pronouns specifically mean, not merely imply, "personalities" and not "natures."

Furthermore, in saying that Jesus was faithful, and thereby counted worthy, this passage in Hebrews reiterated what was said in Psalms 45:7: "You have loved righteousness, and hated wickedness. *Therefore* God, *your God*, has anointed you with the oil of gladness above *your fellows*." It is in this context that God designated, exalted, and anointed Jesus above all *his fellow human beings*.

How do we know that Jesus was exalted above his fellow human beings? For one, because Jesus told us so in yet another "Because... Therefore" passage found in John:

> [19]Jesus therefore answered them, "Most assuredly, I tell you, *the Son can do nothing of himself*, but what he sees the Father doing. For whatever things *he* does, these *the Son* also does likewise. [20]For the Father has affection for the Son, and shows him all things that *he Himself* does. *He will show him* greater works than these, that you may marvel. [21]For as the Father raises the dead and gives them life, even so the Son also gives life to whom he desires. [22]For the Father judges no one, but *he has given* all judgment to the Son, [23]that all may honor the Son, even as they honor the Father. He who doesn't honor the Son doesn't honor the Father *who sent him*.

> ²⁴Most assuredly I tell you, he who hears my word, and *believes him who sent me*, has eternal life, and doesn't come into judgment, but has passed out of death into life. ²⁵Most assuredly, I tell you, the hour comes, and now is, when the dead will hear the Son of God's voice; and those who hear will live. ²⁶For as the Father has life in himself, *even so he gave to the Son* also to have life in himself. ²⁷*He also gave him* authority to execute judgment, <u>because he is a son of man</u>. ²⁸Don't marvel at this, for the hour comes, in which all that are in the tombs will hear his voice, ²⁹and will come out; those who have done good, to the resurrection of life; and those who have done evil, to the resurrection of judgment. ³⁰*I can of myself do nothing*. As I hear, I judge, and my judgment is righteous; <u>because I don't seek my own will</u>, but the will of my Father who sent me." (John 5:19–30)

This passage is simply packed with personal pronouns. The son is explicitly shown to be personally distinct from the Father through Jesus' use of "myself" in contrast to the Father (verses 19 and 20). Then, Jesus clearly explains again why he has the authority to judge: because *the Father gave* all judgment to the Son (verse 22). This means exactly what it says: that personality number one (God the Father) bestowed an authority upon personality number two (Christ Jesus), who did not previously have any authority inherent to his *person*. Thus, according to Jesus himself, he was neither co-equal with the Father (as in Trinitarianism), nor was he simply an incarnation of the person of the Father (as in Onenessianism), clearly and explicitly *because* this authority was given to "him" by another "He" [i.e., Himself, verse 20] being God the Father.

Verse 27 clears up any issue or so-called mystery by stating again ever so clearly that Jesus was given this authority from God "because he is a son of man." Thus, it isn't talking about a deific nature giving His human nature its own inherent personal authority. Rather, the one personal God is bestowing upon another personal son this specific authority.

Finally, in verse 30, Jesus declares that his judgment is righteous not because he is God, but <u>*because he doesn't seek his own will*</u>. Think of how nonsensical this all becomes if this is the non-personal flesh of the person of the Father speaking.

These are biblically stated purposes and reasons, and not guesswork, jumped-to conclusions, or speculation.

All these Scriptures are made totally and completely of no effect by Onenessianism. This means that it is impossible to believe Jesus' words and the Scriptures we've cited while at the same time believing in Onenessianism. They are as incompatible as the Trinity is with Jesus' assertion that Jews know what they worship. Likewise, the apostles never explained Jesus as one individual that was made of two natures.

Onenessians Substitute Christ's Qualifications

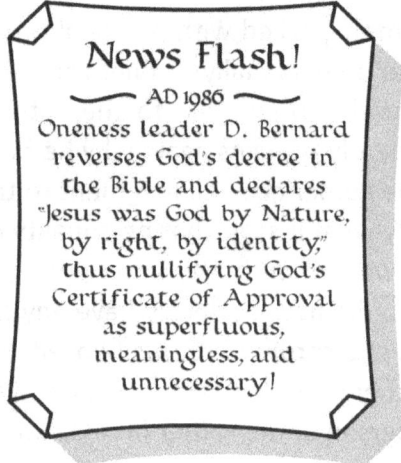

News Flash!
— AD 1986 —
Oneness leader D. Bernard reverses God's decree in the Bible and declares "Jesus was God by Nature, by right, by identity," thus nullifying God's Certificate of Approval as superfluous, meaningless, and unnecessary!

Compare the Scriptures we've discussed thus far with what Onenessianism says:

> While on earth Jesus differed from an ordinary human... in that he had all of God's nature within him. He possessed the unlimited power, authority, and character of God. *He was God by nature, by right, by identity*; he was not merely

deified by an anointing or indwelling. In contrast to a Spirit–filled believer, the Spirit of God was inextricably joined with the humanity of Jesus. *Without the Spirit of God there would have been only a lifeless human*, not the living Christ. Only in these terms can we describe and distinguish the humanity and deity in Jesus...[1]

This statement attempts to defend and justify what the term antichrist (against the anointed) explicitly means. Note very carefully that *Bernard described Jesus' humanity as being lifeless without the Spirit of God*. In contrast, Jesus had declared that all authority had been given to him. That would mean, in the Oneness view, that Christ's human, lifeless flesh was given god-like authority. That is nonsense. Christ declared that authority was given to his "person" and that is why he said "given to me." In clear contradiction to Jesus' declaration, Bernard's definition of Christ is simply not of a man who was made in all things like you and me, to whom was given all authority. For Bernard, Jesus was "God by nature, by right, by identity." This is the exact opposite of what it means to be "given" authority which is what the term Christ explicitly means and identifies about Jesus! And thus, Onenessianism, is "against-the-anointed" which is anti-christ.

If Christ "possessed the unlimited power, authority, and character of God" and was "God by nature," then in no way, shape, or form would any of the above "because and therefore" Scriptures have any real meaning whatsoever. But words do have meaning. So if this Oneness position is true, then the Bible is full of meaningless gibberish! The truth is simply that Onenessianism makes all these Scriptures, and many more, of "no effect."

Bernard goes on to write:

How were Christ's humanity and deity united? How did God become man?...First, the Bible does not give us complete information in this area. It does not describe Christ's child-

---

[1] David K. Bernard, *Symposium on Oneness Pentecostalism 1986*, 130.

hood, for example, nor does it reveal the inner workings of Christ's mind. Secondly, the very nature of the subject places it beyond the comprehension of the finite human mind.[2]

Contrary to Mr. Bernard's position, the Bible actually tells us that it thoroughly furnishes us with all good teachings and doctrines (2 Timothy 3:16–17). His problem is that this thoroughly furnished doctrine does not anywhere describe the essential tenets of the Oneness belief system. Furthermore, *the Scriptures we've been quoting do exactly what he claims the Bible does not do*. The Scripture does describe Christ's childhood to the extent that as a son he "learned obedience by the things he suffered" (Hebrews 5:8), and "he increased in wisdom and stature and in favor with God and man" (Luke 2:52). These passages describe a different upbringing than Onenessians should be comfortable with, in the same way that Trinitarians should be uncomfortable because the Bible doesn't anywhere describe a relationship of a "God the Father" with a "God the Son." The real issue is that neither of those relationships exist in the Bible (let alone are they explained in the Bible) because they are mythological and unbiblical! And they both deny and negate what the Bible *does* describe.

As far as we are concerned, the Scriptures have made Jesus' relationship to the Father very understandable. They've even explained that we are to have the same "inner workings of Christ's mind" in us as Christ had (Philippians 2:5, 12; Luke 22:42). The Scriptures have put the explanation of Christ's relationship to the Father well within our ability to understand, for one in particular, by using the very understandable terms of father and son to describe their relationship. These Scriptures have, as the Scripture says, "thoroughly provided" us with every good thing we need to know. What is absent from the Scriptures is any kind of systematic explanation of Modalism, just as there is no systematic description of the Trinity. Such positions must be "read into" the text.

---

[2] Ibid., 131–132.

So we see that the problem isn't that the Bible doesn't give us complete information. The Onenessian problem is simply that *the biblical information we do have does not fit the antichristian dual nature doctrine, or the incarnation doctrine* which Onenessianism embraces, preserves, and defends.

Believers on Jesus simply must listen to Jesus, and that means not being taken in by traditions of men. We pray that those who are more interested in hearing what Jesus says than being justified in their false teachings, will "come out of her my people" and really start to hear Jesus, who said:

> ...*I am not alone*, but I and the Father that sent me. (John 8:16, KJV)

> ...*I am not alone*, because the Father is with me. (John 16:32, KJV)

> [17]It's also written in your law that the testimony of two people is valid. [18]*I am one who* testifies about myself, *and the Father who* sent me testifies about me. (John 8:17–18)

> Therefore the Father loves me, because I lay down my life... I received this commandment from my Father. (John 10:17–18)

CHAPTER SIXTEEN

Foreknowledge vs. Preexistence

In the beginning man has a "**Plan**"	"In the beginning was **The Plan**"	And **The Plan** was... "Him being delivered up..."
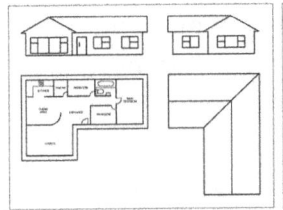		
	"Christ who was foreknown before the foundation of the world" (1 Peter 1:19 - 20)	"By the determined foreknowledge of God!" (Acts 2:23)

²²Men of Israel, hear these words! Jesus of Nazareth, a man approved by God to you... which *God did by him*... even as you yourselves know, ²³him, being *delivered up by the determined counsel and <u>foreknowledge</u> of God*, you have taken by the hand of lawless men, crucified and killed... (Apostle Peter, Day of Pentecost, Acts 2:22–23)

¹...An apostle of Jesus Christ, to the chosen ones... ²according to the <u>foreknowledge</u> of God the Father... ¹⁸knowing that you were redeemed... ¹⁹...with precious blood, as of a faultless and pure lamb, the blood of Christ; ²⁰*who was <u>foreknown</u> indeed before the foundation of the world*, but was revealed at the end of times... (1 Peter 1:1–2, 18–20)

All his works are known to God from eternity. (Acts 15:18)

This chapter will demonstrate that God's *foreknowledge* is biblical. Foreknowledge means knowing something before it comes to pass. The opposite view, which comes from pagan philosophy, is literal *preexistence.* This refers to something or someone actually existing (typically in the heavens or spiritual realm) before being known, or making an appearance, in our world.

According to historian Adolf von Harnack,[1] ancient Jews held the view that God foreknew everything that He planned that would ever come to pass on earth. That is, everything in God's plan existed in God's "foreknowledge." This truth is clearly spelled out in the NT:

> ...as it is written, 'I have made you a father of many nations'... *God... calls those things which do not exist as though they did...* (Romans 4:17–18, NKJV)

Paul explained that God talks about things that *do not actually yet exist,* in a manner *as if* they already do exist. That is the biblical explanation of God's foreknowledge and the key to understanding how God speaks of what He foreknows. The key words are not so much the words "*as though they did*"; rather, the key words are "which do *not* exist."

This NT passage is an explanation of something we see acted out in the OT. Paul was explaining the meaning of God's word when He said this to Abraham:

> Neither will your name any more be called Abram, but your name will be Abraham; for *I have made you* the father of a multitude of nations. (Genesis 17:5)

God told this to Abraham before he even had a child. Abraham's future children were just as real to God in His foreknowledge as they would be when they finally came to be. But that doesn't mean they actually existed...yet. That is why the key words really are "things which <u>do not</u> exist." People often have a hard time accepting that God talks like this. So they imagine that any time God speaks of something as if it already existed, they feel they can conclude that

---

[1] (Adolf von Harnack, "On the Conception of Pre-Existence," in *History of Dogma,* Vol. I, Appendix I).

it must already exist and that is the only acceptable way to understand it. Some people even falsely assume God would be lying by speaking from His position of absolute foreknowledge. That would be imposing our understanding on how God is supposed to be and speak. It is also a way of denying the understanding of God from a biblical Jewish view.

To further muddy the waters, pagan cultures did have theories of literally preexistent deific beings. Such ideas seem to fit God's speaking in the past tense of things "which do not exist <u>as though they did</u>." So rejecting the Jewish view necessarily includes adopting a pagan view in its place.

Let's look more closely at the biblical concept of God's foreknowledge, and then we will compare it with the pagan view. To do that, let's examine some examples of things that were in God's foreknowledge, but which we know did not exist at the time God spoke of them. Harnack pointed out some examples, saying, "*So the Tabernacle and its furniture, the Temple, Jerusalem, etc., are before God and continue to exist before him in heaven, even during their appearance on earth and after it.*"[2]

Harnack derived his list, in part, from Exodus 25:9, 40, when God told Moses to build all things *according to the pattern* that was shown to Moses on the mountain.

Again, what we saw acted out in the OT is explained for us in the NT. The writer of Hebrews tells us:

> [1]Now in the things which we are saying, <u>the main point is this. We have</u> such <u>a high priest</u>, who sat down on the right hand of the throne of the Majesty in the heavens, [2]a minister of the sanctuary, and *of the true tabernacle*, which the Lord pitched, not man. [3]*For every high priest is appointed* to offer both gifts and sacrifices. Therefore it is necessary that this high priest also have something to offer. [4]For if he were on earth, he would not be a priest at all, seeing there are

---

[2] Adolf von Harnack, *History of Dogma*,
http://www.ccel.org/ccel/harnack/dogma1.ii.iv.i.html.

> *priests who offer the gifts according to the law;* ⁵*who serve a copy and shadow of the heavenly things,* even as Moses was warned by God when he was about to make the tabernacle, for he said, "See, you shall *make everything according to the pattern that was shown to you on the mountain."* (Hebrews 8:1–5)

Let's try to follow the train of thought here. The writer emphasizes that we now have Jesus as a high priest of a heavenly tabernacle. Then he goes on to explain that the heavenly tabernacle had a copy and a shadow, or example, in the earthly tabernacle. The reason the writer gives is that the first tabernacle was to be made according to the pattern Moses was shown in the mountain. That is to say, the first tabernacle was made to pattern the heavenly tabernacle that was to come, which in turn was in God's plan. But it was more than just a plan: it was foreknown before the very foundation of the earth. More on that in a moment.

This next passage speaks of the heavenly tabernacle in the past tense, which for us is still actually in the future (just as Abraham's offspring would be in the future). Thus, it is one of "those things which do not exist" that God speaks of and sees "as though they did."

> ¹⁸For you have not come to a mountain that might be touched, and that burned with fire... ²²But *you have come [perfect tense] to Mount Zion, and to the city of the living God, the heavenly Jerusalem,* and to innumerable multitudes of angels, ²³to the general assembly and assembly of the firstborn who are enrolled in heaven, to God the Judge of all, to the spirits of just men made perfect, ²⁴to Jesus, the mediator of a new covenant, and to the blood of sprinkling that speaks better than that of Abel. (Hebrews 12:18–24)

We know that the city of the living God, the heavenly New Jerusalem, is a city yet to be revealed. That is, it is for the future. And yet the Scriptures talk as if we've already arrived. In one sense we have because of its assurance in God's plan, but it has not been actualized yet. The New Jerusalem exists as one of "those things which do not exist" that God speaks of and sees "as though they did" exist.

Now here's an amazing thing. Having faith in the coming future city of the living God is to share in God's foreknowledge of that which is to come. This is something we learn from the following Scripture:

> [8]*By faith*, Abraham, when he was called, obeyed to go out to the place which he was to receive for an inheritance. He went out, not knowing where he went. [9]*By faith*, he lived as an alien in the land of promise, as in a land not his own, dwelling in tents, with Isaac and Jacob, the heirs with him of the same promise. [10]*For <u>he looked for</u> the city which has the foundations, whose builder and maker is God*. (Hebrews 11:8–10)

Our faith is very much related to God's foreknowledge. Our faith is a faint "reflection" or "image" of God's foreknowledge of what He has in mind for our future. And that future is a city whose builder and maker is God, a city which we look for by faith, just as Abraham did.

> Now *faith is assurance of things hoped for, proof of things not seen*. (Hebrews 11:1)

> [22]For we know that the whole creation groans and travails in pain together until now. [23]Not only so, but *ourselves also*, who have the first fruits of the Spirit, *even we ourselves* groan within ourselves, *waiting for adoption, the redemption of our body.* [24] *For we were saved in hope, but hope that is seen is not hope. For who hopes for that which he sees?* [25] But if *we hope for that which we don't see, we wait for it with patience.* (Romans 8:22–25)

So we see that although Hebrews 12:18–24 had told us we "have come to Mount Zion, and to the city of the living God, the heavenly Jerusalem," here in Romans 8:22–25 we are told we really are still hoping for something we do not yet see. In other words, our hope for the coming city, whose builder and maker is God, is also one of those things of which "...God... calls those things which do not exist as though they did..." Just as Abraham, by faith, looked for a city whose builder and maker is God, so the same goes for us.

Romans 8:22–25 also shows us how foreknowledge by definition excludes the possibility of preexistence. You can't *fore*know something that currently exists any more than we can see what we hope for at the same time we hope for it. Thus "foreknowledge" means knowing of things that are not but shall be, in the same exact way that "God... calls those things which do not exist as though they did..."

All of this means that you and I, and everyone who ever lived, already existed *in God's foreknowledge*. That isn't to say we *actually* existed before we were born. It is only to say that God knew exactly who, what, and when we were to be before He even set creation into being. This is what Peter was telling us in the very start of his letter to the assemblies:

> ¹Peter, an apostle of Jesus Christ, to the chosen ones... ²according to the <u>foreknowledge</u> of God the Father.
> (1 Peter 1:1–2)

The Lamb Slain from the Foundation of the World

Before we contrast God's foreknowledge with the pagan belief in preexistence, there is one more powerful piece of evidence showing just how real God's foreknowledge is to God.

> All who dwell on the earth will worship him, whose names have not been written in the Book of Life of *the Lamb slain from the foundation of the world*. (Revelation 13:8, NKJV)

Now, there are a great many theories about this verse put forth by a lot of different voices. We're not going to chase down every proverbial rabbit hole trying to make our case. Suffice it to say, for example, that we are not talking about Calvin's version of "predestination," which is another jumped-to conclusion to be dealt with in a different study.

But there is one false idea that we do want to address here because it should help clarify the topic of God's foreknowledge. Because of passages that speak as if Jesus actually did preexist (e.g., Revelation 13:8), some people believe that Jesus literally existed before he was born of Mary. Keeping with the topic of God's foreknowledge, let's look at some passages that utterly refute that jumped-to conclusion of Revelation 13:8, and also indicates how it should be rightly interpreted with the understanding of God's foreknowledge.

We are talking about the scriptural truth that in actuality Christ only died once for sins. This is very clearly explained in the following passages:

> ¹Now indeed even the first covenant had ordinances of divine service, and an earthly sanctuary... ⁶Now these things having been thus prepared, *the priests go in continually into the first tabernacle, accomplishing the services...* ¹¹ But Christ having come as a high priest of the coming good things... ¹²...<u>entered in once for all</u> into the Holy Place, having obtained eternal redemption... ²⁴For Christ hasn't entered into holy places made with hands, which are representations of the true, but into heaven itself, now to appear in the presence of God for us; ²⁵<u>nor yet that he should offer himself often</u>, as the high priest enters into the holy place year by year with blood not his own, ²⁶*or else he must have suffered often since the foundation of the world*. But now <u>*once at the end of the ages*</u>, he has been revealed to put away sin by the sacrifice of himself. ²⁷Inasmuch as it is *appointed for men to die once*, and after this, judgment, ²⁸*so Christ also, <u>having been once offered</u>* to bear the sins of many, will appear a second time, without sin, to those who are eagerly waiting for him for salvation. (Hebrews 9:1, 6, 11–12, 24–28)

> ⁵Therefore when he comes into the world, he says, "Sacrifice and offering you didn't desire, But a body did you prepare for me..." ⁷Then I said, "Behold, I have come (In the scroll of the book it is written of me) To do your will, God." ⁹...then he has said, "Behold, I have come to do your will." He takes away the first, that he may establish the second, ¹⁰by which will we have been sanctified *through the offering of the body of Jesus Christ <u>once for all</u>*. ¹¹Every priest indeed stands day by day ministering and often offering the same sacrifices, which can never take away sins, ¹²*but he, when he had offered <u>one sacrifice for sins forever</u>, sat down on the right hand of God;* ¹³*from that time waiting until his enemies are made the footstool of his feet.* ¹⁴For <u>by one offering</u> *he has perfected forever those who are being sanctified...*¹⁸Now *where remission of these is, there is no more offering for sin.* ¹⁹Having therefore, brothers, boldness to enter into the holy place by the blood of Jesus, *by the way which he dedicated for us, a new and living way, through the veil, that is to say, his flesh.* (Hebrews 10:5, 7, 9–14, 18–20)

No less than six times (as underlined above, plus once in the negative at verses 9:25), this passage teaches and reiterates that Christ only died once, and it was not before the world began! But that isn't to say that this didn't happen in God's foreknowledge. Revelation 13:8 is one of those examples where "*... as it is written... God... calls those things which do not exist as though they did...*" (Romans 4:17–18, NKJV).

All this points to the simple truth of God's foreknowledge. God foreknew absolutely that Christ was going to have to die for our sins; in fact, God planned it that way from before the foundation of the world. This was God's plan, His "logos/word/plan," which was made flesh when Christ was born and lived out this plan. This view of Christ remained in God's foreknowledge before Christ was born, during the time that Christ lived on the earth, and continues ever afterward. In a manner of speaking, we could say that Christ's life and sacrifice is forever etched into the forefront of God's mind!

The following graphic is a representation of God's foreknowledge. In the top half, we see that in God's mind's eye, He always sees what is in the future in a manner that is just as clear as our view of our world. This graphic illustrates how Jesus could say, "No one has ascended into heaven, but he who descended *out of* heaven, the Son of Man, *who is in heaven*" (John 3:13). It is through the biblical concept of God's foreknowledge that Jesus could quite properly say that the Son of Man, literally, the "offspring of humanity" (himself) was both in heaven and had come out of heaven *at the same time.*

"The Lamb slain from the foundation of the world."
(Revelation 13:8)

"The Son of Man, who is in heaven."
(John 3:13)

"He offered one sacrifice for sins forever."
(Hebrews 10:5-20)

"Came down from heaven, not do his own will."
(John 6:38)

In the top view we see God's foreknowledge expressed in Revelation 13:8. In the bottom half, we have the actual scene wherein Christ was crucified "once at the end of the world," according to Hebrews 9:12, 25, 26, 28; 10:10, 12, 14.

This is how Christ could be said, without contradiction, to have suffered before the foundation of the world and yet, in actuality, only suffered once at his crucifixion. It is because Jesus himself, and the crucifixion, were *always in God's foreknowledge* and became a reality in our world only on that fateful day some 2,000 years ago. God has the same foreknowledge of each and every one of us.

Foreknowledge is a biblical word and is mentioned or described in Romans 4:17–18, Acts 2:1–23, 1 Peter 1:20, and Acts 15:18.

The Pagan Idea of Preexistence

When preexisting pagan gods came down to earth in the likeness of men...

What they look like to God - Zeus, Hermes

What they look like to men - Hermes, Zeus

Now then, to present the opposite position, that of actual preexistence, we're not going to spend a lot of time introducing examples. We're just going to point back to Harnack and let the great historian of Christian dogma tell us what the difference is.

> According to the [pagan] Hellenic conception, which has become associated with Platonism, *the idea of pre-existence is... based on the conception of the contrast between spirit and matter...* In the case of all spiritual beings, life in the body or flesh is at bottom an inadequate and unsuitable condition, for the spirit is eternal, the flesh perishable... *In the case of the higher and purer (spirits)... if they resolved for some reason or other to appear in this finite world, they cannot simply become visible, for they have no 'visible form.' They must rather 'assume flesh,'* whether they throw it about them as a covering, or really make it their own by a process of transformation or mixture.[3]

If you ever wondered where the saying, "God robed Himself in flesh" originated, here we have it. The Oneness doctrine of Jesus being "God incarnate" who "robed Himself in flesh" has its basis,

---

[3] Adolf von Harnack, *History of Dogma*, Vol. I, Appendix I, 320.

not in the OT schoolmaster, but in pagan mythology, just as the concept of the Trinity of three persons in the godhead does. They both originate from ultimately the same source, they have just reached slightly different positions, neither of which is actually spelled out or explained in the Bible.

Let us try to simplify what Harnack has said. In classical philosophy, spirit and matter were incompatible. (This is known as "dualism," which is the philosophic idea that only that which is spirit can be good, while that which is flesh can only be evil or corrupt.) Spirit beings were, of course, believed to be invisible to us. Therefore if they wanted to show themselves, they would have to do one of two things. They either would have to *"robe themselves in flesh"* (which is a common, unbiblical "Oneness" description for God in Christ), or somehow mix with flesh. The point is, in the pagan view these spiritual entities, or gods, preexisted in one form and then had to *change form* in order to become visible in our world.

This idea of a preexistent being "taking on a change" is one of the big reasons it is the opposite of the biblical concept of God's foreknowledge, because God sees in His foreknowledge that which is to be on earth exactly as it is to be without any change. This is a very important distinction that betrays the pagan influence or not of the two views. In the pagan view, the preexistent entity has to change forms somehow; in the biblical view, what appears on earth is exactly as it was in God's foreknowledge. In the Oneness view, God had to robe Himself in flesh to appear to be something He really isn't. That fact of a "change" alone is enough to betray its pagan influence and source. In a previous chapter we brought up wolves in sheep's clothing as a method of deception. That analogy would be very fitting here also for what we've just described as the pagan view.

Even after Christ's resurrection and ascension, the "only wise God" (referring to the Father) is still said to be *invisible* (1 Timothy 1:17). In the Bible Jesus is said to be the *"image of* the invisible God..." (Colossians 1:15). An image is something completely different than an incarnation of a preexistent being. An image is like the picture of President Lincoln we see on a US penny. If we carry a penny in our pocket with the image of Lincoln on it, it specifically means that we don't have Lincoln himself; we have an image of him.

How someone views the Scriptures' descriptions of God and Christ depends on the influences upon that person. The first step in being able to see this involves being honest with the biblical information and with history. It also means being able to accept that we can be and have been preconditioned with biases that are not in line with the OT Schoolmaster and will not bring us to the correct view of Christ.

Unfortunately, many people feel they have a more special relationship with God than others do. They seem to feel that, since they know God called them, they couldn't possibly have been led to believe a lie. This attitude is clearly shown to be wrong through the Jews who believed in Jesus in John 8:30–47. They were not willing to allow Jesus to point out to them they were in bondage to sin. Rather, they seemed only interested in having him justify their supposed "right-standing" with God and expected him to recognize their assumed relationship with God. This is one of the main stumbling blocks that keep "believers" from rejecting errors and advancing into greater truth. Paul explained it by saying, "when I was a child, I thought as a child, but when I became a man I put away childish things" (1 Corinthians 13:11). Possibly no other area has held Christians in more bondage to error than their pagan-influenced, pre-conceived notion that Christ is literally an incarnation of "preexistent" deity.

Harnack pointed out that the pagan ideas of preexistence, incarnation of deity, and such were clearly and absolutely contrary to the biblical, Jewish view of God's foreknowledge. The two concepts, he observed, were "as wide apart as the poles." The biblical Jewish view contained no assumption of the flesh or mixing of spirit and flesh.

Harnack had this to say about *the Jewish view of foreknowledge* in contrast to the *pagan view of preexistence*:

> In becoming visible to the senses, the [Jewish] object in question assumes no attribute that it did not already possess with God. Hence its material nature is *by no means an*

inadequate expression of it, <u>nor is it a second nature added to the first</u>. The truth rather is that *what was in heaven before is now revealing itself upon earth, without any sort of alteration taking place in the process.* There is no *assumptio naturæ novæ*, and no change or mixture. The old Jewish theory of [foreknowledge] is *founded on the religious idea of the omniscience and omnipotence of God*, that God to whom the events of history do not come as a surprise, but who guides their course. As the whole history of the world and the destiny of each individual are recorded on His tablets or books, so also each thing is ever present before Him.[4]

To believe "God is one" is to believe, not only that He is one in personality, but that He is also one in nature. Where Trinitarians destroy the truth that "God is one" by assigning Him multiple persons; Onenessians destroy the truth that God is one by making Him out to personally be Christ whom they define as a dual natured individual. Neither is biblical oneness. They are both based in pagan ideas rather than in Jewish Biblical categories of thought; in particular God's foreknowledge.

The basis and effect of the two contrasting views can be seen in this table:

	Biblical Jewish View	Pagan/Gnostic/Philosophic View
Basis	God's foreknowledge is based on God's omniscience (All-knowing).	Preexistence is based on dualism, the contrast between spirit and matter.
Effect on Appearance	What appears on earth is *exactly* as God foresaw it would appear.	Spiritual beings must "put on," be "joined to," or "mix with" flesh in order to become visible.

---

[4] Adolf von Harnack, *History of Dogma*, Vol. I, Appendix I, 318.

The biblical Jewish view was based on God's omniscience, which is His ability to know all things even into the future. The pagan view was based on the idea of the incompatibility of spirit and matter. Recall from Genesis that, "God saw everything that he had made, and, behold, it was very good" (Genesis 1:31). Thus, God views His physical creation as good, which is the opposite of the pagan philosophic view called "dualism" which has been adopted and modified into the unbiblical Oneness doctrine called "Dual Natures in Christ."

From the perspective of Trinitarian dogma, just as with the pagan view of preexistence, the Son of God was an actually preexistent, spiritual person, who joined to a lower, human nature. From the perspective of Onenessianism, it was the Father Himself who "robed Himself in flesh" and thereby joined Himself "hypostatically" (or personally) to a lower, impersonal human nature, but kept his deific personality. Of course, another problem with the Oneness theory, beyond the fact that it is a pagan concept, is that it negates the Scriptures that describe Jesus as being a separate personal individual from the Father even after his resurrection and subduing of all things under him.

> [25]For he must reign until he has put all his enemies under his feet. [26]The last enemy that will be abolished is death. [27]For, "He put all things in subjection under his feet." But when he says, "All things are put in subjection," it is evident that he is excepted who subjected all things to him. [28]When all things have been subjected to him, then the Son will also himself be subjected to him who subjected all things to him, that God may be all in all. (1 Corinthians 15:25-28)

Passages such as this clearly maintain a permanent state of personal separation and distinction from God and Jesus. Only by dishonestly negating what passages such as this clearly teach, can Onenessians empower themselves to adopt the pagan doctrine of incarnation and dual natures.

In the final analysis, both of these "isms" (Trinitarianism and Onenessianism) have been spoiled by philosophy and traditions of men and have rejected the truth of God's foreknowledge of His Son that He foreknew and foresaw before He ever set one piece of creation into motion. The son that the Bible talks about did not assume any nature that God in heaven did not foresee that he would have on earth.

Hence, there is no scriptural basis for the Oneness concept that Jesus Christ was *"God in creation, Son in redemption, and Holy Spirit in sanctification"* as they often say. John doesn't say that Jesus' human nature would have a different will; rather, Jesus Christ spoke this of his "own" will:

> [41]He was withdrawn from them about a stone's throw, and he knelt down and prayed, [42]saying, "Father, if you are willing, remove this cup from me. Nevertheless, *not my will, but yours, be done."* (Luke 22:41–42)

Jesus said, "Not my will, but yours be done." He didn't say, "Not the will of my human nature be done, but the will of my deific nature," as Onenessians assume he must have meant. This event of Jesus faithfully submitting his personal will to the Father is the pinnacle and epitome of Christianity! It was this very attitude and action of Christ, which God foresaw and ordained, that made God exalt this solitary individual above all the rest of creation (Hebrews 1:9 and Philippians 2:8–9). But the Oneness view runs roughshod over this whole concept and turns it into a complete sham of a playacting god, making God himself into a deceiver in sheep's clothing (Matthew 7:15)! The Oneness view isn't a "high" view of Christ; it is an appalling tragedy that misunderstands and misrepresents the very heart of the gospel: "Jesus of Nazareth, *a man approved by God to you* by mighty works and wonders and signs which God did by him..." (Acts 2:22).

The Onenessian God must have had some form of multiple personality disorder in heaven; either that or Onenessians have been influenced by the pagan doctrine of incarnation of Gods (Acts

14:11)! Trinitarians have the same problem: somehow two of their deific all-knowing persons had conflicting wills throughout all eternity past! In truth, Jesus is perfectly reflecting the Jewish view that Christ is and was the man whom God did always foreknow.

> No one has ascended into heaven, but he who descended out of heaven, the *Son of Man, who is in heaven.* (John 3:13)

Jesus stated quite explicitly that "the Son of Man" (that is, the offspring of humankind) was in heaven at the same time that he was speaking on earth! If we interpret this through pagan ideas of preexistence, we would have to conclude there was more than one son of man—the one on earth and the one that remained in heaven! But if we view the verse through biblical lenses, we know that Jesus was referring to God's plan, God's foreknowledge. In other words, even when he was in heaven—that is, in God's foreknowledge—the "will" that Jesus had in heaven was not the will of the Father. Thus, he and God the Father were *always* separate persons: in God's foreknowledge, during his time on earth, and after his resurrection. Onenessianism contradicts this truth. Only God had always existed, while the Son was actually made in the process of time (in the fullness of time) and made of a woman (Galatians 4:4)! This perfectly fits the concept of God's foreknowledge of His Anointed One.

And this is exactly what Harnack said about the Jewish view. Christ was born just exactly as God foreknew he would without any change or admixture or assumption of the flesh or by being "robed in flesh" or any of those pagan ideas. Thus, the biblical Christ is not at all compatible with the pagan view of preexistence. The biblical Christ was made of a woman in the fullness of time, and what he was made into was exactly as God foreknew him to be before that time, when as yet he actually "was not."

The Jewish view of God's foreknowledge is what John was talking about when he said the plan (*logos*/word) was made flesh. Thus it is written,

> [19]So then you are... [20]being built on *the foundation* of the apostles and *prophets*, Christ Jesus himself being the chief cornerstone. (Ephesians 2:19–20)

> [19]...Christ (the Anointed One) [20]...*was foreknown... before the foundation of the world...* (1 Peter 1:19–20)

> Be careful that you don't let anyone rob you through his philosophy and vain deceit, after the tradition of men, after the elements of the world, and not after The Anointed One. (Colossians 2:8)

Now let's take a look at how the plan of God can be subtly changed into something different by Oneness theology. Note in the following passage how David Bernard slipped the idea of "incarnation" into the discussion.

> John 1 beautifully teaches the concept of God manifest in flesh. In the beginning was the Word (Greek, *Logos*). The Word was not a separate person or a separate god any more than a man's word is a separate person from him. Rather *the Word was a thought or a plan, or mind of God*. It was with God in the beginning and was a part of Him (John 1:1). *The **Incarnation** existed in the mind* of God before the world began. Indeed, in the mind of God the Lamb was slain before the foundation of the world (1 Peter 1:19–20; Revelation 13:8). *In Greek usage, logos can mean the expression or plan as it exists in the mind of the proclaimer*—as a play in the mind of a playwright—or it can mean the thought as uttered or otherwise physically expressed–as a play that is enacted on stage. John 1 says the Logos existed in the mind of God from the beginning of time. When the fulness of time was come, God put that plan in action. He put flesh on that plan *in the form of the man Jesus Christ*. The Logos is God expressed.[5]

---

[5] David K. Bernard, *The Oneness of God*, 60.

Neither the word nor the definition of *incarnation* is in the Bible. It is uncertain how you would even say that in Biblical Hebrew! The onus would be on Onenessians to prove their claim, which they certainly have not. The idea of "incarnation" is just as lacking in the Bible as the Trinity doctrine. But that doesn't mean people won't attempt to interject what they think it should say. By interjecting the pagan doctrine of incarnation, Bernard has imposed pagan views of God upon the Scriptures in the same way Onenessians accuse Trinitarians of doing.

The reader may recall how we quoted Carl Brumbach in Chapter Eleven and showed the way he attempted to be technically accurate, *and yet changed and omitted just enough details to make what he said totally misleading.* Mr. Bernard has done the same type of thing in this passage. As we showed in the last section, there are no OT biblical grounds to believe that the Messiah was to be an "incarnation of God Himself." What Bernard implied in the passage above is contrary to what the OT clearly taught. The word "manifest" and the word "incarnation" are simply not synonymous. So Bernard simply played a shell game with words and concepts in order to make you think that the Bible refers to incarnation when it really only says that Jesus made God known to us (because he was a human being who emulated God's attitudes, attributes, and characteristics).

Certainly it is true that *God's plan of Jesus was always in the mind of God*, and certainly that plan/word/*logos* was with God and in a sense was God (just as anyone else's "word" communicates who they are). But *not until Christianity was influenced by the pagan idea of incarnations of deity was Christ's birth spoken of as an "incarnation."* The word *incarnation* embodies in its meaning the idea of a preexisting being coming to be in the world in a different form from which it previously existed. The word *incarnation* refers directly to the antichristian doctrine of the dual natures of Christ. It is used to represent the act of the preexistent deific nature joining ontologically to the impersonal human nature. So it is not a biblical word, and it does not represent the biblical theme of Christ's genesis/birth at Bethlehem.

As we quoted above, Jesus said that *what* God had planned, and *was* in heaven even while Christ was on earth, *was* "the Son of Man" that was in heaven. God's word says that God is not a man, neither the Son of man (Numbers 23:19). The term "son of man" is just normal poetic biblical parallelism of the sort used in Psalms, with the meaning of human being. It is parallel to "man," and has the same meaning. Furthermore, that "son of man" that was in God's plan had a different personal "will" than God, which signifies to us God's foreknowledge of the Son's will was exactly as it would be in reality on earth. Remember, "God calls *those things that are not as though they were.*" When we read the Bible, we need to keep the things that it does say in context if we want to hear what it is saying rather than imposing our own ideas upon it, especially when those ideas actually originated in antichristian Gnosticism and the paganism that Gnosticism adopted and adapted to appear to "fit" biblical words and ideas.

We will return to God's foreknowledge in Chapter Twenty-Seven.

In Closing Section Three

In this section we have attempted to present some very simple, biblical doctrines and show how they have been hijacked through the influence of similar sounding pagan ideas. However, when the Bible is allowed to speak, the impostors can be exposed, and those pagan ideas can be shown to be far from what the Bible actually describes.

Those doctrines are:
- The biblical Christ being made of a woman of the offspring of David versus the antichristian doctrine of dual natures of flesh and deity.
- The biblical Christ being a man approved of God versus the pagan doctrine of gods coming to earth in the form of mankind.
- The biblical doctrine of God's foreknowledge versus the pagan view of preexistence of deities.

To this list could be added the following contrast that was brought out in Chapter Three, pages 63–66:

- The biblical concept of agency versus the pagan view of incarnation of deities.

    The words...I speak not from myself; but the Father who lives in me. (John 14:10)

We've placed this section of topics here because without first dealing with these concepts, many readers would simply keep reading the pagan views into the NT Scriptures we are going to present in the next section.

We hope we've given you, dear reader, enough information that you will be open to reading the words of the NT through lenses that are made clear through the light of Scripture and not darkened through the influences of paganism, which comes from "the gods that are round and about you."

SECTION FOUR

The New Testament Presentation of Jesus Christ

CHAPTER SEVENTEEN

The Overwhelming Majority of Passages Distinguishing Jesus from God

²²Men of Israel, hear these words! <u>Jesus of Nazareth, a man approved by God</u> to you by mighty works and wonders and signs <u>which God did by him</u> in the midst of you, even as you yourselves know, ²³him, being delivered up by the determined counsel and foreknowledge of God, you have taken by the hand of lawless men, crucified and killed; ²⁴whom God raised up, having freed him from the agony of death, because it was not possible that he should be held by it... ³⁶Let all the house of Israel therefore know assuredly that <u>God has made him</u> both Lord and Christ, this Jesus whom you crucified. (Acts 2:22–36)

This section contains manifold Scriptures that clearly state and prove that Jesus is personally distinct from the Father and that he is completely human. This is in contrast to the Oneness and Trinitarian ideas that Jesus is an incarnation of deity. In this section, the reader may wish to skim the data, or spot check it in certain places, if they would like. Of course we'd like to think the reader would want to, at least eventually, read every reference. But part of our point here is the sheer volume of this information. We understand it may become overly tedious. We'd rather readers skim this section rather than get so bogged down they fail to finish.

In our passage above, Jesus of Nazareth, a man approved by God, <u>*was made*</u> both Lord and Christ. These simple and clear words state *exactly what we are intended to believe*. These words also happen to lay the foundation of the true apostolic assembly of Jesus Christ by way of his apostles.

People holding other views simply cannot quote Scripture like this that simply and clearly states their positions. No apostle ever simply preached that God is a Trinity of Persons and the Second Person of the godhead who robed himself in flesh and came to earth. Similarly, no apostle ever simply preached that Jesus Christ is the very person of YHWH God who incarnated Himself as a man. Neither one of these man-made doctrines is simply stated as such anywhere in the Bible.

Our opening passage is not alone, nor has it been taken out of context. In no way is it an exception to other usual and customary descriptions of Jesus. And yet, for some entirely groundless reason, this description of the Anointed One is considered miserably inadequate, even heretical, by the great majority of professing believers if it is not immediately supplemented and "improved" upon by man's extrabiblical ideas! That is, if you tell most people that you believe Jesus is a man who was approved of God, whom God made Lord and Christ and raised from the dead and that's all he is, they will call you a heretic and dissociate from you. We know this by experience. How can it be wrong, let alone heretical, to confess belief in Christ exactly the way that the apostles *constantly and consistently preached and clearly explained him to be*?

So in this section we are going to address what could suitably be called "the elephant in the room." That is, we are going to look at *a great many* Scriptures that *matter-of-factly describe* and explain that Jesus the Messiah is the human descendant of King David who was foreknown by God and has been highly exalted by God. In doing so we will also describe and defend our view that *those other positions have misinterpreted Christ's role as God's perfect representative to mankind* and have confused such passages by "identifying" Christ as "personally" being that God whom Jesus represented, which idea Jesus himself clearly denounced many times!

But first let's ask whether "Representative" is a good choice of words for describing Jesus. What Scriptures give us the authority or set the precedence for this word and the view it symbolizes? Well, it's the following, some of which we've already mentioned:

> [22]For Moses indeed said to the fathers, "The Lord God will raise up a prophet for you from among your brothers, like me. You shall *listen to him in all things* whatever he says to you." (Acts 3:22)

> [1]God, having in the past spoken to the fathers through the prophets at many times and in various ways, [2]has at the end of these days *spoken to us by his Son*, whom he appointed heir of all things, through whom also he made the worlds. (Hebrews 1:1–2)

> For I spoke not from myself, but *the Father who sent me, he gave me a commandment, what I should say*, and what I should speak. (John 12:49)

These verses embody the meaning of what the word "Representative" means. In Jesus, God raised up a prophet, through whom God would speak to us; therefore, in that capacity Jesus represents the Father to us. Jesus himself testifies that he spoke by commandment from God. This language couldn't be clearer in explaining that Jesus was, in this sense of speaking for God, God's representative.

In Trinitarianism, it is theorized that it was "God the Son" who was incarnated somewhat in the pagan sense of Acts 14:11, and that is who was speaking the words that God the Father gave. In Onenessianism, it is imagined that it was God the Father Himself who incarnated Himself, thereby becoming a son to Himself. *Neither of these views are what Jesus ever said of himself*. They are both, however, clearly contradicted by Jesus' words. In the first case it was the Lord God who would raise up a prophet, not the second person in a Trinity. In the second case, Jesus clearly said he didn't speak from himself, which utterly demolishes the Onenessian view that Jesus is just an incarnation of the person of the Father.

Let's consider how similar these two positions are to each other:

> A) There are absolutely no Scriptures saying that God consists of three persons. This is a huge problem for those supporting the Trinity. And yet, as many of us have discovered, Trinitarians seem totally unfazed by this glaringly obvious problem. They have literally hundreds of verses that they feel "prove" the Trinity, even though no biblical passage ever calls God that or describes Him as such, and many verses can be quoted to refute the theory. Furthermore, most Trinitarians are quite adamant that if you don't believe in the Trinity you are most likely, if not definitely, not saved. The Trinity is, thus, an extrabiblical "revelation," which really means you have to believe beyond what the Bible says in order to receive it.

> B) Likewise with Onenessianism, there is *not one verse* that simply and clearly states that Jesus is an incarnation of God the Father, or that Jesus is the very person of YHWH God Himself, or that God became a son to Himself, or that the person of Jesus is made of dual natures of humanity and deity, or that when the Bible talks about Jesus as son it is referring to his impersonal flesh, but when it is speaking of God or Father it is speaking of his deity. And yet these are fundamental "truths," according to most Onenessians, and if you don't believe in them, according to them, you most likely aren't a true, saved believer! Oneness is, thus, an extrabiblical "revelation," which really means you have to believe beyond what the Bible says in order to receive it.

So you see, even though the results appear different, the method Onenessians use is actually very similar to that of Trinitarians. The end result is to destroy the actual faith spelled out in the Bible and replace it with a man-made imitation, which is idolatry.

Furthermore, there are *literally hundreds of verses that clearly and consistently teach against* the Oneness view by stating or showing that *God the Father is numerically personally distinct from His Son*, Jesus *Christ*. Usage of the very title *Christ* is really all the evidence that many passages need because being *anointed* is by biblical definition a role *someone cannot take upon himself*. And yet Onenessians often *seem* just as *unfazed* as Trinitarians are at the complete lack of Scriptures that state, explain, or expound on their position in simple terms.

We are not at all saying that either group *ignores* the problem. Rather, we are asserting that both groups have their ready-to-order responses (we could honestly call them "excuses") that make these volumes of Scriptures of no effect through their respective traditions of men.

For example, according to Oneness writer Jason Dulle, quoted below, those hundreds of verses are, ironically, a huge *"problem."* They are definitely a problem for them, but not for us. For us that would be like saying that "the commandment not to tempt God is a problem, but... " We would expect a response like this from someone expecting Jesus to jump from a pinnacle to prove he is God's Son. But we wouldn't expect such a statement from someone who wanted to live by every word of God. It begs the question, *why is the sheer volume of descriptions of Jesus throughout the Bible a problem*? Why are the bulk of the descriptions of Jesus not rather the true descriptions of what we are really supposed to believe, understand, and confess about Jesus the Anointed One? Why is the practice of *"reading into a small number of verses what they don't actually say or expound on"* not counted as *"the problem,"* instead of the clear bulk of Scriptures to the contrary?

I will tell you the answer without the sugar coating of political correctness: it is because Gnosticism is all about reading a hidden, esoteric meaning into the text that *allows them to feel a certain "spiritual exceptionalism" over other "less spiritually enlightened" individuals*. In a word, it is spiritual *arrogance*. The opposite of that spiritual arrogance is to "receive with meekness the engrafted word which is able to save your souls" (James 1:21). But don't take my word for it—here's what Jesus says:

> ¹⁶Jesus therefore answered them, "*My teaching is not mine, but his who sent me.* ¹⁷*If anyone desires to do his will, he will know about the teaching, whether it is from God, <u>or</u> if I am speaking from myself.* ¹⁸*He who speaks from himself seeks his own glory*, but he who seeks the glory of *him who sent him* is true, and no unrighteousness is in him." (John 7:16–18)

Jesus said he was speaking from God, not from himself. He didn't claim the Oneness position at all! So Jesus himself tells us that even his doctrine isn't his, but the Father's who sent him. He also says that those who speak from themselves, who add to and take away from the word of God according to their own opinions, do so to seek their own glory, and by that act reveal their unrighteousness. That is what Jesus said; don't shoot the messenger.

Thus all Christians should give great caution to any teachings *or attitudes* that originated outside the Bible and especially those extrabiblical opinions and formulations that originated in Gnosticism. And the truth is, historically speaking, Gnosticism was where that *hidden meaning* or *spiritual revelation* type of attitude originated.

In contrast to the secrecy of Gnosticism, with its hidden mysteries and unwritten traditions, the apostles had quite an open attitude toward what they were preaching and teaching. That is, they expressed no inclination toward hiding the truth in mysterious sayings. Quite to the contrary, they wrote such things as these...

> ¹²Having therefore such a hope, we use great boldness [or plainness/openness] of speech, ¹³and *not as Moses, who put a veil on* his face...

> ¹Therefore seeing we have this ministry, even as we obtained mercy, we don't faint. ²But we have *renounced the hidden things* of shame, not walking in craftiness, nor handling the word of God deceitfully; but *by the manifestation of the truth* commending ourselves *to every man's conscience* in the sight of God. ³Even if our Good News is veiled, it is veiled in those who perish; ⁴in whom *the god of this world has blinded the minds of the unbelieving*, that the light of the Good News of the glory of Christ, who is the image of God, should not dawn on them. (2 Corinthians 3:12–4:4)

Whereas Jesus had told the disciples that he spoke in parables, this was not the method the apostles used to preach and teach the gospel. In fact, they said that *if* what they were saying was veiled or hidden at all, it was *only hidden to those who were unbelievers!* That means that if someone believes in a teaching or doctrine *that is not clearly spelled out, explained, and expounded upon in the Scripture provided by the apostles*, but instead is something different than what is spelled out, *that doctrine is a teaching of disbelief in the apostles' doctrines*, and thus not a biblical truth!

In order to make his message clear, Paul contrasted verse 3:12 with the veil over Moses' face. The contrast he made was between that which was hidden and that which is now made clear. The Greek word Paul used (which is translated as "boldness" in the quote above) carries with it the idea of freedom of speech:

> NT:3954 parreesia, refers properly to one's *freedom to say anything*... and thence to *straightforwardness and openness in speech*. In the Greek realm this word group occurs above all among political authors. *Parressia is virtually the equivalent of the "freedom (of speech)"* of free citizens in the Attic democracy (Demosthenes Or. 111.3 f.), which admittedly existed only among equals...[1]

---

[1] *Exegetical Dictionary of the New Testament*

Paul used great freedom of speech in making known what he was teaching. All of this should tell us that we shouldn't be looking for hidden or veiled meanings in the teachings of the apostles. Rather, *we should be looking for what they were plainly, clearly, and openly telling us*. Does this not indicate that any idea viewing the very large bulk of Scriptures on a topic as "problematic" should be instantly held with the highest suspicion?

This begs yet another question: if the apostles used such great plainness of speech, why didn't their speech sound like that of Trinitarians or Onenessians? The answer is simple. It's because that isn't what they were preaching or teaching! The apostles were preaching and teaching something different from the Trinity or Oneness!

So not only should we read the Bible in such a way as to glean what it is simply saying; we should also shun teachings that can only be found by reading between the lines, particularly those ideas that make other Scriptures null and void. If we observe anything about the way both Trinitarians and Onenessians try to show their doctrines in the Scripture, it is their *constant negating and denigrating of what the Bible clearly and abundantly explains and describes, particularly about who and what Jesus Christ truly is*.

This is what we come up against in considering Jason Dulle's attitude regarding the very numerous Scriptures that speak directly on the topic of Christ's relationship to his Father. Dulle himself notes he is up against a problem of some "magnitude" (in support of Onenessianism) in explaining why such passages can't really mean what they so clearly and plainly state. Here is how Dulle explains this problem:

> To convey a sense of <u>the magnitude of the problem confronting us</u>, consider this small sampling of passages in which a clear distinction is made between the Father, Son, and Spirit: In the Great Commission, Jesus said all power was given to Him in heaven and in earth (Matthew 28:18). To be given something implies a distinction between one who gives and one who receives, and thus a distinction between Jesus and the one who gave Him all power.

Jesus said the Father was greater than Himself (John 14:28). 'Greater' is a comparative term that implies the presence of two distinct entities. Surely Jesus did not mean to say He was greater than Himself! On another occasion He said, 'The Son can do nothing of himself, but what he sees the Father do; for whatever he does, the Son does likewise. For the Father loves the Son and shows him all things that he himself does' (John 5:19–20; see also 3:32). Here we have one showing, and one doing. *Clearly Jesus is not showing Himself what to do*. In another context He plainly said of His own ability, 'I can of mine own self do nothing' (John 5:30). Even the words Jesus taught were first given Him by the Father (John 12:49–50). Once again we have one giving, and one receiving. *All such statements point to a genuine distinction between Father and Son*.

Furthermore, Jesus said, '... even as I have kept my Father's commandments, and abide in his love' (John 15:10b). One cannot keep their own commandments and abide in their own love. Such a statement implies the existence of *one who gives* the commandment, *and one who keeps* the commandment; one who loves, and one who abides in that love. Jesus spoke of the Father as being with Him (John 8:29), and Himself as proceeding from and being sent by the Father (John 8:42; 14:24; 16:27–28; 17:8, 18), returning to the Father (John 16:5, 7, 10), and as being sanctified by the Father (John 10:36). The Father is even said to honor the Son (John 8:55).

Jesus told His disciples He would pray to the Father to send them the Spirit. The Spirit is said to proceed from the Father, speaking not of Himself, but speaking that which He will hear (Hear from whom? Himself?). The Spirit is even said to glorify Jesus (John 14:16–17; 15:26; 16:13–14). On another occasion Jesus said that if we love Him, then His Father will love us, and they will come to us and make their abode with us (John 14:23). If there is only one God, and both Jesus and the Father are that God, why does Jesus

> speak of the Father and Himself in the plural? Finally, Jesus said, 'My Father has not left me alone; for I always do those things that please him' (John 8:29). Did He mean to say He always pleased Himself? It seems <u>evident</u> that Jesus was speaking of the Father as being <u>someone other than Himself</u>.[2]

It is simply amazing that such verses are a *magnitude* of a *problem,* as if they are a threat to a core teaching. For us, Dulle has just captured exactly what these verses are saying... *and then swiftly rejected their clear and obvious meaning!* What, we ask, needs to be added to them by man's reasoning abilities? What, pray tell, is wrong with looking at these Scriptures and accepting that these aren't the problem, but that these "*hundreds of distinctions* we find in the NT between Father and Son" (quoting Dulle) *are the gospel truth, and anything that doesn't align with these hundreds are actually the problem?* Mr. Dulle is right about one thing: there are, at our count, roughly 578 verses at a minimum in the NT where God and Jesus the Anointed are clearly and irrefutably referred to as "personally" different individuals in one way or another. There are even more if one counts the verses that have "unclear" mentions of both Father and son together in the same passage.

The actual "problem" is that Mr. Dulle has simply failed to "receive with meekness" (James 1:21) what he admits these Scriptures describe! We quote from above, "Such a statement *implies* the existence *of one who gives* the commandment, *and one who keeps* the commandment..." Here we have Dulle himself noting there are two "who's" being testified to in the Scriptures. But for Dulle these passages only "imply" something, and this then has become Dulle's "yea, has God said" declaration: "Yea, has God's word said that there are two who's, the Father and the Son? No, that can't be right, for

---

[2] Jason Dulle, http://www.onenesspentecostal.com/ugstsymposium.htm (emphasis mine).

God knows that... xxx," and thus he proceeds to insert his idea of what God's word means but never even says let alone explains! Truly *that* is what we should consider to be "a magnitude of a problem!"

Following, then, is the way that Jason Dulle proposes his own brand-new solution to the so-called problem that the magnitude of the Scriptures impose against the Oneness position. Unfortunately, the true Son of God doctrine, which Dulle himself admits is spelled out in hundreds of Scriptures, is not given even as an *unviable option* here, since he had already ruled that out prior to this next passage of his:

> When it comes to reconciling the Biblical distinctions between Father and Son with Biblical monotheism we are met with *only a few viable options*. We could conclude that:
>
> 1. It is a separation between two divine essences (Bitheism, Tritheism).
> 2. It is a distinction between two divine persons within one divine essence (Binitarianism, Trinitarianism).
> 3. It is a distinction within Jesus, between His divine nature (identified as "Father") and His human nature (identified as "Son").
> 4. *It is a distinction between YHWH's transcendent (cosmic) and incarnate modes of existence.*
>
> ... I will argue that *only option four can do full justice to the Father-Son distinction, while at the same time maintaining God's uni-personal nature, the deity of Christ, and the unity of His person.*[3]

---

[3] Jason Dulle, accessed 8/3/2015, "Avoiding the Achilles Heels of Trinitarianism, modalistic monarchianism, and Nestorianism: The Acknowledgement and Proper Placement of the Distinction Between Father and Son," http://www.onenesspentecostal.com/ugstsymposium.htm.

This is a clear case of starting with a preconceived denominational bias, and then proceeding to justify it at any cost. It betrays a loyalty to the error of man's traditions rather than to the word of God preached by the apostles, which is truth. The proof of this is in the acknowledgement of the sheer volumes of scriptures that need to first be explained away through artificial, man-made ideas, rather than to receive them as the truth that sets free.

In case you didn't notice, Dulle listed and ruled out the common Oneness "dual-nature" belief in point three. Yet for whatever reason he decided not to label it as such. Then, instead of going to the Scriptures for his position, he simply took the liberty of inventing and proposing *yet another new doctrine*. There is no Scripture teaching that Christ consists of distinctions "between YHWH's transcendent (cosmic) and incarnate modes of existence." Apparently Mr. Dulle has forgotten the exhortation to "teach no other doctrine" and "to teach no other Jesus" either! Otherwise, perhaps Mr. Dulle would care to quote chapter and verse where this teaching of YHWH's "modes of existence" is spelled out and explained, or better yet preached by the apostles, and further yet is taught in the OT schoolmaster that brings us to the true Christ. Perhaps it is right next to the lost biblical verse where the word Trinity is coined and its doctrinal elements of "one substance in three persons" are spelled out.

For the record, our Bible doesn't exhort us to give respect to misrepresentations of the gospel of truth. It tells us ever so clearly that if anyone preaches any other gospel than the apostles preached, they are to be accursed (Galatians 1:6–11).

What is the difference between the Trinitarians saying that God is one substance in three persons and Dulle saying the difference between Christ and the Father is a difference between God's "transcendent (cosmic) mode and incarnate mode"? There is no difference apart from some holding one opinion while others hold another: they are both man-made opinions and nothing more! Furthermore, they are both equally contrary to what the Bible actually describes! Remember, again, that no father was ever a son to himself and no son was ever his own father. These very terms are all we need to express and explain the personal and moral relational differences between Jesus and the Father. We don't need man-made theories such as Dulle has invented and imagined.

Dulles' basic problem is simply that he recognizes that hundreds of Scriptures aren't in harmony with the Oneness position, so rather than discarding Onenessianism in favor of what the Bible actually says (as many of us have done), he is left searching for an alternate meaning to *explain away what those verses do say*. This is exactly how the Trinitarians deal with Scriptures that refute their false teaching. The problem isn't in the Scriptures themselves, but in people's willingness to receive them. The symptom of this unwillingness shows itself in methods of interpretation used to weaken, neutralize, and then ultimately contradict what the Scriptures actually do teach.

The real solution is simply to get back to what the Bible *clearly* teaches. So in this section that is what we are going to do. We are going to bring to light a hearty sampling of this *"magnitude of Scriptures"* that clearly teaches the *personal distinctions* between Jesus the Anointed One and his God and Father, who is also our God and Father. That is the purpose in this fourth section.

> [16]Jesus said to her, "Mary." She turned and said to him, "Rhabbouni!" which is to say, 'Teacher!' [17]Jesus said to her, "Don't touch me, for I haven't yet ascended to my Father; but go to my brothers, and *tell them, I am ascending to my Father and your Father, to my God and your God."* (John 20:16–17)

CHAPTER EIGHTEEN

The Synoptic Gospels

The book of the generation [literally *genesis/beginning*] of Jesus Christ, the Son of David, the Son of Abraham. (Matthew 1:1)

With this verse begin the Synoptic Gospels, which are traditionally held to be three out of four of the writings from eyewitness accounts of the Lord Jesus' time on earth.

Early in my writing ministry, I put together a collection of all the biblical purposes and reasons for being baptized into the name of Jesus Christ. It is still, I believe, a very pertinent study. You can find it in Appendix Four at the back of this book. The intent was to show just how firmly established in the Bible the practice of calling on Jesus' name at the time of water baptism is. The point was that not only do we have biblical examples of baptism, but there are also several *clearly stated purposes* for being baptized "into Jesus Christ"; for example, "for remission of sins" (Luke 24:47, Acts 2:38, 10:43), or to be "buried with him by baptism into death" (Romans 6:4 and Colossians 2:12).

In contrast with these many Scriptures and examples, the Trinitarians have their one, sole verse referring to water baptism: Matthew 28:19. It doesn't explain what the Trinitarians claim, nor did anyone in the Bible ever apply it to support the Trinitarian claim.

Such lack of biblical support is also true of the Oneness position that Jesus Christ is supposedly an incarnation of the very person of God the Father. It isn't that they, like Trinitarians, don't have a number of Matthew 28:19 *type* verses to turn to; rather, it's that they have absolutely no Scriptures that simply explain or expound upon this belief, or any examples of an apostle preaching such a concept. The Oneness doctrine can only be taught the way the Trinity is: by quoting proof texts and claiming they really mean something they don't actually say, all the while negating and neutralizing absolutely all the Scriptures that set out to describe the relationship of Jesus the Anointed One to His God and Father who anointed him.

This is absolutely not the case in connection with the true, biblical Son of God doctrine. Declaring and defending the Son of God doctrine over against the Oneness doctrine is very much like comparing baptism in Jesus' name over against the Trinitarian use of the titles. To the contrary of Modalism, the Bible is brimming with example after example and explanation after explanation of the relationship, meaning and ramifications of the true Son of God's relationship to his God and Father.

The three books of Matthew, Mark, and Luke contain a total of 76 passages that clearly, distinctly, and irrefutably describe Jesus the Anointed One as personally distinct from God. Those verses are listed in a footnote for anyone who wishes to look them up.[1] We won't be quoting or covering all of them, just a significant amount suitable for this study.

We covered what the gospels say about the birth of Christ in Chapter Twelve, so we won't discuss that again here. Suffice it to say that he was made and born of a woman of the offspring of David according to the flesh, and his birth (nativity, genealogy, and beginning) happened in Bethlehem some 2,000 years ago according to all three of the Synoptic Gospel accounts.

---

[1] The following verses are the places where Jesus is clearly and irrefutably held in personal distinction from God the Father in the Synoptic Gospels:
Matthew 2:15; 3:16, 17; 7:24; 9:6–8; 10:32, 33; 11:25, 27; 12:18, 32, 50; 14:33; 15:13; 16:15–16, 17, 27; 17:5; 18:10, 11–14, 19, 35; 19:4; 20:23; 22:43–44; 23:9–10; 24:34–36; 25:34; 26:29, 39, 42, 53; 27:46, 54;
Mark 1:1, 11–12; 8:38; 9:7, 37; 10:27(w/Jn 5); 12:35–36; 13:32; 14:36, 61–62; 15:34; 16:19;
Luke 1:31–32, 35; 2:22, 26, 27–30, 40, 49, 52; 3:21–22; 4:18, 41; 6:12; 7:15–16; 9:20–22, 26, 35–36, 47–48; 10:16, 21, 22; 12:8–10; 18:19; 20:41–42; 22:29, 41–42, 69; 23:34, 46; 24:19, 49.

**Jesus' Baptism and God's Testimony Regarding Jesus
(It is <u>impossible</u> for God to lie.)**

Father   Mother   Son
Not "My beloved human nature!"

In Matthew 2:15, we read that Jesus was called out of Egypt as God's Son (that is, not God calling to Himself, but rather, as in the case of Aaron, no man takes this honor upon himself, Hebrews 5:4). Then in Matthew 3:16–17, we come to the scene of Jesus' baptism. This is where God Himself makes a certain very clear and meaningful testimony regarding Jesus:

> [16]Jesus, when he was baptized, went up directly from the water: and behold, the heavens were opened to him. He saw the Spirit of God descending as a dove, and coming on him. [17]Behold, a voice out of the heavens said, *"This is my beloved Son*, with whom I am well pleased." (Matthew 3:16–17; also found in Mark 1:11 and Luke 3:22)

Here we have God's explicit revelation and confession of who Jesus the Anointed is: he is God's Son. He isn't "God the Son," and he isn't "God incarnate." He is God's Son whom God is *with*. It is impossible for God to lie, but it is certainly possible for men to lie about what God said and meant by what He said! In saying this, the Bible used a Greek relative pronoun. In other words, this is another case where we have God as one "who" in clear distinction from His Son as another "who." *But this time it is God Himself making this proclamation.* How many other messages did God audibly preach in the Bible? And yet still Onenessians and Trinitarians won't hear!

So this distinction in "whos" is God-who-can't-lie's testimony of His Son. God had no reason not to be clear, open, and truthful here. Onenessianism treats God's straightforward declaration as a lie that has to be interpreted and rephrased to mean what they want it to mean. That is because what God said here does not at all mean, "This is me, YHWH, robed in human flesh." Are we to believe that God Himself was ashamed of the Oneness gospel? That's ludicrous!

Furthermore, Jesus' baptism isn't the only place where God made this audible declaration.

> While he was still speaking, behold, a bright cloud overshadowed them. Behold, a voice came out of the cloud, saying, "This is my beloved Son, in whom I am well pleased. Listen to *him*" (Matthew 17:5; also Mark 9:7 and Luke 9:35).

Again, God who cannot lie (i.e., Titus 1:2 and Hebrews 6:18) called Jesus *someone third person to Himself*. He said this by referring to His Son with the personal pronoun "him," [Gr. *autoú*] in contradistinction to Himself as "I." This statement, out of the very mouth of God Himself, *clearly and concisely refutes Onenessianism.*

What arrogance Onenessians have, then, to think they know better than God Himself!

What reason would God have to lie or be at all misleading about this relationship, which He reiterated exactly as He had stated at Jesus' baptism? We can think of none. So we have it out of the mouth of God at two different events as testified by three different writers! Why is this simple, profound truth so hard for so many professing Christians to accept? God had told King David that a son would proceed out of David's bodily organs and would be God's Son, and here that very same God is calling this offspring of David His "son in whom He is well pleased." God agrees with Jesus that He is with and in Jesus, but apparently God Himself could not, would not, and did not bring Himself to agree with Onenessians that He *is* Jesus or that Jesus is He!

Recall also that Jesus said regarding God being "in" him:

> ²¹That they may all be *one; even as you, Father, are in me, and I in you*, that they also may be one in us; that the world may believe that you sent me. ²²The glory which you have given me, I have given to them; that they may be one, even as we are one; ²³I in them, and you in me, that they may be perfected into one; that the world may know that you sent me, and loved them, even as you loved me. (John 17:21–23)

This is biblical oneness: whatever oneness Jesus shares with the Father is the very same oneness that we will share with the Father. This is not what Onenessians are implying when they proclaim their idea of Jesus' "oneness" with the Father. This is the Bible interpreting the Bible, the clear passages interpreting the less clear verses. God is in Jesus, and Jesus is in God, in the same way in which God is in us and we in Him when he dwells in us and we walk in His ways and His will... just exactly as Jesus did! There is no biblically stated reason to believe that the Father meant or was referring to anything other than this unity of Him being "in" (as in dwelling in) the relative pronoun "who" of Jesus Christ. That is God's publicly proclaimed testimony of Jesus, and the Bible says let God be true and every man a liar (Romans 3:4)! It is a tragedy to our Christian faith that Trinitarian and Oneness philosophies have brought such complexity and confusion to these matters. But, glory to God for being so clear and articulate!

Jesus' Temptation

We read that directly after Jesus' baptism he was led into the wilderness to be tempted. Here is another very clear and powerful testimony that Jesus is not the person of God.

> Then Jesus was led up by the Spirit into the wilderness to be tempted by the devil. (Matthew 4:1)

Just as we have a number of Scriptures that reiterate and strengthen baptism into the name of Jesus Christ, we also have other Scriptures that reiterate how Jesus Christ was tempted. To begin with, we know that he was neither God nor the person of God because of very clear passages such as this:

> [13] Let no man say when he is tempted, "I am tempted by God," *for God can't be tempted by evil*, and *he himself tempts no one.* [14] But each one is tempted, when he is drawn away by his own lust, and enticed. [15] Then the lust, when it has conceived, bears sin; and the sin, when it is full grown, brings forth death. (James 1:13–15)

When Trinitarians put forth their doctrine, they do so by redefining certain established biblical truths. For example, they redefine the lone God of the OT to be One God substance in three persons. Well, in order to make the temptation passages "fit" their doctrine, Onenessians likewise simply redefine both "self" and "temptation" to be something other than what the Bible describes. This is probably the most important place where Jesus' "wolves in sheep's clothing" analogy fits the Oneness doctrine of God "robing Himself in flesh." If God merely robed Himself in flesh while Jesus remained 100% God, then it could only have been the person of God that was tempted when Jesus was tempted.

But James taught that the very person, the "himself" (Gr. "*autós*"), of God cannot be tempted, nor does He tempt anyone. Contrary to both the Trinity and Oneness doctrines, the Son of God was tempted as to his personal self, his "*autós*"; thus, explicitly, "he himself" and not just his so-called human nature:

> ¹⁷Therefore *he was obligated in all things to be made like his brothers*, that he might become a merciful and faithful high priest in things pertaining to God, to make atonement for the sins of the people. ¹⁸For in that <u>he himself</u> has suffered being tempted, he is able to help those who are tempted. (Hebrews 2:14–18)

The Greek "*péponthen autós*" ["he himself"] here explicitly states that he personally experienced temptation. This is speaking of his very person, not merely his "human nature." (Keep in mind that <u>no</u> Scripture describes Jesus as distinct between a mythological "deific" nature in contrast to a "human" nature; such an idea is as artificial and man-made as the Trinity is). This Scripture *totally refutes the false notion that Jesus was personally God but was only tempted as to his human nature*. It absolutely proves that those who interpret other verses to mean Jesus was somehow God incarnate are absolutely mistaken. To the contrary, this passage explains in specific detail that Jesus was tempted in his very person, which would be utterly impossible if he were God. This is how Incarnationists make a sham of Jesus' overcoming: by implying he was only tempted as to his human nature and not that he was tempted to the very core of his personal being, as the Bible clearly teaches!

In the previous passage, James described what it means, biblically, to be tempted. Applying this to Jesus clearly shows how repulsed Onenessians and Trinitarians actually are by Scripture. James said, "Every *man* is tempted when *he* is drawn away *of his own lust* and enticed." That is Scripture, penned by James. Nowhere does the Bible say that Jesus was only tempted in his impersonal human nature while remaining personally God as to his deific nature. That is how both Onenessians and Trinitarians reinterpret the Bible to make it fit their theories, rather than allowing their minds to conform to what it says.

Typically, Onenessians will say that Jesus was 100% man and 100% God. If they truly believe so, we need to ask, was the "man" part of Jesus also God? If not, then why are they so adamantly against the Scriptural teaching we uphold; namely, that Christ, personally, was only a man? We further need to ask, if he was (as in Onenessianism) inseparably both man and God at the same time, in what way could or did he stop being God long enough to be tempted in all points as a man, since God cannot be tempted? In order to "change natures," did he do something like the equivalent of jumping into a proverbial phone booth like Superman? Or perhaps he wiggled his nose like Samantha in the TV show *Bewitched*?

This is a legitimate question because Onenessians do say things like this:

> ...Whenever Jesus speaks in Scripture *we must determine* whether He is speaking as man or as God... Sometimes it is easy to get confused when the Bible describes Jesus in these two different roles, especially when it describes Him acting in both roles in the same story. For example He could sleep one minute and calm the storm the next minute. He could speak as a man one moment and then as God the next moment.[2]

---

[2] David Bernard, *The Oneness of God*, 87–88.

The initial false dilemma with such a position is that Jesus said he was given such authority; which is not the same as it being inherent to his person as Onenessians teach. The major problem with the above Oneness opinion is that it contradicts what the Bible explicitly teaches. The Bible doesn't teach that Jesus was only tempted as far as his human nature goes. It explicitly teaches that "he himself" was tempted:

> ...he also himself... *he was obligated in all things to be made like his brothers...* in that *he himself* has suffered being tempted, he is able to help those who are tempted. (Hebrews 2:14–18)

"He himself" was made like his brother, just as "he himself" was tempted. The Bible doesn't separate Jesus into dual natures, or any kind of "roles" for that matter! This shows how clearly the Onenessians must add to and take away from what the Bible clearly teaches in order to support and defend their beliefs regarding Jesus.

The Oneness position obviously teaches another doctrine and another Christ in a way that we are not supposed to do! No human has the authority to add teachings to the Bible! The crux of the matter is that everything Jesus said or did, he said or did as a man who was fully authorized by, and yet remained in submission to, God. As we've seen, Jesus reiterated this truth repeatedly!

The Onenessian response is that this dual nature thing is a mystery and that is why it isn't spelled out in the Bible. Well, if it is a "mystery" religion, then how is their mystery any different than the mystery of the Trinity? For when Trinitarians can't explain how three persons can be one God, they just claim it is a mystery no one can understand. The reason the Bible doesn't explain how Jesus can change back and forth from man to God at will is the same reason the Bible doesn't explain how God can be three persons and yet still be one God. It is because that isn't what the Bible means, and too many people don't sufficiently believe the Bible when it does say and explain what it means! That is the real problem with both the Oneness and the Trinity doctrines.

For more evidence of this, let's consider what Oneness preacher Anthony Mangun said about Jesus, which starkly reveals his actual view of Christ. As you read his view and consider what the Scriptures say about Jesus' very real temptations, ask yourself if this Jesus that Mangun is talking about could ever have been sincerely tempted in all things the way you and I are truly tempted, as the Bible clearly states. In this passage, Mangun is comparing his view of Jesus to that of Dan Brown's in *The Da Vinci Code*.

> They called him a man because he was flesh and blood, but he was housing the Father Almighty God... I'm going to tell you Mr. Da Vinci Code, he never married... He had enough pressure on him being God, he didn't need to be married. Can you imagine [him] coming home and sitting down... Mary [speaking to Jesus]: 'Why you ten minutes late? Where've you been today? Who you been talking to? What you getting me for Christmas? I didn't approve that new bass boat!' He had enough pressure on him without being married... But can you imagine the pressure on her? 'Hey, God, what's happening today? What went on over the other side of the world today?' He never had a child in spite of what Dan Brown has written; blasphemous!... He never had a child. He was the absolutely almighty God, born without sin.[3]

So you see, in the Onenessian view, Jesus personally is thoroughly and inseparably God incarnate. He "has" flesh, but that is only an impersonal temple that his deific person "dwells in." The "human" part of Jesus, in the Oneness view, is not really 100% human, because he has no human personality; that part of him is all God. This is how the Oneness doctrine makes a sham out of Jesus' true overcoming of sin, just as Trinitarianism makes a sham out of the Shema, the biblical statement that God is indivisibly one.

---

[3] Anthony Mangun, *The Dual Natures of Christ*, Disc 5, "Jesus the Man," track 8 at 0:00–1:55.

Now let's get back to discussing what the Bible teaches about lusts and see if the Onenessian view of Jesus fits the Bible or not.

The Bible says that Jesus was tempted, and in order to be tempted, as James 1:14 states, he had to have "lusts" that could even be tempted in the first place! Only a human could have these kinds of "lusts" (or desires) that "every man" is tempted by. God cannot be tempted; so then, to believe that Jesus could in any way be tempted by sin is to declare absolutely that Jesus is *not* personally God. With God there is no variableness or shadow of turning; you can't temporarily suspend God's repugnance to the evil fruit that sin produces. So in order to claim that Jesus is an incarnation of God, it would first be necessary to redefine the person of God as someone who has lusts that could even be tempted, all of which is totally contrary to Scripture.

As we've said, some try to redefine Jesus' humanity by saying he was only tempted in his impersonal "human nature." This claim redefines Jesus in a way contrary to how he was described in the Bible. Some say that he was only tempted externally by the devil, but not internally; yet that would be to redefine temptation. Biblically, as we've read above, temptation is something that appeals to a human individual's internal (that is, *personal*) lusts. Without redefining God, Christ, and temptation, there is no way around Jesus having been a man. As such, he could not have been God because he *was* truly tempted.

The Bible gives us yet another very clear, "it is written again" type passage that should silence anyone who presumes that Jesus was God incarnate. It says this:

> ¹⁵For we don't have a high priest who can't be touched with the feeling of our infirmities, but one who *has been in all points tempted like we are*, yet without sin. (Hebrews 4:15)

This is what makes all those other excuses invalid. They go against what the Bible definitively describes in detail about Jesus' temptations: *he was tempted in every way, the same way we are.* That's pretty simple, isn't it? Most of all, it is clearly descriptive and definitive! All Christians know very well what it is like for us to be tempted. It isn't all external. It isn't all just some outward appeal. Somehow temptation has a way of sneaking right into the very core of our being and catching us unawares. In fact, real temptation has a way of making us feel as if the sin we want to commit is actually part of who we are! The Bible says Jesus was tempted like that, because he was tempted in all points like we are yet without sin. Anyone who is honest about his temptations will have to agree, because such is common to all mankind.

One of humanity's biggest temptations is the temptation to believe that God doesn't exist, isn't around, or simply doesn't care about our humble situation in the first place. This being the case, how many of us experience temptation while fully aware that we are God incarnate, as in the Oneness view about Jesus? If Jesus was God and was personally tempted like us in all things, how was he tempted not to believe in Himself (God)? How many of us are tempted to believe we don't exist? Furthermore, how many of us are tempted to believe we personally don't exist, *all the while knowing full well that we are God incarnate*? You see, saying that Jesus was tempted *in all points like we are* yet without sin quite simply destroys the theory that Jesus was "Almighty God incarnate." If Jesus was God who cannot be tempted by sin, then he absolutely could not have been tempted in all points the way we are tempted because these are mutually exclusive ideas. That is why James 1:13–15 is an "it is written again" Scripture that destroys any and all "incarnation of God" theories for those whose faith "comes by hearing the word of God."

Let us remember that no Scripture exists that described Jesus' temptation in any terms other than that he was personally tempted. If the word of God had said or explained that Jesus was "tempted as to his human nature but not as to his deific nature," then that position would be called scriptural. It is not in the Scriptures, and that is what makes it extrabiblical, unbiblical and therefore man-made.

We aren't by any means saying that Jesus was a sinner. If you will notice, both James 1 and Hebrews 4 differentiate temptation and lust from the act of sin and its resultant death. "Then the *lust, when it has conceived*, bears sin; and the sin, *when it is full grown, brings forth* death" (James 1:13–15). So we see how James described lust as having to conceive and bear sin. This description makes lust itself like a womb, and sin an act that comes forth from that womb; thus "lust" is not the same as "sin," any more so than every young maiden who has a womb is by that fact pregnant. On the other hand, because every maiden has a womb, that gives them the capacity to bear children. It is in that manner, James tells us, that we, by our lusts, have the capacity to sin; so also Christ, who was tempted in all things like you and me. I heard one pastor explain it like this: "Just because you can't keep the birds from flying overhead, doesn't mean you have to let them nest in your hair. Likewise, just because you have lusts, doesn't mean you have to give in to them and act on them." Putting this last analogy in more biblical terms, the Scriptures say this:

> [16]Don't you know that to whom you present yourselves as servants to obedience, his servants you are whom you obey; whether of sin to death, or of obedience to righteousness? [17]But thanks be to God, that, whereas you were bondservants of sin, you became obedient from the heart to that form of teaching whereunto you were delivered. [18]Being made free from sin, you became bondservants of righteousness. (Romans 6:16–18)

This is why Jesus is called God's servant. He alone out of all mankind truly served God in the kind of obedience described here throughout his entire life.

The Bible clearly defines sin as transgression of the law. Sin isn't a "nature." Rather, sin is something we either commit or omit. It is doing something we shouldn't have done or not doing something we should have done in order to be obedient to the law of God. This is what James described in saying that sin is what is brought forth, as in the act of delivery, out of our lusts, because we acted upon them.

When the Bible says Jesus was tempted and yet without sin, it is simply saying that he never submitted his bodily members (heart, mind, body, or soul) to commit sin. When the devil tempted him, he stayed obedient to God. There is simply no Scripture that teaches that Jesus was made of a different form of humanity than the rest of us. Rather, it clearly teaches that he was made like us in all things. To say that Jesus was not a sinner means nothing more than to say he never committed sin.

> Everyone who sins also commits lawlessness. Sin is lawlessness. (1 John 3:4)

This verse plainly tells us that sin is something we commit. It is only in pagan philosophy that our physical flesh is sinful in "nature" (namely, that sin is somehow in the makeup of physical substance). When God created mankind, he saw that it was very good. In Ezekiel 18, God spoke very clearly to the Israelites, renouncing what is known today as the doctrine of "Original Sin," which is the idea that our flesh itself is sinful. That idea is not true, and God expressed His repugnance at the very idea. God's view is that we each commit sin and thus become corrupted.

Paul wrote that "death passed upon all men..." (Romans 5:12). That is what we "inherited" from our original parents, Adam and Eve, according to God's warning (Genesis 2:17). Those who believe otherwise have been spoiled by the philosophy of later Philosopher-Christians like Augustine, who, after the Gnostics, was the first to interpret Paul in such a philosophical way. For our purposes, we just need to reiterate the Scripture that says Jesus was tempted in all points like us, without sinning. This is one of the strongest points in counteracting the false notion that Jesus was God incarnate as a human. His very temptations prove that theory false. The Scripture stands: *God cannot be tempted by sin or evil.* No Scripture teaches that Jesus was only tempted as to his impersonal human nature; rather, it says he was tempted in all points just like you and me are tempted. He just never yielded to temptation. This is precisely what makes Jesus so worthy of his honor and position, and why God made him "Lord and Christ."

Jesus Was Given Authority

Let's look next at the place where Jesus claimed to have the authority to forgive sins.

> ⁶"But that you may know that *the Son of Man has authority on earth to forgive sins...*" (then he said to the paralytic), "Get up, and take up your mat, and go up to your house." ⁷He arose and departed to his house. ⁸But when the multitudes saw it, they marveled and glorified God, who had <u>given such authority to men</u>. (Matthew 9:6–8)

Here is a perfect example of why we need to interpret the acts and sayings of Jesus through the foundation of the Messiah as an OT concept (see Section Three). Jesus, ever so clearly, defined his authority for us: it was bestowed upon him as *"the son of man," which explicitly refers to the fact that he is a true human being.* Another clear indication was the response of the crowd. They recognized that this authority had been expressly *"given... to men."* We've reiterated over and over that Jesus testified: "*All authority* has been given *to me* in heaven and earth" (Matthew 28:18). In Matthew 11:27, Jesus also said, "All things have been *delivered to me* by my Father." Conversely, nowhere does Jesus ever claim inherent power, authority, or ability. Rather, he is consistently adamant "that I do nothing of *myself*; but as my Father taught me, I speak these things" (John 8:28).

All that is left for us to do then is to believe Jesus at his word. People contrarily believe that the traditions of men explain what he was about better than he. We choose to believe Jesus' clear words.

Jesus was God's Servant

In Matthew 12 we come to another testimony from the Father through a prophecy given to Isaiah:

> Behold, *my servant whom I have chosen*; My beloved in whom my soul is well pleased: I will put my Spirit on him. He will proclaim justice to the nations. (Matthew 12:18)

Here Matthew quoted a prophecy that helps us understand how the disciples interpreted and understood who Jesus was. Clearly God did not have it stated anywhere in the Bible that His servant would be God Himself. Accordingly, in no way did the disciples believe that this servant was an incarnation of the very God who originally uttered these words.

Peter's Confession:
"You are the Anointed One, <u>the Son of</u> the Living God"!

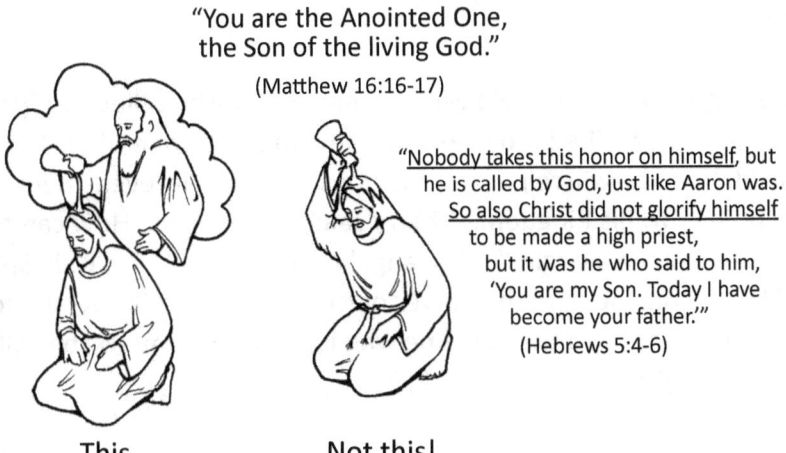

"You are the Anointed One, the Son of the living God."
(Matthew 16:16-17)

"<u>Nobody takes this honor on himself</u>, but he is called by God, just like Aaron was. <u>So also Christ did not glorify himself</u> to be made a high priest, but it was he who said to him, 'You are my Son. Today I have become your father.'"
(Hebrews 5:4-6)

This   Not this!

Now we come to the biblically acceptable confession of Christ:

> ¹⁶Simon Peter answered, "You are **the Christ, the Son of** the living God." ¹⁷Jesus answered him, "Blessed are you, Simon Bar Jonah, for flesh and blood has not revealed this to you, but my Father who is in heaven." (Matthew 16:16–17)

We must keep in mind that our writer, Matthew, would have derived the meaning of the Messiah as God's Son from the descriptions given in the OT Scriptures that we covered in Chapter Six. In particular, the designation refers to the oath from God that David's offspring would be God's Son.

We saw earlier, in Matthew 3:17, that *God had testified that Jesus was His Son*. The fact is that God wasn't the only one to make this confession, nor was Peter. We have it from many witnesses in addition to God and the Apostle Peter...

Jesus— ³⁵"Jesus heard that they had thrown him out, and finding him, he said, 'Do you believe in <u>the Son of God</u>?' ³⁶He answered, 'Who is he, Lord, that I may believe in him?' ³⁷Jesus said to him, 'You have both seen him, and it is he who speaks with you'" (John 9:35–37).

The angel Gabriel— ³²"'He will be great, and will be called <u>the Son of the Most High</u>. The Lord God will give him the throne of his father, David, ³³and he will reign over the house of Jacob forever. There will be no end to his Kingdom.' ³⁴Mary said to the angel, 'How can this be, seeing I am a virgin?' ³⁵The angel answered her, 'The Holy Spirit will come on you, and the power of the Most High will overshadow you. Therefore also the holy one who is born from you will be called <u>the Son of God</u>'" (Luke 1:32–35).

The devil— "The tempter came and said to him, 'If you are <u>the Son of God</u>, command that these stones become bread'" (Matthew 4:3).

The demons— "Behold, they cried out, saying, 'What do we have to do with you, Jesus, <u>Son of God</u>?'" (Matthew 8:29, also Luke 4:41).

The Jews, including the High Priest— ⁷⁰"They all said, 'Are you then <u>the Son of God</u>?' He said to them, 'You say it, because I am.' ⁷¹They said, 'Why do we need any more witness? For we ourselves have heard from his own mouth!'" (Matthew 26:63–65; Mark 14:61 and Luke 22:70–71). Also: "The Jews answered him, 'We have a law, and by our law he ought to die, because he made himself <u>the Son of God</u>'" (John 19:7).

The Centurion— "And the centurion who was standing over-against him, having seen that, having so cried out, he yielded the spirit, said, 'Truly this man was *Son of God*'" (Mark 15:39, YLT).

John the Baptist— "I have seen, and have testified that this is <u>the Son of God.</u>" (John 1:34)

Nathanael— "Nathanael answered him, 'Rabbi, you are <u>the Son of God</u>! You are King of Israel!'" (John 1:49)

The Disciples— "Those who were in the boat came and worshiped him, saying, 'You are truly <u>the Son of God</u>!'" (Matthew 14:33)

Mark— "The beginning of the Good News of Jesus Christ, <u>the Son of God.</u>" (Mark 1:1)

John the Beloved— "But these are written, that you may believe that Jesus is the Christ, <u>the Son of God</u>, and that believing you may have life in his name." (John 20:31)

The Ethiopian— "Then Philip said, 'If you believe with all your heart, you may.' And he answered and said, 'I believe that Jesus Christ is <u>the Son of God.</u>'" (Acts 8:37, NKJV)

The Apostle Paul— "Immediately in the synagogues he proclaimed the Christ, that he is the Son of God." (Acts 9:20)

Alongside all these consistent testimonies of believers and non-believers alike, there is no such list of anyone claiming or believing that Jesus was an incarnation of the very person of the Father, or that God would be a son to Himself.

Furthermore, there is no Scripture teaching that the phrase the "Son of God" means the unbiblical "God the Son." Such an idea would never have entered the minds of any of the saints in this list. To confess Jesus as *"truly"* the Son of God is a biblical, right, and proper confession.

Not My Will But Thine Be Done

Oneness Father and Son

Jesus had an opposing will to that of God the Father. This simply means he was obviously not coequal with God, nor was he an incarnation of the person of God.

> ⁴¹He was withdrawn from them about a stone's throw, and he knelt down and prayed, ⁴²saying, "Father, if you are willing, remove this cup from me. Nevertheless, *not my will, but yours, be done.*" (Luke 22:41–42)

This confession is similar in strength to the truth that Jesus was truly tempted. In this passage Jesus affirmed his very real and personal separation and distinction from the Father: his will. His will, what he personally desired, was radically at odds with the Father's will. We don't find Jesus getting down on his knees and praying, "Hello Father, it's me: you. If my spirit is willing, I could remove this cup from me. Nevertheless, not as my impersonal flesh wills, but as my Spirit which is God the Father wills." Is it really not obvious what a mess and mockery the Oneness position makes out of Jesus' prayer?

We don't find any such description or language anywhere in the Bible that would affirm the Oneness position. But here we have Jesus, as consistently as ever, speaking of the Father in the second person as "you" and of himself in the first person as "me." How could words get any plainer?

This was the very defining moment of Jesus' life. This is where he fulfilled what God had prophesied through Isaiah that God would do with and through him. That is, he was ³"a man of suffering, and acquainted with disease... he was despised and we didn't respect him. ⁴Surely he has borne our sickness, and carried our suffering; yet we considered him plagued, struck by God and afflicted. ⁵But he was pierced for our transgressions, he was crushed for our iniquities... and by his wounds we are healed... ¹⁰Yet it pleased YHWH to bruise *him; he has put him* to grief: when you shall make his soul an offering for sin..." (Isaiah 43:3–5, 10).

It was always God's plan that His Son would die a horrible death to make reconciliation for the sins of His people.

The Parables of Jesus

Teaching by parables was one of Jesus' favorite methods. In one instance he said he wouldn't even teach non-believers without using parables. Of the many parables of Jesus, not one teaches in any way that Jesus is an incarnation of God the Father. The majority of the parables don't even address the relationship of Jesus with God the Father. Those parables that do refer to God and Jesus teach quite plainly that Jesus is not the Father. Here they are:

The Parable of the Marriage— "The Kingdom of Heaven is like a certain king, who made a marriage feast _for his son_..." (Matthew 22:2)

The Parable of the Ten Talents— ¹⁴"For it is like a man, going into another country, who called his own servants, and entrusted his goods to them. ¹⁵To one he gave five talents, to another two, to another one; to each according to his own ability... ³¹But when _the Son of Man_ comes in his glory, and all the holy angels with him, then he will sit on the throne of his glory. ³²Before him all the nations will be gathered, and he will separate them one from another, as a shepherd separates the sheep from the goats... ³⁴Then the King will tell those on his right hand, _'Come, blessed of my Father_, inherit the Kingdom prepared for you from the foundation of the world.'" (Matthew 25:14–15, 31–34)

The Parable of the Wicked Husbandmen— ³³"Hear another parable. There was a man who was a master of a household, who planted a vineyard... leased it out to farmers, and went into another country... ³⁴When the season for the fruit drew near, he sent his servants to the farmers, to receive his fruit. ³⁵The farmers took his servants, beat one, killed another, and stoned another... ³⁷But _afterward he sent to them his son_, saying, 'They will respect my son.' ³⁸But the farmers, when _they saw the son_, said among themselves, '_This is the heir_. Come, let's kill him, and seize his inheritance.' ³⁹So they took him, and threw him out of the vineyard, and killed him. ⁴⁰When therefore the lord of the vineyard comes, what will he do to those farmers?" (Matthew 21:33–40)

The Parable of the Shepherd— ¹¹"I am the good shepherd. The good shepherd lays down his life for the sheep. ¹²He who is a hired hand, and not a shepherd, who doesn't own the sheep, sees the wolf coming, leaves the sheep, and flees... ¹⁴I am the good shepherd. _I know my own, and I'm known by my own;_ ¹⁵_even as the Father knows me, and I know the Father_. I lay down my life for the sheep.. ¹⁷_Therefore the Father loves me, because I lay down my life_, that I may take it again. ¹⁸No one takes it away from me, but I lay it down by myself. I have power to lay it down, and I have power to take it again. _I received this commandment from my Father._" (John 10:11–18)

The Parable of the Unjust Judge— ¹⁸"He also spoke a parable to them that they must always pray, and not give up, ²saying, 'There was a judge in a certain city who didn't fear God, and didn't respect man'... ⁶The Lord said, 'Listen to what the unrighteous judge says. ⁷_Won't God avenge his_ chosen ones, who are crying out to _him_ day and night, and yet he exercises patience with them? ⁸I tell you that _he will_ avenge them quickly. Nevertheless, when the _Son of Man_ comes, will he find faith on the earth?'" (Luke 18:1–8)

In all of the above parables, Jesus presented himself as personally distinct from the Father. Jesus offered no parable in which he presented himself as an incarnation of his Father. Perhaps the following parable is the clearest of them all.

The Parable of the True Vine and the Farmer— *"I am the true vine, and my Father is the farmer.* Every branch in me that doesn't bear fruit, He takes away. Every branch that bears fruit, He prunes, that it may bear more fruit... *I am the vine. You are the branches.* He who remains in me, and I in him, the same bears much fruit, for apart from me you can do nothing." (John 15:1–5)

"I am the Vine and My Father is the Farmer"
- John 15:1

Let's consider this parable in more detail. This is, after all, one of the "I am" statements of Jesus. In this parable God is the farmer, Jesus is the vine, and we are branches of the vine. In this analogy, we are the same substance as Jesus. Just as clearly, Jesus is a different substance and creature from God the Father.

Secular scientists have categorized all life forms in relation to the following hierarchy moving from the top down: kingdom, phylum, class, order, family, genus, and species. You and I are of the animal kingdom, the chordate (backbone) phylum, the mammal class, the primate order, the mankind family, the genus Homo, and the species sapiens. In Jesus' analogy, *Jesus isn't even in the same kingdom as God* the Father. "Kingdom" is the top level of hierarchies of life forms, but Jesus is not there with God, let alone is he the same species or anything in-between. Remember that it was God Himself who authorized man to name all living things.

According to the biblical doctrine of Christ, Jesus was made like us, his brothers, *"in all things."* This analogy of Jesus' fully reiterates and supports this truth. But Jesus takes it to yet another level. According to Jesus, in this analogy, he is the very same organism as those of us who are "in him."

This analogy teaches us that Jesus submitted to the Father, partly as an example to us. It teaches how essential it is that we bear the spiritual fruits of righteousness, and act so as to be pleasing to the Father in the same way as he was and did. This analogy gives us great hope, promise, and direction for our lives. It even addresses God's purpose in creating us: so that we can bear fruit. This analogy, as consistently as anything else in Jesus' teachings or the Synoptic Gospels in general, very clearly and soundly repudiates Modalism and supports, defends, and describes the "true Son of God" doctrine.

In each of the Synoptic Gospels, we find Jesus presented as personally distinct from the Father. This is true in each and every case and context where the gospels are clearly trying to explain things to us.

CHAPTER NINETEEN
The Gospel of John

The Plan became flesh, and lived among us. We saw his glory, such glory as of the one and only Son of the Father, full of grace and truth. (John 1:14)

In the Book of John there are at least 149 passages that teach a clear personal distinction between the Anointed One (Christ) and God the Father.[1] This is an incredible number of Scriptures in light of the fact that John is considered the biblical figure most responsible for establishing a basis for believing Jesus was an incarnation of the Father Himself. In light of these many passages, it is a legitimate question to ask whether or not John believed that Jesus was an incarnation of the Father (as many believe but which he never actually said), or whether these great number of passages to the contrary are the ones that explain John's belief.

---

[1] The following verses are the places where Jesus is clearly and irrefutably held in personal distinction from God the Father in the Book of John:

We've already discussed John 1:1–2, 14 in Chapter Three and will do so again in Chapter Twenty-Seven, so we won't spend much additional time here on that passage. What we would like to note here is that verse 14 describes the one who is made flesh as "the Son of the Father." Again we must observe that nowhere does Scripture ever claim that anyone, including God and Christ, was ever a son to himself or a father to himself. The very words "son" and "Father" should be descriptive enough. Otherwise, it would be like saying it is biblical for one to be a husband to one's self or a wife to one's self.

Trinitarians like to claim that Jesus is a son to the Father, but they don't believe that makes him either subordinate or inferior to the Father, other than in his temporary role as a human. The problem is: that view redefines the very roles of father and son and goes against God's moral code for parents and children.

> [2]"Honor your father and mother," which is the first commandment with a promise: [3]"that it may be well with you, and you may live long on the earth." [4]You fathers, don't provoke your children to wrath, but nurture them in the discipline and instruction of the Lord. (Ephesians 6:2–4 and Exodus 20:12)

We know that Trinitarians are wrong in their extrabiblical tradition because a son is not coequal in time or authority with his father. Therefore, the Trinity is a redefinition of the meaning of the very word "son" and the concept that it represents.

This is likewise the case with the modalistic Oneness practice of *redefining* "son" to mean "the flesh" of the person of Jesus, and "Fa-

---

John 1:14, 18, 29, 36, 49, 51; 2:16; 3:2, 16–17, 34–35; 4:34; 5:17, 19, 20–24, 26–27, 30–31, 36–38, 43, 45; 6:27, 29, 32, 37, 39, 40, 44, 46, 57, 65, 69; 7:16–18, 28–29, 33; 8:16, 18–19, 26–29, 38, 40, 42, 49–50, 54–55; 9:4; 10:15, 17–18, 25, 29, 30, 32, 35–37; 11:22, 27, 41–42; 11:51–52; 12:13, 27, 30, 44, 49–50; 13:1, 3–4, 20, 31–32; 14:1–2, 6–7, 10, 12–13, 16, 20–21, 23–24, 26, 28, 31; 15:1–2, 8–10, 15–16, 23–24, 26; 16:3, 5, 10, 15–17, 23, 25–28, 30, 32; 17:1–15, 18, 21–26; 18:11; 20:17, 21, 31; 21:19.

ther" as "the deity" of the person of Jesus. The only difference is that the former is the Trinitarian result of adding to the word of God, while the latter is the Oneness result of adding to the word of God. Both are also a "taking away," or "subtracting from," because they take away from the biblically established contexts, meanings and usages of the terms as the Bible writers would have given them.

Furthermore, John didn't say that God transmutated into flesh, or that God 'joined' to flesh, or any other of those extrabiblical ideas, suppositions, and inventions that men come up with. John said the word, or plan, was *made* flesh. This also has specific meaning. If it really said what these groups assert it means, then John said that God was made into flesh. That's because they unashamedly declare that since John said the plan "was with God and the plan was God... and the plan was made flesh," it means (to them) the same as saying "God was made flesh." But the Scripture doesn't say "God was made flesh" for very good reason: God cannot change. What did change was that God's plan became a reality. God's plan went from being only in the mind of God to being a reality in our physical universe. God's word/plan is/was conceptual until that concept was made into a human being. This way of understanding John agrees completely with how the writer of Hebrews explained the same event from a different angle:

> [1]God, having in the past spoken to the fathers through the prophets at many times and in various ways, [2]has at the end of these days *spoken to us by his Son*, whom he appointed heir of all things, through whom also he made the worlds. (Hebrews 1:1–2)

Simply stated, God used to speak through prophets, but now He speaks through His Son. God appointed His Son as heir of all things, so, just as Jesus claimed, all power and authority was given to him. Now some (as the Trinitarians do with Genesis 1:26–27) will focus on just the part they want, and say, "See here, it says 'through whom also he made the worlds.'" We'll explore this passage more fully when we examine Hebrews, but in brief, the Trinitarian idea comes from viewing this passage through the pagan notion of an incarnation of deity, as described in Acts 14:11, and also polytheism (many-god-ism), as was renounced by Paul in 1 Corinthians 12. This is why we must keep in mind the biblical idea of God's foreknowledge, which we covered in Chapter Sixteen. If we view these issues within the biblical, Jewish view of God's foreknowledge, we can keep ourselves from being "spoiled by philosophy," as we are warned in Colossians 2:8.

Take, for example, the words of God to Jeremiah the prophet:

> [4]Now the word of YHWH came to me, saying, [5]Before I formed you in the belly I knew you, and before you came forth out of the womb I sanctified you; I have appointed you a prophet to the nations. (Jeremiah 1:4–5)

Are we to believe, by these words, that Jeremiah preexisted his earthly life? Absolutely not. Rather, this is how God speaks based on His absolute foreknowledge. Now, if Jeremiah were to believe God and go out and say, "before I was born God knew me and sanctified me," would we be correct in presuming Jeremiah was claiming that he literally preexisted? No, we'd just be jumping to conclusions and not listening to what was said in context.

This type of "foreknowledge" language is the manner of speaking that the Bible uses for Jesus, and that Jesus uses of himself. This is why it is important to align our way of thinking with the OT law as our Schoolmaster, and not the world of paganism with its ideas of preexistent beings and incarnations of deity.

And just as importantly, we have the rest of the Book of John to help us understand what is meant. That is, unless we willfully choose to be ignorant of all the Scriptures where the gospel speaks quite clearly.

So let's do that instead. Let's look through the Book of John and see whether or not it clearly explains things for us. Let's start with verses where John described Jesus:

> No one has seen God at any time. The one and only Son, who is in the bosom of the Father, he has declared him. (John 1:18)

What does it mean that the Son is in the bosom of the Father? Well, in Luke 16:22–23 we read a parable from Jesus where a man named Lazarus died and was carried by the angels into Abraham's *bosom,* and a beggar is spoken of as seeing Lazarus in Abraham's *bosom.* The word (*kolpos*) in this context simply means lap, or perhaps breast. In John 13:23 we find the disciple John leaning against Jesus' *bosom.* In other words, it is saying that Jesus was held close to God in a place of honor with God, like John was to Jesus. So then, no one has seen God, but they most definitely both saw and touched Jesus (John 1:14 and 1 John 1:1). Jesus is as close as a person can get to God. That's what these passages are telling us.

Now let's consider John the Baptist's testimony. As we read, try to resist the tendency to interpret the way your traditions have conditioned you to read, and try to understand John's language in the Jewish idiomatic way that he would be speaking:

> [26]John answered them saying... [27]"He is *the one who comes after me,* who *is preferred before me*..." [29]The next day, he saw Jesus coming to him, and said, "Behold, *the Lamb of God,* who takes away the sin of the world! [30]This is he of whom I said, 'After me comes a man who is *preferred before me, for he was before me.*'... [34]I have seen, and have testified that *this is the Son of God.*" [35]Again, the next day, John was standing with two of his disciples, [36]and he looked at Jesus as he walked, and said, "Behold, *the Lamb of God!*" (John 1:26–35)

Very simply, the individual whom John is describing is, first the Lamb of God, and secondly the Son of God. From the OT perspective, the title Son of God means he is the promised son of David that God swore by an oath would come out of David's body.

The title "Lamb of God" has to do explicitly with the fact that Christ came into this world to lay down his life for our sins. We've covered this in Isaiah 53:3–12: he was wounded for our transgressions, and his soul was made an offering for sin.

We've also covered God's foreknowledge of the event of Christ's passion. There are those who would jump to conclusions because he was the lamb slain from the foundation of the earth (Revelation 13:8). Yet Hebrews 10:5, 7, 9–14, 18–20 teaches us that in actuality Christ was slain only once, in the end of the earth. So John is using typical biblical imagery to declare that this is the man, sent from God, who would sacrifice his life in payment of our sins.

Moving on, we come to Nathanael's confession of who Jesus is:

> [49]Nathanael answered him, "Rabbi, you are <u>the Son of God</u>! You are <u>King of Israel</u>!" [50]Jesus answered him... [51]... "Most assuredly, I tell you, hereafter you will see heaven opened, and the angels of God ascending and descending on <u>the Son of Man</u>." (John 1:49–51)

So then, within the first chapter of John we have the words of the Bible explaining for us exactly what all these things really mean. It is all so very simple if we allow the Bible to set the meanings for the terms and words it uses. Incarnationists want us to believe that John said one thing in John 1:1–2, 14, but then described something else throughout the rest of his writings! We believe John clearly explained what he meant. The problem is that some readers jump to conclusions over unclear passages that are explained elsewhere differently in John's writings.

If we read John's words through the words of the OT Schoolmaster, we will come up with these conclusions: Jesus is the promised son of David that would come and be the Son of God; and he is also, as was spoken by Isaiah, the one who would lay his life down for our sins as the Lamb of God; and all of this was the plan of God since before the world began. And thus we understand what John meant when he said, and "the plan was made flesh."

Destroy This Temple and in Three Days I Will Raise It Up

In John 2 is found one of the incarnation theorist's favorite proof texts:

> [18]The Jews therefore answered him, "What sign do you show us, seeing that you do these things?" [19]Jesus answered them, "Destroy this temple, and in three days I will raise it up." [20]The Jews therefore said, "Forty-six years was this temple in building, and will you raise it up in three days?" [21]But he spoke of the temple of his body. (John 2:18–21)

The way that some people interpret this passage is a classic case of not seeing the forest for the trees. It's also a classic case of jumping to conclusions. But worst of all, it's a case of not "hearing" Jesus, something he often admonished his disciples to do. And indeed, those who truly are his disciples hear his word, which means all of his word, not just selected portions taken out of context and in isolation from all other Scriptures on the subject.

One thing you will never hear Jesus saying or explaining is that he did this or any other thing of his own inherent power. You will never read anywhere in the Bible that Jesus was able to raise himself from the dead because he was God incarnate. We do have places where Jesus expressly explained how he could make statements like the one above and yet not be God himself. Will you hear him, or man's traditions to the contrary? That is the question.

> [19]Jesus therefore answered them, "Most assuredly, I tell you, *the Son can do <u>nothing</u> <u>of himself</u>*, but what he sees the Father doing. For whatever things he does, these the Son also does likewise. [20]For the Father has affection for the Son, and shows him all things that he himself does. He will show him greater works than these, that you may marvel. [21]For as the Father raises the dead and gives them life, even so the Son also gives life to whom he desires. [22]For the Father judges no one, but *he has given* all judgment to the Son... [26]For as the

Father has life in himself, even so *he gave to the Son also to have life* in himself. ²⁷He *also gave him authority* to execute judgment, because he is a son of man... ³⁰*I can of myself do nothing.*" (John 5:19–30)

¹⁷Therefore the Father loves me, because *I lay down my life, that I may take it again.* ¹⁸No one takes it away from me, but I lay it down by myself. I have power to lay it down, and I have power to take it again. <u>I received this commandment</u> from my Father. (John 10:17–18)

In what way did Jesus explain himself to be the very person of God incarnate who was operating through his own impersonal human nature? In no way! Rather, he clearly explained the exact opposite:

- The son can do nothing of himself
- The Father *gave* to his son authority *and* to have life in himself (therefore, the Father's life is inherent, but the son's life was not inherent—it was given to him)
- Jesus received the power to take up his life again *by commandment* from the Father

So in one passage Jesus claimed that he would raise his body up, but in many subsequent explanations he clarified that he could actually do nothing of himself and that the Father actually gave him the authority by commandment to rise from the dead. As for the bulk of the Scriptures on the subject, the rest all teach that God, who raised Jesus from the dead, was personally distinct from the one whom God raised from the dead. Here are some of those passages:

¹⁴But you denied the Holy and Righteous One, and asked for a murderer to be granted to you, ¹⁵and killed the Prince of life, *whom God raised from the dead*, to which we are witnesses. (Acts 3:14–15)

Acts 3:14–15 tells us that the Holy and Righteous One who was the Prince of life was killed, and was a distinctly different "who" from God, who raised him from the dead.

> [10] Be it known to you all, and to all the people of Israel, that in the name of Jesus the Anointed One of Nazareth, whom you crucified, *whom God raised from the dead*, in him does this man stand here before you whole. [11] He is "the stone which was regarded as worthless by you, the builders, which has become the head of the corner." [12] There is salvation in none other, for neither is there any other name under heaven, that is given among men, by which we must be saved! (Acts 4:10–12)

Acts 4:10–12 tells us that Jesus, the Anointed One of Nazareth, was killed, and he was yet again a distinct "who" from God, who raised him from the dead.

> [32] We bring you good news of the promise made to the fathers, [33] that God has fulfilled the same to us, their children, in that *he raised up Jesus*. As it is also written in the second psalm, *"You are my Son. Today I have become your father."* [34] *Concerning that he raised him up from the dead*, now no more to return to corruption, *he has spoken thus: "I will give you the holy and sure blessings of David."* (Acts 13:32–34)

Acts 13:32–39 shares some additional crucial details about how the resurrection fits into God's prophetic plan. According to the apostle's interpretation, the resurrection was the actualization of God's sworn oath to raise up a son. They applied God's phrase, "Today I have become your father," to that day. Next we are told, again in reference to the resurrection, that it was also a fulfillment of God's promise to give the sure mercies of David, a covenantal oath, to the offspring of David. And finally, we are told that the resurrection of

Jesus was the actualization of David's prophetic words, "You will not allow your Holy One to see decay." It must be kept in mind that this phrase in the Hebrew was not a reference to God, but a clear and distinct reference to a, that is one, saint of God.

Therefore, if we do away with man's jumped-to conclusions and pet theories and rely on what the word of God says and explains for us, we find the Scriptures are quite descriptive about how God was a person distinct from the man whom He raised from the dead.

> [30]The times of ignorance therefore *God* overlooked. But now *he commands that all people everywhere should repent,* [31]because he has appointed a day in which he will judge the world in righteousness *by the man whom he has ordained*; of which he has given assurance to all men, in that *he has raised him* from the dead. (Acts 17:31)

With regard to the resurrection, Acts 17:30–31 makes very clear that the one who is ordained *is necessarily by definition personally distinct from the one who does the ordaining.* This is evidence of God's assurance to all the rest of us "men," or humankind. So this passage reiterates that, like Aaron, Christ didn't take this honor on himself (Hebrews 5:4). So then once again, *by definition,* Jesus can't be "the Anointed One" and also be the one who anointed or ordained himself.

Another point made in Acts 17:31 is that God gave assurance to all men by the resurrection of Christ. If Christ's resurrection were merely a matter of God raising His own impersonal flesh from the dead, in what way would this equate to assurance to all men? If God merely raised Himself from the dead, that would hardly equal any assurance to the rest of us mortals. So the incarnation of God theory neutralizes the very real and true hope that God has given and shown to all men by raising Jesus from the dead.

> [6]But *the righteousness which is of faith* says this, "Don't say in your heart, "Who will ascend into heaven?" (that is, to bring Christ down); [7]or, "Who will descend into the abyss?"

> (that is, to bring Christ up from the dead.)" ⁸But what does it say? "The word is near you, in your mouth, and in your heart;" that is, the word of faith, which we preach: ⁹that if you will confess with your mouth that Jesus is Lord, and *believe in your heart that God raised him* from the dead, you will be saved." (Romans 10:6–9)

Romans 10:6–9 is a very popular and well-known passage. And it offers yet stronger and more powerful words with regard to the resurrection. It doesn't say that God raised Himself, or for us to believe Jesus raised himself, but that God raised the Anointed One (the one who didn't take this honor on himself). Then it clearly says it is the righteousness of faith to believe that *"God raised him"* from the dead. So then those of us who believe in the two "whos" are the true people of the righteousness which is of faith.

> ¹²Now if Christ is preached, that he has been raised from the dead, how do some among you say that there is no resurrection of the dead? ¹³But if there is no resurrection of the dead, neither has Christ been raised. ¹⁴If Christ has not been raised, then our preaching is in vain, and your faith also is in vain. ¹⁵Yes, we are found false witnesses of God, because *we testified about God that he raised up Christ*, whom he didn't raise up, if it is so that the dead are not raised. (1 Corinthians 15:12–15)

The context for 1 Corinthians 15:12–15 is the apostle's certainty of the resurrection of Jesus the Anointed One. And part of that established truth is the element about God: "that He raised up the Anointed One." These very terms indicate in the strongest manner that, in raising Christ, God did not raise Himself up from the dead.

Those who claim to the contrary, saying that God raised Himself from the dead, either don't believe that He was truly dead, or they must redefine death. For the Scripture says, "there is no work, nor device, nor knowledge, nor wisdom in the grave" (Ecclesiastes 9:10).

> Paul, an apostle (not from men, neither through man, but through Jesus Christ, and God the Father, *who raised him from the dead*). (Galatians 1:1)

In Galatians 1:1, we are told that Jesus the Anointed One is a distinct "who" from God the Father who raised him from the dead. Paul used very clear, biblical terminology that did not mean God raised Himself from the dead.

> [20]Which *he worked in Christ, when he raised him from the dead*, and made him to sit at his right hand in the heavenly places, [21]far above all rule, and authority, and power, and dominion, and every name that is named, not only in this age, but also in that which is to come. [22]He put all things in subjection under his feet, and *gave him to be* head over all things for the assembly. (Ephesians 1:20–22)

Consistently, when the Bible is allowed to explain Christ's resurrection, it is shown to be God who raised Jesus, while whatever part Jesus played, *he did so by commandment* from his Father. Jesus said, "I have power to lay it down, and I have power to take it again. *I received this commandment* from my Father" (John 10:17–18).

This saying of Jesus brings to mind two examples where Jesus actually did raise people from the dead. Notice his wording in doing so:

> ...Turning him to the body said, Tabitha, arise. And she opened her eyes: and when she saw Peter, she sat up. (Acts 9:40, KJV)

> And when he thus had spoken, he cried with a loud voice, Lazarus, come forth. (John 11:43, KJV)

In both examples, we see Jesus commanding the dead people to act. Note that Jesus didn't say, "I am God and I say you are alive," or anything like that. No, he gave them a commandment to come to life! So not only do we have Jesus' express statement that he received a commandment from his Father to take up his life, but he also exemplified for us through his actions how such a commandment looks.

Trinitarians love to quote Matthew 28:19 as the source of their baptismal formula, but they have no examples of any biblical figure being baptized the way they do it. Those who baptize into the name of Jesus Christ have many examples in the Bible, including Jesus himself indirectly telling Paul to be baptized into his name (Acts 9:5–6, in conjunction with Acts 22:16 and Romans 6:3). Likewise, we who hold the true Son of God doctrine not only have clearly explained Scriptures that testify to our position, but the words and examples of Jesus himself as well.

To this list could be added many other Scriptures teaching that God, who raised Jesus, was personally distinct from the one He raised: Acts 10:40, Acts 13:30; Eph. 1:20; Col. 2:12; 1Th. 1:10; 1Pe. 1:21; Rom. 4:24, Rom. 6:4, Rom. 8:11; 1Co. 6:14; 2Co. 4:14; Heb. 13:20.

In contrast to all these Scriptures, there is not one verse of Scripture anywhere that says that Jesus' deific nature raised his impersonal human flesh-nature from the dead, or that Jesus raised himself because he was inherently God. So even when they quote John 2:18–21, neither it, nor any other verse actually goes on to say, proclaim, or teach what Onenessians believe to be the case. Once again, they have to interpret it and interject their preconceived ideas before they can try to use it as one of their proof texts.

The resurrection of the dead has to be held as one of the most important doctrines that the apostles preached in the Book of Acts. This doctrine represents the great hope that God offers to humankind. The specific hope the apostles preached to humanity is actually thwarted and made suspect if Jesus was an incarnate deity that raised himself from the dead. We've already quoted four places in Acts where the apostles preached the resurrection. Notice in the following verses how the apostles indicated that the resurrection was a central part of their message of Jesus.

²⁹Brothers, I may tell you freely of the patriarch David, that he both died and was buried, and his tomb is with us to this day. ³⁰ Therefore, being a prophet, and knowing that God had sworn with an oath to him that of the fruit of his body, according to the flesh, he would raise up the Christ to sit on his throne, ³¹he foreseeing this <u>spoke about the resurrection of the Christ</u>, that neither was his soul left in Hades, nor did his flesh see decay. (Acts 2:29–31)

¹As they spoke to the people, the priests and the captain of the temple and the Sadducees came to them, ²being upset because they taught the people and *proclaimed in Jesus the <u>resurrection from the dead</u>*. (Acts 4:1–2)

But *God <u>raised him from the dead</u>*. (Acts 13:30)

²Paul, as was his custom, went in to them, and for three Sabbath days reasoned with them from the Scriptures, ³explaining and demonstrating that the Christ had to suffer and *<u>rise again from the dead</u>*, and saying, "This Jesus, whom I proclaim to you, is the Christ." (Acts 17:2–3)

Men and brothers, I am a Pharisee, a son of Pharisees. *Concerning the hope <u>and resurrection of the dead</u>* I am being judged! (Acts 23:6)

Having hope toward God, which these also themselves look for, that there will be *a <u>resurrection of the dead</u>*. (Acts 24:15)

Unless it is for this one thing that I cried standing among them, '*Concerning <u>the resurrection of the dead</u>* I am being judged before you today!' (Acts 24:21)

Why is it judged incredible with you, if *God does <u>raise the dead</u>*? (Acts 26:8)

How the Christ must suffer, and how, <u>*by the resurrection of the dead*</u>, *he would be first* to proclaim light both to these people and to the Gentiles. (Acts 26:23)

Instead of man's traditions negating the bulk of the Scriptures we've covered here, we have chosen to believe Paul: "... I fear, lest somehow... he who comes preaches another Jesus whom we have not preached... you may well put up with it!" (2 Corinthians 11:2–4, NKJV).

As a comparison, we ask our Oneness neighbors to consider how similar their attitude on this subject is to the Trinitarian use of Matthew 28:19 in defense of their practice of baptizing into the titles. Against the bulk of the Scriptures that teach to baptize into the name of Jesus, and in spite of the examples of the apostles doing only just that, the Trinitarians still stubbornly cling to their baptismal formula because of what Jesus said in one verse. In opposition to their position, we even have Jesus himself, in Acts 9:6, telling Paul what he "must do"; namely, to "call on the name of the Lord" (Acts 22:16), and that name was provided to Paul by Jesus himself back in Acts 9. So really it is those of us who baptize into Jesus' name who hear Jesus, because we listen to his explanation and do not just jump to conclusions over one verse.

In like manner Onenessians have their one sole verse (John 2:18–21) they also tenaciously cling to against the bulk of the Scriptures to the contrary. Jesus himself said he could do nothing of himself (John 5:19–30) and that he was given the authority to rise from the dead by commandment from God (John 10:17–18).

Onenessianism completely disregards Paul's dire warning in 2 Corinthians:

> ³But I fear, lest by any means... ⁴... if he that cometh preacheth another Jesus, *whom we have not preached*, or if ye receive another spirit, which ye have not received, *or another gospel*, which ye have not accepted, *ye might well bear with him*. (2 Corinthians 11:3–4, KJV)

Paul's warning isn't exactly stated as a commandment; however, others that are very similar are commandments. Note that he mentioned another gospel along with another Christ. Any incarnation theory definitely is another gospel because it is preaching that God Himself became Christ, not that Christ was a man approved of God. We are commanded to call accursed those who present any other gospels than the one the apostles preached.

> [9]*If any man preach any other gospel unto you than that ye have received, let him be accursed.* (Galatians 1:6–9, KJV)

In addition, we are commanded to "teach no other doctrine" (1 Timothy 1:3).

No incarnation doctrine is spelled out in the Scriptures. The idea of "incarnation" can only be concluded by interpreting the way the devil interprets. Even clearer is the fact that no apostle even came close to preaching an Incarnationist view of Christ. This distortion of the Scriptures is devastating for those who love the word of God!

In Summary

The idea that Jesus was an incarnation of YHWH who raised Himself from the dead negates a great many Scriptures and supplants them with an idea that is never clearly spelled out or explained in the Scriptures.

Since we cover many other passages in John throughout this book, we'll leave John for now and go on next to the Acts of the Apostles.

CHAPTER TWENTY

The Acts of the Apostles

Acts Chapter Two – A Man Approved by God

...I fear, lest somehow... he who comes preaches another *Jesus whom we* have not *preached*... you may well put up with it! (2 Corinthians 11:2–4, NKJV)

Here are all the places they preached Jesus as a man

1) Acts 2:14 - 36
2) 3:12 - 26
3) 4:8 - 12
4) 5:29 - 32
5) 7:2 - 53
6) 8:32 - 37
7) 10:34 - 43
8) 13:16 - 41
9) 17:22 - 31
10) 18:4 - 5
11) 26:2 - 23

Here are all the places they preached Jesus as God incarnate...

0

Paul was very clear. He feared that people were going to be deceived away from believing in the simplicity of Jesus *as they preached him to be*. The Book of Acts is where we find exactly what the apostles preached about Jesus. What they preached was Jesus as a man anointed by God, in distinction from God. They never once preached a Onenessian or Trinitarian version of Jesus, not ever.[1]

---

[1] Following, for your reference, are all the passages in which Christ is "preached" without ever once being preached as an incarnation of the Father

When confronted with the fact that the apostles preached only a human Christ, Onenessians use the excuse that the apostles taught something deeper after they became disciples. This is the same excuse that Trinitarians use. Both are simply rejections of what Paul wrote. No Scriptures say that the apostles taught a different, deeper Christ later. So let's obey the Scripture of 2 Corinthians and resolve to believe in Jesus as the apostles openly preached him to be.

The first preaching, on the Day of Pentecost, laid the foundation for the assembly (ecclesia), the body of Christ. Keep in mind that those who heard these words had been brought to a saving knowledge of Jesus Messiah if they chose to accept it.

> [22]Men of Israel, hear these words! Jesus of Nazareth, <u>*a man approved by God*</u> to you by mighty works and wonders and signs *which* <u>*God did by him*</u> *in the midst of you, even as you yourselves know,* [23]*him, being delivered up by the determined counsel and* <u>*foreknowledge*</u> *of God, you have* taken by the hand of lawless men, *crucified and killed;* [24]*whom God raised up*, having freed him from the agony of death, because it was not possible that he should be held by it.
> [25]*For David says concerning him,*
> *"I saw the Lord always before my face,*
> *For He is on my right hand, that I should not be moved.*
> [26]*Therefore my heart was glad, and my tongue rejoiced.*
> *Moreover my flesh also will dwell in hope;*
> [27]Because you will not leave my soul *in Hades,*
> *Neither will you allow your Holy One to see decay.*
> [28]*You made known to me the ways of life.*

---

or as the second person in a mythological Trinity: Acts 2:14–36; 3:12–26; 4:8–12; 5:29–32; 7:2–53; 8:32–37; 10:34–43; 13:16–41; 17:22–31; 18:4–5; 26:2–23. The following verses are the places where Jesus is clearly and irrefutably held in personal distinction from God the Father in the Book of Acts: Acts 1:4, 7; 2:22, 23, 24, 26–30, 32, 33, 34–35, 36, 38–39; 3:6–9, 13, 15, 18, 20, 22, 23, 24, 26; 4:10, 26, 27, 4:29–30; 5:30, 31; 7:37, 55, 56; 8:12, 37; 9:20; 10:36, 38, 40, 42; 11:17; 13:23, 30, 33, 37; 15:10–11; 16:17–18, 31–32; 17:30–31; 20:21; 26:8–9, 22–23; 28:31.

> *You will make me full of gladness with your presence."*
> ²⁹Brothers, I may tell you freely of the patriarch *David*, that he *both died and was buried*, and his tomb is with us to this day. ³⁰Therefore, *being a prophet, and knowing that God had sworn with an oath to him that <u>of the fruit of his body, according to the flesh, He would raise up the Christ</u>* to sit on his throne, ³¹he foreseeing this spoke about the resurrection of the Christ, that *neither was his soul* left in Hades, *nor did his flesh see decay*. ³²*This Jesus* God raised up, to which we all are witnesses. ³³Being therefore exalted by the right hand of God, and having received from the Father the promise of the Holy Spirit, He has poured out this, which you now see and hear. ³⁴For David didn't ascend into the heavens, but he says himself, "The Lord (*YHWH*) said to my Lord (*adoni*), 'Sit by my right hand, ³⁵Until I make your enemies a footstool for your feet.'" ³⁶Let all the house of Israel therefore know assuredly that God has *made him both Lord and Christ, this Jesus* whom you crucified. (Acts 2:22–36)

Peter describes Jesus the Messiah as a Judean king descended by a sworn oath from the seed (or, offspring) of David—no more and no less. He is a male, human descendant of King David, with a human soul. The only significant difference Peter notes between this man Jesus and any other man is that his office and position were both *foreknown* (v. 23) and foretold by God.

Peter's predominant message in this passage is the truth that God raised Jesus from the dead. That message seems not to be as profound as it was in their time, but it should be.

What is profound today about this passage is what Peter did *not* say. Nowhere in this passage did Peter in any way preach that Jesus was a hybrid God-man. Nowhere did Peter say anything to the effect that this Jesus was a deific member of a Trinity of persons in the godhead. Nowhere in this passage did Peter preach Jesus to be inherently God. *These doctrines were all developed after the death of the apostles and are read back into the Scriptures.* Rather, while preaching the saving gospel of Jesus Christ, Peter consistently held

God in clear, personal distinction from the man Jesus Christ.

This passage is not at all out of the norm in the Book of Acts. When Jesus was preached, he was consistently referred to as only human. This man is the Jesus of the gospel. This is the Jesus that the apostles preached, in whom people should believe for salvation. It is this Jesus who is *not to be changed or perverted*. You may disagree, but that would only be because the traditions of men that have been delivered to you have clouded your vision. What you have read in the passage above is the word of God.

In this passage, God explicitly said that *it was David's seed who would be His (God's) son*. Thus, God Himself refuted one of the first major assumptions of Trinitarianism. For early, "official" Trinitarians, God's Son was *made of no other substance than the essence of the Father*. However, that is entirely unbiblical. God swore by an oath, not that His Son was going to be made of deific material, but rather that he would be made of human substance, "of the seed of David." This couldn't be clearer. Furthermore, this was an unconditional promise that David received from God concerning his own, personal lineage.

This passage also described "the sure mercies of David"; for example:

> Turn your ear, and come to me; hear, and your soul shall live: and *I will make an everlasting covenant* with you, *even the sure mercies of David.* (Isaiah 55:3)

Isaiah's prophecy clearly demonstrates to us that Jesus, as the Son of David, was *in a specific covenant* with God. Namely, Jesus' covenant was an extension of David's covenant with God, which in turn was God's unconditional promise to David and David's offspring. In other words, Jesus wasn't an incarnation of God; rather, he was the fulfillment of God's promise to David.

God called this covenant "the *'sure'* mercies of David" because He swore that it would come to pass. Apostle Paul considered this prophecy to have been conferred on Christ when God raised him from the dead.

> ³⁴And that He raised him from the dead, no more to return to corruption, He has spoken thus: "I will give you <u>the sure mercies of David</u>." ³⁵Therefore he also says in another Psalm: "You will not allow Your Holy One to see corruption." (Acts 13:34–35, NKJV)

The prophecy in Isaiah 55:3 referred only to the human offspring of David. Like Peter, Paul also assigned this prophecy to Jesus (Acts 13). Paul did not change or revise Peter's preaching of a human Jesus. The sure mercies of David meant the unconditional promise, or covenant, spoken by God to David because of David's wanting to build God a house for His name. All of these Scriptures, when tied together, further teach us that this human Jesus was also called God's "Holy One" (see Acts 2:27 and 13:35 above).

The title "Holy One," quoted at Acts 2:27, raises some questions, but that is only because of the way it is translated into English in certain versions. In Hebrew the word *qadosh* is used in numerous passages (such as Isaiah 10:20, 43:15; Hosea 11:9; and elsewhere) exclusively in reference to God Himself. (Here are the 41 occurrences where this word was translated into "Holy One" in English, and in not one of them is it applied to human saints: 2Ki 19:22; Job 6:10; Ps. 71:22, 78:41, 89:18; Isa. 1:4, 5:19, 24, 10:17, 20, 12:6, 17:7, 29:19, 23, 30:11, 12, 15, 31:1, 37:23, 40:25, 41:14, 16, 20, 43:3, 14, 15, 45:11, 47:4, 48:17, 49:7 (twice), 54:5, 55:5, 60:9, 14; Jere. 50:29, 51:5; Ezek. 39:7; Hosea 11:9; Hab. 1:12 and 3:3.)

However, in Psalm 16:10, which the apostles applied to Jesus in Acts, the phrase "Holy One" (Acts 2:27 and 13:35) comes from the Hebrew word *chasid*. This word means "kind (i.e., religiously), <u>pious (a saint)</u>" (from *Strong's Numbers and Concordance*). *It is used <u>not</u> for God, but for saints of God in twenty-nine out of thirty-two occurrences in the Bible.* Here are those passages: 1 Sam. 2:9; 2 Sam. 22:26; 2 Chr. 6:41; Ps. 4:3, 12:1, 16:10, 18:25, 30:4, 31:23, 32:6, 37:28, 43:1, 50:5, 52:9, 79:2, 85:8, 86:2, 89:19, 97:10, 116:15, 132:9, 16, 145:10, 148:14, 149:1, 5, 9; Prov. 2:8; and Micah 7:2. It is used of YHWH in Deut. 33:8; Ps. 145:17; and Jere. 3:12.

This means that the passage in Psalms 16:10, as applied in reference to Jesus as the "Holy One," simply means, paraphrased, "you will not allow *this saint of yours* to see corruption." It is *not* saying, "you will not allow *God the Holy One* to see corruption," as could be presumed by the English.

That Peter understood this verse as referring to the human Jesus can be seen very clearly in Acts 2:31. Here, *he explicitly interprets the Psalm as referring to Christ's flesh*, which is to say, his humanity.

> "Because you will not leave my soul in Hades, *Neither will you allow your Holy One to see decay..."*
> He foreseeing this spoke about the resurrection of the Christ, that neither was his soul left in Hades, *nor did his flesh see decay*. (Acts 2:27, 31)

Through the use of a couplet (a phrase meant to convey a synonymous thought in two ways) Peter has provided a scriptural, Holy Spirit-anointed interpretation of the meaning of "Holy One" as it was used in Psalms 16:10. Biblically, it explicitly means *the human flesh; that is, the humanity of Jesus Christ*. Thus, according to Peter's clear interpretation, it is definitely *not* referring to God the Holy One (*qadosh*). To receive God's word is to receive this interpretation of God's word from Acts 2:31. Peter simply reiterated God's vow that David's seed would be the Savior.

In Acts 13:35–39, as we have begun to see, Paul preached from the same passage as Peter. From Psalms 16:10, Paul preached a human Jesus, without any implication whatsoever that he was a hybrid God-man.

> [35]Therefore he says also in another psalm, "You will not allow <u>your Holy One to see decay</u>." [36]For David, after he had in his own generation served the counsel of God, fell asleep, and was laid with his fathers, and saw decay. [37]But <u>he whom</u>

> *God raised up saw no decay.* ³⁸Be it known to you <u>therefore</u>, brothers, that *through <u>this man</u> is proclaimed to you remission of sins,* ³⁹and <u>by him</u> *everyone who believes is justified* from all things, from which you could not be justified by the law of Moses. (Acts 13:35–39)

Clearly Paul was preaching the same human Jesus that Peter was preaching. Paul emphatically reinforced Peter's interpretation of Psalm 16. Both of them provided explicit interpretations regarding the "Holy One" who did not see "decay." For Peter, the interpretation was the flesh of Jesus (Acts 2:31). For Paul, the interpretation was "he whom God raised up... this man" (Acts 13:37–38). Notably, Paul added that it is through him, this human raised by God, that justification comes. *According to Paul, salvation comes through believing in a glorified and resurrected human.* As with Peter's message, Paul's gospel indicates it isn't a Trinitarian or a Onenessian Jesus who saves.

Another notable point of Paul's is in agreement with what he wrote in Romans 10:6–9: "... if you will confess with your mouth that Jesus is Lord, and believe in your heart that *God raised him from the dead*, you will be saved." We addressed this in Chapter Nineteen. Accordingly, faith that saves is particularly defined as believing that Jesus is Lord (as heir to the throne of David), and believing that "*through this man* is proclaimed to you *remission of sins*, and *by him everyone who believes* is justified from all things."

Onenessians are particularly fond, as we are, of quoting Acts 2:38, where Peter proclaimed that we are baptized unto Christ for the remission of sin. Now, in Acts 13:39, Paul explicitly tells us *what we are to believe about this man Jesus* by whom we receive remission of sins; and quite frankly, he isn't "preaching" the modalistic Oneness version of Jesus at all!

Acts Chapter Three – A Prophet Like Moses

We already discussed Acts 3:13–26, the second recorded preaching of the gospel after the day of Pentecost, in Chapter Eight. Briefly here, Peter clearly contrasted and distinguished the God of the Jews from the man whom God calls *His Servant*.

> [13]*The God of Abraham, Isaac, and Jacob, the God of our fathers, has glorified <u>His Servant</u> Jesus, whom you delivered up, and denied...* [15]*whom God raised from the dead, to which we are witnesses...*
> [18]*...the things which God announced by the mouth of all His prophets, that Christ should suffer, He thus fulfilled...* [22]*For Moses indeed said to the fathers, "<u>The Lord God will raise up a prophet for you from among your brothers, like me</u>. You shall listen to him in all things whatever he says to you.* [23]*It will be, that every soul that will not listen to <u>that prophet</u> will be utterly destroyed from among the people."...* [26]*God, having raised up <u>His servant, Jesus,</u> sent him to you first, to bless you, in turning away everyone of you from your wickedness.* (Acts 3:13–26)

Thus, Jesus was far from being preached as God incarnate. The servant (Jesus) whom God glorified was distinct from God (the God of their fathers), who glorified him.

Acts Chapters Five and Seven – Jesus at God's Right Hand

In these two passages, Jesus is preached as being at God's right hand. We read...

> [29]But Peter and the apostles answered... [30]The God of our fathers raised up Jesus, whom you killed, hanging him on a tree. [31]God <u>exalted him with his right hand</u> to be a Prince

and a Savior, to give repentance to Israel, and remission of sins. ³²We are His witnesses of these things; and so also is the Holy Spirit, whom God has given to those who obey him. (Acts 5:29–32)

³⁷This is that Moses, who said to the children of Israel, 'The Lord our God will _raise up a prophet_ for you from among your brothers, _like me_...' ⁵⁴Now when they heard these things, they were cut to the heart, and they gnashed at him with their teeth. ⁵⁵But he, being full of the Holy Spirit, looked up steadfastly into heaven, and saw the glory of God, and _Jesus standing on the right hand of God_, ⁵⁶and said, "Behold, I see the heavens opened, and _the Son of Man standing at the right hand of God_!" (Acts 7:37, 7:54–56)

As a Onenessian, I was taught that Jesus being at God's right hand was symbolic and meant Jesus was at the "right hand of power." This was supposed to mean that God now does everything through Jesus just as a man's own right hand is part of his person. However, I now know that view is pure speculation created by mixing truths and half-truths. It is a half-truth because, yes Christ embodied God; but we also embody God and that doesn't make us incarnations of the person of God any more than that was so of Jesus. The question is, does "being at the right hand" _only or definitively_ mean we're talking of a literal extension or part of a single personality? If we search the Scriptures, we find that being on someone's right hand, even in the Bible, was very much the same figure of speech as it is today for a right-hand man.

For example, we find this in Psalms:

I have set YHWH always before me. Because he is at my right hand, I shall not be moved. (Psalms 16:8)

Are we to believe that YHWH is the person of the Psalmist because He is at the Psalmist's right hand? Of course not!

In Romans we come to a similar passage:

Who is he who condemns? It is Christ who died, yes rather, who was raised from the dead, <u>who is at the right hand of God</u>, who also makes intercession for us. (Romans 8:34)

> **"Christ who died... who was raised from the dead,**
> who is at the right hand of God,
> who also makes intercession for us."
> (Romans 8:34)

Oneness Father and Son

According to Onenessian doctrine, the Son is the impersonal, inanimate human flesh of God, or he is God acting in a "mode" of son. Are we to believe either that an impersonal flesh is now our intercessor with God the Father, or that the Father needs to intercede with Himself on our behalf? The Onenessian idea is simply nonsense when looked at within the biblical context.

Now watch how James and John ask to be seated at the right and left hand of Jesus when he comes into his kingdom. Are we to suppose they were asking to also become incarnations of God, just like Jesus supposedly was in the Oneness view? The answer is obviously not. This passage shows that being at one's right hand means the same as it does today: being someone's closest assistants or advisors.

> [35]James and John, the sons of Zebedee, came near to him, saying,.. [37]..."Grant to us that we may sit, one at your right hand, and one at your left hand, in your glory." [38]But Jesus

said to them, "You don't know what you are asking... ⁴⁰...to sit at my right hand and at my left hand is *not mine to give*, but for whom it has been prepared." (Mark 10:35–40)

Here were two of Jesus' closest disciples. These two disciples were clearly not asking to be the same person of Jesus simply because they used the phrase "at your right hand." Jesus showed that he was willing to hear, and likely do for them as they asked. *But what they asked of him was beyond his personal authority.* If Jesus was truly God, then he had just lied to and deceived his closest disciples.

Now let's go back and look at the context of Stephen's vision of Christ: ⁵⁵"But he, being full of the Holy Spirit, looked up steadfastly into heaven, and saw the glory of God, and *Jesus standing on the right hand of God*, ⁵⁶and said, "Behold, I see the heavens opened, and the Son of Man *standing at the right hand of* God!" (Acts 7:55–56).

One thing is obvious: no one speaks of someone's own literal right hand as "standing at the right hand of" so-and-so. Therefore, the passage can only be read symbolically, with the meaning of someone being a close assistant to some other personality. Stephen did not declare that Jesus was God Himself.

The Context of Stephen's Preaching of the Anointed One

Let's look at some of the highlights of Stephen's sermon in Acts 7. There is a specific theme that Stephen was trying to get across that jumps right out at us if we would just let him speak:

> v.2 God raised up Abraham...
> v.6 God said that (Abraham's) seed would be aliens in a strange land...
> v.9 The patriarchs sold Joseph into Egypt...
> v.11–14 There came a famine... the fathers found no food... but Joseph summoned Jacob (Israel) his father with all his relatives...

v.20 Moses was born...
v. 25 God, by Moses' hand, was giving them deliverance...
v.35 This Moses they refused, saying, "Who made you a ruler and a judge?"...
v.37 Moses said, "the Lord our God will raise up a prophet for you from among your brothers, like me"...
v.39 To whom (Moses), Stephen said, "our fathers wouldn't be obedient"...
v.41 They made a golden calf... and sacrificed unto the idol...
v.45–47 David found favor with God... but Solomon built him a house...
v.48 However the Most High doesn't dwell in temples made with hands...
v.51–53 You stiff-necked and uncircumcised in heart and ears, you always resist the Holy Spirit! As your fathers did, so you do!
v.56 "Behold, I see the heavens opened, and the Son of Man standing at the right hand of God!"

The theme that Stephen preached was that God always sent a man whom He worked through. Moses even clearly described that man to come. There was no theme or hint of an incarnated deity in Stephen's speech, or in any other preaching by a true disciple of Christ. That idea only came from those who disbelieved and bore false witness against Jesus. Therefore, those who resisted the men sent by God have become the types of those who resist receiving Jesus under the same exact conditions: a man sent by God whom they refuse to obey, but choose rather to turn and sacrifice to their man-made idols.

Paul and Moses

We go now to Paul's conversion in the Book of Acts. As you consider Paul's encounter with the Lord Jesus Christ, it is interesting to compare his reaction with that of Moses. Let's read...

> [1]But Saul, still breathing threats and slaughter against the disciples of the Lord... [3]As he traveled, it happened that he got close to Damascus, and suddenly a light from the sky shone around him. [4] He fell on the earth, and heard a voice saying to him, "Saul, Saul, why do you persecute me?" [5] He said, "Who are you, Lord?" The Lord said, "I am Jesus, whom you are persecuting. [6]But rise up, and enter into the city, and you will be told what you must do." (Acts 9:1–6)

This is the passage that first explains how Saul received a personal visitation. Saul calls out to the voice, "who are you Lord?" And this individual responds by telling him his name, and tells Saul what he has done wrong and what he needs to do. One of the most striking parts of this event is lost on most people: it is how Jesus describes himself to Saul. He said, "I am Jesus, *whom you are persecuting.*" But Saul hadn't been persecuting Jesus; he'd been persecuting his disciples. Yet Jesus identified himself so closely with his disciples that he spoke of them in the first person. This is a prime example of idiomatic speech that should be easy for us to understand: the saints that Paul preached were not the literal person of Jesus Christ, but Jesus spoke of them that way because believers make up the body of Christ without negating their individual personalities. If we can understand this when Christ speaks this way in the context of his relationship with us, we shouldn't be surprised when he seems to speak the same way in context with his relationship with God his Father.

Well before this point, Jesus had ascended to heaven, leaving behind his followers. Paul would later describe Christ's disciples as Christ's body. So, if we interpret this passage the way Onenessians do, we'd have to conclude that these followers of Christ, whom Saul had been persecuting, were all personal incarnations of Jesus himself. That is, after all, how Onenessians and Trinitarians apply the same type of language to Christ, that since God is his head and God indwells Christ, then by that fact, Jesus must be an incarnation of deity. But no, that's not the case. Jesus was actually the firstborn of many brothers. The ones Saul was persecuting were those many brothers that make up Christ's body, and being many, they are even still one body. But that is a long way from the unbiblical, nonsensical idea that they are all personal incarnations of Jesus, let alone of God.

Saul's encounter with Jesus could have been very similar to Moses' encounter with God. Since Onenessians believe Jesus was personally YHWH, then it would stand to reason, from their view, that Saul's encounter would have been his first direct encounter with YHWH Himself. But is that how either Saul or Jesus described the encounter? To answer that, let's look at Moses' encounter with the true, Almighty God YHWH and let's see if we can find any distinguishing similarities or differences.

> [2]The angel of YHWH appeared to him in a flame of fire out of the midst of a bush. He looked, and behold, the bush burned with fire, and the bush was not consumed. [3] Moses said, "I will turn aside now, and see this great sight, why the bush is not burnt." (Exodus 3:2–3)

> [13]Moses said to God, "Behold, when I come to the children of Israel, and tell them, "The God of your fathers has sent me to you;" and they ask me, "What is his name?" What should I tell them? [14]God said to Moses, "*I AM WHO I AM,*" and he said, "*You shall tell the children of Israel this: I AM has sent me to you.*" [15]God said *moreover* to Moses, "*You shall tell the children of Israel this, 'YHWH, the God of your fathers, the God of Abraham, the God of Isaac, and the God of Jacob, has sent me to you.' This is my name forever, and this is my memorial to all generations.*" (Exodus 3:13–15)

> Moses told Aaron all the words of YHWH with which he had sent him, and all the signs with which he had charged him. (Exodus 4:28)
>
> Afterward Moses and Aaron came, and said to Pharaoh, *This is what YHWH, the God of Israel, says,* "Let my people go, that they may hold a feast to me in the wilderness." (Exodus 5:1)

In this encounter, God was very straightforward with Moses in revealing His identity to him. When Moses was approached and called by God, he understood that he had been given a message, just as Saul understood. The message that Moses began preaching was completely straightforward: "the God of your fathers has sent me to you." No ambiguity here.

Now imagine if you were Saul and you had a similar encounter with Almighty God YHWH. I can tell you that if you were a Trinitarian, you'd run out preaching "the second person of the Trinity has sent me to you," and if you were a Onenessian, you'd run out preaching "YHWH the Father Himself incarnate has sent me to you to tell you that His name is now Jesus." How do I know that? Because that's exactly what they preach about their respective views of Christ. But our question is, what was Saul's view? What did the person who actually had that experience with Christ think and understand and preach about who and what approached him?

Well, here's what Saul had to say:

> [20]Immediately in the synagogues he proclaimed the Anointed One, that he is the Son of God. [21]All who heard him were amazed... [22]But Saul increased more in strength, and confounded the Jews who lived at Damascus, proving that *this is the Anointed One.* (Acts 9:20–22)

Do you see the difference between what Saul testified of and what Moses testified of? Moses had an encounter with YHWH Himself and said so. Saul had an encounter with the Messiah—Christ the Anointed One—the Son of God, and said so. But here, don't take my word for it, let's hear Saul (Paul) himself describe what he preached about the Anointed One. Note as you read how similar his theme is to Stephen's regarding God anointing men. Keep in mind the contrast here with Moses's testimony after encountering YHWH God. If you are honest with this comparison you will have to admit that Saul did not make the same claim as Moses did; in particular, Saul claimed to have witnessed and exalted man, not God Himself:

> [16]Paul stood up, and beckoning with his hand said, "Men of Israel, and you who fear God, listen. [17]The God of this people chose our fathers, and <u>exalted the people</u> when they stayed as aliens in the land of Egypt, and with an uplifted arm, he led them out of it... [20]After these things <u>he gave them judges</u> until Samuel the prophet. [21]Afterward <u>they asked for a king</u>, and God gave to them Saul...[22]When he had removed him, <u>he raised up David</u> to be their king, to whom he also testified... [23]From <u>this man's seed</u>, God has brought salvation to Israel according to his promise... [26]Brothers... the word of this salvation is sent out to you. [27]For those who dwell in Jerusalem... [28]Though they found no cause for death, they still asked Pilate to have him killed... <u>[30]But God raised him from the dead</u>, [31]and he was seen for many days by those who came up with him from Galilee to Jerusalem, who are his witnesses to the people. [32]We bring you <u>good news of the promise made to the fathers,</u> [33]that God has fulfilled the same to us, their children, <u>in that he raised up Jesus</u>. As it is also written in the second psalm, "<u>You are my Son. Today I have become your father</u>." [34]Concerning that <u>he raised him up from the dead</u>, now no more to return to corruption, he has spoken thus: 'I will give you the holy and sure blessings of David.' [35]Therefore he says also in another psalm, 'You will not allow your Holy One to see decay.' [36]For David, after he had in his own generation served the counsel of God, fell asleep, and was laid with his fathers, and saw decay. [37]But <u>he whom God raised up saw no decay</u>. [38]Be it known to you therefore, brothers,

that *through this man is proclaimed to you remission of sins*, ³⁹and *by him everyone who believes is justified* from all things, from which you could not be justified by the law of Moses. ⁴⁰Beware therefore, lest that come on you which is spoken in the prophets: ⁴¹ "Behold, you scoffers, and wonder, and perish; For I work a work in your days, A work which you will in no way believe, if one declares it to you." (Acts 13:16–41)

So Paul never preached that Jesus was God incarnate, or even that he had encountered YHWH as Moses had. Either Paul was ashamed of the "Oneness" gospel, or it wasn't the "Oneness" gospel that Paul believed and preached. Paul's theme was almost identical with both Peter's and Stephen's. After consistently emphasizing the OT concept that God exalted people, he preached Jesus, the man through whom everyone who believes is justified. Therefore, *if you believe in a different Jesus, then you have no right to partake in this Jesus* whom Peter with all the apostles, Stephen, and Paul, all in one accord consistently preached him to be.

Now let's compare the testimony of Jesus to Saul, to the testimony that God gave of Himself to Moses:

I (Saul) answered, "Who are you, Lord?" He said to me, *"I am Jesus of Nazareth*, whom you persecute." (Acts 22:8)

¹⁴God said to Moses, *"I AM WHO I AM,"* and he said, "You shall tell the children of Israel this: I AM has sent me to you." ¹⁵God said moreover to Moses, "You shall tell the children of Israel this, *'YHWH, the God of your fathers*, the God of Abraham, the God of Isaac, and the God of Jacob, has sent me to you.' This is my name forever, and this is my memorial to all generations." (Exodus 3:13–15)

These are radically different responses from someone who is supposed to be the same individual. Jesus is not "I am that I am," either here or anywhere else in the Bible. Remember that Jesus said, "Most assuredly, I tell you, the Son *can do nothing of himself...*" (John 5:19). And again Jesus said, "I can *of myself* do nothing" (John 5:30).

In describing himself to Saul, Jesus also gave a very important clue regarding another verse in Acts that some people use to conclude that Jesus was God incarnate. Here is that verse:

> Take heed, therefore, to yourselves, and to all the flock, in which the Holy Spirit has made you overseers, to shepherd the assembly of the Lord and God which he purchased with his own blood. (Acts 20:28)

Some people claim that since Jesus' blood is referenced here as God's "own blood," that alone is proof that Jesus was God. But Paul had another explanation, quite likely based on Jesus' identity with his people, which Paul learned about from his first encounter with Jesus:

> [11]But the one and the same Spirit works all of these, distributing to each one separately as he desires. [12]For as the body is one, and has many members, and all the members of the body, being many, are one body; so also is Christ. [13]For in one Spirit we were all baptized into one body, whether Jews or Greeks, whether bond or free; and were all given to drink into one Spirit. [14]For the body is not one member, but many... [24]...God composed the body together, giving more abundant honor to the inferior part, [25]that there should be no division in the body, but that the members should have the same care for one another. [26]When one member suffers, all the members suffer with it. Or when one member is honored, all the members rejoice with it. [27]Now *you are the body of Christ, and members individually.* (1 Corinthians 12:11–14, 24–27)

Do you see that last sentence? "*You are the body of Christ, and members individually.*" Paul explained it as plain as day. We are not little incarnations of Jesus Christ, any more than Christ was an incarnation of God. Rather, Paul explains:

> ...you are Christ's, and Christ is God's. (1 Corinthians 3:23)

> But I would have you know that the head of every human is Christ, and the head of the wife is the husband, and the head of Christ is God. (1 Corinthians 11:3)

He that has ears let him hear. In the same way a wife is one flesh with her own husband, who is her head in the marriage relationship, yet she retains her own personal individuality (1 Cor. 12:27), so is every human under Christ, while retaining his human individuality. *So also is Christ under God*, who (Christ) in the same manner also retains his human individuality. This is the truth that Onenessianism destroys.

Now then, if this passage is true, that the head of Christ is God, just as the head of man is Christ, then these explanations in 2 Corinthians are the ones we need to use to "interpret the Scripture by the Scripture," wherein it is written that "the members should have the same care for one another" (1 Corinthians 12:25). And if so, "Christ is God's," and for that biblical reason, it could be said that God purchased the assembly of believers "with his own blood." The Bible never says Christ is an incarnation of God, but it does explicitly explain that we are Christ's, in the same way that Christ is God's.

This is also to lean, *not* on paganism for answers, but on the OT view of God's empathy with his people, as it is also written:

> [8]For he said, Surely, they are my people, children who will not deal falsely: so he was their Savior. [9]*In all their affliction he was afflicted*, and the angel of his presence saved them: in his love and in his pity he redeemed them; and he bore them, and carried them all the days of old. (Isaiah 63:8–9)

"In all their affliction He [God] was afflicted!" Well then, per the way Onenessians interpret things the Israelites must have also been God Himself just like Jesus was! Preposterous! Rather, simply, by this we see that God so intimately empathized with His people, that when they were afflicted, He felt every pain. Just as the NT

describes: "When one member suffers, all the members suffer with it" (1 Corinthians 12:26). If we can understand this is so with God and his saints without them being incarnations of God, we have no excuse for not understanding and believing that it is the exact same case with Jesus in whom God dwelled as in a temple. This is what allowing the Scriptures (as opposed to pagan ideas of incarnation and the like) to explain things to us looks like.

So then it is perfectly biblical to call Jesus' blood "His own blood," since Christ is God's just as we are Christ's, and all together we are one body. Acts 20:28 does not in any way teach or imply that Jesus is God incarnate!

Christ that Paul Preached

Let us now summarize the key points of Paul's first fully recorded preaching in Acts 13. These are the important points that this man who encountered Jesus himself felt was his duty to preach:

> v.17 God chose our fathers and exalted people...
> v.20 He gave judges...
> v.21 God gave Saul...
> v.22 removed him and raised David...
> v.23 Of this man's [David's] seed has God raised unto Israel a Savior Jesus...
> v.30 God raised him from the dead...
> v.33 God has fulfilled... in that he has raised Jesus... Thou art my Son this day have I begotten you...
> v.34 [God said] I will give you the sure mercies of David [the Davidic covenant]...
> v.37 *He whom God raised...*
> v.38 *Through this man is preached unto you* the forgiveness of sins and by him all that believe are justified from all things.

Paul preached Christ as a man; not as God incarnate! These are the elements of the "preached" Jesus that Paul warned us not to be moved away from. In none of these is the Trinity or Oneness doctrine set forth or even implied. Thus yet again, the true, preached, Son of God doctrine that we have been pointing to is the true saving view of Jesus Christ.

Note: to this chapter could be added the topic of the resurrection from the dead, but we covered that already in Chapter Nineteen.

CHAPTER TWENTY-ONE
The Epistles

Romans

¹Paul, a servant of Jesus Christ, called to be an apostle, set apart for the Good News of God, ²which he promised before through his prophets in the holy Scriptures, ³concerning *his Son, who was born of the seed of David according to the flesh*, ⁴who was *declared to be the Son of God* with power, according to the Spirit of holiness, *by the resurrection from the dead*, Jesus Christ our Lord. (Romans 1:1–4)

The Book of Romans, the first book of the letters (epistles), begins by describing Jesus, the Anointed One. Paul doesn't call him "God, the second person of the Trinity," nor does he call him "God Incarnate." To the contrary, he is the Anointed One and the Son of God who was "born of the seed of David according to the flesh and *was declared to be* the Son of God... *by the resurrection from the dead.*" This is a specific definition and it is maintained without alteration throughout the book.[1] This explanation of Jesus is totally reversed by the false idea that Jesus was an incarnation of God.

Before going on with Paul, let's look at some statements from James D. G. Dunn regarding the way in which Paul spoke of Jesus. Dunn is a highly respected, often quoted contemporary scholar. The following insights he provides are quite enlightening.

> Within Jewish thought there was a fair amount of speculation about exalted heroes... Jewish monotheistic faith could accommodate the idea of one highly exalted, without (apparently) any thought that Jewish monotheism was compromised or would have to be rethought... Equally striking is the repeated formula in the Pauline letters in which God is spoken of as 'the God and Father of our Lord Jesus Christ' (Rom. 15:6; 2 Cor. 1:3; 11:31; Col. 1:3; Eph. 1:3, 17; also 1 Pet. 1:3). The striking feature is that Paul speaks of God not simply as the God of Christ, but as 'the *God...* of our *Lord*

---

[1] The following verses are the places where Jesus is clearly and irrefutably held in personal distinction from God the Father in the epistles of Romans through Jude:
Romans 1:1, 2–3, 7, 8, 9, 16; 2:16; 3:22, 25; 4:24; 5:1, 8, 10, 11, 15; 6:4, 10, 11, 23; 7:4, 25; 8:3, 9, 11, 17, 29, 32, 34, 39; 9:5, 33; 10:3–4, 9; 14:18; 15:5, 6, 7, 8, 16, 17, 19, 30; 16:20, 25, 27.
1 Corinthians 1:1, 2, 3, 4, 24, 30; 2:16; 3:22–23; 4:1; 6:11, 14, 15; 8:6; 9:21; 10:4–5; 11:3; 12:27–28; 15:15, 24, 25, 27, 28, 57.
2 Corinthians 1:1, 2, 3, 18–19, 20, 21; 2:14, 15, 17; 3:3, 4–5; 4:4, 6, 14; 5:18, 19, 20, 21; 9:13; 10:5; 11:31; 12:2, 19; 13:4, 14.
Galatians 1:1, 3, 4, 15–16; 2:21; 3:17, 21–22, 26; 4:4, 6, 7, 14; 6:14.
Ephesians 1:1, 2, 3, 4, 5, 10, 17, 19–20; 2:4–5, 7, 10, 12, 16, 18, 19–20; 3:1–6, 9, 10–11, 14, 21; 4:32; 5:2, 5, 20; 6:6, 23.
Philippians 1:2, 8, 11; 2:5–6, 9, 11; 3:3, 9, 14; 4:7, 19–20.
Colossians 1:1, 2, 3, 12–13, 15, 19, 27; 2:2, 12; 3:1, 3, 16–17; 4:3, 12.
1 Thessalonians 1:1, 3, 9–10; 2:14, 15; 3:2, 11, 13; 4:16; 5:9, 18, 23.
2 Thessalonians 1:1, 2, 8, 12; 2:14, 16–17; 3:5.

Jesus Christ.' Even as Lord, Jesus acknowledges his Father as his God. Here it becomes plain that *kyrios* [lord] is not so much a way of *identifying* Jesus with God, but if anything more a way of *distinguishing* Jesus *from* God... That is, that Jesus' lordship is a status granted by God, a sharing in his authority. It is not that God stepped aside and Jesus has taken over. It is rather that God shared his lordship with Christ, without it ceasing to be God's alone.[2]

Does Paul speak of Jesus as 'God/god'? The debate here revolves around one text in particular—Rom. 9:5 What is at issue is whether the final clause would be more fairly translated: 'from them, according to the flesh, comes the Messiah, who is over all, God blessed for ever. Amen' (NRSV). This is stylistically the most natural reading, and it accords with Paul's style elsewhere... On the other hand, the theology implied in referring the benediction to the Messiah would almost certainly jar with anyone sensitive to the context... It is equally notable that it is precisely the other Pauline benedictions which bless 'the God and Father of our Lord Jesus (Christ).' In other words, to infer that Paul intended

---

1 Timothy 1:1, 2, 16–17; 2:5; 4:5–6; 5:21; 6:13.
2 Timothy 1:1, 2, 9; 2:8–9, 19; 3:15–16; 4:1.
Titus 1:1, 4; 2:13.
Philemon 1:3.
Hebrews 1:1, 3, 5, 6, 8, 9, 13; 2:3, 9, 12, 13, 17; 3:1–2; 4:14; 5:5, 6, 7, 8–10; 6:1; 7:21–22, 25; 8:1; 9:14, 9:24; 10:7, 9, 12–13, 21; 11:25–26; 12:2, 22–24; 13:20–21.
James 1:1.
1 Peter 1:2, 3, 17–19, 21; 2:4, 5, 20–21, 23; 3:15–16, 18, 21, 22; 4:1–2, 11, 14; 5:1–2, 10.
2 Peter 1:1, 2, 17.
1 John 1:3, 5–7; 2:1, 22, 23, 24; 3:8–9, 23; 4:2, 3, 9, 10, 14; 5:1, 5, 9, 10, 11, 20.
2 John 1:3, 9.
Jude 1:1, 4, 21.
[2] James D. G. Dunn, *The Theology of Paul the Apostle* (Grand Rapids, MI: Eerdmans, 1998), 252–254.

> Rom. 9:5 as a benediction to Christ as 'God' would imply that he had abandoned the reserve which is such a mark of his talk of the exalted Christ elsewhere. And this would be no insignificant matter... So, in terms of reconstructing Paul's theology, we would be wiser to hear the benediction as a moment of high exultation (for Israel's blessings) and not as a considered expression of his theology.
> We need not discuss other possible references in the Pauline corpus. They either depend on contentious or little supported readings of the text, or are later... . Particularly Tit. 2:13—'awaiting the blessed hope and appearance of the glory of our great God and Saviour, Jesus Christ.' This is the most probable rendering... And is 'Jesus Christ' in apposition to 'our great God and Saviour' or to 'the glory of our great God and Saviour' (cf. particularly to John 1:14 and 12:41)?[3]

The point here, in observing that God is the "God and Father of our *Lord* Jesus Christ," is that Paul speaks of Christ in radically different ways than Onenessians or even Trinitarians do. In fact, Dunn is strongly insinuating that to read into Paul's words the idea that Paul taught Jesus to "be" God, would be to misrepresent what Paul was saying overall.

Furthermore, Dunn makes an excellent case that the term "Lord" for Christ is not a code word for deity, as some seem to suppose. The issue is that later theologians keep insisting on interpreting Paul, not through the lens (language and viewpoint) of a first-century Jew, but in the context of post-Nicene Trinitarianism and even post-gnostic views of Christ as an incarnation.

Getting back to our opening verse for this chapter, Paul's description of Christ is foundational. This explanation is not a side note, as if it were so full of allegory as to be barely understandable. These are clearly terms of definition. Christ means the anointed one, who, like Aaron, hasn't taken this honor unto himself. Son means off-

---

[3] James D. G. Dunn, *The Theology of Paul the Apostle* (Grand Rapids, MI: Eerdmans, 1998), 255–257.

spring, just as we've learned. A son isn't a root, a spring from a well, or a ray of light from the sun. Biblically, Jesus wasn't God's Son because he was of the same essence of the Father. Rather he was led by the Spirit and was *declared to be the Son of God by the resurrection from the dead.*

Romans 1 is remarkably similar to John 1. In fact, when both are considered synonymous—that is, one can be used for interpreting the other—then only one possible view emerges. Let's take a look at John 1:

> ¹In the beginning was the Word, and the Word was with God, and the Word was God. ²The same was in the beginning with God. ³All things were made through him. Without him was not anything made that has been made. ⁴In him was life, and the life was the light of men. ⁵The light shines in the darkness, and the darkness hasn't overcome it... ¹⁴The Word became flesh, and lived among us. We saw his glory, such glory as of the one and only Son of the Father, full of grace and truth. (John 1:1–14)

Now let's compare the two passages and let them interpret each other:

John 1	Romans 1
¹In the beginning was the Word, and the Word was with God, and the Word was God. ²The same was in the beginning with God.	¹...Jesus The Anointed One...of God, ²...which He had promised before through his prophets in the holy Scriptures.
¹⁴The Word became flesh, and lived among us. We saw his glory, such glory as of the one and only Son of the Father.	³...concerning his Son, who was born of the seed of David according to the flesh, ⁴who was declared to be the Son of God...by the resurrection from the dead, Jesus Christ our Lord.

It is obvious that John was using poetic, allegorical language, whereas Paul was speaking in plain descriptive language to believing disciples. Paul's words are the Scriptures that should be used to explain John's meanings, rather than man's opinions that are influenced by pagan Greek ideas of the *logos*. Why? Because, Paul's words reiterate plainly what the OT Schoolmaster taught about the coming Messiah. It would be unfounded to think that John was using language to support pagan ideas. Pagans would interpret John's "*logos*" as one of their deities of the same name. On the other hand, Jews like the apostles would interpret John's "word" as God's plan for a Messiah that was always in the mind of God (God's foreknowledge) and would be revealed in God's time. Furthermore, there are no other Scriptures in the entire Bible that corroborate the pagan-influenced view that the Messiah would be an emanation of the material or spiritual essence of God's substance. That idea came directly from paganism and to jump to such a conclusion would be to ignore the way Jesus taught us to interpret Scriptures: by using clear statements, not by jumping to conclusions. It's just that simple.

In fact, practically every epistle in the NT begins by establishing itself on the authority and model of the true Son of God doctrine. The pattern is always God over Christ over the apostle or author. Here are two examples:

> Paul, an apostle of Christ Jesus through the will of God. (2 Corinthians 1:1)

Here, to take the terms literally, Paul was saying he was an apostle under Jesus the Anointed One, and both he and Jesus were such by the will of God.

> Paul, an apostle (not from men, neither through man, but through Jesus Christ, and God the Father, who raised him from the dead). (Galatians 1:1)

Paul wasn't an apostle ordained by men, but through Jesus who was anointed by God the Father, who raised him from the dead. This is simple enough language. Jesus died, so Paul was not talking about some person who was coequal with God who could not die, nor was he saying that Jesus the Anointed One was himself God or God's "human nature." And so it goes in the following: Eph. 1:1; Phil. 1:1–2; Col. 1:1–2; 1 Thes. 1:1; 2 Thes. 1:1–2; 1 Tim. 1:1–2; 2 Tim. 1:1–2; Titus 1:1; Phil. 1:3; Heb. 1:1–2; James 1:1; 1 Peter 1:1–3; 2 Peter 1:1; 1 John 1:3; 2 John 1:3; Jude 1:1.

All the epistles begin by simply and consistently reiterating the hierarchy that Paul made so clear in Corinthians:

> But I would have you know that the head of every man is Christ, and the head of the woman is the man, and the head of Christ is God. (1 Corinthians 11:3)

Christ	Husband	God
Man	Wife	Christ

It is wrong to think that since God is the head of Christ they must be personally the same. That would mean a man and his wife would have to be personally the same in order for the man to be the "head" of the wife and the wife to be the "body" of the man in the marriage relationship. In fact, in the next chapter Paul teaches us that a "body" necessarily means there are "many members" that make up the "body."

> [12]For as the body is one, and has many members, and all the members of the body, being many, are one body; so also is Christ. [13]For in one Spirit we were all baptized into one body, whether Jews or Greeks, whether bond or free; and were all given to drink into one Spirit. [14]For *the body is not one member, but many*. (1 Corinthians 12:12–14)

The point is that in one sense Jesus is the bodily temple of God, just as much as we are all the one body of Christ and husbands and wives are one "body" or "flesh" in their own marriage. No one would claim that my wife and I are therefore the same person, or that each personal member of Christ's body is the person of Christ. In this same manner, neither do these verses teach that Christ is the person of God.

The Greek Word *kai*

Does "*Kai*" Always Mean "That is"?		
God	And Even That is	Our Bro. Sosthenes

Some Onenessian theologians claim that the introductions to the epistles teach Onenessianism. They lean on the fact that the word *kai* in Greek means not only "and," but can also mean "even" or "that is." For example, they interpret Galatians 1 in this way... "Paul, an apostle... (through Jesus Christ, [that is] God the Father, who raised him from the dead)" (Galatians 1:1). However, this is just interpreting by presupposed bias. That is, they are just cherry-picking an option that suits them, regardless of the context, when they should instead be using a holistic approach to Paul's theology of Messiah as the Son of God, and God as his Father. For example:

> Blessed be the God and Father of our Lord Jesus Christ. (Ephesians 1:3)

Onenessians simply have no biblical explanation of how the "*Lord*" Jesus Christ could "have" a God and a Father!

We simply need to ask ourselves what the writers were actually trying to say. If the Oneness position was what they were trying to say, did they do a very good job of it? Or were they really trying to say something else?

What we really need to do is simply to read the passages in their context. For example, let's look at this verse: ¹"Paul, called to be an apostle of Jesus Christ through the will of God, *and* our brother Sosthenes, ²to the assembly of God which is at Corinth..." (1 Corinthians 1:1). If it were a hard and fast rule to interpret *kai* as "even/that is," we would read something like this: "... God even/that is our brother Sosthenes..." Certainly no Onenessian would confuse this sentence to mean that dear brother Sosthenes was thereby meant to be understood as also being the person of God the Father. And yet basically that is exactly what they are assuming it says of Christ in relation to the Father. Conversely, there is not one instance of these introductions where *kai* is unquestionably used to mean that God and His Anointed One are one and the same individual. It is yet another way that Onenessians interject their ideas upon the text, rather than being something that is simply stated by the text. *Thus, the key is simply reading the texts in context.*

The key word in all of these instances is "Christ." In all the introductions we've just listed, Jesus is called Christ (the Anointed One), which means the one who didn't take this honor upon himself but was called as Aaron was. If Jesus is the one who is anointed *and* the one who anointed himself, then Galatians 1:1 would have to be interpreted like this: "Paul, an apostle... through Jesus the anointed one [who didn't take this honor upon himself], [that is] God the Father [who anointed himself even though that contradicts the meaning of being anointed by another and], who raised him[self] from the dead)." Do you see how nonsensical the Onenessian use of *kai* becomes?

They are able to make that nonsensical conclusion simply by not keeping in mind, or purposely concealing, what the word Christ truly means.

Did you notice also, at the end of Galatians 1:1, that Paul used two personal pronouns ("who raised him") to distinguish between God and Christ? In other words, Paul wasn't referring to Jesus' impersonal human nature in distinction with his deific nature; he was referring clearly and plainly to two personally distinct individuals.

Do you see how reading these words in context and with the

plain meanings in sight allows us to see right through false, jumped-to conclusions of what they "could" mean. This is exactly how the Trinitarians interpret passages that "could mean" God is a Trinity when they actually don't say so. The key is simply letting the Bible interpret the Bible, rather than using man's opinions.

Romans Teaches Christ is a Man

Nowhere in the Book of Romans does Paul expound on the pagan idea of Jesus being an incarnation of God the Father. Rather, we continue to find the same types of explanations of what Jesus Christ is. For example, he writes:

> [10]For if, while we were enemies, we were reconciled to God through the death of his Son, much more, being reconciled, we will be saved by his life. [11]Not only so, but we also rejoice in God through our Lord Jesus Christ, through whom we have now received the reconciliation. [12]Therefore, *as sin entered into the world through one man, and death through sin; and so death passed to all men*, because all sinned. [13]For until the law, sin was in the world; but sin is not charged when there is no law. [14]Nevertheless death reigned from Adam until Moses, even over those whose sins weren't like Adam's disobedience, who is a foreshadowing of him who was to come. [15]But the free gift isn't like the trespass. *For if by the trespass of the one the many died, much more did the grace of God, and the gift by the grace of the one man, Jesus Christ*, abound to the many. (Romans 5:10–15)

This passage is very clear: the freely given gift of saving grace, and with it the promise of eternal life, came by one man who reversed the curse of death that also came upon mankind by one man. It begins by talking about Christ as God's Son; that is, neither as an emanation of the Father's essence, nor as the "impersonal human nature" in contrast to Jesus' deific nature. Rather, Jesus is treated as though on the same level as Adam, and the passage contrasts

Adam's disobedience with Christ's obedience. This means, in reality, that if Jesus were God incarnate he really didn't do any great thing by being obedient to Himself.

What we see in Romans 5:10–15 is what Paul clearly taught in an explanatory way. We never find Paul clearly "teaching" an explanation of either the Oneness or Trinity view. Thus, these latter views are a way of negating what Paul actually did teach and explain in passages such as this one.

Let's consider one final passage in Romans:

> [5]Now the God of patience and of encouragement grant you to be of the same mind one with another according to Christ Jesus, [6]that with one accord you may with one mouth glorify the God _and_ Father of our Lord Jesus Christ. (Romans 15:5–6)

Here then, in verse six, is a good place where "and" could easily be interpreted as "even/that is," because of the clear context. But that being the case, watch how it would look if we try to interpret it in a Onenessian sense:

> ...With one accord... with one mouth glorify the *Deific Nature and Father* of our Lord Jesus the impersonal *Human Nature*.

This ridiculous parody shows what Onenessians do by saying the humanity and deity of Christ are to be understood in such distinctions, and not as the personal distinctions the words father and son plainly mean. Do Onenessians really believe that the impersonal human nature of Jesus is our Lord? Of course not. The point is that they only interpret *kai* as "even/that is" when it fits their theology and is helpful for their cause to do so, regardless of the context. In context, the passage is simply reiterating a truth that Jesus clearly explained to us:

> Jesus said to her, "Don't touch me, for I haven't yet ascended to my Father; but go to my brothers, and tell them, 'I am ascending *to _my Father_ and your Father, to _my God_ and your God.*" (John 20:17)

Jesus is clearly telling us that first, he has a God and Father, and second, that His God and Father is the same God and Father as ours—and in the same way that He is God and Father to us.

So we have gone through the Book of Romans, but we have not yet heard Paul discuss Jesus as an incarnation of God, either in a Trinitarian or in a Onenessian sense. Rather, he taught and explained something different: he has consistently upheld the Son of God doctrine just as it was understood in the OT Schoolmaster.

1 Corinthians – Jesus is God's Son

As we read through the epistles to the Corinthians, we come upon this passage:

> God is faithful, through whom you were called into the fellowship of *his Son*, Jesus Christ, our Lord. (1 Corinthians 1:9)

This statement is pretty straightforward and continues the Son of God theme. However, what would it look like if it were interpreted through the lens of Onenessianism? For example, one Oneness preacher states their position like this:

> And when you speak of Jesus Christ you are speaking of a dual nature. You are speaking of flesh and you are speaking of Spirit. And the flesh is the Son and the Spirit is the Father.[4]

> "Our Great God and our Savior, He's a dual nature. He's Father and He's Son, He's God and He's man. He's absolutely God; He's absolutely man."[5]

So then, in the Onenessian understanding, 1 Corinthians 1:9 should be interpreted something like this:

---

[4] Anthony Mangun, *The Dual Nature of Christ*, Disc 5, track 6, just over 2 minutes in.

[5] Ibid., Disc 6, Track 1, 1:53.

...The [deific nature of Jesus] is faithful, through whom you were called into the fellowship of his [impersonal human nature], Jesus the [anointed impersonal human nature], our Lord.

If that is what it meant, I wonder why that isn't what it says, here or anywhere else? The truth is that when the Bible speaks of Christ, it is speaking of an anointed man, period. The very term "Christ" (the Anointed One) directly refutes any interpretation claiming that Christ was a dual-natured individual. As we have shown, the idea of calling Jesus Christ a dual-natured individual is antichrist in nature, because it completely negates the truth of Jesus' source of authority: his anointing that he did *not* take upon himself. Although it may seem sacrilege to criticize their position, in reality it is the Oneness position that is sacrilegious to what the Scriptures actually teach and explain about Jesus the Anointed One, God's Son!

The True Apostolic Doctrinal Discourse on the Nature of Christ

When we get to 1 Corinthians 15, we find Paul explaining about Jesus. This is "Son of God Doctrine" through and through, spelled out plainly for us, with no mention of either Trinity or Oneness.

> [20]But now Christ has been raised from the dead. *He became the first fruits* of those who are asleep.[21]For *since death came by man, the resurrection of the dead also came by man.* [22]For as in Adam all die, so also in Christ all will be made alive. [23]But each in his own order: Christ the first fruits, then those who are Christ's, at his coming. [24]Then the end comes, when he will deliver up the Kingdom to God, even the Father; when he will have abolished all rule and all authority and power. [25]For he must reign until he has put all his enemies under his feet. [26]The last enemy that will be abolished is death. [27]For, "He put all things in subjection under his feet." But when he says, "All things are put in subjection," it is evident that *he is excepted who subjected*

all things to him. ²⁸When all things have been subjected to him, *then the Son will also <u>himself</u> be subjected to him who subjected all things to him,* that God may be all in all. (1 Corinthians 15:20–28)

In this passage Paul purposely *explains and defines* who and what Christ is. There are no comparable explanations of the Trinity or the Onenessian incarnation doctrines. Therefore, those man-made opinions are *substitutes* that attempt to replace the truth Paul explained above.

In Paul's explanation, Jesus is a man like Adam. Christ is the *first fruits of those who sleep;* that is, of those who die, which obviously means all the rest of us human beings. The reference to fruit is an agricultural and sacrificial term; Jesus himself is part of God's harvest of souls, and Jesus was the first one because he was the first one to be resurrected from the dead into the presence of God forevermore!

In the latter part of the passage, Christ is personally distinct from God, *who* subjected all things unto *him.* There *is no suggestion that this was Jesus' deific nature in contrast to his impersonal human nature.* To the contrary, in the end, Paul clearly says, the Son "*himself*" will be subject to God, *just as the rest of us are,* so that God may be all in all. So Paul *explicitly described this as one personal self in contrast to another personal self.* This language is clear enough when theologians aren't interjecting esoteric meanings that only they really understand. There is no Oneness talk here or Trinitarian talk. This is pure, simple and true "Son of God" teaching all the way.

2 Corinthians – God is the Father

In 2 Corinthians, we find again that God is the Father of Jesus, with no mention that Jesus the Son is code for the human nature of the person of God.

> Blessed be the God and Father of our Lord Jesus Christ. (2 Corinthians 1:3)

> The *God and Father of* the Lord Jesus Christ, he who is blessed forevermore, knows that I don't lie. (2 Corinthians 11:31)

These two passages are reminiscent of these sayings of Jesus:

> Jesus said to her, "...I haven't yet ascended to my Father; but go to my brothers, and tell them, 'I am ascending to *my Father* and your Father, to *my God* and your God.'" (John 20:17)

> He who overcomes, I will make him a pillar in the temple of *my God*, and he will go out from there no more. I will write on him the name of *my God*, and the name of the city of *my God*, the new Jerusalem, which comes down out of heaven from *my God*, and my own new name. (Revelation 3:12)

> About the ninth hour Jesus cried with a loud voice, saying... "*My God, my God*, why have you forsaken me?" (Matthew 27:46)

Again, these statements explicitly refer to personal whos, not impersonal natures.

Furthermore, when Paul gets down to the task of explaining who and what Jesus is, he is very clear and to the point:

> [18]But all things are of God, who reconciled us to himself through Jesus the Anointed One, and gave to us the ministry of reconciliation; [19]namely, that God was in the Anointed One reconciling the world to himself, not reckoning to them their trespasses, and having committed to us the word of reconciliation. [20]We are therefore ambassadors on behalf of Christ, as though God were entreating by us. We beg you on behalf of Christ, be reconciled to God. [21]For *him who* knew no sin *he made to be sin* on our behalf; so that in *him* we might become the righteousness of God. (2 Corinthians 5:18–21)

This is one of those passages that Onenessians take out of context in order to use it to "prove" their position. They claim that since God reconciled us to "himself" through Christ, that can only mean that Christ is the "himself" of God. However, that conclusion simply ignores the grammar of the passage. If that is *necessarily* the case based only on this wording, then when we have God dwelling in us and working through us it would also have to mean that we too are the "himself" of "God in us."

The real meaning of the passage can be found in Paul's explicit interpretation in verse 21. Yet again Paul uses distinct personal pronouns in personal distinction from each other. Thus, "*Him who* knew no sin" is personal pronoun #1. Then Paul says "*He*," which is personal pronoun #2, made (personal pronoun #1) to be sin on "our" (personal pronoun #3) behalf. Personal pronoun #1 is the person of Christ, who is held in personal distinction to God (personal pronoun #2). There is no explanation that these meant or were intended to be interpreted as impersonal natures of the one person of Jesus. So whoever claims they mean other than they say, without any scriptural support saying so, is really saying they don't believe this or other Scriptures like it!

In our final passage from 2 Corinthians, Christ is once again held in personal distinction from God in the same exact way that we are also held in personal distinction to God.

> For he was crucified through weakness, yet he lives through the power of God. For we also are weak in him, but we will live with him through the power of God toward you. (2 Corinthians 13:4)

"He" (Christ) was weak in the same way that "we" are also weak, and we as with him will live through the power of God. We are not God any more than Christ is God, for we are just as personally weak as he is without God. This we have explicitly from Jesus, who said, "Most assuredly, I tell you, the Son can do nothing of *himself*..." (John 5:19), and again, "I can *of myself* do nothing" (John 5:30). The word that Christ uses, "himself," explicitly contradicts and thus refutes the antichristian notion that Christ is a dual-natured individual.

Galatians

> Paul, an apostle (not from men, neither through man, but through Jesus Christ, and God the Father, who raised him from the dead) (Galatians 1:1)

Paul continues his description of Christ being personally distinct from God, who raised him from the dead. The two personal pronouns are all we need to understand he is reiterating the same hierarchy he gave us in 1 Corinthians 11.

> [15]But when it was the good pleasure of God, who separated me from my mother's womb, and called me through his grace, [16]to reveal his Son in me, that I might preach him among the Gentiles, I didn't immediately confer with flesh and blood. (Galatians 1:15–16)

Paul still holds Jesus to be God's Son, not God incarnate. Furthermore, Paul explains to us, yet again, what this son is that he is referring to:

> [4]But when the fulness of the time was come, God sent forth his Son, made of a woman, made under the law, [5]To redeem them that were under the law, that we might receive the adoption of sons.. (Galatians 4:4–5, KJV)

There is no discussion of how "son" really means God's impersonal flesh, no teaching on how Christ is an incarnation of the third person of the Gnostic Trinity. Rather in specific terms, God sent forth his son made of a woman. It thus refutes the ancient Trinitarian and Gnostic idea that the Son is made of no other essence or substance than that of the Father. It also refutes the idea that the Son was made of a purer "pre-fall" humanity, as many Onenessians would like to presume. What Paul certainly did not say is that "God made Himself a body and incarnated Himself into human form." That is what we would expect this to say if Onenessianism were at all actually biblical.

Paul's language here is quite reminiscent of Jesus' words that we are to believe not in him, but in Him who sent him. There is a sender and a sent one, and if you believe they are the same, then you simply don't believe what the Bible says:

> ⁴¹So they took away the stone from the place where the dead man was lying. Jesus lifted up his eyes, and said, "Father, I thank you that you listened to me. ⁴²I know that you always listen to me, but because of the multitude that stands around I said this, that they may believe that you sent me." (John 11:41–42)

Imagine how this looks in the Oneness view: "Father, I thank me, that I have listened to me. I know that I always listen to me, but because of the multitude... I said this that they may believe that I sent me." This is nonsense. But it is the same nonsense to think that is what Paul "was trying to say" or that he "really meant to say" (but didn't) in Galatians 4:4–7.

It means what it says. When the time came, God sent His Son made of a woman.

Ephesians

> Blessed be *the God and Father of our Lord Jesus Christ*, who has blessed us with every spiritual blessing in the heavenly places in Christ. (Ephesians 1:3)

> That *the God of our Lord Jesus Christ*, the Father of glory, may give to you a spirit of wisdom and revelation in the knowledge of him. (Ephesians 1:17)

> ¹⁴For this cause, I bow my knees to *the Father of our Lord Jesus Christ*, ¹⁵from whom every family in heaven and on earth is named, ¹⁶that he would grant you, according to the riches of his glory, that you may be strengthened with power through his Spirit in the inward man; ¹⁷that

the Anointed One may dwell in your hearts *through faith*;
to the end that you, being rooted and grounded in love.
(Ephesians 3:13–17)

These passages are clear and descriptive. The terms used are "Father" and "son," not natures in one personal individual. Don't forget that father means father, not deific nature, and son or Christ doesn't mean impersonal human nature. That is the way Onenessians read it, but that isn't what Paul said, wrote, or meant. He explained what he meant. God is the Father of Christ. A Father is always and consistently a distinct personal entity to a son.

But it says Christ dwells in our hearts, so must that mean he is God? After all, a person can't be in two places at once, let alone in the hearts of all believers. No, that would be the *wrong* conclusion. When Paul wrote "...you being gathered together, and my spirit" (1 Corinthians 5:4), did he mean to imply he was God or omnipresent? Of course not. The scriptural concept is this: "...he that is joined unto the Lord is one spirit" (1 Corinthians 6:17). So the answer is to continue reading what Paul said. He said, in Ephesians 3:17, that Christ dwells in our hearts "...by faith." And what does Paul say about faith?

> Now faith is assurance of *things hoped for*, proof of *things not seen*. (Hebrews 11:1)

> [24]For we were saved in hope, but *hope that is seen is not hope*. For *who hopes for that which he sees*? [25]But if we hope for that which we don't see, we wait for it with patience. (Romans 8:24–25)

So then, when we walk in Christ, we let his spirit—that is, his attitude—work in and through us. We have counted ourselves dead to sin, but alive to God through the righteousness of Christ. Does that mean we are actually righteous? Only as long as we are righteous in Christ working through us. Let's see how the Bible talks about the Spirit of Christ dwelling in us:

> ¹⁶Let the word of Christ dwell in you richly; in all wisdom teaching and admonishing one another with psalms, hymns, and spiritual songs, singing with grace in your heart to the Lord. ¹⁷Whatever you do, in word or in deed, do all in the name of the Lord Jesus, giving thanks to God the Father, through him. (Colossians 3:16–17)

In this passage, having Christ dwell in us means that we allow the word of Christ to lead us in wisdom teaching, and admonishing one another with spiritual songs.

Now let's look at the "Spirit" that was in Christ:

> ¹A shoot will come out of the stock of Jesse, And a branch out of his roots will bear fruit. ²The Spirit of YHWH will rest on him: *The spirit of wisdom and understanding, The spirit of counsel and might, The spirit of knowledge and of the fear of YHWH.* ³His delight will be in the fear of YHWH. He will not judge by the sight of his eyes, Neither decide by the hearing of his ears; ⁴But with righteousness he will judge the poor, And decide with equity for the humble of the earth. He will strike the earth with the rod of his mouth; And with the breath of his lips he will kill the wicked. ⁵Righteousness will be the belt of his waist, And faithfulness the belt of his waist. (Isaiah 11:1–5)

Through these words we see that having the Spirit of Christ in us is to take on his attitudinal characteristics. The opposite way of viewing these traits is as the pagans do, in assigning to each characteristic a separate personality. Thus they come up with gods for the skies and the seas and so forth. Such is carnal, pagan thinking!

The Spirit of Christ is the attitude of Christ, for these are the "spirits" that were in him: wisdom, understanding, counsel and might, the spirit of knowledge, and yes, even the fear of YHWH was in Christ! Is the Spirit of YHWH a distinct person in the godhead? No? Then neither is Christ a distinct person in the godhead or an incarnation of God.

Philippians

We first addressed this next passage in Chapter Seventeen, when we discussed Jesus' prayer "not my will, but yours be done." Here we will focus on it in greater detail.

> [5]Have this in your mind, which was also in Christ Jesus, [6]who, existing in the form of God, didn't consider it robbery to be equal with God, [7]but emptied himself, taking the form of a servant, being made in the likeness of men. [8]And being found in human form, he humbled himself, becoming obedient to death, yes, the death of the cross. [9]Therefore God also highly exalted him, and gave to him the name which is above every name; [10]that at the name of Jesus every knee should bow, of those in heaven, those on earth, and those under the earth, [11]and that every tongue should confess that Jesus Christ is Lord, to the glory of God the Father. [12]So then, my beloved, even as you have always obeyed, not only in my presence, but now much more in my absence, work out your own salvation with fear and trembling. (Philippians 2:5–12)

This passage is extremely simple if read without attempting to impose pagan ideas of incarnation and the like into it. Nothing in this passage says anything about a preexistent Christ humbling himself before coming to earth. However, it does explicitly say, in verse 8, that this humbling happened while Jesus was a human being. It goes on to teach how and why this human being was exalted by God. Note how Young's Literal Translation has this passage:

> [7]But did empty himself, the form of a servant having taken, in the likeness of men having been made, [8]and in fashion having been found as a man, he humbled himself... (Philippians 2:7-8, YLT)

Christ was "having been made" in the likeness of men, and it was in that state that he emptied himself and took the form of a servant, not before. This says nothing at all of him "divesting himself" of his personal deific powers or nature. That idea is something that men have read back into the text, but the context betrays the error in such an interpretation.

Keeping things in context, Paul began this passage by telling us *how we are to think*: "Have this in *your* mind." His main purpose was to establish what *our* attitude should be regarding *our* position before God. The passage uses Christ *as an example for us* to help us understand what should be in *our* minds. The apostle reiterated that purpose in the conclusion in verse 12. This he began by saying, "So then..." Through this phrase, he linked what was said about the mind of Christ to what he said next. "So then... as you have always obeyed... now... work out your own salvation..." (Philippians 2:12). To paraphrase, he was primarily saying to us, "Here's how you are to think of yourself: the way Christ thought of himself."

Obviously, none of us consciously remembers being in heaven and thinking, "Being as I am God, I am going to become a human in order to show people how submissive to God I can be and how they should be." That isn't what Paul said, but some people want us to believe that is what Paul implied Christ was thinking. When we see the stated purpose of the passage, which was how we are to think of ourselves, we can see the passage actually refutes that whole idea.

Next, it says that Jesus found himself "in the *form* of God." What it does *not* say is, "Jesus Christ *being* God..." There are perfectly good biblical reasons why Jesus could think of himself as being *in the form of* God without meaning he actually was God. Genesis 1:26–27 provides an ideal context for interpreting what is meant here, since that is where the Bible first mentions mankind being in the form of God:

> God said, "Let us make man in our image, after our likeness: and let them have dominion..." God created man in His own image. In God's image He created him... (Genesis 1:26–27)

This Scripture teaches us that when God made man He *made man in His own image*, and in doing so, God gave man dominion, which means rule and domination over the rest of creation. This is the "form of God" that Jesus found himself in: having dominion, from God, over the rest of creation. That isn't to say he was God, or was even equal to God, for it is written again:

> For, "He put all things in subjection under his feet." But when he says, "All things are put in subjection," it is evident that he is excepted who subjected all things to him. (1 Corinthians 15:27)

So then, the authority given to Jesus (Matthew 28:18), is what causes people, who weren't and aren't used to seeing such authority in humans, to wrongly assume such authority was his inherently, by personality. But clearly, the Bible teaches Jesus' authority was not inherent and, in fact, was not unlimited. He was still, and always will be, under authority to God.

In the Book of Romans, Paul taught, "that to whom you present yourselves as servants to obedience, his servants you are whom you obey; whether of sin to death, or of obedience to righteousness" (Romans 6:16). God had given Adam and Eve dominion over all things, including over the serpent, when He created them. When Adam and Eve submitted to the serpent, they gave up their God-given dominion to the serpent and became servants of unrighteousness. That is, they turned God's divine order of authority upside down. On the other hand, Jesus never relinquished his God-given dominion to anyone. Rather, Jesus took responsibility for it and acted on it in a righteous manner. This was actually the whole point of the passage in Philippians. Jesus' attitude in finding himself in the form of God was that he didn't think it was stealing from God to wield that authority. After all, it was God who gave him all authority. But he still recognized that the true God, the Father, still had authority over him.

Whereas the worldly mind thinks, "If I'm in charge, I'm going to do things my way," Jesus had the better way. He determined not to build his own reputation. Instead, he made himself a servant to God and mankind and became a complete reflection of God's character traits. It was just this kind of thinking that God foresaw and foreordained in Jesus. It was that kind of thinking that God loved Jesus for. And it was that attitude for which God exalted him. Thus, Philippians continues by saying, in verse 9, "Therefore God also highly exalted him." The very fact that it says God exalted him is the internal evidence that this passage is not saying Jesus was first God, who then later made himself human, as many suppose.

We see, then, that Paul was simply reiterating biblical teachings in Philippians. Jesus' thinking of himself *in the form of* God is how we should expect Christ to think of himself as the second Adam. As the second Adam, he was created with the same dominion as the first Adam.

> So also it is written, "The first man, Adam, became a living soul." The last Adam became a life-giving spirit. However that which is spiritual isn't first, but that which is natural, then that which is spiritual. The first man is of the earth, made of dust. The second *man* is[50] from heaven. (1 Corinthians 15:45–47)

The idea of Christ as second Adam aligns perfectly with the proclamation that God explicitly *made* Jesus Lord and Christ. There are no biblical grounds for interpreting Philippians in a way that assigns preexistence or deity to Jesus. To interpret the passage as if the word "form" was not there and imply it means Jesus simply was "being… God" would be to tamper with the Bible. To claim that it says Jesus humbled himself before being made human would be adding to the Bible which is strictly forbidden.

There is, then, no reason to believe this wasn't the type of "form of God" that Paul had in mind in Philippians 2:6. The main purpose of the passage was to teach us how we are to think. Theologians *jump to the conclusion* that this passage was primarily meant to explain Christ's pre-human God-Person choice to be incarnated. That idea has no parallel to the way we could realistically think of ourselves.

Colossians

> We give thanks to *God the Father of our Lord Jesus Christ*, praying always for you. (Colossians 1:3)

> Who delivered us out of the power of darkness, and translated us into *the Kingdom of the Son* of his love. (Colossians 1:13)

With these words, the apostle set the context for what he went on to say in the rest of the epistle. That is, he talked about Jesus being the Son of God, but not about Jesus being an incarnation of God, or the shell of a human without personality other than God's person.

Father   Mother   Son   Oneness Father & Son

The point is, Paul started out by specifically referring to the father and son relationship portrayed on the left, not the Oneness theory on the right. Paul established that foundation and context first of all.

Secondly, it will also be helpful to recall our discussion in Chapter Sixteen about the difference between the biblical concept of God's foreknowledge and the unbiblical, pagan idea of incarnated deities.

With these two thoughts in mind, let's see if we can read the next passage, Colossians 1:15–22, without jumping to the false, unbiblical conclusion that Paul was "trying to say" that Jesus was an incarnation of God.

> v.15: who is the *image* of the invisible God, *the firstborn of all creation*...

Note that Paul described Christ as "the image of the invisible God"—not God Himself—and then, "the firstborn of all creation." With these thoughts in mind, we begin to untangle the preconceptions that Onenessians impose on these texts.

> v.16: For by him (image/firstborn) were all things created, in the heavens and on the earth, things visible and things invisible, whether thrones or dominions or principalities or powers; all things have been created through him, and for him.
> v.17: He is before all things, and in him all things are held together.
> v.18: He is the head of the body, the assembly, who is *the beginning, the firstborn from the dead*; that in all things he might have the preeminence.

Remember, "God calls the things that are not, as though they were" (Romans 4:17). So we have two choices here, interpret these verses by the pagan idea of "Gods come to the earth in the form of man" (Acts 14:11), or interpret them in the light of the Scriptures, including this one, which reiterates twice that we are talking about "the first of all *creation*" (not the Creator Himself, mind you, but the first creation of God).

This man who is the firstborn from the dead was God's *plan* from before He set creation in motion. Creating the world through and by Christ was not an afterthought. And, having foreknown that man, God planned the following for him:

> v.19 For all the fullness was pleased to dwell in him;
> v.20 and through him to reconcile all things to himself, by him, whether things on the earth, or things in the heavens, having made peace through the blood of his cross.
> v.21 You, being in past times alienated and enemies in your

mind in your evil works,
v.22 yet now he has reconciled in the body of his flesh through death, to present you holy and without blemish and blameless before him,

So then, Colossians 1:15–22, when interpreted in the light of all the "beginning oracles of God" that we've covered thus far, reveals there is only one way to understand this passage. God had this plan of this man in His mind from before time. God's plan was for this man to save mankind from our sins, and this plan included God dwelling in this man, just as He would dwell in us. This is the plan that existed from the beginning. In fact, it was through this planned man and *for* this planned man that God created this world in the first place!

We will address Colossians 2:9 in Section Five.

1 Thessalonians

> [9]...you turned to God from idols, to serve a living and true God, [10]and to wait for his Son from heaven, whom he raised from the dead—Jesus, who delivers us from the wrath to come. (1 Thessalonians 1:9–10)

First Thessalonians continues the theme that Jesus is God's Son that God raised from the dead.

1 & 2 Timothy

> [3]God our Savior... [4]... desires all people to be saved and come to full knowledge of the truth. [5]For there is one God, and one mediator between God and men, *the man* Christ Jesus (1 Timothy 2:3–5).

There is one God, and the man Christ Jesus is the one mediator between God and men. How does this verse imply that it is only speaking of Jesus' humanity as his impersonal human nature? The same word is used to describe both Jesus and all other men. Does Jesus only mediate between God and our impersonal human natures? Absolutely not. In fact, we are supposed to be dead to the flesh. So then, this passage is very clear if not interpreted through the dark lenses of man's preconceptions. God is God, and Jesus is the man distinct from God who mediates between God and mankind on our behalf.

Titus

> ³I was entrusted according to the commandment of God our Savior; ⁴to Titus, my true child according to a common faith: Grace, mercy, and peace from God the Father and the Lord Jesus Christ our Savior. (Titus 1:3–4)

This book starts out with the usual distinction between God the Father and Jesus the Anointed One. There is no confusion here as long as we keep in mind that one doesn't anoint himself, and God needs no anointing. Thus the statement itself supports the true Son of God doctrine.

> ¹⁰...that they may adorn the doctrine of God, our Savior, in all things. ¹¹For the grace of God has appeared, bringing salvation to all men, ¹²instructing us to the intent that, denying ungodliness and worldly lusts, we would live soberly, righteously, and godly in this present world; ¹³looking for the blessed hope and <u>*appearing of the glory of*</u> *our great God and Savior*, Jesus Christ; ¹⁴who gave himself for us, that he might redeem us from all iniquity, and purify for himself a people for his own possession, zealous for good works. (Titus 2:10–14)

This is a perfectly legitimate way of rendering Titus 2:13. This is how it is translated in the World English Version, Revised Standard Version, American Standard Version, New American Standard, New Revised Standard Version, English Standard Version, Douay-Rheims,

New American Standard Bible, Complete Jewish Bible, New Living Translation, Young's Literal Translation and New Century Version. In each of these translations Titus 2:13 reads in accordance with the World English Bible above: *"the appearing of the glory of our great God and Savior Jesus Christ."*

The problem is that there are other translations that put these words together differently. For example, the New International Version, King James Version, New King James Version, New English Translation, and Noah Webster's Bible translate Titus 2:13 like this: "...the *glorious appearing of* our great God and Savior Jesus Christ."

To say "looking for the appearing of the glory of..." and "looking for the glorious..." God and savior, is saying two completely different things. The former is talking about an event in time and place precipitated by God, the latter makes it about two individuals which Onenessians try to squeeze into one. So how can we tell what is the correct translation and word order?

Well, the first problem with this translation is that it isn't true to the Greek grammar. It changes the Greek noun "glory" (*doxees*) into an adjective "glorious." This is what the Bible calls "handling the word of God deceitfully."

The next thing we need to do is to interpret the way Jesus taught us: by looking for clear verses on the subject that will help us to keep from stretching the Scriptures beyond what they intend. And so, it is written again:

> For the Son of Man will come *in the glory of his Father* with his angels, and then he will render to everyone according to his deeds. (Matthew 16:27)

> The *glory which you have given me, I have given to them*; that they may be one, even as we are one. (John 17:21)

These verses support the "appearing of the glory" translation of Titus 2:13. They also tell us that Jesus' glory, like his name and authority, was not inherent to his person; they were derived from the Father. Furthermore, the glory that Jesus was given from the

Father is a glory he is also able to turn and give to the saints, so that we may be one in the same way that the Father and the Son are one.

Next, let's look at the context of Titus 2:13 and see what it tells us. For one thing, we don't find Paul saying his intention was to explain anything new here. In other words, he didn't say this passage was meant to explain the nature or relationship between Jesus and the Father. Rather, the context of the passage was, according to Paul, "instructing to the intent" of "denying ungodliness" and instead living "soberly, righteously and godly in this present world." So to claim the intent was to teach that Christ was an incarnation of God is to take the passage wildly out of context to say the least!

The proper, biblically influenced way to understand what this passage is saying is simply to accept that Paul was using typical language that reflected Jesus' words; namely, that Jesus' doctrine was not his own and that he did only what the Father commanded him. And furthermore, that Christ was never alone for the Father was always with him. How much more so, then, when Christ returns to earth!

> He who sent me is with me. The Father hasn't left me alone, for I always do the things that are pleasing to him. (John 8:29)

Thus, when Christ returns, we don't expect him to return alone or under the power of his own human authority. Rather, we look "for the blessed hope and *appearing of the glory of our great God and (our) Savior* Jesus Christ." That is, we expect Christ, the living temple of the living God to return in the same oneness that Christ promised we would share with him and the Father.

> ⁹Whoever transgresses and doesn't remain in the teaching of Christ, doesn't have God. He who remains in the teaching, *the same has both the Father and the Son.* ¹⁰If anyone comes to you, and doesn't bring this teaching, don't receive him into your house, and don't welcome him. (2 John 9–10)

Hebrews

Whose image and inscription are on it?
Luke 20:24

Jesus is the "image" of God (2 Cor. 4:4) like this image of Caesar on this coin. Thus he is not God anymore than this coin image is Caesar himself.

> ¹"God, having in the past spoken to the fathers through the prophets at many times and in various ways, ²has at the end of these days *spoken to us by his Son*, whom he appointed heir of all things, through whom also he made the worlds. ³His Son is the radiance of his glory, *the very image of his substance*, and upholding all things by the word of his power, when he had by himself made purification for our sins, sat down on the right hand of the Majesty on high." (Hebrews 1:1–3)

This passage seems pretty clear, but let's look more closely at what it says. In verse two, Jesus is again called God's Son, not an emanation like a ray from the sun or a river from a well or spring as in Trinitarianism. Nor is he called an impersonal nature of flesh as part of an incarnation of God the Father, as in Onenessianism. Now look at the details: God speaks to us through His Son. How many of us go around saying things like, "Bob speaks to me through his impersonal human nature"? Do you see how out of context that is? The word "son" isn't a code word here; it means what it says.

In verse 3, Christ is called the radiance of God's glory and the image of God's "substance." The word "image" is a word that is also applied to all human beings, so it should be obvious that this doesn't mean he is God. Rather, in Colossians we get the impression that being the image of God has to do with him being the firstborn of all creation by the resurrection of the dead.

> God said, "Let us make man *in our image, after our likeness*: and let them have dominion..." God created man in His own image. In God's image He created him... (Genesis 1:26–27)

> Who is the image of the invisible God, the firstborn of all creation... (Colossians 1:15)

The definition of "image" in Strong's is: "*charakter* (khar-ak-tare') from the same as NT:5482; a graver (the tool or the person), i.e. (by implication) engraving (["character"], the figure stamped, i.e. an exact *copy or [figuratively] representation*)."

Recall from Chapter Sixteen our example of Abraham Lincoln's image on a penny. The reason the image is there is to represent the person in place of the person. Jesus Christ is like that image of Lincoln on a penny. Christ is the "very image" of God's person specifically because he is not the person of God. One difference is that the image on the penny is incomplete. Jesus Christ is a complete *image* (or representation) of *almost all* of the personal, attitudinal characteristics of the Father. What the verse doesn't say is that Christ is the very same substance of God the Father. One instance where Jesus isn't a perfect image of God is that God is invisible but Jesus is visible. Another is that Christ was unwilling ("not my will...") to die within his own personality; nevertheless, he submitted in obedience to God's will ("...but thy will be done...").

Although the word for *image* was only used once in the NT, we are not totally without backup material. Note that Strong's says this word is related to another word, #5482, which is the word *charax*. In defining this word, Strong says it is "from *charasso* (to sharpen to a point; akin to NT:1125 through the idea of scratching); a stake, i.e. (by implication) a palisade or rampart (military mound for circumvallation in a siege)."

This analogy indicates that Christ is a scratched-out image of the person of God. An "image" or "scratching," like a kind of engraving, hardly fits the Trinity dogma that he is of exactly the same substance of God the Father, or the Oneness view that he is a mode of the person of the Father. In the biblical analogy, Jesus is the image of God, particularly so that we can see Him. The Father remains invisible, while the Son is the visible character of the person of God the Father. Thus Jesus can say,

> [7] If you had known me, you would have known my Father also... [9] *He who has seen me has seen the Father.* How do you say, "Show us the Father?" [10] Don't you believe that I am in the Father, and the Father in me? *The words that I tell you, I speak not from myself;* but the Father who lives in me does His works. (John 14:7–10)

What the idea of the image teaches us is that Jesus was a visible representation of the very person of God the Father. It is in this way that if you've seen Jesus, you've seen the Father, because Jesus is the visible representation, the exact image, of the Father made flesh, or human. In this passage Jesus himself refuted the idea he was trying to say he was the Father when he said he didn't speak from himself.

Next is the word "substance," in that Jesus is called the express image of God's "substance."

The word that is translated here as "substance" simply does not mean physical substance. The Greek word is *hupostasis,* and it is the same word that is found in Hebrews 11:1:

> ...faith is the substance of things hoped for, the evidence of things not seen (Hebrews 11:1, KJV and NKJV).

Although the old and the New King James versions use the word substance here, other versions say "being sure of" (NIV), "the assurance of" (WEB, NRSV, NASU), or "being confident of" (CJB). Thus, all versions agree that faith is defined as an attitudinal concept and not a physical or material reality.

If we were to translate Hebrews 1:3 in the same way these versions translate that word, it would look like this: "His son is the radiance of his glory, *the very image of his assurance."* This should show that the word *hupostasis* simply doesn't mean some physical substance. Rather, it is like faith to the Christian, which is totally substantial, yet it is not physical.

Other verses using the word *hupostasis* are usually also interpreted as a non-physical thing that they call "confidence." For example:

> ...If there come with me any of Macedonia and find you unprepared, we (to say nothing of you) should be disappointed in this <u>confident</u> boasting. (2 Corinthians 9:4)

> That which I speak, I don't speak according to the Lord, but as in foolishness, in this <u>confidence</u> of boasting. (2 Corinthians 11:17)

> For we have become partakers of Christ, if we hold fast the beginning of our <u>confidence</u> firm to the end. (Hebrews 3:14)

All this means is that the Bible, in Hebrews 1:3, by using the word *hupostasis* (substance, confidence, or assurance), described God in a manner similar to how it described faith. As we know, faith is an attitude, and not by any means is it a physical or material substance.

So then, all Hebrews was saying in calling Jesus the very image of God's substance was that Jesus perfectly reflected God's character traits in a way that we can see and understand, just as Jesus said in John 14:7–10, which we quoted above.

The passage continues by saying, today I have become your Father:

> For to which of the angels did he say at any time, "You are my Son, Today have I become your father?" and again, "I will be to him a Father, And he will be to me a Son?'" (Hebrews 1:5)

Once again we find Jesus being called the Son of the Father at a certain point in time. He wasn't called the impersonal flesh, or an eternal person of the mythological Trinity. He was born and became the Son of the Father at a certain time.

Jesus Prayed to One: "He" Who Was Able to Save Him

In reading through the Book of Hebrews, we come to this passage:

> ⁷He, in the days of his flesh, having offered up prayers and petitions with strong crying and *tears to him who was able to save him from death*, and having been heard for his godly fear, ⁸though he was a Son, yet learned obedience by the things which he suffered. ⁹Having been made perfect, he became to all of those who obey him the author of eternal salvation, ¹⁰named by God a high priest after the order of Melchizedek. (Hebrews 5:7–10)

The passage clearly speaks about a human Jesus ("in the days of his flesh"). In this case, Jesus was a real man who prayed to a God whom he held in reverential fear. This man learned obedience, so it obviously wasn't part of his nature. He also had to be made perfect, indicating he didn't start out perfect. Since the context of the discussion is obedience and godliness, we know it is moral "perfection" that Jesus had to learn. Finally, it wasn't until after he was perfected that he "became" the author of eternal salvation and was named by God to be a priest after the order of Melchizedek.

Each of these simple, matter-of-fact descriptions of Christ completely demolishes any idea that he was an incarnation of a preexistent deity. This shows that biblical descriptions and explanations of Christ must be explained away by Trinitarians and Onenessians alike.

But for us, these are true, biblical descriptions about our Lord Jesus the Anointed One. There are no such matter-of-fact Scriptures that describe Jesus as the second person of the Trinity or the incarnation of God the Father Himself.

Believing on the Son of God really comes down to simply accepting what the Bible describes about him.

Various Other Sub-Topics on the Son of God Found in Hebrews But Addressed Elsewhere

There are many additional verses in the Book of Hebrews addressing the distinctions and reasons for them between Jesus the Son and God the Father. But we have covered these already in other places. So rather than repeat them here, we will list them and allow the reader to cross-reference those chapters as they will.

Hebrews 1:6 will be addressed in Chapter Twenty-Six on worshiping Jesus in Section Five.

Hebrews 1:13 ("right hand") is addressed in Chapter Twenty.

Hebrews 1:8 ("your throne, O God") was addressed in Chapter Six.

Hebrews 1:9 ("anointed... above your fellows") was addressed in Chapter Fifteen.

Hebrews 2:17–8 ("Obligated in all things to be made like us") has been addressed in many places, for example Chapters Three, Four, Five, Seven, Twelve, and Fourteen.

Hebrews 3:1–6 ("faithful to him who appointed him") has also been addressed in many places, such as Chapters Six and Fifteen.

Hebrews 5:4–6 ("nobody takes this honor on himself") has been addressed in several places and is the major subject of Chapter Nine.

James

> [13]Let no man say when he is tempted, "I am tempted by God," for God can't be tempted by evil, and he himself tempts no one. [14]But each one is tempted, when he is drawn away by his own lust, and enticed. [15]Then the lust, when it has conceived, bears sin; and the sin, when it is full grown, brings forth death. (James 1:13–15)

> Then Jesus was led up by the Spirit into the wilderness to be tempted by the devil. (Matthew 4:1)

James presents us with yet another powerful passage of Scripture *that totally refutes* the idea that Jesus was God incarnate. Since God cannot be tempted by sin, Jesus absolutely could not have been tempted as a man while possessing deific characteristics at the same time.

Since we already covered the topic of Jesus' temptation in Chapter Twelve, we won't repeat it here other than to note James' major contribution toward our understanding that the apostles did not view Christ as God, since Jesus was tempted and God cannot be tempted.

1 Peter

> Who, when he was cursed, didn't curse back. When he suffered, didn't threaten, but committed himself to him who judges righteously. (1 Peter 2:23)

In this passage we see that Jesus was distinct from the person of God because he committed his trust to "Him who judges righteously." This passage is much like Philippians 2:5–9 in that it also tells us how we are to think. In 1 Peter 2:21–24 it says, "For to this you were called, because Christ also suffered for us, leaving you an example, that you should follow his steps... *Who his own self* bore our sins in his body on the tree, that we, having died to sins, might live to righteousness..."

Clearly this passage was not talking about a human nature in distinction from a deific nature. Rather it spells out that this is the "his own self" of Jesus in contrast to another "who," being "Him who judges righteously."

Very similar passages showing that Jesus was personally distinct from God with reference to his atoning death, are found in Hebrews:

> [1]Therefore, holy brothers, partakers of a heavenly calling, consider the Apostle and High Priest of our confession, Jesus; [2]*who was faithful to him who appointed him*, as also was Moses in all his house. (Hebrews 3:1–2)

> ¹⁷Therefore he was obligated in all things to be made like his brothers, that *he might become a* merciful and *faithful high priest in things pertaining to God, to make atonement for the sins of the people.* ¹⁸For in that he himself has suffered being tempted, he is able to help those who are tempted. (Hebrews 2:17–18)

These passages clearly teach us that Jesus was a faithful priest in things pertaining to God. As we build on this thought, let's keep in mind that by definition a priest is a man who offers sacrifices to God on man's behalf:

> ¹For every high priest, being <u>taken from among men</u>, is appointed for men in things pertaining to God, that he may offer both gifts and sacrifices for sins. ²The high priest can deal gently with those who are ignorant and going astray, because he himself is also surrounded with weakness. ³Because of this, he must offer sacrifices for sins for the people, <u>as well as for himself</u>... ⁵<u>So also Christ</u> didn't glorify himself to be made a high priest, but it was He who said to him, 'You are my Son. Today I have become your Father. (Hebrews 5:1–3)

So Jesus was taken from among men and made to be a priest *to offer gifts and sacrifices* for sins for the people, *as well as for himself*. Chances are very, very high that you never heard that from your Oneness preacher, that it says Jesus also had to sacrifice for himself! This is Scripture, and those who don't believe it and twist it to mean other than it says just prove they don't really believe what their Bible says about the biblical Christ. Although Jesus never committed sin, it does nevertheless say that "he himself is also surrounded with weakness. Because of this, he must offer sacrifices for sins of the people *as well as for himself*." That is because he was human, and also explains why he had to pray daily, for one example. He himself was surrounded by weakness, and that was why he had to sacrifice for himself. For the people, however, he had to sacrifice for their sins.

This passage must be understood in light of the following explanations:

> For him who knew no sin *he made to be sin* on our behalf; so that in him we might become the righteousness of God. (2 Corinthians 5:21)

> For what the law couldn't do, in that it was weak through the flesh, God did, sending his own Son in the likeness of sinful flesh and for sin, he condemned sin in the flesh. (Romans 8:3)

> Christ redeemed us from the curse of the law, *having become a curse* for us. For it is written, 'Cursed is everyone who hangs on a tree.' (Galatians 3:13)

Jesus had to sacrifice for himself, not because he personally committed sin, but because he was made to be sin on our behalf. It's hard to imagine anyone thinking for a moment that God Himself could be "made to be sin for us on our behalf." Of course, we don't have to. It is written that there were two individual personalities involved here: the one who was made to be sin on our behalf, and the one who made him so. This was another important element of being a priest that Jesus could only accomplish by not being the God to whom he offered such gifts and sacrifices to.

Keeping this definition of the duties of the priest in mind, we go back to Hebrews 3:1–2 and Hebrews 2:17–18 above, and we note again that Jesus performed his duty of a priest *faithfully*.

That is the key word that ties these discussions on Christ's role as "priest in things pertaining to God" back to 1 Peter, when he said that Jesus "committed himself to him who judges righteously." That is, Jesus had faith in God and therefore performed the duties of a priest faithfully. That Jesus had faith in God is more evidence that he was not himself personally God.

So what does it mean for Christ himself to have been faithful? *Faith* is biblically defined as *hope that is not seen* (Romans 8:24). It is also defined as the "assurance of things *hoped for*, proof of things *not seen*" (Hebrews 11:1; see also 2 Corinthians 5:6–7; Romans 3:21–22; and Galatians 2:16). Our faith in God exists in contrast to any ability to see God, "for we walk by faith, not by sight" (2 Corinthians 5:7). To be our example of faith, Jesus also had to walk by faith, not by sight. The only way Jesus could walk by faith was to have had a human self-awareness that could not "see" God. These are things the Bible tells us about Jesus when it says he was made like us *in all things*.

When anyone insists that Jesus had to have a deific self-awareness, or even some form of pre-human existence, they *reject and deny* the biblical teaching that Christ was in submission to the Father *through faith*. That is because one cannot consciously *be* God and *hope to see* God at the same time. They are mutually exclusive concepts. Therefore, if Christ did not submit to the Father through faith, then he is no true example of the "faithfulness of Christ" that we are to emulate. Also, if Christ is God and fully aware of his deity, then we have no hope of ever actually being like Christ.

The testing of our faith is the ultimate test of our Christianity. To be a Christian literally means to be like Christ. So then, we are to have faith after Christ's example in order to be Christ-like. Christ was tempted *like us* in *all* things and yet, as Peter says, committed himself to him who judges righteously. Therefore, to assign inherent deific characteristics to the human Christ is to negate the faith of Christ. Yet the faith of Christ is the very heart and core of the practice of being Christ-like (Christianity).

2 Peter

> ¹⁷For he received from God the Father honor and glory, when the voice came to him from the Majestic Glory, 'This is my beloved Son, in whom I am well pleased.' ¹⁸This voice we heard come out of heaven when we were with him in the holy mountain. (2 Peter 1:17–18)

Very simply, Peter was using common expressions about God the Father in relation to His Son Jesus Christ. He was talking about God testifying to us, not that God was the Son, not that God incarnated himself as a man, and not that what they touched and felt was just God's impersonal human nature—none of that. God who can't lie called Jesus His Son and said He was pleased in him. It hardly seems to need any more commentary than that.

1–3 John

Let's take a walk through the epistles of John and see what he has to say about Jesus Christ, the Son of God. What we want to discover is whether John understood things the way Onenessians and Trinitarians claim, or if he held Jesus as a true Son of God.

> ...our fellowship is with the Father, and with his Son, Jesus Christ. (1 John 1:3)

Here we have, yet again, the same consistent testimony: there is a father and there is a son. No mention of these being code words. We have no reason to believe that "father" meant something different than it always does. These words always indicate a relationship between separate and distinct individuals.

> If anyone sins, we have a Counselor with the Father, Jesus Christ, the righteous. (1 John 2:1)

John doesn't say we have a counselor with the Father that is the impersonal human flesh of the person of Jesus. Do we ever find in Scripture that something impersonal can be a counselor to someone personal? Since there aren't such Scriptures, let's just let these passages mean what they simply and clearly say.

> [22]*Who is the liar but he who denies that Jesus is the Anointed One?* This is the Antichrist, he who denies the Father and the Son. [23]Whoever denies *the Son*, the same doesn't have *the Father*. He who confesses *the Son* has *the Father* also. (1 John 2:22–23)

In this verse John identified a very clear and understandable term to describe people who don't believe in a true Father and son: "liar." He used this word five times in his first epistle, three of them for people who claim to love God but don't keep His commandments, and two of them for those who deny the Father and the Son and deny that Jesus is the Anointed One. John didn't say, "Who is a liar but he who denies that Jesus is a dual-natured God-man hybrid wherein his flesh is one nature and his deific nature is another and the two natures make up his single personality." John also did not say, "Who is a liar that denies that Jesus *isn't just an Anointed One* but is also God Himself incarnate." Rather, we recall that it was in John's gospel where Jesus said many times and in many ways:

> [16]"*I am not alone*, but I am with the Father who sent me... [26]... However *he who* sent *me* is true; and the things which *I heard from him*, these I say to the world..." [28]Jesus therefore said to them, "When you have lifted up the Son of Man, then you will know that I am he, and *I do nothing of myself*, but as my Father taught me, I say these things." (John 8:17–28)

So then, whoever denies that Jesus is the Anointed One is of an antichrist spirit. Also, whoever denies the Father and the Son that John refers to is of an antichrist spirit. These statements are according to the apostle that wrote John 1:1–2, 14 and John 10:30, and John 8:58, and other such verses. John heard Jesus say he could "do nothing of himself," and John heard Jesus say, "I am not alone."

If I redefine "father" and "son" to mean "mother" and "daughter," would that be acceptable? How about if we describe the Father as the first eternal coequal person in the godhead in contrast to the Son as the second eternal coequal person, would these be acceptable? No, because father and son have meaning, and a father is always prior in time and functionally superior, whereas a son is always after in time and inferior or subject.

How then do Onenessians believe they can redefine the terms father and son at their whim and count themselves guiltless of John's accusation that if you don't have the Father and the Son you are antichrist? Onenessians redefine explanations given in God's word just as Trinitarians do, but they come up with a different conclusion. They are both, however, just as unbiblical and antichristian because they redefine the terms father and son and deny that Jesus is an anointed man.

> [9] *By this was God's love revealed* in us, *that God has sent his one and only Son* into the world that we might live through him. [10] In this is love, not that we loved God, but that he loved us, and sent his Son as the atoning sacrifice for our sins. (1 John 4:9–10)

Did God send the second eternal person in the Trinity godhead into the world that we might live through him? This passage doesn't state or imply that anymore than it says He sent his impersonal human nature into the world to save us. Why then don't people who claim to love God accept what the apostles say God did for us through the man He calls His Son?

> We have seen and testify that the Father has sent the Son as the Savior of the world. (1 John 4:14)

Once again, do we read "Father and Son" here in the common meaning, or as unbiblical "deific nature sent his own impersonal human nature" as the Savior of the world? Hopefully by now it's getting easier and clearer for you.

> Whoever believes that Jesus is the Anointed One is born of God. Whoever loves the father also loves the child who is born of him. (1 John 5:1)

What does this say? It says that he who believes that Jesus is an anointed man is born of God. Does it say he who loves God also loves the impersonal nature *that* is born of Him, or that he loves the child *who* is born of Him? Is the child a *that* or a *whom*?

> Who is he who overcomes the world, but he who believes that Jesus is the Son of God? (1 John 5:5)

Who is it who overcomes the world? This verse does not say it is he who believes that Jesus is an incarnation of God is an overcomer, rather it says that he who believes that Jesus is the Son of God is the person who overcomes the world. Do you want to be a biblical overcomer, or a succumber to man-made teachings that make the word of God of no effect?

> [10]He who believes in the Son of God has the testimony in himself. *He who doesn't believe God has made him a liar*, because he has not believed in *the testimony that God has given concerning his Son.* [11]The testimony is this, that God gave to us *eternal life*, and this life *is in his Son.* (1 John 5:10–11)

We've read where God Himself spoke from the heavens calling Jesus His Son. Has God called from the heavens and said, "You can redefine what the terms father and son mean; it will still be the same thing"? No! He did not! He gave us testimony that Jesus was His Son and that in His Son He was well pleased. He didn't say, "being *as* I am my son I am well pleased." Why then do people who claim to love this same God feel they know better how to declare and describe God's relationship with His Son than God does?

> We know that the Son of God has come, and has given us an understanding, that we know him who is true, and *we are in him who is true, in his Son* Jesus *Christ*. This is the true God, and eternal life. (1 John 5:20)

What a perfect verse to pick for jumping to conclusions. See, it calls Jesus "the true God and eternal life." Right? Really? Let's back up a minute and remember the first principles of the oracles of God: "we are in him who is true, in his son Jesus Christ."

Did that stop meaning "son," as in one who was born after the Father in time and who is someone who is inferior or subordinate to the father? If it did, then is it saying that the inferior son who was made in the process of time was the "true God"? Or, as in the Onenessian view, where the flesh is the impersonal human nature, is this saying that the inhuman personal nature is God? And again, it calls Jesus the "Anointed One" (Christ), which we've learned necessarily means a role that someone doesn't take upon themselves. Was it this one who was anointed who is the true God? No, because the meanings of these words (son and Christ) are incompatible with the definition of "true God."

True God is truly "I Am that I Am," who needs nothing from anyone, who is subordinate to no one, who is eternally the same, and who is the Father of eternity and not the offspring of humanity, nor needs anyone to anoint Him to be God!

So what is the biblical truth? It is just as Jesus simply said:

> I am not alone, but I am with the Father who sent me. (John 8:16)

> He who sent me is with me. The Father hasn't left me alone, for I always do the things that are pleasing to him. (John 8:29)

"I AM NOT ALONE"

> ...I am not alone, because the Father is with me... (John 16:32)

> Believe in God. Believe also in me. (John 14:1)

So then, John says, this is the true God (i.e., the Father who is with Jesus and sent Jesus), **and** eternal life which life is in the Son—not the impersonal human nature, but rather the Son of God, which means he that is personally distinct, inferior in authority, and definitely much younger in time as he is God's creation rather than God's coequal.

Of course, John actually spells this all out for us. We just need to hear what he is saying and describing without redefining his words to mean something he never meant or intended:

> [11]The testimony is this, that God gave to us *eternal life*, and this life *is in his Son*. [12]He who has the Son has the life. He who doesn't have God's Son doesn't have the life. [13]These things I have written to you who *believe in the name of the Son of God*, that you may know that you have eternal life, and that you may *continue to believe in the name of the Son of God*. (1 John 5:11–13)

Here John sets out to explain to us "the testimony." The Son of God was John's unifying theme when summarizing the important elements he wanted to relay. Not the Trinity theme and not the Oneness theme and not any other God incarnate theme. Eternal life can only be found in the doctrine of God's true son. Only by redefining John's words is it possible for these others to use John as a proof text for their theories.

Not in pretense, not in redefinition, not in twisting the words of the Scriptures to our destruction, here it is one more time as clear as can be in John's second epistle:

> Grace, mercy, and peace will be with us, from God the Father, and from the Lord Jesus Christ, *the Son of the Father, in truth* and love. (2 John 3)

> I rejoice greatly that I have found some of your children *walking in truth, even as we have been commanded by the Father.* (2 John 4)

> Whoever transgresses and doesn't remain in the teaching of Christ, doesn't have God. He who remains in the teaching, *the same has both the Father and the Son.* (2 John 9)

In verse 3 John exhorts us to believe in the Son of the Father *in truth*. That means don't distort what father and son mean! Then in verse 4 he says it is a commandment from the Father to walk in truth. That means it is a sin to make up untrue meanings and teach people to believe them! He reiterates this in verse 9: it is a transgression not to remain in the teaching of the Anointed One, whereas one should remain in the teaching of the Father and the Son.

Why was he writing these things? Because in his time the antichristians were starting to interject extra meanings to *Christ* and *son* that so blurred the truth that they were teaching sinful lies!

Keeping in the truth, then, is so incredibly simple with John: believe in the Anointed One and believe that there is a true father and a true son.

CHAPTER TWENTY-TWO

The Book of Revelation

Description: The Revelation that God gave to Jesus, who gave it to his angel, who gave it to John, who gave it to us

The point is: We know who was speaking by the characteristics and attributes of the speaker, not by jumping to conclusions!

¹This is the Revelation of *Jesus Christ*, which *God* gave him to show to his servants the things which must happen soon, which he sent and made known by his *angel* to his servant, *John*, ²who testified to God's word, and of the testimony of Jesus Christ, about everything that he saw. (Revelation 1:1–2)

The first thing to notice in the introduction to the Book of Revelation is that there are four distinct individuals involved in delivering the message:

1. God
2. Jesus Christ
3. An angel
4. John

This is a simple chain of transmission of the messages that have been delivered in the Book of Revelation. These characters are all listed in the context of being personally distinct from each other in the same way. That is, according to the way this is written, John is as distinct from the angel as the angel is from Jesus Christ, who is likewise as distinct from God. This distinction is, again, maintained throughout the book.[1]

Now notice how each of these individuals is referred to, in context, by some distinguishing characteristic:

> ⁴*John, to the seven assemblies that are in Asia: Grace to you and peace, from God, who is and who was and who is to come*; and from the seven Spirits who are before his throne; ⁵and *from Jesus Christ, the faithful witness, the firstborn of the dead*, and the ruler of the kings of the earth. To him who loves *us*, and washed us from our sins by his blood; ⁶and he made *us* to be a Kingdom, priests *to his God and Father*; to him be the glory and the dominion forever and ever. Amen. (Revelation 1:4–6)

John was identified in verse 1 (above) as a servant of Jesus and God. In this passage he was identified by the word "us" as one of those whose sins were washed, and made to be a priest to God.

Jesus is identified as the faithful witness, the firstborn from the dead, and ruler of the kings of the earth. So there is our clue of what the titles "first and last" may mean as applied to Jesus Christ.

Jesus is the FIRST born from the dead:

> He is the head of the body, the assembly, who is *the beginning, <u>the **firstborn** from the dead</u>*; that in all things he might have the preeminence. (Colossians 1:18)

---

[1] The following verses are the places where Jesus is clearly and irrefutably held in personal distinction from God the Father in the Book of Revelation: Revelation 1:1, 2, 4–5, 6, 9; 2:7, 26–27; 3:2, 5, 12, 14, 21; 5:7, 9–10, 13; 6:16; 7:10, 17; 11:15; 12:5, 10, 12:17; 14:1, 4, 10; 15:3; 19:6–7, 9; 20:6; 21:22, 23; 22:1, 3–4.

> We know that all things work together for good for those who love God, to those who are called according to his purpose. For whom he foreknew, he also predestined to *be conformed to the image of his Son, <u>that he might be the firstborn among many brothers</u>.* (Romans 8:28–29)
>
> He is the head of the body, the assembly, who is the beginning, *the **first**born from the dead; <u>that in all things he might have the preeminence</u>.* (Colossians 1:18)

And we also know that he is the LAST Adam:

> [35]But someone will say, "How are the dead raised?" and, "With what kind of body do they come?" [36]You foolish one, that which you yourself sow is not made alive unless it dies. [37]That which you sow, <u>you don't sow the body that will be</u>, *but a bare grain*, maybe of wheat, or of some other kind... [42]So also is the resurrection of the dead. It is sown in corruption; it is raised in incorruption... [45]So also it is written, "The first man, Adam, became a living soul." *The **last** Adam became <u>a life-giving spirit</u>.* [46]However <u>that which is spiritual isn't first</u>, but that which is natural, <u>then that which is spiritual</u>. [47]The first man is of the earth, made of dust. The second man is the Lord from heaven. (1 Corinthians 15: 35–37, 42, 45–47)

On the other hand, God is identified as He who is and who was and who is to come. He is also, in verse 6, identified as the God and Father of Jesus Christ. So Incarnationists attempt to fit puzzle pieces together that just don't fit.

The first real issue of confusion comes between these two passages:

> [8]'I am the Alpha and the Omega,' says the Lord God, 'who is and who was and who is to come, *the Almighty.*' (Revelation 1:8)

> ¹⁷...He laid his right hand on me, saying, 'Don't be afraid. I am the first and the last, ¹⁸and the Living one. *I was dead, and behold, I am alive* forevermore. Amen. I have the keys of Death and of Hades. (Revelation 1:17–18)

At this point people tend to jump to the conclusion they were taught and say, "See, Jesus is called by the same title that God Almighty was called, and therefore they are one and the same person!" But that would be interpreting the way the devil interprets Psalm 91:12 without allowing for Deuteronomy 6:16, which says not to tempt the Lord.

So rather than interpret like that, let us keep in mind what the Bible also says. For example, Jesus said, "Most assuredly, I tell you, the Son *can do nothing of himself*..." (John 5:19), and again, "*I can of myself do nothing*" (John 5:30). Additionally, the Scripture, which Jesus says cannot be broken, states that "with God nothing shall be impossible" (Luke 1:37), and again, "with God all things are possible" (Matthew 19:26). In this way we can rule out that Jesus considers himself to be God *Almighty,* who has no such limitations but with whom nothing is impossible.

Further, we need to keep in mind that Jesus said, "All things whatever the Father has are mine; therefore I said that he takes of mine, and will declare it to you" (John 16:15). So it does not follow biblically that just because Jesus the Anointed One and God his Father share many of the Father's characteristic titles that they are the same personal individual. In fact, there is not one verse in the whole Bible that simply states that Jesus is the person of God.

Keep in mind that there are *no Scriptures* explicitly stating or explaining that since God and Jesus share some of the same titles, that should be taken as evidence they are the same personal individual. To say they are, then, is another way of adding a new doctrine that the Bible doesn't teach.

Furthermore, we do know there are Scriptures stating that God is the first and the last uncreated being (Isaiah 43:10). We do have Scriptures teaching that Jesus is the only begotten son (John 3:16, 18; Hebrews 11:17; 1 John 4:9), so it is not out of line to say that

Jesus was the first and last only begotten son. Adam was made of the dust of the earth, and Eve was made from the side of Adam, but neither of them is called God's only son or daughter.

Is John the Alpha and Omega?

In the following verses we see just how important it is to keep the context and the descriptions in mind and use them to help us understand who and what is being referred to. Look how this passage reads without any references or punctuation (which is what the biblical *koine* Greek looks):

> I am the Alpha and the Omega says the Lord God who is and who was and who is to come *the Almighty I John your brother* and partner with you in oppression Kingdom and perseverance in Christ Jesus was on the isle that is called Patmos because of God's Word and the testimony of Jesus Christ. (Revelation 1:8–9)

Without the uninspired, later punctuation marks, this passage could mean that John was declaring himself to be the Lord God. And interpreting in just such a manner is how some folks come to the conclusion that Jesus is God. This means that the only way we know that this passage isn't John saying, "I am Alpha and Omega says the Lord God I John," is because of the qualifying descriptions. The Alpha and Omega spoken of here are God, because He tells us so. John, however, isn't God, because he is our brother and partner with us in oppression and in the kingdom and in perseverance, as he also tells us.

It is the same with "the first and the last" in verse 17. This isn't the same first and last that was Almighty God, because he tells us he was dead and now lives...

> [17]...I am the first and the last, [18]and the Living one. *I was dead, and behold, I am alive* forevermore. Amen. (Revelation 1:17)

We know of no one who seriously believes that the Almighty God died. So this is someone else, but that doesn't stop people from interpreting these verses through the traditions they have been taught. The proper way to interpret is to let the clear passages interpret unclear ones. That is why we have taken the time to show the hundreds of verses that contradict people's conclusions about these unclear ones.

Some people will say that this is one more passage among many "strongly implying" (without clearly saying) that Jesus is God. These people would argue that there are enough such verses to conclude this must be what they mean when taken altogether. Well, then, let's ask it this way: if there were, say, two or three dozen Scriptures saying that believers could take up serpents and not be harmed, would those dozens of verses then be enough to override the commandment not to tempt the Lord our God? Obviously not. The point is, it doesn't matter how many verses may be thought to imply something. One passage of Scripture that clearly refutes such a conclusion is enough to negate that conclusion.

So then, let's look at the rest of Revelation, and the Bible, and see if it maintains distinctions between the persons of the Father and Son (as in Onenessianism) or treats the Son as a coequal person in the godhead (as in Trinitarianism).

Jesus Received from his Father, and Other Clear Statements

> ²⁶He who overcomes, and he who keeps my works to the end, to him I will give authority over the nations. ²⁷He will rule them with a rod of iron, shattering them like clay pots; *as I also have received of my Father*... (Revelation 2:26–27)

Jesus asserted that we receive authority from him in the same exact way that he *received authority* from his Father. If he were an incarnation of the Father, this promise would be impossibly ridiculous, since none of us are incarnations of Jesus. The same would hold true if he were a coequal person in the godhead. The only way this makes sense is if Jesus is the human, Anointed Son of God.

> He who overcomes, I will make him a pillar in the temple of my God, and he will go out from there no more. I will write on him *the name of my God*, and the name of the city of *my God*, the new Jerusalem, which comes down out of heaven from *my God*, and my own new name. (Revelation 3:12)

Jesus has a God. This verse alone should be more than enough evidence that he is not God, since there is only one God and no one is higher than He.

> ¹⁴To the angel of the assembly in Laodicea write: The Amen, the Faithful and True Witness, the Head of God's creation, says these things... ²¹He who overcomes, I will give to him to sit down with me on my throne, *as I also overcame*, and sat down with my Father on his throne. (Revelation 3:14, 21)

Jesus is the head of God's creation. This is reminiscent of 1 Corinthians 11, where God is the head of Christ, and Christ is the head of the man, and the man is the head of the woman. The Greek word for head, above, is *arche* and can mean beginning, corner, first, etc.

If this isn't clear enough, verse 21 concludes by promising to share his throne with those who overcome, even as he overcame. Because none of us know that we are God in the back of our minds, there is no way we could hope to overcome "even as he overcame" if such were the case. Thankfully we *can* overcome even as he overcame.

One of the ways he overcame was in recognizing and renouncing the way the devil jumped to conclusions and negated parts of God's clear word. That is what we are trying to teach people to overcome in this study.

The passage also states that we will sit with Jesus on his throne, as he sits with his Father on His throne. So in context, according to Jesus himself, we are as personally distinct from Jesus, as Jesus is from his Father. Furthermore, sitting on the Father's throne is obviously not meant to mean he is the Father on whose throne he sits "with." Therefore, Revelation 3:21 is another "I am not alone" type passage refuting Onenessianism.

> ⁶I saw in the midst of the throne and of the four living creatures, and in the midst of the elders, a Lamb standing, as though it had been slain, having seven horns, and seven eyes, which are the seven Spirits of God, sent out into all the earth. ⁷Then <u>he came</u>, and <u>he took</u> it out of the right hand <u>of him</u> who sat on the throne. (Revelation 5:6–7)

Here we clearly see that Jesus as the slain lamb is being depicted in a manner personally separate and distinct from God who sits on the throne. Of course, many would like to say this is merely symbolic of Jesus' lifeless human nature receiving the scroll out of the hands of His deific nature. If that is the case, show us the Scripture that in any way says this is what it means.

As for us, rather than rely on traditions based on inventions of antichristians, we will continue to use clearly stated Scriptures to state our case. Such as the following:

> I saw, and behold, the Lamb standing on Mount Zion, and with him a number, one hundred forty-four thousand, *having his name, and the name of his Father*, written on their foreheads. (Revelation 14:1)

Jesus has a Father and the Father has a son. And until someone can show that there ever was a father that was a son to himself, or fathered his own impersonal human nature and called that his son, then we will stick to what the Bible actually describes and spells out. Sticking with the Bible is not a difficult or complicated position to take:

Son = Son
Father = Father
Christ = Anointed One

All we need to do is remember John's warning about those who deny what these words mean.

³Grace, mercy, and peace will be with us, from God the Father, and from the Lord Jesus Christ, *the Son of the Father, in truth* and love. ⁴I rejoice greatly that I have found some of your children walking in truth, even as we have been commanded by the Father. (2 John 3–4)

⁹Whoever transgresses and doesn't remain in the teaching of Christ, doesn't have God. He who remains in the teaching, the same has both the Father and the Son. ¹⁰If anyone comes to you, and doesn't bring this teaching, don't receive him into your house, and don't welcome him, ¹¹for he who welcomes him participates in his evil works. (2 John 9–11)

We will address Revelation 22:16 in its own chapter.

CHAPTER TWENTY-THREE
The Root and the Offspring of David

Revelation 22:16

I, Jesus, have sent my angel to *testify* these things to you for the assemblies. *I am the root and the offspring of David*; the Bright and Morning Star. (Revelation 22:16)

This is the last actual description of Jesus the Anointed One in the Bible. (You will recall that the first description said he was to be the seed of the woman who would crush the head of the serpent.)

This is Jesus' final personal testimony of himself in the Bible.

To reject this testimony is not only to reject Jesus as he solemnly declares himself to be, but to make him out to be a liar.

A lot of people don't realize how clearly Jesus testified to his being "just a man." That's because a lot of people mistakenly believe that when Jesus said he was *"the root and the offspring of David"* that the "root" part was a reference to his supposed "deity." I confess I used to believe and teach that myself. For Onenessians, "root" is supposedly a code word that refers to Jesus' deific nature, while "*the offspring*" supposedly refers to his human nature. However, that idea is a completely man-made fabrication with absolutely no basis in Scripture. Even worse, it negates what Jesus was clearly and explicitly testifying to.

In all of the occurrences of the word "root" in the Bible, *not once* can any one of them be shown to be ascribed to God *in any way*. That's 42 times in the World English Bible and 44 times in the KJV.

In common, everyday language, what would you think the word "root" means or signifies? Wouldn't you think of an integral part of a plant that plays a certain role in supporting that plant? For example, a carrot is a root. Does a carrot preexist the plant, or is it part of the whole organism of the carrot plant? The latter, right?

That is precisely how the Bible uses the term root. For example, take a look at Job 14:10, where we can see the contrast between "man," who does not have roots, and "trees," which actually do take root. As you read the description of the tree that takes root, ask yourself if this is in any way a clear reference to God.

> [1]Man, who is born of a woman, Is of few days, and full of trouble. [2]He comes forth like a flower, and is cut down. He also flees like a shadow, and doesn't continue... [7]For there is hope for *a tree, If it is cut down*, that it will sprout again, That the tender branch of it will not cease. [8]Though the **root** of it grows old in the earth, And the stock of it dies in the ground; [9]Yet through the scent of water it will bud, And put forth boughs like a plant. [10]*But man dies, and is laid low.* Yes, man gives up the spirit, and where is he? (Job 14:1–10)

As we can see, the root is part of the tree. The point here is that man isn't entirely like a tree; if man is cut down, he is dead. A tree, on the other hand, can still regrow because its life is still in the root; thus, in the cut-down tree there is still hope. It is precisely in this way that Jesus said he was the root of David. He is of the lineage of David that will bring productive, visible life back to the kingdom of David as God promised.

On the other hand, nothing in this analogy of the "root" is said to represent God.

One of the classic uses of "root" in the OT was God's promise to the remnant people of Judah, who would escape from Sennacherib, king of Assyria.

> ³⁰The remnant that has escaped of the house of *Judah* shall again take *root* downward, and bear fruit upward. ³¹For out of Jerusalem shall go forth a remnant, and out of Mount Zion those who shall escape: the zeal of YHWH shall perform this. (2 Kings 19:30–31)

In this case, the "root" analogy was applied to the whole family of Judah. Although much of the family may die off or be scattered, there is a remnant, a small number of individuals that can be likened to the root of a tree. So the word "root" was being used in a similar way to the analogy we saw in Job 14. Paul explained in Romans 9:27 that a "remnant shall be saved." He elaborated this point very clearly in Romans 11:5, where he wrote that in his time there was a remnant of the seed of Israel. Accordingly, the word "root" points to the word "remnant," which in turn points to the people of God. It never refers in Scripture to God, or deity, or Jesus' deific nature. It is always used in a context such as this, with reference to human beings.

Jesus explained what he meant by being the root when he said this: ¹"I am the true vine, and my Father is the farmer... ⁵I am the vine. You are the branches" (John 15:1–5).

According to Jesus, in this analogy *he is the same organism (vine/vegetation) as we are*. On the other hand, and quite to the contrary, the Father alone (being typified as the "farmer") is in a kingdom, phylum, class, order, family, genus, and species all His own, quite exclusive of the rest of us—including Jesus!

Note carefully that Jesus is only part of the plant, and still a very physical part of this organism. This passage is very much like Paul's discussion in 1 Corinthians 12 saying that we are the body of Christ. All of this is still very much in line with the picture of the Israelite *remnant* as a single organism.

Thus, this analogy of Jesus being the vine and his followers being the branches refutes both modalism and Trinitarianism.

Now then, what do the scriptural prophecies specifically teach about Jesus being the "Root" of David?

> It will happen in that day that the nations will seek *the root of Jesse*, who stands as a banner of the peoples; and his resting place will be glorious. (Isaiah 11:10)

Jesse was the father of King David. The subsequent passages in Isaiah explain who the root is, and it is the remnant of God's people.

> It will happen in that day that the Lord will set his hand again the second time to recover *the remnant that is left of his people* from Assyria, from Egypt, from Pathros, from Cush, from Elam, from Shinar, from Hamath, and from the islands of the sea. He will set up a banner for the nations, and will assemble the outcasts of Israel, and gather together the dispersed of Judah from the four corners of the earth. (Isaiah 11:11–12)

So, quite explicitly, a root can signify a remnant of people. Such is the biblical context for Jesus claiming in Revelation 22:16 that *he is the root and offspring* of David. In making this statement, Jesus was referring completely to his humanity and descent from David, his being of the human lineage of David and the ultimate reason and purpose for the Davidic kingdom that Jesus was to inherit. Nowhere in the Bible does "root" mean God the Father; that idea is just a man-made assumption that hides and changes Jesus' real meaning in his self-testimony.

In the NT, Paul referred to the above prophesy of Isaiah's and testified that Jesus was the root *that was to come*; thus, not a root that had always existed (such as God always existed).

> Again, Isaiah says, "There will be the root of Jesse, He who arises to rule over the Gentiles; On him will the Gentiles hope." (Romans 15:12)

Another interesting thing about the "root of Jesse" is that "the Spirit of Yahweh will rest on him... The Spirit of knowledge and the fear of Yahweh... his delight will be in the fear of Yahweh" (Isaiah 11:1–3). Would God need to have his own Spirit rest upon him? Would God need to be filled with the Spirit of the fear of Yahweh? Would God fear Himself? Such ideas are, of course, ridiculous and show that the root of Jesse was simply not an incarnation of Yahweh Himself.

Note that in Revelation 22:16, Jesus also referred to himself as the bright and morning star. The OT Scriptures also tell us what this means. And once again we find the same theme being reiterated; namely, the theme of human descent.

> [17]I see him, *but not now*; I see him, *but not near*: There shall come forth *a star out of Jacob*, A scepter shall rise *out of* Israel... [19]*Out of* Jacob shall one have dominion... (Numbers 24:17, 19)

Numbers 24:17–19 teaches that a star will arise "out of" Jacob, once again indicating offspring. The star did not exist at that time ("not now"), and was not "near" at that time. And most importantly that star was to bear a scepter and have dominion. All of these concepts point to the predictions of the kingship of Jesus, which were made *before he existed*; that is, before he was born to Mary in Bethlehem. Thus these Scriptures show that it was ultimately Jesus who would be the prophesied ruler. And it is very clear that he comes out of Jacob and Israel. No word about him being the Father who would incarnate himself in the flesh; except in systems influenced by pagan ideas of incarnated gods (Acts 14:11) and Gnostic antichristian "dual nature" teachings like Tertullian's.

So far, which of these ideas about a "root" does the word of God teach and support: that Jesus somehow actually preexisted his own birth, or that God foreknew what Christ would be as the "root and the offspring" of David? The latter is the truth; the former idea derives from pagan notions about incarnations of deity.

The bottom line is, it is Jesus' own testimony of himself that Onenessians refute when they claim him, contrary to his self-testimony, to be a dual-natured, God-man.

Jesus declared himself to be the offspring of David, thus not a recreated form of humanity. He also testified to being the root of David, meaning the remnant of David's lineage that would rise out of Israel and have dominion. This is the revelation of Jesus the Anointed One. He never reversed his earlier testimony that he was not alone and that he could of his own self do nothing.

Closing Section Four

In this section we have presented hundreds of Scriptures, either quoted or referenced for the reader, that clearly and explicitly hold the person of Jesus the Anointed One in distinct separation from God the Father. Any serious Bible student should take all these Scriptures very seriously in their view of Christ. In the following section, we will show that the proof texts of Onenessians are relatively small in number and are anything but clear in establishing, let alone stating, their doctrine.

SECTION FIVE

REFUTING ONENESS "PROOF-TEXTS"

CHAPTER TWENTY-FOUR
Laying Out The Plan to Refute Oneness

Which foundation is built on a solid Rock?

True Son of God?   ...or...   God incarnate?

* Biblically stated
* Preached by the apostles
* 578 NT verses alone
* From Gen. 3:15 to Rev. 22:16
(beginning of the Bible to the end)

* Antichristian dual natures doctrine
* Pagan gods come to earth
* Trinitrian language
* Council of Chalcedon
* Never preached

⁸Therefore he says, "When he ascended on high, he led captivity captive, and gave gifts to men."... ¹¹He gave some to be apostles; and some, prophets; and some, evangelists; and some, shepherds and teachers; *¹²for the perfecting of the saints to the work* of serving to the *building up of the body of Christ* ¹³*until we all attain to the unity of the faith and of the knowledge of the Son of God* to a *full grown man*, to the measure of the stature of the fullness of Christ [the Anointed One]; ¹⁴that we may *no longer be children, tossed back and forth and carried about with every wind of doctrine, by the trickery of men, in craftiness, after the wiles of error;* ¹⁵but speaking truth in love, we may grow up in all things into him, who is the head, the Anointed One. (Ephesians 4:8–15)

This passage is quite amazing just because of the amount of things it teaches in such relatively few words. It introduces Jesus and briefly describes what he's been through. It establishes some of the more influential ministerial giftings. Then it lays out the mission and the intended purposes for growth and mission in the body of Christ. And it also speaks to the aims and challenges of the same.

Notice that one goal of these ministries is to bring all the saints of God unto a spiritual "full grown man." Along this line of thought, Paul wrote in Galatians 4 that an "heir, *as long as he is a child*, differs nothing from a servant... but *is under tutors and governors until* the time appointed of the Father" (Galatians 4:1–3). This means that people of God who are held under "governors and tutors" indefinitely are being suppressed and treated like children, when they should be developed by their spiritual leaders into mature, spiritual adults having full, equal legal status within the ecclesia so that they also can join in the work of building up the body of Christ. In other words, the real purpose of the ministry isn't to permanently oppress a congregation under an overlord to whom the people are ever to be beholden. Rather, the very job and purpose of the ministry is to empower and develop each and every saint *to move into their coequal potential of being also contributors in the kingdom of God*. But this topic is a whole other subject from our study at hand, so that isn't going to be our focus in this awesome passage. Still, we did want to point that out because the oppression that God's people are under is part of what has caused them to submit to the untruths and false teachings that are our subject matter.

What we do want to focus on here, in this passage, is the ultimate goal the apostle just described; namely, to "attain to *the unity of the faith* and of *the knowledge of the Son of God*." Note carefully that it doesn't say "unto the knowledge of the third person of the Trinity." It also doesn't say "unto the knowledge of the incarnation of God the Father." It says that *"the knowledge of the Son of God"* is part of what is involved <u>*in our perfecting and attaining to the unity of the faith*</u> that will bring the body of Christ, you and I, unto a "full grown man," meaning spiritual adulthood. And if we're still unclear, he's talking about the "fullness of the Anointed One," which as we've been reiterating over and over is not something God can do unto Himself, since being anointed is something no one takes upon themselves.

Bringing the saints of God unto *the knowledge of the Son of God* in truth is one of the prescribed and prophetic goals of all the ministry types given by Christ to mankind. So, in this book regarding the Son of God, not only are we on the right side of biblical doctrine, *we are also on the right side of biblical prophecy*. That's because we are working toward the goal expressed by Paul!

Having addressed the positive side of the passage, now let's take a look at the negative side. Let's ask, what has been hindering Christ's saints from coming into the fullness of the knowledge of the Son of God? It is spelled out for us: we have been held as children and have been *"tossed back and forth and carried about with every wind of doctrine, by the trickery of men, in craftiness, after the wiles of error."* Those who hinder saints of God from coming into the knowledge of the Son of God are detractors of the very ministry and mission of the body of Christ!

And that is what we are going to address in this section: the craftiness and trickery of "winds of doctrine" that are following the "wiles of error." We've already shown many of the actual methods of the "wiles of error," but we're not quite done yet.

Now we are ready to demonstrate, beyond any doubt, that Onessianism is derived by the trickery of men and imposed artificially upon certain passages.

> For my people have committed two evils: they have forsaken me, the spring of living waters, and hewed them out cisterns, broken cisterns, that can hold no water. (Jeremiah 2:13)

As this verse says, the ultimate problem with the Oneness doctrine is *twofold*. Not only is Modalism "read into" the texts of the Bible, but the true Son of God doctrine is diluted, explained away, and ultimately taught not to be believed.

As we've stated many times, the Oneness doctrine can't be readily found in the Bible like all other essential biblical teachings:

- Want to know what baptism is for? Go to Romans 6 and read about it.
- Want to know about the death, burial, and resurrection of Christ? Go to 1 Corinthians 15 and read about it.
- Want to know about the virgin conception of Christ? Go to such passages as Matthew 1:18 and Luke 1:26–35 and read about it.
- Want to know how the Bible says Christ was made like us in all things? Go to Hebrews, particularly 2:17, and read about it.

But there is no passage that clearly and simply states that Jesus is the very person of God the Father incarnate. There are verses that seem to imply this, but it is never clearly stated or taught. This inherent contrast exists between Onenessianism and all other clear biblical teachings. It makes it obvious that it is *only through interpretational methods* that Onenessians can try to make the Bible appear to say what they believe. This method, from the very beginning of the fall of mankind, is the same exact method the devil uses, and teaches people to use, for interpreting the Bible. In fact, it is the same method of interpretation used to support all false teachings.

Probably worst of all, Onenessianism makes a liar out of Jesus, who claimed to be the truth. According to Onenessianism, Jesus must have only been telling the truth when he spoke in unclear terms. For example, according to Onenessianism, Jesus wasn't speaking the clear truth when he said he was "not alone" and could do "nothing" of his own "self." Instead of listening to what Jesus said, Onenessians have developed a plethora of unbiblical explanations about who and what Christ is, making a complete mockery of the many places that describe Jesus' personal distinction from the Father.

Onenessianism's "Trickery of Men" and "Wiles of Error"

Let's take a look at some of the biblical teachings that Modalism must make a mockery of, if their interpretation is true. According to the Onenessian position (and contrary to the otherwise plain reading of these passages):

- It was Jesus himself who counseled with himself to come to earth to save mankind (Philippians 2:6–11).
- It was Jesus himself who impregnated his own mother Mary with himself so that he could become his own father and his own son to himself (Matthew 1:18), contrary to every biblical meaning and definition of the terms "son" and "father."
- It was Jesus himself who swore an oath to himself that he would make himself a priest forever after the order of Melchizedek (Hebrews 7:21).
- And then, even though he was God himself, he still had to become human before he could actually be touched by our weaknesses (Hebrews 4:15), or could become a surety of a better covenant (Hebrews 7:22), or even be able to save us or intercede on our behalf (Hebrews 7:25). (So much for God being so all-powerful that nothing was impossible for him (Luke 1:37); that is, at least, before he became human!)
- So then, when the time came to reveal himself he called out to himself at his baptism saying, "This is me in whom I am well pleased" (Matthew 3:17), yet somehow the words that slipped out otherwise may confuse us to believe he was personally distinct from his Father.
- It was at that time that he anointed himself and sent himself, even though the Bible says he couldn't anoint himself because that would be contrary to the biblical teaching that anointing yourself disqualifies you from the anointing (Hebrews 5:4–5).
- After his baptism he led himself into the wilderness to be tempted (Hebrews 2:18), which is something that is actually impossible for him personally (James 1:13). In other words,

the Oneness Jesus pretended to be someone he was not, so He could not do something that was impossible for him, personally, to do (lie or sin) in order to show us how to be what we're truly supposed to be.
- Then of course there was the Garden of Gethsemane, where he prayed to the point of bloody sweat, "Please, Myself, if it be possible, let this cup pass from Me; nevertheless, not My will be done but My will be done" (Luke 22:41–44). At least, that is what Onenessianism claims he meant, even though that wasn't what he actually said.
- Then came the time while he was on the cross that he called out to Himself asking Himself why He had forsaken Himself (Matthew 27:46). Hmm, what would He have answered to Himself if He had answered?
- And then after he died, he of course raised Himself from the dead, which was a particularly neat trick since the Bible says there are no works, or even knowledge or wisdom, in the grave (Ecclesiastes 9:10), which means if he was conscious and could work (the work of raising himself), then he didn't really ever fit the biblical definition of death, which implies that *Onenessians really don't believe or accept that Jesus fully and completely died*, which would make our faith vain according to Paul (1 Corinthians 15:12–15).
- Then after he had raised himself from the dead, he told the apostles not to touch him because he hadn't ascended to Himself, which Himself was his God and their God and his Father and their Father.
- Some time after that he told his disciples he had given himself all authority in heaven and earth (Matthew 28:18).
- At this present time, that is after having sacrificed himself to Himself, he is now currently under an oath to Himself that he will sit on the right hand of Himself until he makes his own enemies his own footstool (Psalm 110:1; Matthew 22:44; Hebrews 10:7–14).
- Finally, although he is reigning now, he will only reign until death has been destroyed, at which point, in the future,

once he has subdued all things under himself he will also himself be subject to Himself, by delivering the kingdom up to Himself, so that He, God, may be all in all (1 Corinthians 15:24–28).

All of this, and more, is what the "revelation" of Onenessianism will get you, regardless of what these Scriptures actually say about Jesus. And then, of course, if you come to believe such passages at face value, rather than what Onenessians interpret them to mean, then Onenessians will accuse you of not having a true "revelation" of Jesus' deity (just as Trinitarians accuse Onenessians for not having a "revelation" of the Trinity).

For us, all of these "Oneness views" are certainly examples of the "trickery of men" and "wiles of error" that are keeping a large block of God's people from coming into a mature knowledge of the true Son of God.

Do Onenessians Even Hear the Words of Jesus?

Everyone who hears these words of mine, and doesn't do them will be like *a foolish man, who built his house on the sand*. The rain came down, the floods came, and the winds blew, and beat on that house; and it fell, *and great was its fall*. (Matthew 7:26)

So far, we have shown that the teaching we call the Son of God doctrine is not built on sand, but that it is built on an *extremely rock-solid* foundation throughout the Bible from beginning to end. The true Son of God doctrine, with flying colors, satisfies all the *biblical rules* for interpreting God's word, particularly including the words of Jesus to "hear him." Like any true teachings of the Christian faith, this "Son of God" teaching is clearly stated in Scriptures and does not require jumping to conclusions, or stringing Scriptures together to attempt to arrive at a "logical conclusion" or a "solution" to an assumed problem, or proof-texting.

On the other hand, this is not the case with the Oneness position. In this section we intend to show that the Oneness view is built on nothing more than a sandy foundation of presumptions, opinions, and jumping to conclusions.

Of course, that isn't to say Onenessians don't believe they see their doctrine clearly in their Bible. How can this be? Let us try to explain through a similarity of interpretation.

Recently, in July of 2015, there was news floating around the Internet of a Pentecostal man in Jenson, Kentucky, who died from being bitten while practicing *snake handling*. This tragedy reminds us how very real and literal the Scriptures are that say, *"there is a way that seems right to a man, but it is the way that leads to death"* (Proverbs 14:12 and 16:25)! Most of us are aware that these misguided folks use verses such as Mark 16:18 and Luke 10:19 to justify their practice. Certainly, these passages do clearly promise that believers "will take up serpents..." that "will in no way hurt them."

The point is, snake handlers have good Scriptures that they use in wrong, even disastrous, ways.

We do not discount the Scriptures they use that promise us protection. We wholeheartedly believe such words, *when taken in context*. But we are sure that certain misguided souls believe they are being true to God's word, but are not. That is because *they have an imbalanced view of the whole of the Scriptures*.

That is, we are *equally aware of the Scriptures, such as the one Jesus quoted, that command us not to tempt or test the Lord our God* (e.g., Deuteronomy 6:16). Using *qualifying* Scriptures to interpret unclear Scriptures allows us to see the error of false doctrines like snake handling. Purposely doing such a thing like snake-handling is very much "tempting" the Lord God every bit as much as when the devil tempted Jesus to jump from a pinnacle. Jesus' method of searching the Scriptures for clear statements, also allows us to see the errors in Trinitarianism and Onenessianism because those doctrines necessarily must ignore the qualifying Scriptures that speak against their positions.

Moreover, we have yet *another biblical advantage* beyond comparing each other's "interpretations" of what these Scriptures may state or imply: we have the apostle's examples. As a case in point, the only place in the Bible where we find an NT believer bitten by a snake was in Acts 28:3–6, where Apostle Paul was *accidentally* bitten.

> ³But when Paul had gathered a bundle of sticks and laid them on the fire, a viper came out because of the heat, and fastened on his hand... ⁵However he shook off the creature into the fire, and wasn't harmed. (Acts 28:3–5)

As we see here, Paul did not institute the practice of taking up snake handling; he merely happened to be accidentally bitten, and, true to the Scriptures, he was not harmed. But he also stayed true to the commandment not to tempt the Lord, as exemplified by Jesus.

So in the case of snake handling, we have a) the scriptural promise that we won't be hurt, and b) the apostle's example of how that looked in real life. No snake handler, however, can point to a Scripture where anyone purposely took up the practice of handling poisonous snakes to prove their faith!

Likewise, we have a similar contrast between the Son of God doctrine and the Oneness doctrine. We have a) the apostle's examples to support the true Son of God doctrine, and b) all the examples where the apostles preached Jesus as a man anointed by God. Onenessians, however, do not have a single example of anyone ever preaching their jumped-to conclusion that Jesus is a "God-man"!

It is a matter of biblical record that no apostle ever preached that Christ was an incarnation of God the Father. No apostle ever preached a modalistic view of Jesus, just as no apostle ever preached a Trinitarian view of Jesus. Just as consistently as they preached the Son of God, so also did the apostles practice "baptism into the name of Jesus Christ" and not the Trinitarian formula. And likewise, the apostles *always and consistently preached Jesus as a man who was anointed by God and never, ever preached him as personally being God the Father himself incarnate.*

Modalism is just as illegitimate, biblically speaking, as is the doctrine of taking up snake handling to prove your faith!

Onenessianism's Magical House of Cards

Now imagine someone building a huge house of seemingly dozens of cards with a foundation of only a few cards supporting the whole structure. It would look like an upside down pyramid. Imagine how precarious it would be if the foundation were unsettled. The whole structure would come tumbling down. We are going to show that this card tower analogy is very much what the Oneness doctrine is like. When it comes right down to it, there are really only about eight or so key verses that Onenessians use to support and defend their teaching. If those eight verses were to be removed from the base of their theory, the whole tower (that is to say, all the rest of their other minor proof texts) would go tumbling down like so many cards. Those key supporting verses are Matthew 4:10, John 1:1 and 14, John 8:24, John 8:58, John 20:28, 1 Tim. 3:16, and Colossians 2:9. (We could add Hebrews 1:8, but we already covered that in Chapter Six.) Let me state categorically that if these verses were not in our Bibles, there would be no Oneness doctrine.

We're going to limit our direct refutation of modalism in this section by showing that these eight verses just don't say what the Oneness view requires them to mean for the doctrine to be true.

We hope that once people see how the Scriptures are taken out of context to bolster the Oneness position, then those who have a sincere love for the truth will see Onenessianism as the spiritual *optical illusion* that it really is. Once you see how their magic trick is performed, it is hoped you won't ever fall for such a hoax again.

It is amazing to the point of shocking just how much Scripture is provided in plain sight, but some still refuse to see. But it isn't really a vision problem. It is a heart issue. God's word also calls it a sifting of the wheat (Luke 22:31), whereby those who are determined to live by every word that proceeds out of the mouth of God can be distinguished from those who only love the word of God in pretense and appearance.

¹²Yes, they made their hearts as hard as flint, lest they might hear the law, and the words which Yahweh of Armies had sent by his Spirit by the former prophets. Therefore great wrath came from YHWH of Armies. ¹³It has come to pass that, as he called, and they refused to listen, so they will call, and I will not listen, said YHWH of Armies. (Zechariah 7:12–13)

But he said, "On the contrary, blessed are those who hear the word of God, and keep it." (Luke 11:28)

Most assuredly I tell you, he who hears my word, and believes him who sent me, has eternal life, and doesn't come into judgment, but has passed out of death into life. (John 5:24)

He who is of God hears the words of God. For this cause you don't hear, because you are not of God. (John 8:47)

A cloud came, overshadowing them, and a voice came out of the cloud, "This is my beloved *Son. Listen to him.*" (Mark 9:7)

CHAPTER TWENTY-FIVE

Matthew 4:10 Worship God Only: Part 1, Old Testament Schoolmaster

Jacob was worshiped	Joseph was worshiped	King Saul was worshiped	King David was worshiped

Was Jacob God? No! (Gen. 27:29)	Was Joseph God? No! (Gen. 37:7, 42:6)	Was King Saul God? No! (1 Sam. 24:8)	Was King David God? No! (1 Sam. 26:23, 41)

Then Jesus said to him, "Get behind me, Satan! For it is written, 'You shall worship the Lord your God, and him only shall you serve.'" (Matthew 4:10)

Onenessians (and Trinitarians) conclude and claim that because of this commandment Christ must be God because he was worshiped. They conclude that if Christ were a mere man, then "worshiping" him would be idolatry. But is it really so clear, or is this an example of building a doctrine on what certain verses appear to say (like snake handling), without regard to the clearer verses to the contrary?

In reality the idea that Jesus must be God because he was worshiped comes from ignoring the bulk of the Scriptures on the topic.

One of the first things we need to establish is that there was indeed a remarkable, and consistent, difference between the veneration that was given Jesus and the true worship that was reserved only for God. To explain this, we will quote the words of the eminent scholar James D. G. Dunn:

The significance of the veneration offered to the exalted Christ. The use of *kyrios* for Christ in itself suggests that veneration was indeed offered to the exalted Lord in earliest Christian worship. There is certainly evidence that Jesus was invoked or besought in Christian worship and prayer. 1 Cor. 1:2 and Rom. 10:13 indicate that from very early on believers identified themselves as 'those who call upon the name of the Lord (Jesus Christ)'... At the same time an equivalent caution... must also be observed here. This is indicated in the care which Paul seems to take in his use of the normal worship terms. His thanks (*eucharistein, eucharistia*) are always addressed to God and never to Christ or 'the Lord.' This is not simply because traditional formulation is being used, for Paul modifies the formulation on several occasions by adding 'through Jesus Christ' or through him.' The point, then, is that Christ is neither simply the content of the thanksgiving, nor its recipient. In his exalted state he is envisaged as somehow mediating the praise to God. It is equally notable that the normal prayer terms (*deomai, deēsis*) are usually addressed to God and never to Christ. So too with the term *doxazō*, 'glorify.' For Paul, properly speaking, only God is to be glorified. The same is true of *latreuō*, 'serve (religiously, cultically),' and *latreia*, 'service, worship,' and the one use of *proskyneō*, 'worship, reverence' in Paul (1 Cor. 14:25). It is equally noticeable that Christ is absent from the passage which speaks most explicitly about worship in the Pauline churches. In 1 Corinthians 14, the speaker in tongues speaks 'to God' (14:2, 28); thanks are given to God (14:18); the worship is to God (14:25). Such uniformity in Paul's usage should certainly make us hesitate before asserting that Paul 'worshiped' Christ, since the evidence more clearly indicates otherwise... If we observe the ancient distinction between 'worship' and 'veneration,' we would have to speak of the veneration of Christ, meaning by that something short of full-scale worship.[1]

So then, any honest discussion of the veneration or worship of Jesus has to include the acknowledgment that his veneration was not on a par with that worship given only to God.

This being the case, is it dealing with the scriptures honestly to claim that Jesus must have been God because he was worshiped as Onenessians often conclude? In reply we could say, in a sense, that this issue is to the Oneness position what the issue of Jesus plucking grain and healing on the Sabbath was to the Pharisees (see Matthew 12:1–8). The question Jesus asked back to the Pharisees was, "have you not read...?" And then he pointed out that David ate of the shew bread in the temple, and the priests profaned the Sabbath and were all guiltless. The point of Jesus' question then, and ours here, is this: does God have the authority to define the limits of His own commandments or not?

So let's ask Jesus' question back to the Onenessians: "haven't you read" that in the Bible the human Hebrew kings, patriarchs, and even some of their prophets were "worshiped," as in venerated, honored, or paid homage to, and the people were guiltless of idolatry?

If God's servants, the priests and David, "profaned" the Sabbath and were guiltless, then surely God Himself is in full authority to define His own commandments. And furthermore, if nothing is impossible for God, then God also has full authority to *bestow His authority* on His only begotten son and *expect people to honor (or revere) the Son in the position to which God has exalted him*, just as the Bible clearly states:

---

[1] James D.G. Dunn, *The Theology of Paul the Apostle* (Grand Rapids, MI: Eerdmans, 1998), 257–260.

> ²²For the Father judges no one, but he has *given all* judgment to the Son, ²³*that all may honor the Son, even as they honor the Father.* He who doesn't honor the Son doesn't honor the Father who sent him. (John 5:22–23)

> ⁷Your divine throne is everlasting; your royal scepter is a scepter of equity. ⁸You love righteousness and hate wickedness; rightly has God, your God, chosen you *to anoint you with the oil of gladness over all your peers.* (Psalms 45:7–8, Tanakh)

The problem with the idea that "*if* Jesus was worshiped, *then* Jesus had to be God" reveals a profound lack of understanding of the role of the Judean king, which Jesus was called and anointed by God to be. So we need to go back to the OT Schoolmaster and reestablish this apparently lost or at least neglected foundational truth. We are going to spend some time on this topic because it explains so much about Jesus' role as our king. We will start with the OT Schoolmaster and see if it teaches that God's people understood the first commandment the way Onenessians and Trinitarians do.

The first thing to note is that the verse Jesus quoted was Deuteronomy 6:13. The word used in that passage (Heb. *yare'*) was actually *not* "worship," but *"fear."* It was the same word that Adam used when answering God in the Garden, saying, "I was <u>afraid</u>, because I was naked" (Genesis 3:10). But it is also the word that was used of Joshua (who had the same name in Hebrew as Jesus) in this passage:

> On that day YHWH magnified Joshua in the sight of all Israel; and they <u>feared</u> him [Joshua], as they <u>feared</u> Moses, all the days of his life. (Joshua 4:14)

Now, how is it that they *feared/worshiped* the man (Moses) that delivered the same law that said to *fear/worship* the Lord God only? Onenessians like to say that Jesus should have rebuked the people for worshiping him if he was not God. By the same token, then, why didn't Moses or Joshua rebuke the people for *fearing/worshipping* them, in accordance with the same reasoning that Onenessians use? The answer is in yet another written again Scripture:

> YHWH said to Joshua, This day *will I begin to magnify you* in the sight of all Israel, that they may know that, *as I was with Moses, so I will be with you.* (Joshua 3:7)

This is where the fear comes from. It wasn't because they feared "any other gods"; it was because it was the one true God who was with the leader and who had sent him. So, the key in this passage is in accepting who was doing what to or for whom!

Contrary to the Oneness jumped-to conclusion, *God Himself tells us* Joshua would be magnified because, "YHWH said,...'I will be with you.'" If it is the same God who sent these men, how is it serving "another" god (idolatry) *to honor the one* that God Himself *sent*? And that is the point in God's commandment to serve Him *rather than* other "gods." You see, there is a specific context in which this is stated. It is not that His servants who come in His name shouldn't be honored; *rather, it is quite pointedly that those other gods or those who come in the names of those other gods should not be so honored.*

With that thought in mind, now recall Jesus' words:

> *He who sent me is with me.* The Father *hasn't left me alone, for I* always do the things that are pleasing to *him.* (John 8:29)

What we are seeing in these passages is the OT foundation for Jesus' words in the following:

> [19]Jesus therefore answered them, "Most assuredly, I tell you, the Son can do nothing of himself, but what he sees the Father doing. For whatever things he does, these the Son also

does likewise... ²²For the Father judges no one, but he has given all judgment to the Son, ²³that all may honor the Son, even as they honor the Father. He who doesn't honor the Son doesn't honor the Father who sent him." (John 5:19–23)

Here, Jesus renounced any claim to being "I am that I am" by clearly saying he could "do nothing of himself." After making that clear, he then goes on to say that all should honor the Son explicitly because he was sent by the Father. Therefore, all Jesus did was explain that he was to be honored because he was sent in a fashion similar to men such as Moses and Joshua, who also were honored (though not so highly) because they too were sent by the Father.

Similar to the way that God was with Moses, so He was with Joshua, and so He was *with* Jesus (and thus not the same as Jesus)! That's what the Bible teaches. Why should we expect anyone to respect and honor Jesus Christ the only begotten Son of God *any less* than people were to honor Moses and Joshua? Remember Jesus' parable, where such prophets as Moses and Joshua were merely caretakers over God's kingdom, but Jesus was the Son and rightful heir of all (Matthew 21:33–40; Mark 12:1–9; Luke 20:9–16). This clearly shows that the idea that "Jesus had to be God because he was worshiped" is a false argument.

Now, Jesus didn't explain anywhere that he wasn't alone because his deific nature was always with his human nature! Not at all, here or anywhere else in the whole Bible! But that isn't to say he didn't give a reason and an explanation. The point is, it is the explanation that Jesus clearly gave that Onenessianism negates and diminishes from the word of God. That reason is simply that God was *with* Jesus! And the reason the Father was with him was explicitly because he always did the things that are pleasing to the Father! This is something completely different and contrary to saying Jesus was an incarnation of the Father.

Did Jesus mean to tell us that God loves *Himself* because God always does the things that are pleasing to Himself? Of course not, God isn't that shallow or ridiculous. But rather than hear these words of explanation, and apply them, Oneness teachers twist them in a way that makes them mean something different than what Jesus clearly and simply said.

Moving on then, let's look now at another word often translated as *worship* and some of the ways it was used in the OT. This is the Hebrew word *shachah*, which simply means to prostrate oneself in homage to deity or royalty.

For example, it is written that Abraham, ²"Lifted up his eyes and looked, and *saw that three men* stood opposite him. When he saw them, he ran to meet them from the tent door, *and bowed himself* [worshiped] to the earth, ³and said, '*My lords* [*adonai*], if now I have found favor in your sight, please don't go away from your servant.'" (Genesis 18:2–4)

Here we have Abraham seeing three men and worshiping them. This is the word for *worship* that is most often used for that *worship* that is given to God. But it isn't reserved for God alone by God's people. For it is written again:

> ⁵Joseph dreamed a dream, and he told it to his brothers, and *they hated him all the more*. ⁶He said to them, "Please hear this dream which I have dreamed: ⁷for behold, we were binding sheaves in the field, and behold, my sheaf arose and also stood upright; and behold, <u>your sheaves came around, and bowed down to [worshiped] my sheaf.</u>" ⁸His brothers said to him, "*Will you indeed reign over us*? Or will you indeed *have dominion over us*?" *They hated him* all the more for his dreams and for his words. (Genesis 37:5–8)

Here we see that God gave Joseph a dream wherein his brothers would bow down and worship him. Does that mean, using Oneness reasoning, that Joseph must have been God incarnate? Of course not. Rather, the OT is schooling us on Christ. Do you see why Joseph's brothers hated him? They were jealous of him because he was going to reign and have dominion over them. That is the same reason the Pharisees rejected Jesus—they were jealous of him and didn't want this man Jesus, who renounced their man-made traditions, reigning over them!

The same was written of Abraham, that he bowed down to [worshiped] the people of the land:

> ⁷"Abraham rose up, and bowed himself [worshiped] to the people of the land, even to the children of Heth... ¹²Abraham bowed himself down [worshiped] before the people of the land" (Genesis 23:7, 12).

Notice these other "it is written again" examples of worship:

> The two angels came to Sodom at evening. Lot sat in the gate of Sodom. Lot saw them, and rose up to meet them. He bowed himself (worshiped) with his face to the earth. (Genesis 19:1)

> Isaac blessed Jacob, saying, "Let peoples serve you, And nations bow down (worship) to you. Be *lord over your brothers; Let your mother's sons bow down (worship) to you.* Cursed be everyone who curses you; Blessed be everyone who blesses you." (Genesis 27:29)

> David... cried after Saul, saying, *My lord* the king. When Saul looked behind him, David bowed with his face to the earth, and *did obeisance [worship]*. (1 Samuel 24:8)

> ²³When Abigail saw David, she hurried, and alighted from her donkey, and fell before David on her face, and bowed herself to the ground [worshiped]... ⁴¹She arose, and *bowed herself [worshiped]* with her face to the earth, and said, Behold, your handmaid is a servant to wash the feet of the servants of my lord. (1 Samuel 25:23, 41)

> ⁴When the woman of Tekoa spoke to the king, she fell on her face to the ground, and *did obeisance*, and said, Help, O king... ²²Joab fell to the ground on his face, and did obeisance, and blessed the king: and Joab said, Today your

servant knows that I have found favor in your sight, my lord, king, in that the king has performed the request of his servant... ³³So Joab came to the king, and told him; and when he had called for Absalom, he came to the king, and *bowed himself* on his face to the ground before the king: and the king kissed Absalom. (2 Samuel 14:4, 22, 33)

Mephibosheth, the son of Jonathan, the son of Saul, came to David, and fell on his face, and *did obeisance [worshiped]*. David said, Mephibosheth. He answered, Behold, your servant!. (2 Samuel 9:6)

The sons of those who afflicted you shall come bending to you; and all those who despised you *shall bow themselves down [worship] at the soles of your feet*; and they shall call you The city of YHWH, The Zion of the Holy One of Israel. (Isaiah 60:14)

Behold, I will make them of the synagogue of Satan, which say they are Jews, and are not, but do lie; behold, I will make them *to come and worship before thy feet,* and to know that I have loved thee. (Revelation 3:9)

When the sons of the prophets who were at Jericho over against him saw him, they said, The spirit of Elijah does rest on Elisha. They came to meet him, and bowed themselves [worshiped] to the ground before him. (2 Kings 2:15)

Onenessians think that if Jesus wasn't God, he should have rebuked anyone who worshiped him. Why then didn't Elijah rebuke the sons of the prophets for worshiping (prostrating themselves) before him?

Here's the thing that makes the difference: the commandment of the Lord is to worship God in contrast to <u>not</u> worshiping <u>other gods</u>. "You shall have no other gods before me" (Exodus 20:3). What is different, is this, wherein it is written again,

> Jesus cried out and said, "Whoever believes in me, believes <u>not</u> in me, but <u>*in him who sent me.*</u>" (John 12:44)

By what stretch of the imagination is Jesus saying he really is the Father here? By what stretch of the imagination is he saying, "whoever believes in my human nature is really believing in my deific-nature"? No, he is saying something completely different. He is clearly saying that if you believe in him (personal pronoun), you *aren't* believing on him (personal pronoun), but on another "Him" (the Sender)! Jesus consistently described his position with God in terms that perfectly align with the doctrine of agency, or *shaliah*. Again, he said,

> [22]For the Father judges no one, but he has *given* all judgment to the Son, [23]*that all may honor the Son, even as they honor the Father*. He who doesn't honor the Son doesn't honor the Father who sent him. [24]Most assuredly I tell you, he who hears my word, and believes him who sent me, has eternal life, and doesn't come into judgment, but has passed out of death into life. (John 5:22–24)

This is very much like what happened, as is written again, in the case when, "David said to all the assembly, Now bless YHWH your God. All the assembly blessed YHWH, the God of their fathers, *and bowed down* their heads <u>*and prostrated [worshiped]*</u> themselves before YHWH <u>*and the king*</u>" (1 Chronicles 29:20).

This is also very much like what happened when it was written again that, "...*Solomon sat on the throne of YHWH as king* instead of David his father, and prospered; *and all Israel obeyed him*" (1 Chronicles 29:23).

It is all spelled out so very clearly in the OT that it really shouldn't need any further explanation! Solomon sat on the throne of YHWH, not *as* YHWH, but as His representative *agent*. And that is the sonship that Jesus inherited as David's heir!

And it was that very same kingdom that the apostles were still anticipating when they asked the Lord Jesus, "Lord, will You at this time restore the kingdom to Israel?" (Acts 1:6–7, NKJV). What kingdom were they talking about? Did they believe that God had stopped having a kingdom such that God's eternal kingdom needed to be restored? Of course not. They were talking about the kingdom of David, which God had promised, wherein people bowed down before and obeyed the sons of David because God was with them!

As we said, in the same way that Onenessians use all the other Scriptures on baptism to refute the Trinitarian jumped-to conclusions, there are many more that can be brought against the false interpretation that Jesus must have personally been God to receive "worship." This shows that the "Jesus must be God because he was worshiped" conclusion is a false dilemma. It makes it appear there is only one true option, theirs, and that any other option would make the Bible contradict itself; when in fact that is not true at all. The apostle Paul wrote, "We have renounced the hidden things of shame, not walking in craftiness, nor handling the word of God deceitfully" (2 Corinthians 4:2). If creating false conclusions isn't a form of handling the word of God deceitfully, what is?

The Snake-Handler Factor: The idea that Jesus must be God because he was worshiped, ignores the context of his being heir to the throne of David. The real contrast in the Bible came with the commandment not to bow down to, or give honor or worship to any other gods or those who came representing other gods. The ironic thing is that Onenessianism is just such a false way, because it leads people to the pagan doctrine of incarnation of deities and the antichristian invention of the dual natures of Christ.

We will continue with the Scriptures on worship in the following chapter covering the same type of worship in the NT.

CHAPTER TWENTY-SIX

Matthew 4:10 Worship God Only: Part 2, Behold, your King

| King Saul was worshipped | King David was worshipped | King Jesus was worshipped just like the other kings |

King Saul was not worshipped as God (1 Sam. 24:8)

King David was not worshipped as God (1 Sam. 25:23, 41)

King Jesus was not worshipped as God (Matt. 9:8, 18; 15:22-28; Mark 5:21-23 with 35-36)

¹⁴[Pilate] said to the Jews, "Behold, your King!" ¹⁵They cried out, "Away with him! Away with him! Crucify him!" Pilate said to them, "Shall I crucify your King?" The chief priests answered, "We have no king but Caesar!"...¹⁹Pilate wrote a title also, and put it on the cross. There was written, "JESUS OF NAZARETH, THE KING OF THE JEWS." (John 19:14–19)

Having prepared our minds in the last chapter with the OT Schoolmaster, we should be suitably prepared to see how King Jesus was received in the NT. As you read each of these passages, ask yourself honestly, based on the context: were they seeking to worship their Messiah as a king after the manner of David, or as God incarnate? We believe the context reveals the answer.

As it is written, "The multitudes... who followed kept shouting, 'Hosanna to *the son of David*! Blessed is he who comes *in the name of the Lord*! Hosanna in the highest!'" (Matthew 21:9).

It is written, ¹"Now when Jesus was born... wise men... came... saying, 'Where is he who is *born King of the Jews*? For we saw his star in the east, and have *come to worship him.*' 3 When Herod the king heard it... ⁷Then Herod...⁸... sent them to Bethlehem, and said, 'Go and search diligently for the young child. When you have found him, bring me word, *so that I also may come and worship him*'" (Matthew 2:1, 3, 7–8).

It is written again, ⁸"But when the multitudes saw it, they marveled and glorified God, who had given such *authority to men*...¹⁸While he told these things to them, behold, *a ruler came and worshiped him*, saying, 'My daughter has just died, but come and lay your hand on her, and she will live'" (Matthew 9:8, 18).

It is written again, ¹⁶"Fear took hold of all, and *they glorified God, saying, 'A great prophet has arisen among us!*' and, 'God has visited his people!' ¹⁷This report went out concerning him in the whole of Judea, and in all the surrounding region" (Luke 7:16,17).

It is written again, ¹"Jesus said these things, and lifting up his eyes to heaven, he said, 'Father, the time has come. Glorify your Son, that your Son may also glorify you; ²*even as you gave him authority over all flesh, he <u>will give</u> eternal life to* all whom you have given him. ³This is eternal life, that they should know *you, the only true God, and <u>him</u> whom <u>you</u> sent*, Jesus Christ. ⁴I glorified you on the earth. I have accomplished the work which you have given me to do. ⁵Now, Father, glorify me with your own self with the glory which I had with you before the world existed'" (John 17:1, 3, 5).

It is a curiosity that Onenessians will skip right over the first four clearly stated verses and jump to the fifth verse that is unclear (Glorify me with your own self). They do this so that they can jump to the pagan conclusion of literal preexistence and dual natures. This is how they end up accepting doctrines that are taught by pagans and antichristians but which are never clearly spelled out in the Bible. Remember that jumping to conclusions is the big daddy of all sin!

The way Jesus taught us to interpret the Scriptures is by interpreting the unclear verses by means of the clear verses. There is no clear verse that says Jesus intended us to understand that being glorified by the Father meant he was to be considered the person of the Father. Now look at this next verse that qualifies Jesus' statement:

> The glory which you have given me, I have given to them; that they may be one, even as we are one... (John 17:22)

Biblical Truth

...that they may **be one even as we are one**
- John 17:22

The Oneness view: Is it true to the Scriptures?

Oneness Father and Son

...that they may **be one even as we are one**
- John 17:22

Are we going to be lifeless puppets controlled by God like the Oneness Jesus was? No! But, "We shall be like him; for we shall see him just as he is." - 1 John 3:2

If Oneness is true, then Jesus was praying for us all to be "lifeless empty shells without the spirit of God in us," in accordance with David Bernard's description of Jesus. Jesus' prayer only makes sense if he were as human as we are and was praying that we, personally, join in the unity with the Father that he has, which is a unity of purpose and attitude, not a unity of personality.

We continue...

Similarly to John 17, it is written, ^{32}"When Elisha was come into the house, behold, the child was dead, and laid on his bed. ^{33}He went in therefore, and... prayed to YHWH... ^{35}...*and the child opened his eyes.* ^{36}"He called Gehazi, and said, Call this Shunammite. So he called her. When she was come in to him, he said, Take up your son. ^{37}Then *she went in, and fell at his feet, and bowed herself to the ground [worshiped]*; and she took up her son, and went out" (2 Kings 4:32–37).

Was Elisha God? If not, why didn't he rebuke the Shunamite woman for worshiping at his feet? Why is it so hard for us to believe that Elisha was part of the OT Schoolmaster to help bring us to Christ and understand how a man like Jesus, who was greater than Elisha, could be given authority over all flesh and be worthy of our worship because he is the Son of God?

It is written again, ^{21}"When Jesus had crossed back over in the boat to the other side, a great multitude was gathered to him; and he was by the sea. ^{22}Behold, one of the rulers of the synagogue, Jairus by name, came; and seeing him, *he fell at his feet [worshiped]*, ^{23}and begged him much, saying, 'My little daughter is *at the point of death*. Please come and lay your hands on her, *that she may be made healthy*, and live'" (Mark 5:21–43).

By what stretch of the imagination would anyone believe that one of the "rulers of the synagogue" believed that Jesus was YHWH God incarnate? The man was desperate for the life of his daughter, but that doesn't mean he'd forgotten everything he knew as a Jewish leader.

Furthermore, we don't have to guess what the people thought Jesus was, because the Bible tells us, as it is written, "While he was still speaking, they came from the synagogue ruler's house saying,

'Your daughter is dead. Why bother *the Teacher* anymore?' But Jesus, when he heard the message spoken, immediately said to the ruler of the synagogue, 'Don't be afraid, only believe'" (Mark 5:35–36).

I would think that the apostles, or Jairus, or Jesus himself would have rebuked those who came from the ruler's house. They should have said something like, "Teacher? This is not just a teacher! Why this is YHWH God Himself come down to earth as a man!" Doesn't any Onenessian think it is just a little bit odd that *no one in the Bible ever confessed the theory they hold so dear and so "primary"— that "Jesus is the Father incarnate"*? This question is like the question we and Oneness Pentecostals ask, saying, "Doesn't any 'just believer' think it is a little bit odd that no one in the Bible was ever told to 'accept the Lord as their personal savior'?" The absent Oneness confession in the Bible not only shows the utter weakness of the Oneness conclusion, but also the double-mindedness of Onenessians in their methods.

And again, as the story is told in Matthew, ²⁷"As Jesus passed by from there, two blind men followed him, calling out and saying, 'Have mercy on us, *son of David*!' ²⁸When he had come into the house, the blind men came to him. Jesus said to them, 'Do you believe that I am able to do this?' They told him, 'Yes, Lord.' ²⁹Then he touched their eyes, saying, 'According to your faith be it done to you'" (Matthew 9:27–29).

According to what faith did they have? Well, what did they confess? Was it belief that Jesus was God incarnate, or that he was the son of David? If they thought he was God incarnate, wouldn't Jesus' question have been a little silly? Would any Jew not believe that God was able to heal?

It is written again, "When they got up into the boat, the wind ceased. Those who were in the boat came and *worshiped him*, saying, 'You are truly *the Son of God*!'" (Matthew 14:32–33).

Recall what we learned about what the term "Son of God" meant to the Jews? That he was the Son of David, whom God said would be His Son. So they worshiped him as David's heir, just like David himself was seen doing before his king, Saul, as it is written, "David also arose afterward, and went out of the cave, and cried after Saul, saying, *My lord the king*. When Saul looked behind him, *David bowed with his face to the earth, and did obeisance [worship]*" (1 Samuel 24:8).

If Oneness reasoning is true, shouldn't we believe that King Saul was also God incarnate? Of course not.

It is written yet again, ²²Behold, a Canaanite woman came out from those borders, and cried, saying, "Have mercy on me, *Lord, you son of David*! My daughter is severely demonized!" ²³But he answered her not a word. His disciples came and begged him, saying, "Send her away; for she cries after us." ²⁴But he answered, "I wasn't <u>sent</u> to anyone but the lost sheep of the house of Israel." ²⁵But *she came and worshiped him*, saying, "Lord, help me." ²⁶But he answered, "It is not appropriate to take the children's bread and throw it to the dogs." ²⁷But she said, "Yes, Lord, but even the dogs eat the crumbs which fall from their masters' table." ²⁸Then Jesus answered her, "*Woman, great is your faith*! Be it done to you even as you desire." And her daughter was healed from that hour" (Matthew 15:22–28).

Was her confession of faith in Jesus as the "son of David" or as "YHWH incarnate"? The fact is, in not one example out of all the places where Jesus was "worshiped" did anyone ever confess they worshiped him as "YHWH incarnate."

It is written again, ²⁰"Then the mother of the sons of Zebedee came to him with her sons, *kneeling [worshiping] and asking* a certain thing of him. ²¹He said to her, "What do you want?" She said to him, "Command that these, my two sons, may sit, one on your right hand, and one on your left hand, in your Kingdom" (Matthew 20:20–23). The Jews were expecting the Son of David to restore the kingdom of David to Israel. It would simply be jumping to conclusions to believe that this mother was asking that her sons be at the right and left hand of God's throne in the heavens.

It is written again, ⁸"They departed quickly from the tomb...⁹As they went... behold, Jesus met them, saying, 'Rejoice!' They came and took hold of his feet, and worshiped him. ¹⁰Then Jesus said to them, 'Don't be afraid. *Go tell my brothers* (or siblings) that they should go into Galilee, and there they will see me' (Matthew 28:8–10). This passage doesn't seem to tell us whether they worshiped because Jesus was the Son of David or because he was YHWH incarnate. But if we have ears to hear Jesus, he tells us, "Go tell my brothers". Does YHWH have siblings? But He must if the Oneness theory is to be believed. Rather, this verse is reminiscent of Psalms 45:7 and Hebrews 1:6–9: "Therefore God, your God, has *anointed you* with the oil of gladness *above your fellows*." Thus the Jesus that was being worshiped here was the one that Moses spoke of, "For Moses indeed said to the fathers, 'The Lord God will raise up *a prophet* for you *from among your brothers, like me*. You shall *listen to him* in all things whatever he says to you. It will be that *every soul that will not listen* to that prophet *will be utterly destroyed* from among the people'" (Acts 3:22–23). People who don't listen to this prophet Jesus jump to conclusions and think he is YHWH incarnated, but that isn't something Jesus ever said or claimed of himself.

It is written again, ¹⁶"The soldiers led him away...¹⁷...They clothed him with purple, and weaving a crown of thorns, they put it on him. ¹⁸They began to salute him, 'Hail, King of the Jews!' ¹⁹They struck his head with a reed, and spat on him, and bowing their knees, did homage [worship] to him" (Mark 15:16–19). Obviously these soldiers didn't mock-worship Jesus as YHWH, but as the king of the Jews.

It is written again, ³⁶"He answered, 'Who is he, Lord, that I may believe in him?' ³⁷Jesus said to him, 'You have both seen him, and it is he who speaks with you.' 38 He said, 'Lord, I believe!' and he *worshiped* him" (John 9:35–38). Did this man see YHWH? It is written again, "No one has seen God at any time. The one and only Son, who is in the bosom of the Father, he has declared him" (John 1:18).

We would like to think that the evidence we've provided against the Oneness theory can be found in the above words of God in the Bible, not in our commentary. But that doesn't mean there isn't more to say. If it still isn't clear how Jesus could be worshiped even though he is not an incarnation of God the Father, compare the following and see if this doesn't help reveal the biblical viewpoint to you.

> You shall have *no other* gods before me. (Exodus 20:3)

On the other hand,

> Hosanna to the son of David! Blessed *is he who comes in the name of* the Lord! Hosanna in the highest! (Matthew 21:9)

> For the Father judges no one, but *he has given all* judgment to the Son, *that all may honor the Son, even as they honor the Father.* He who doesn't honor the Son doesn't honor the Father who sent him. (John 5:22–23)

> [6]Again, when he brings in the firstborn into the world he says, "*Let all* the angels of God *worship him.*" [7]Of the angels he says, "Who makes his angels winds, And his servants a flame of fire." [8]but of the Son he says, "Your divine throne is forever and ever; The scepter of uprightness is the scepter of your Kingdom. [9]*You have loved righteousness, and hated iniquity; Therefore* God, your God, *has anointed you... above your fellows.*" (Hebrews 1:6–12)

We hope the reader can see the difference between honoring someone who has been sent by the true God versus following after other gods. The passage in Hebrews says this "firstborn" had a God who anointed him to be worshiped of angels, and anointed him above his "fellows," much as could have been said of Joseph.

Now we ask the reader to consider what all these passages we've read so far are saying as compared to the Oneness position.

> If Christ is just a man in whom God dwells in a special way, as opposed to *being the very incarnate person of God Himself, then worship of Christ is idolatrous*, for we would be worshipping [sic] someone other than God. *Only if Jesus' human nature shares an essential and metaphysical union with the divine person/nature can the man from Galilee be considered to be God and be worthy of worship.*[1]

You have just read the subtlety of deceit, as a theologian expresses how to have an antichrist spirit; that is, a spirit that is *against the idea of an anointed man* being our savior as Jesus Christ was. As we have seen, the Bible contains many examples where men of God were worshiped without actually being God. So what the above words present is nothing more than false conclusions. The option not being accepted in this case is Jesus' lordship and kingship as the Son of David, king of the Jews, which was given to him by God.

Along these lines is another often overlooked biblical contrast that may be helpful to point out here. That is the simple truth that Jesus is, even now, the only true human king anointed by God over all other humans; in contrast, no other human has such authority within the body of Christ.

> [49]Nathanael answered him, "Rabbi, you are the Son of God! You are King of Israel!" [50]Jesus answered him, "Because I told you, 'I saw you underneath the fig tree,' do you believe?" (John 1:49–50)

> These will war against the Lamb, and the Lamb will overcome them, for *he is Lord of lords, and King of kings...* (Revelation 17:13–14)

---

[1] Jason Dulle, accessed 2/27/2015, http://www.onenesspentecostal.com/ugstsymposium.htm.

These verses, among many others, show that Jesus is even still rightly called our king. On the other hand, the following Scriptures are very clear that no one else among us should have such authority over others in the body of Christ:

> ²⁵He [Jesus] said to them, "The kings of the nations lord it over them, and those who have authority over them are called 'benefactors.' ²⁶*But not so with you.* But one who is the greater among you, let him become as the younger, and one who is governing, *as one who serves.*" (Luke 22:25–26)

> ²Shepherd the flock of God which is among you, exercising the oversight, not under compulsion, but voluntarily, not for dishonest gain, but willingly; ³ *neither as lording it over* the charge allotted to you, but making yourselves examples to the flock. (1 Peter 5:2–3)

So then, when John was rebuked in the Book of Revelation for worshiping the messenger, it wasn't evidence that if Jesus were so worshiped the only conclusion would be that Jesus must be God. No, John was rebuked because the messenger that John was speaking to was one of his fellow servants.

> ⁸Now I, John, am the one who heard and saw these things. When I heard and saw, I fell down to worship before the feet of the angel who had shown me these things. ⁹He said to me, 'See you don't do it! *I am a fellow bondservant with you and with your brothers, the prophets*, and with those who keep the words of this book. Worship God.' (Revelation 22:8–9)

The same was true when the devil tempted Jesus to worship him. The devil has no authority from God as a king over anyone. So it is simply creating a false conclusion to adamantly claim with no possibility of exception that if Jesus was worshiped it could only mean that he is God. Creating or defending such a false conclusion is to ignore completely all the OT Schoolmaster Scriptures we've quoted, along with the context in which Jesus was being worshiped (as the heir of the throne of King David). Such a false argument is nothing short of handling the word of God in a deceitful manner.

Have we exaggerated our opening comment in this chapter that the Oneness rejection of worshiping a human Jesus is their "working on the Sabbath" issue? Is the Oneness position a fair estimation that harmonizes all the Scriptures we've seen in this and the previous chapter? Or is it rather a subtle rejection of *the man who has been anointed above his fellows, whom he calls his siblings*? We believe we've made a very strong case, but that doesn't mean all will see it.

Maybe not everyone will see it, but here's what we see: the subtlety of the Oneness rejection of the biblical Jesus is found in the *"redefinition"* of Christ into something (an incarnation of the person of God the Father) *that the Bible never clearly articulates*. And isn't a redefinition another way of *creating a man-made counterfeit* instead of the real thing? And isn't worshiping a *counterfeit* a genuine form of *idolatry*?

If this still isn't clear, let's ask this: how many passages could be listed from the beginning to the end of the Bible that declare plainly that the "Messiah should be worshiped *because he is and was to be an incarnation of the person of YHWH God*"? Answer: zero! It is the same number of Scriptures you would find looking for a clear statement about the Trinity in the Bible!

Rejecting the Messiah is nothing new. Rejecting God's authority is nothing new. What is "unique" about the Oneness position is that it rejects the truth that there is one individual *who* has been sent, and there is another individual *who* anointed the other sent *who*. This is two whos, not one.

The Trinitarians reject the truth of the "one sender and the other one sent" also being "worshiped" by making them both co-equal "persons" in the godhead. The Onenessians reject the truth by making the sender and the one sent merely two natures of the same individual person. Both are doctrines by deduction rather than scriptural explanation. The result is that both fail to see and accept the simplicity of Jesus Christ, and therefore they come up with another "Jesus" that the Bible quite frankly does not describe anywhere in all its pages.

> *But I am afraid* that somehow, as the serpent deceived Eve in his craftiness [or subtlety], so your minds might be corrupted from the simplicity that is in Christ. For if he who comes preaches <u>another Jesus, whom we did not preach</u>... you put up with that... (2 Corinthians 11:3)

The Snake-Handler Factor: The idea that Jesus "must be God because he was worshiped," based on the NT, ignores the context of Jesus' position amidst the rest of the saints of the NT. When John was told not to bow down to the angel in heaven, he was told precisely why: because that "angel" (or messenger, which is what the word really means) was really a fellow saint of God, who also came out of great tribulation! Thus the messenger was not John's "king." Such is not the case with the Lord Jesus, the Anointed One. Right now, today, he is and has been "anointed with the oil of gladness above his fellows!" Jesus is, even now, our Lord, our Liege, our King! The Oneness contention is like comparing Brother Joe to Brother Larry and saying because Brother Larry can't worship Brother Joe, then neither can King Jesus be worshiped without actually being God. This is a non sequitur; the conclusion does not follow the reasoning. It is therefore a false and deceptive way to attempt to prove "doctrine."

Jumping to Conclusions versus "It is written": The Oneness and Trinitarian idea that *"Only if Jesus' human nature shares an essential and metaphysical union with the divine person/nature* can the man from Galilee be considered to be God and be worthy of worship" is jumping to conclusions and adopting pagan incarnation ideas not found in the Bible. On the other hand, we are told by the Lord Jesus that, "...the Father... <u>has given all</u> judgment to the Son, <u>that all may honor the Son, even as they honor the Father</u>. He who doesn't honor the Son doesn't honor the Father who sent him"

(John 5:22–23). Thus both Onenessians and Trinitarians reject the thoroughly biblical truth of a highly exalted, human Son of God and Son of Man in whom God dwelled and through whom God worked.

The OT Schoolmaster: "YHWH said to Joshua, This day *will I begin to magnify you* in the sight of all Israel, that they may know that, *as I was with Moses, so I will be with you*" (Joshua 3:7). Joshua was a type of Jesus Christ that taught us to fear and worship Jesus as God's anointed representative above the rest of us.

Teach No Other Doctrine: The concepts that Oneness and Trinitarians have of Christ come straight from antichristian Gnosticism, as we covered in Chapter 12. It is not a doctrine that is clearly stated in the Scripture. Thus, teaching that Christ was an incarnation either of the person of God the Father or of an eternal God the Son is teaching other doctrines, which is forbidden by the Christian Scriptures and thus an open and unrepentant sin.

CHAPTER TWENTY-SEVEN

John 1:1,14 The Word was with God and the Word was God

> ¹In the beginning was the word, and the word was with God, and the word was God. ²The same was in the beginning with God... ¹⁴And the word was made flesh, and dwelt among us, (and we beheld his glory, the glory as of the only begotten of the Father,) full of grace and truth. (John 1:1–2, KJV)

Here is a verse that Onenessians typically turn to as a proof text for their incarnation-of-the-Father doctrine. But is that what it says? Does this passage clearly and simply say or teach that Jesus is an incarnation of the person of God the Father? For anyone with any sense of open honesty, this passage is far from explaining itself in either a Onenessian or Trinitarian manner. First off, it simply doesn't say that "God was made flesh." It doesn't clearly state the Trinitarian position, nor does it clearly state the Oneness position. It simply says that God's word was, past tense, with God, and was, past tense, God, but that at some point in time, "the word" was made flesh. Thus, it does not say that "God was made flesh" by any means. Saying that "the word was made flesh" is to say something different than Onenessians interpret it to mean.

So once again, we are faced with an issue of "interpretation" and not an issue of the Bible actually stating something that negates or contradicts what the Bible elsewhere consistently states and reaffirms the Son of God to be!

Since John didn't simply say, "God became flesh," let's consider honestly what he actually did say.

What he did say is, "and the word became flesh." If we were to say that "your word was you and was with you and then your word became flesh," would that be saying the same as saying, "you became flesh"? Would that mean an exact clone of you was made? Or would that mean that you, personally, were transformed into flesh (assuming you hadn't been flesh before)?

If "God was made flesh," that would have meant that God "was transformed" into something he wasn't before. And who was it that performed the action of transforming God into something else?

On the other hand, when God's word/plan/expression was made flesh, His word/plan/expression was transformed into something it hadn't been before: flesh. And yet that doesn't mean that there was a "word" that was transformed into something and didn't remain what it was.

Why is it true to say that about the "word," but it wouldn't be true to say about God? It's because God is an entity, whereas "word/plan/expression" is a concept. If we were to say that you were made flesh, we would be saying you were transformed into something else because you are an entity. When a concept is made into reality, the concept itself doesn't stop being the same concept it was before it was made real.

This is why John did not say that God was made flesh and why it is so terribly wrong for Incarnationists to claim that's what he meant.

Besides, the fact is, neither Trinitarians nor Onenessians actually believe that God was made flesh. Quite to the contrary, what you do hear Onenessians say is that the Son is the flesh, and the deity is the Father, so they disprove their own reliance on this verse by their own confession! Since God stayed God, then God wasn't "made" flesh, was He? That is why they have to change the wording of the Scriptures and conclude by saying that God was joined to flesh or robed Himself in flesh. In this way, you can make the Bible appear to say anything if you redefine what the words mean.

But John also did not say that God joined to flesh or robed Himself in flesh, nor did he say that the word joined to flesh or that the word robed itself in flesh.

It was the word that was made flesh; that is to say, God's plan and self-expression of Himself was made flesh. Thus it wasn't God Himself that was made flesh, and that is another reason John did not say it was God that was made flesh.

Furthermore, the Bible actually explains for us how God's word was made flesh, and it has nothing at all to do with God incarnating Himself as a human. It is written again, that, "...When the fullness of the time was come, God sent forth his Son, *made **of*** a woman, made under the law" (Galatians 4:4).

God's self-expression was made *of* a woman; that is, made flesh from the woman's humanity. God's plan was made human by being made out of a woman.

Do you see the difference between jumping to conclusions as opposed to letting the Bible explain itself?

It is the difference between imposing man-made ideas into the Bible to make it say something it never actually says, in contrast to letting the Bible explain something to you so that you take out of the Bible what it is saying. They are completely different approaches. The former is unrighteous, and the latter is righteous. Why? Jesus explained it like this:

> [16]Jesus therefore answered them, "My teaching is not mine, but his who sent me. [17]If anyone desires to do his will, he will know about the teaching, whether it is from God, or if I am speaking from myself. [18]*He who speaks from himself seeks his own glory, but he who seeks the glory of him who sent him is true, and no unrighteousness is in him.*" (John 7:16–18)

When we change the Bible's message from what it is telling us to what we want it to say, or what we think it should say, then we aren't being righteous; we aren't being true to the message that we are sent as messengers to deliver.

This Son of God doctrine is not something someone made up after the apostles. This Son of God doctrine is what the apostles taught clearly, completely, and thoroughly throughout the NT.

Christ Did Not Glorify Himself

Of all of the Scriptures, perhaps the one that is most devastating to the modalistic Oneness interpretation of John Chapter One, is this one:

> ¹For every high priest, being taken *from among men*, is appointed... ⁴*Nobody takes this honor on himself*, but he is called by God, just like Aaron was. ⁵*So also Christ didn't glorify himself to be made a high priest, but it was he who said to him, "You are my Son. Today I have become your father."* (Hebrews 5:1–5)

Here we have a verse that clearly states that the same personal "self" who was made the high priest, whose name was "Jesus" and who was titled "the Anointed One," *could not have glorified himself* to be made a high priest. That biblical truth in itself rules out the Onenessian conclusion that Jesus is the same self as the Father. Furthermore, what ties this very same biblical truth straight back to John Chapter One is the very next sentence. God Himself said, "You are my Son. *Today I have become your father.*" So God Himself, by using personal pronouns, refutes the modalistic Oneness conclusion that He was made into the Son.

This is how the Bible clearly teaches that the Son who was made flesh was very specifically not the same personal individual who said to him, "Today I have become your father."

The simple, biblical truth is, if Jesus was God Himself incarnate, then by God's own decree, He was *not biblically qualified* to be Christ, the "Anointed One." And that is because in order to be "the Anointed One," according to the biblical rules of this spiritual race we are in, *someone else MUST anoint you*, you cannot take the honor of being "anointed" upon yourself. This verse explicitly applied to Christ! And that is exactly what the title "Christ" means every time someone says it! So every time a Onenessian or Trinitarian calls Jesus "Christ," they are saying he was a man anointed by God who didn't take this honor upon himself.

That is what the Bible says, and what the God of the Bible says. And that is what the Bible says *against the antichristian idea that Christ is the person of the Father incarnate!* In order to get around the biblical truth that "Christ didn't glorify himself" (as the Scripture says), they simply adopted the antichristian "dual nature" doctrine and, without any biblical support whatsoever, redefined Christ's true "self" into a mere "nature."

What Was The Plan That Was Made Flesh?

Now let's look at some Scriptures that actually describe what plan was made flesh.

> No one has ascended into heaven, but he who descended out of heaven, the *Son of Man*, who is in heaven. (John 3:13)

> ...I have come down from heaven, *not to do my own will, but the will of Him* who sent me. (John 6:38)

These Scriptures express the "face," or the "person" of the "plan" (or *logos*) that was *"with"* God. How do we know this? Because John 1:14 said, "and *the plan was made flesh.*" That plan who was made flesh (human), and became *the true Witness* after being made flesh, testified to us that *he didn't come to do his own will.*

In this way he testified for himself that he wasn't personally God before he was made flesh. That fulfilled and realized plan, when he was in the days of his flesh, said that "the offspring of humanity" was what was in heaven and came down out of heaven. These words, like the word *logos,* have real meaning. Since Jesus was the firstborn of many brethren, he was not an offspring of humanity until he was actually born in Bethlehem. He could only have been "the Son of Man" in heaven, in God's mind, *as God's plan,* because before creation there was no humanity in existence for him to be an offspring of or that would have been there to parent him! So Jesus was quite clearly referring to the fact that God calls things that are not, as though they were. God's plan was *of* Jesus *as* the "son of humanity" that he would one day become.

In fact, Jesus also testified himself that *even in heaven he had a separate and contrary will to that of God.* This is more evidence and explanation so that we can know that, even in heaven, in the mind of God, God didn't plan to incarnate Himself. That is not what He either said He would do or what He claimed to have done. Rather, what this says is that God's plan was for this man, who had a separate and contrary will to God Himself, to submit himself to this God who planned him. God's plan required Jesus, of his plan, to not be God Himself, because He planned him to not have the same will as God Himself!

Not only did Jesus describe himself as distinct from God during the time when he was *only a plan* in God's foreknowledge, but God Himself also testified to us that He (God) was not the Son of Man. This is more evidence that Jesus was not an incarnation of the person of God in any manner.

> *God is not a man*, that he should lie, *Neither the son of man*... (Numbers 23:19)

In the Jewish view, as this verse shows us, "son of man" is simply a synonym for "man," not a technical title. Numbers 23:19 states the complete opposite of what Incarnationists believe John 1:1–2 says. It also stands in stark contrast to these two verses we are looking at:

No one has ascended into heaven, but he who descended out of heaven, the *Son of Man, who is in heaven*. (John 3:13)

...I have come down from heaven, *not to do my own will, but the will of Him* who sent me. (John 6:38)

So, between these two sets of passages, we have God claiming that he is not the son of man, and Jesus claiming that he was the *Son of Man* (offspring of humanity) in heaven who came down out of heaven not to do his own will. Jesus was *not literally the offspring of humanity* in heaven before any other human was born; he was planned by God to be the offspring of Eve, Abraham, and David.

God is not the author of confusion, and what a confusion it makes of God to claim that He came down to earth to do His will by not doing His own will! Yet again, Onenessians make God and Jesus out to be liars!

All of this scriptural talk is simply about God's foreknowledge, about God calling those things that are not, as though they were. This biblical concept completely flies in the face of talk of incarnation, and proves it all wrong and utterly confused and even in denial of the true omniscient power of God! All of that incarnation mumbo-jumbo can be seen in Acts 14:11, which exposed repugnant paganism!

This also explains why John didn't say that God was made flesh, but that the *logos, the thought and plan* of God that was to come to be, was made flesh. John didn't say the "Spirit of God became man." John didn't say "the person of God became man." We just need to learn to weed out such man-made ideas and unbiblical definitions of the words the Bible uses. The Bible calls this "not in the words which man's wisdom teaches, but which the Holy Spirit teaches; comparing spiritual things with spiritual" (1 Corinthians 2:13). That doesn't mean making things up; it means not going to the world's philosophers for wisdom and understanding, but rather letting the words of the Bible teach us!

But What About Melchizedek?

One of the ploys that Incarnationists will reach for is the character Melchizedek. Their position goes something like this: "Well, the same passage that says Christ didn't take this honor upon himself also says Melchizedek had neither beginning of days nor end of life. So this teaches that Jesus also preexisted." Here's the passage they would be referring to:

> [1]For this Melchizedek, king of Salem... [2]...which is king of peace; [3]*without father, without mother, without genealogy, having neither beginning of days nor end of life, but made like the Son of God*), remains a priest continually. [4]Now consider how great this man was, to whom even Abraham, the patriarch, gave a tenth out of the best spoils. (Hebrews 7:1–4)

"See there!" they'll say. "Melchizedek was made like the 'Son of God,' *'having neither beginning of days nor end of life'*!" They'll say, "Aha! See, he was God!" And that is how they get you, and they snag you like a fish taking a baited hook.

But look a little closer. First it says that Melchizedek was "made"; God isn't "made." Next, notice that it also says that Melchizedek *was without father and without mother*. Is that what the Bible says about Jesus? No, in point of fact we are commanded to believe that God is his Father! In fact, if you deny it, you would be antichrist (1 John 2:22). And so the analogy begins to breakdown, as all analogies must, since they are only replicas and not the real thing. Furthermore, according to the Bible, neither was Jesus without a mother like Melchizedek was...

> ...When the fullness of the time came, God sent forth his Son, *made of a woman*, born under the law. (Galatians 4:4)

So then, in fact, *unlike* Melchizedek, *Jesus was not without father or mother* as we are told was the case with Melchizedek. We find throughout Scriptures that the Bible quite clearly and consistently calls Mary, the mother of Jesus! (Matthew 1:18; Luke 2:43; John 2:1,3, 6:42, 19:25).

Do you see what is happening here? We have a tendency to believe that because a train of thought in the Bible leads in one direction, and may even have a common thread with another thought in the Bible, then we are justified in thinking these give us a kind of permission or authority to believe whatever else that train of thought takes us to! This is how people take biblical thoughts too far in a dangerous direction!

Consider how this works with the snake handlers. They have Scriptures they base their ideas on, true enough. But they don't let the rest of the Scriptures temper or qualify their thoughts. Joining thoughts along any possible "train of thought" works as well as if someone built a train track thinking they could connect the rails to either side and the train would still run along the route just fine!

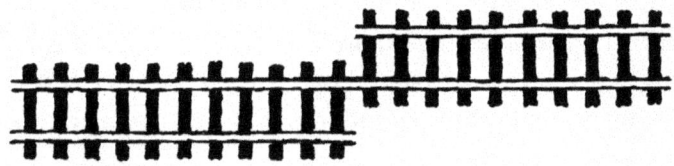

In reality, joining tracks together like this is a sure-fire way to create a train wreck! And that is what people do who don't let the Bible lay every step of every rail along the way!

- Snake handlers join the thought of God's protection from poisonous snakes together with the idea of purposely taking them up to prove their faith. But the Scripture that says not to tempt the Lord warns us that those train tracks don't fully join together!
- Trinitarians see the words Father, Word, and Holy Spirit and claim they must be distinct persons in the godhead, like the pagans understand their god to be. But Scriptures saying

that God is one individual, and not to go after the gods of the people around you, warn us that those train tracks don't join together biblically either.
- Onenessians see the Scripture that says, "The word was with God and the Word was God... and the Word was made flesh," and they assume that means God was made flesh. But the Scriptures that we've quoted above, that Jesus wasn't alone, that he could do nothing of himself, that God said to him, "today have I become your father" (Hebrews 1:5), along with many other verses, warn us that the Oneness interpretation tracks simply don't join together biblically.

In each of these three cases, a theological train wreck is just as absolutely assured as would happen with an actual train. That is simply because there is no way a train can steer itself without tracks, and certainly not if the tracks aren't integrally joined together.

But it isn't this way at all with biblical truth! The Bible is like a train track, and its words are like the rails that will keep us on the trail of truth as long as we follow them and not go off on tangents by laying our own rails toward chaos. If we allow it, the Bible will protect our thoughts from wandering out of the way and will keep us on course.

And so it is with the analogy we are supposed to glean from Melchizedek. What it is actually teaching us is simply that Jesus, God's High Priest of the New Covenant, did not spring from the tribe of Levi and the order of Aaron. *The Bible actually spells out that this is the purpose of the analogy of Melchizedek.* It is up to us to learn to listen and hear what the Bible has to say!

> [6]As he says also in another place, '*You are a priest forever, After the order of Melchizedek.*'... [7]He, in the days of his flesh, having offered up prayers and petitions with strong crying and tears *to him who was able to save him from death*, and *having been heard for his godly fear*, [8]though he was a Son, yet learned obedience by the things which he suffered. [9]*Having been made perfect, he became* to all

of those who obey him the author of eternal salvation, ¹⁰named by God a high priest *after the order of* Melchizedek. (Hebrews 5:1–10)

¹¹Now if there was perfection through the Levitical priesthood (for under it the people have received the law), what further need was there for another priest to arise after the order of Melchizedek, *and not be called after the order of Aaron?* ¹²*For the priesthood being changed, there is of necessity a change made also in the law.* ¹³For he of whom these things are said belongs to another tribe, from which no one has officiated at the altar. ¹⁴For *it is evident that our Lord has sprung out of Judah, about which tribe Moses spoke nothing concerning priesthood.* (Hebrews 7:11–14)

Look at what these passages teach us about Christ! They don't say Melchizedek is Jesus, they say Jesus' priesthood was after the order of Melchizedek. Then it says that Jesus, just like us, had to trust in God, who was someone else from himself, to save him! He had to learn by the things he suffered, and by that suffering he was perfected! Is that the case with God? Does or did God have to go through the learning of suffering in order to be perfected? Absolutely not! But God heard Jesus. Was that because Jesus was God himself? No, it's because he had godly fear! Does God "fear" God? Absolutely not! It is talking about our deep reverential fear, or respect, that convinces us not to want to ever cross God. It's talking about our respectful fear of God, which Jesus also had!

And then, being made perfect, Christ was raised up by God to usher in a new priesthood that was to replace, and be much superior to, the Levitical priesthood of the order of Aaron.

That is what Melchizedek represents: the priesthood being changed from the tribe of Levi to another tribe altogether, that of Judah, of whom Moses said nothing about a priesthood.

Do you see how they completely hijack the analogy of Melchizedek in order to impose their false interpretation of what it signifies?

Again, the point of Melchizedek clearly wasn't to prove that Jesus always existed, because this passage (Hebrews 5:1–5), where we are taught about Melchizedek's similarity to Christ, already had God telling Jesus, "'You are my Son. Today I have become your father.'" So here we have Jesus born at a certain point in time, and having a father, both traits that were unlike Melchizedek.

The bottom line is, in no way does the Bible ever, ever say that God became a father to Himself and a son to Himself. Not in John 1 or any other passage of the Bible. That is pure, unadulterated hogwash and mythology!

The problem with John 1 isn't what it says; it is how it is interpreted. Onenessians disobey the Scriptures in order to go after the views of the gods round about them and end up adopting an antichristian view of Christ in interpreting passages such as John 1.

Jesus' Way of Interpreting John 1

As we've said, there are really only two ways to interpret the Bible. There is the devil's method, and then there is Jesus' method. Most people seem determined to interpret John 1:1–14 using the devil's method. One thing that method will produce is a variety of opinions, but opinions do not equal truth.

We will now demonstrate how to apply Jesus' method, and in doing so, let the Scriptures show us what John was saying. We can know this is what he was trying to say, because he said the same thing in different ways in other places, and so did others in the Bible. So this method is the only one that puts his words in harmony with the rest of the Scriptures.

The first thing to point out is the similarity in language between the prologue of John's gospel and John's epistle:

> ¹*In the beginning* was the word, and *the word* was with God, and the word was God. ²The same was in the beginning with God... ¹⁴And the word was made flesh, and dwelt among us, (and we beheld his glory, the glory as of the only begotten of the Father,) full of grace and truth. (John 1:1–2, KJV)

> ¹That which was *from the beginning*, that which we have heard, that which we have seen with our eyes, that which we saw, and our hands touched, concerning *the Word of life* ²(and the life was revealed, and we have seen, and testify, and *declare to you the life, the eternal life*, which *was with the Father, and was revealed to us*); ³that which we have seen and heard we declare to you, that you also may have fellowship with us. Yes, and our fellowship is with the Father, and with his Son, Jesus Christ. ⁴And *we write these things to you*, that our joy may be fulfilled. ⁵*This is the message* which we have heard from him and announce to you, that God is light, and in him is no darkness at all. (1 John 1:1–5)

Using John's epistle is actually the proper way to interpret John's gospel. While many assume that "in the beginning" in John 1:1 referred to eternity past, that is supposition. John's epistle, on the other hand, leads us to the idea that "the beginning" had more to do with the beginning of the gospel message. For right here he explained what he meant by "from the beginning"; namely, "that which we have heard... seen... touched, concerning the word of life... which we... declare to you..." In fact, this idea (that beginning has to do with the beginning of Jesus' ministry) was shared with other NT writers. For example...

> Even as those who *from the beginning* were eyewitnesses and ministers of the word delivered them to us. (Luke 1:2)

> ¹*The beginning of the Good News* of Jesus Christ, the Son of God. ²As it is written in the prophets, "Behold, I send my messenger before your face, Who will prepare your way before you. ³The voice of one crying in the wilderness, 'Make ready the way of the Lord! Make his paths straight!'" ⁴John came baptizing in the wilderness and preaching the baptism of repentance for forgiveness of sins. (Mark 1:1–4)

In Mark's gospel, the beginning of the good news of Jesus started at John the Baptist. This same idea was also given to us by Luke...

> In the high priesthood of Annas and Caiaphas, *the word of God came to John*, the son of Zacharias, in the wilderness. (Luke 3:1)

When we join the above with what Luke wrote in Acts, we see he again started at the beginning, which was *the beginning of Jesus' ministry...*

> The first book I wrote, Theophilus, concerned *all that Jesus began* both to do and to teach. (Acts 1:1)

This consistency is more than mere coincidence; it is the harmony of the gospel message.

Now notice how similar the language is in the opening of the Book of Hebrews...

> [1]God, having *in the past spoken* to the fathers through the prophets at many times and in various ways, [2]has *at the end of these days spoken to us by his Son*, whom he appointed heir of all things, through whom also he made the worlds. (Hebrews 1:1–2)

This passage was another way of saying that Jesus was God's word made flesh. In the past, God's word was spoken by the fathers; i.e., Abraham, Isaac, Jacob, Moses, the prophets, and so forth. But now it's different; God speaks to us through His Son. This implies God didn't speak through His Son prior to the Son's birth, at least not like He does now. When we start to listen to the Son, we find that not only are his words the words of the Father, but so also is everything he did!

> The words that I tell you, *I speak not from myself*; but the Father who lives in me does His works. (John 14:10)

> *The word* which you hear *isn't mine, but the Father's* who sent me. (John 14:24)
>
> He who sent me is true; and the things which *I heard from him, these I say* to the world. John 8:26
>
> ...I do nothing of myself; but *as my Father taught me, I speak* these things. (John 8:28)
>
> For *I spoke not from myself, but the Father* who sent me, he gave me a commandment, what I should say, and what I should speak. I know that his commandment is eternal life. The things therefore which *I speak, even as the Father has said* to me, so I speak. (John 12:49–50)
>
> Now they have known that all things whatever you have given me are from you, for *the words which you have given me I have given to them*, and they received them, and knew for sure that I came forth from you, and they have believed that you sent me. (John 17:7–8)

It doesn't seem as though Jesus could have been clearer, or more consistent. This was such an important theme that it was reiterated in many ways. The words that Jesus spoke were, not his own words, but God the Father's words! Even John the Baptist, Jesus' forerunner, said the very same thing:

> For he whom God has sent *speaks the words of God*; for God gives the Spirit without measure. The Father loves the Son, and has given all things into his hand. (John 3:34–35)

For those who have ears to hear, these are the passages in which *John himself describes and defines the "word" he was referring to in John 1*. The *words* that Jesus spoke were not his *words*, they were the *words* that God gave and *commanded* him to *speak*. They were words that *taught us about God*, but were more than just words:

the same words *became commandments* to us, because they are God's words to us. It is in this way that the words are "God" to us. These words were with God, and these words were God, and then the Son was born and spoke these words to us. John's words fit perfectly with what John had been explaining, through Jesus' words, which were actually God's words.

Read in this way, in the light of these other Scriptures bearing on the subject of the "word," John 1 has nothing at all to do with the pagan idea of an incarnation. Rather, it has everything to do with the truth that God is the source of authority of all the words spoken by and through Jesus:

> For Moses indeed said to the fathers, "The Lord God will raise up a prophet for you from among your brothers, like me. You shall *listen to him in all things whatever he says to you*. It will be, that *every soul that will not listen to that prophet will be utterly destroyed* from among the people." (Acts 3:22–23)

Why is this so hard for us to understand? Because we have been spoiled by philosophy!

I recently listened to part of an online debate among some Oneness theologians. They were apparently trying to come to a consensus on how they should view the "incarnation" of Jesus. It was a live broadcast. Suffice it to say, they offered several different possibilities, each according to his own opinion. Not one did, or could, provide an "it is written" quote that spelled out their view of the incarnation. One speaker even went as far as to say he really didn't mind having to resort to a little bit of philosophical metaphysical language if it would help explain things the Bible didn't go into.

The reason that neither Onenessians nor Trinitarians can find such words or concepts clearly spelled out and explained in detail in the Bible is simply because that isn't what the Bible teaches! To begin with, according to the Bible, *Jesus was born* (Matthew 1:18, 2:1; John 18:37), *not "incarnated,"* period. So they are both trying to impose a pagan concept upon the biblical message, and it just doesn't fit!

That is exactly the reason why *they can find the words and concepts in pagan views* to describe their view of an incarnation: it is because paganism is the ultimate source (Acts 14:11) of their incarnation view. No matter how it entered their heads, it originated in paganism, not the Bible! And having been spoiled by worldly philosophy, they just can't shake the idea from their minds! The only way out of such spiritual deception is to open your mind and heart to what these Scriptures are actually saying and describing and to "receive with meekness the engrafted word, that is able to save your souls" (James 1:21).

These words, in which Jesus says he doesn't speak from himself, are the words of God, which God gave Jesus to speak. That doesn't mean Jesus simply repeated God's word verbatim. God could never say, "I do nothing of myself." Rather, they were words that God gave Jesus so that Jesus could explain to us how it was between himself and God. In this way, under direct inspiration from God, Jesus speaks directly against the Onenessian idea that "at times he spoke as God, and other times he spoke as man." That is not what Jesus said he did, ever! Those who jump to conclusions (of an incarnation) to the contrary, are simply not hearing God or Jesus and are implying both are liars... just like the devil does! But we have the Scriptures that state and explain what we believe. We don't need to look to pagan philosophers for words or concepts to explain our position. We rely on the "it is written again" Scriptures, such as those above, to define our position and bring it into line with the words of God in the Bible! "For man does not live... but by every word that proceeds out of the mouth of God" (Matthew 4:4).

Now, the really radical and awesome thing John wanted us to know is that it wasn't just the words that Jesus spoke that are God's words to us; rather, that "word" is now Jesus himself, including his whole life! Let's look at 1 John 1:1–3 again in this light:

> [1]That which was from the beginning, that which we have heard, that which we have seen with our eyes, that which we saw, and our hands touched, concerning the Word of life [2](and *the life was revealed, and we have seen, and testify,*

> *and declare to you the life, the eternal life, which was with the Father, and was revealed to us);* ³*that which we have seen and heard we declare to you, that you also may have fellowship with us. Yes, and our fellowship is with the Father, and with his Son, Jesus Christ.* (1 John 1:1–3)

John interprets his earlier words here, saying that instead of the "word" being with God, now it is "the life" that was with God the Father and was "revealed" to them. And in turn, they are *"declaring"* that life to us! So Jesus isn't just the "word" made flesh. He is also the "life" made flesh.

> ¹God, having in the past spoken to the fathers through the prophets at many times and in various ways, ²has at the end of these days *spoken to us by his Son*, whom he appointed heir of all things, through whom also he made the worlds. ³His Son is the radiance of his glory, *the very image of his substance*, and upholding all things by the word of his power, when he had by himself made purification for our sins, sat down on the right hand of the Majesty on high. (Hebrews 1:1–3)

As we can see, this passage in Hebrews conforms completely to our theme, and it adds to our understanding. When we add these last two passages to all the others, we can conclude that Jesus' words, because they are God's words, are speaking "God" to us! For example, Acts 3:22–23 puts it this way: "that every soul that will not listen to that prophet will be utterly destroyed from among the people." It is in this way that we can confidently say, "the word was with God and the word was God." The "word" is none other than God's communication to us. *God's word to us is God actually communicating Himself to us!* And this word/communication to us is through His Son, now that His "word" has been made into a human being!

But that doesn't mean that His "word" doesn't also carry the significance of being God's "plan." In these next verses, we can see that this word to us is the "plan" for us.

> ²Beloved, now we are children of God, and it is not yet revealed what we will be. But we know that, when he is revealed, we will be like him; for we will see him just as he is. ³Everyone who has this hope set on him purifies himself, even as he is pure. (1 John 3:2–3)

> For whom he foreknew, he also predestined to be conformed to the image of his Son, that he might be the firstborn among many brothers. (Romans 8:29)

Now if we are *"predestined"* to be conformed to an *"image,"* and that "image" is Christ, then that "image" before Christ was born was God's "plan"; that is, God's "word," which is to say, God's *logos!* From this perspective, we could even say that God's word to us is God's set of "blueprints" for making us in Christ's image!

Since we are intended to be like him, we can know that Jesus Christ isn't any more of an incarnation of God than we will be when we are glorified to be like him! For it isn't only Jesus who is supposed to speak the words of God, but so are we:

> *If any man speaks, let it be as it were oracles of God*. If any man serves, let it be as of the strength which God supplies, that in all things God may be glorified through Jesus Christ, to whom belong the glory and the dominion forever and ever. Amen. (1 Peter 4:11)

> ¹⁹But when they deliver you up, don't be anxious how or what you will say, for it will be given you in that hour what you will say. ²⁰For it is *not you who speak, but the Spirit of your Father who speaks* in you. (Matthew 10:19–20)

So then, as the firstborn of many brothers, as our image to whom we should conform, Jesus set the pattern that we also may be the mouths that speak the words of God!

All of these Scriptures testify that John had something else completely in mind than the pagan doctrine of an incarnation of deity, which neither he, nor any other biblical writer, ever clearly expounded for us.

The Snake-Handler Factor: To say that because God's word was made flesh can and must only mean that God Himself was made flesh is to jump to conclusions and impose a pagan, preconceived idea of an incarnation of deity. It is to ignore and negate many, many Scriptures that define Christ to the contrary as being made human in all respects. To teach or imply that John would introduce such a radically extrabiblical, pagan concept (as the incarnation of God) in such vague, unclear terms and then leave the body of Christ to work out what he meant is to accuse him of being utterly irresponsible at best and willingly misleading at worst.

~~~

For extra reading, following is more from Adolf von Harnack. These passages will help support the biblical concept of God's foreknowledge of Christ (that is, Christ as God's "plan"), and how John's language would fit very well within a Jewish view of a foreknown, yet not actually yet existent, Messiah.

> According to the theory held by the ancient Jews and by the whole of the Semitic nations, everything of real value that from time to time appears on earth has its existence in heaven. In other words, it exists with God, *that is God possesses a <u>knowledge</u> of it; and for that reason it has a real being...*[1]

---

[1] Adolf von Harnack, "On the Conception of Pre-Existence," in *History of Dogma*, Vol. I, Appendix I. The entire text of von Harnack's *History of Dogma* is available at: http://www.ccel.org/ccel/harnack/dogma1.ii.iv.i.html, and http://www.archive.org/details/historyofdogma01harnuoft, accessed 10/14/2009.

Earthly occurrences and objects are not only regarded as 'foreknown' by God before being seen in this world, but the latter manifestation is frequently considered as *the copy of the existence and nature which they possess in heaven*, and which remains unalterably the same, whether they appear upon earth or not. <u>That which is before God experiences no change</u>... so *the Tabernacle and its furniture, the Temple, Jerusalem, etc., are before God and continue to exist before him in heaven, even during their appearance on earth and after it.*

This conception seems really to have been the oldest one. Moses is to fashion the Temple and its furniture according to the pattern he saw on the Mount (Exod. XXV. 9. 40: XXVI. 30: XXVII. 8: Num. VIII. 4). *The Temple and Jerusalem exist in heaven, and they are to be distinguished from the earthly Temple and the earthly Jerusalem...*

Most <u>Jews... conceived the Messiah as a man</u>. *We may indeed go a step further and say that no Jew at bottom imagined him otherwise; for even those who attached ideas of pre-existence to him, and gave the Messiah a supernatural background,* <u>never</u> *advanced to* <u>speculations</u> *about assumption of the flesh, incarnation,* <u>two natures and the like</u>. *They only transferred in a specific manner to the Messiah the old idea of pre-terrestrial existence with God*, universally current among the Jews. *Before the creation of the world the Messiah was hidden with God, and, when the time is fulfilled, he makes his appearance...* <u>Nowhere do we find in Jewish writings a conception which advances beyond the notion that the Messiah is the man who is with God</u> in heaven; and who will make his appearance at his own time."[2]

---

[2] Adolf von Harnack, *History of Dogma*, http://www.ccel.org/ccel/harnack/dogma1.ii.iv.i.html.

For an excellent video teaching about the Jewish view of conceptual preexistence versus literal preexistence, please check out "John and Jewish Preexistence" by Dr. Dustin Smith[3]

---

[3] www.youtube.com/watch?v=vZE4IhjvOWc.

CHAPTER TWENTY-EIGHT

John 8:24 Unless You Believe That I Am He

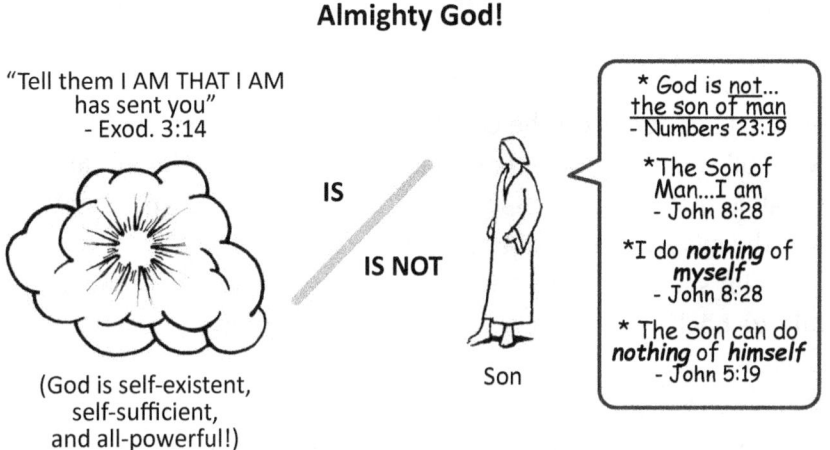

...you will die in your sins; for unless you believe that I am he, you will die in your sins. —Jesus Christ of Nazareth, John 8:24

Some people, particularly Onenessians, believe Jesus claimed to be "I am that I am" of Exodus 3:14 because he used the phrase "I am" (which is translated in Greek as "*ego eimi*"). But is that connection to "I Am that I Am" what Jesus really meant? Is that what Jesus is really expecting us to believe for salvation? Is that what the Scriptures teach when we dig a little deeper and let the Scriptures, and Jesus, explain these statements? Or do we find something completely different when we simply let Jesus explain himself?

The simple answer is that when Jesus is allowed to speak for himself he completely refutes that he is what the term "I am that I am" means. When we allow him to explain himself, all he really told them was to believe what he had been telling them to believe about himself all along: that he is the Son of God.

To explain, let's first consider whether or not it is automatically true that the phrase "I am" is a unique title for God. It is written in Luke 1:19 that an angel said, "*I am* Gabriel, who stands in the presence of God." In John 9:9, a man who was healed of blindness said, "*I am*." In Acts 10:21, Peter said, "Behold, *I am* he whom you seek." All of these used the exact same phrase that Jesus used. Were any of these expecting their hearers to believe they were God, the "I am that I am"? Not any more than any of us would expect someone to believe we were the great "I am" if we said, "I am." The meaning of "I am" depends on the context in which it is used. And Jesus, as we shall see, was quite clear in his context. The real "problem," as usual, is that people simply don't hear him. And if anywhere that was the case, it was with the Jews.

So let's let Jesus explain to us what he was actually saying. For this we back up just a few verses from our opening verse and read these words:

> [16]Even if I do judge, my judgment is true, for *I am* not alone, but *I am* with the Father who sent me. [17]It's also written in your law that the testimony of *two people* is valid. [18]*I am one who* testifies about myself, *and the Father who* sent me testifies about me. (John 8:16–18)

In verse 16 Jesus says he (eimi) is not alone but that he (ego) is with the Father who sent him. Thus Jesus was claiming to be a separate "I am" from the "I am of the Father. Again Jesus said, in verse 18, "*I am* one *who*," and then he said, in distinction to him, there is, "and the Father *who*." One "who" plus one "who" equals two "whos"; thus, 1+1=2. Not two natures but two "whos." In verse 17, Jesus explicitly referred to himself and his Father *in the context of two "people."* Jesus was very consistent with his math in this passage, as he always was. In this case it was actually division, since he always kept himself and the Father divided into two distinct persons (by keeping his "I am" distinct from the person of the Father):

v. 26 There is a sender who (the Father), and there is a sent who (Jesus).

v. 26 There is a speaker who (the Father), and there is a hearer who (Jesus).

v. 28 There is one who does nothing of himself (Jesus), and there is another who (the Father) that taught the first who what to do.

v. 29 There is one who (the Father) that is with the doer who (Jesus) that is never alone.

v. 29 There is one (Jesus) who pleases the other who (the Father).

These are all according to Jesus. We believe he knew what he was talking about. We believe that those who say he meant something other than what is recorded in the Bible are not truly hearing Jesus when he describes himself! Nowhere does the Bible say that he was referring to his dual natures. That idea came into Christianity not by the apostolic Scriptures, but by way of the antichristians who invented the idea via the Trinitarians who adopted the Gnostic/antichristian doctrine of the Trinity.

Look at how the Jews responded in verse 25 to his statement in verse 24.

> [24]"I said therefore to you that you will die in your sins; for *unless you believe that I am* he, you will die in your sins." [25]*They said <u>therefore</u> to him, "<u>Who</u> are you?"* Jesus said to them, "Just <u>what I have been saying to you from the beginning</u>." (John 8:24–25)

It should be obvious that *the Jews did not interpret Jesus to mean that he was clearly claiming to be "I am that I am," as many suppose*. In fact, those who teach you that is what he meant, and the Jews understood that, are simply lying to you. They have either been misled themselves, or they are intentionally false teachers. The important part is that these Jews, just like many today, simply ignore Jesus' own explanation!

To the contrary of what many claim, what Jesus was saying was *very unclear* to the Jews, and *that is why they asked, "who are you?"* It was not "clear" to these Jews, by any means, that he was "claiming to be the Father." But let's give these Jews the benefit of the doubt; perhaps the Jews were just so incredulous they couldn't accept what Jesus really said. So let's assume Jesus had to tell them what he was saying. *And what did he say in explanation of himself?* His reply was to repeat to them the same things he had been saying from the beginning. Clearly, he wasn't trying to bring them to a new truth or sneak in a new revelation. So let's look at those things that he actually did say, or we should say, had said, for in that way we will have Jesus' answer, instead of the answer of men.

In the beginning of the passage, he told them he was the "light of the world." We know that he said we also will be the light of the world (Matthew 5:14). Does that mean we are also "I am that I am"? That would have been a fine way to try to tell them he was their God: by claiming that he was something he expected all of his disciples to be.

If we back up even more and look at what Jesus "had been saying," we come across what he said three chapters earlier. In this case some Jews had taken up stones to kill him because he had broken the Sabbath and thus, in their opinion (according to John's telling of the account), made himself equal to God. As an aside: in point of historical fact, neither breaking the Sabbath nor calling God "Father" would have been considered a "claim" to "being" God or "equal to God" according to Jewish culture. The likely issue the Jews had was that in claiming to be the heir to David's kingdom, Jesus was threatening the harmony of the entire Jewish community because of the Romans who ruled over them. They did eventually experience just such a crisis in both the First Jewish–Roman War (66–73 AD) and the Bar Kochba Rebellion (132–135 AD). Another issue, just as likely, which is strongly implied in Matthew 12, was their jealousy of his spiritual presence, power, and influence with the people.

What we do know for a certainty is Jesus' explanation of himself, in which he told them plainly who he was:

> Jesus therefore answered them, "Most assuredly, I tell you, *the Son can do nothing of himself*, but what he sees the Father doing. For whatever things he does, these the Son also does likewise. *For the Father has affection for the Son, and shows him* all things that He Himself does. He will show him greater works than these, that you may marvel. For as the Father raises the dead and gives them life, even so the Son also gives life to whom he desires. For the Father judges no one, but He has *given all* judgment to the Son, that all may honor the Son, even as they honor the Father. He who doesn't honor the Son doesn't honor the Father who sent him." (John 5:19–23)

This is the consistent explanation, in distinction and separation between himself and the Father, that Jesus had been saying from the beginning, which he referred to in John 8:25. As we've pointed out earlier, *saying he could do "nothing of himself" is the exact opposite of claiming to be "I am that I am."* In this way Jesus himself refuted the idea that he was claiming to be "I am that I am."

The fact is, *Jesus always kept himself personally distinct from God the Father.* He himself was a man sent by God. Again, these are the kinds of things Jesus "had been telling them from the beginning" and that he continued to reiterate to them after he had said to believe in who he is.

> [39]...Jesus said to them, "If you were Abraham's children, you would do the works of Abraham. [40] But now you seek to kill me, *a man who* has told you the truth, which *I heard from* God. Abraham didn't do this. [41] You do the works of your father." (John 8:39–41)

Jesus went on to tell them that they were of their father the devil, and thus they were doing the works of their father the devil.

An example of jumping to conclusions can be seen in the Onenessian interpretation of these words:

> ²⁵Jesus said to them... ²⁶..."he who sent me is true; and the things which I heard from him, these I say to the world." ²⁷They didn't understand that he spoke to them about the Father. (John 8:25–27)

Here Jesus was talking about the two different "whos," himself and the one who sent him. Onenessians claim that Jesus was trying to tell these Jews that he was both the Father and the Son, but that is not what he said here at all. The correct way to understand Jesus is to hear what he actually said in places like this:

> ²⁸Jesus therefore said to them, "When you have lifted up <u>the Son of Man</u>, then you will know that I am he [i.e., "<u>the Son of Man</u>" as he just said], and <u>I do nothing of myself</u>, but as my Father taught me, I say these things. ²⁹<u>He who sent me is with me</u>. The Father <u>hasn't left me alone, for I always do the things that are pleasing to him</u>." (John 8:28–29)

The wrong way to understand Jesus is to take his statements like this and claim "he was trying to explain the differences between his dual nature and his human natures." No, that would be interpreting by imposing traditions of men and also bearing false witness because Jesus did not say that.

Jesus simply did not claim to be personally both the Father and the Son in two natures but still one personality. Rather, he went on to explain, very clearly we might add, that the one who sent him, who was the other "who," was none other than God the Father. In verse 54 Jesus tells them, "If I glorify myself, my glory is nothing. It is <u>my Father</u> who glorifies me, <u>of whom you say that he is our God</u>." So Jesus wasn't saying he was the Father; rather, he was refuting it. And he wasn't saying he was God (as in a future Trinitarian sense either), because Jesus consistently maintained his personal separation from God and the Father!

When Jesus said "I am," this is what Jesus was claiming to be, as it is written: "The son of man" (vs.27), and again, "<u>a man</u> who has told you the truth, which I heard from God" (vs. 39). That is a brief sum total of his "I am" statement in John 8:24 when read in context. Jesus clearly and concisely refuted the idea that he was claiming to be "I am that I am" by simply saying:

> Most assuredly, I tell you, *the Son can do nothing of himself*. (John 5:19)

The great "I am that I am" simply could not say that without lying, and lying is one of the extremely limited few things that the great "I am that I am" cannot do. Onenessians make a liar out of Jesus in one of the very same places they attempt to make him into God!

Jesus' message was summed up quite well in John 8:28: "When you have lifted up *the son of man*, then you will know that *I am he*, and I do nothing of myself, but as my Father taught me, I say these things." By this Jesus clearly stated what he meant by saying "I am he," because he told us: he is the Son of Man.

We will deal with John 8:58 in the next chapter.

The Snake-Handler Factor: The idea that Jesus claimed to be "I am that I am" is a classic case of handling the Scriptures the way the snake handlers do. Very simply, Jesus did not say, "I am that I am" (any more than he said to purposely take up snake handling). Furthermore, what Jesus did clearly and explicitly say was that "*the Son can do nothing of himself*" (John 5:19). These two concepts, one that is clearly spoken out of the mouth of Jesus and one that can only be artificially imposed upon his intentions, are two completely contradictory ideas. By saying what he did say, Jesus himself refutes directly the Onenessian doctrine that Jesus is God, the "I am that I am."

Jesus did not say, "I am that I am." Jesus did say he could do nothing of himself. Jesus spoke explicitly about "himself." Onenessians say he meant "natures." Either Onenessians are liars about Jesus' identity, or Jesus is a liar; there simply is no common ground.

Jumping to Conclusions. As we can see, never once did Jesus clearly explain that he is really God the Father incarnated into a man. Only by jumping to conclusions and putting words in Jesus' mouth can people come up with that idea. The Jews did not understand him to mean that, and Jesus was very consistent in saying that he was a distinct who (never a distinct human nature, etc.) from the Father.

The OT Schoolmaster. The OT never taught, and no true Jew ever believed, that the Messiah would be "I am that I am" incarnated as a human.

Teach No Other Doctrine. Nowhere did the apostles expound on the idea that Jesus claimed to be "I am that I am," nor did Jesus. That idea is definitely a later invention, and so adding that teaching is forbidden by the Scriptures. What that conclusion does do is negate and obscure Jesus' clear explanations that he was a separate and distinct "who" that was *not* left alone, but that the Father "who" was with him and in him.

CHAPTER TWENTY-NINE
John 8:58 Before Abraham Was, I AM

Jesus said to them, "Verily, verily, I say to you, Before Abraham's coming — I am." (John 8:58, YLT)

This is a problematic gray area Scripture that is often abused in much the same way as Trinitarians abuse Matthew 28:19 and snake handlers abuse Mark 16:18.

The key to understanding it, once again, is in looking for Scriptures that qualify and actually explain the topic at hand. One of the clearest is 1 Corinthians 15:45–47, which clearly tells us that he who is spiritual is *not* first...

> [35]But someone will say, "How are the dead raised?" and, "With what kind of body do they come?" [36]You foolish one, that which you yourself sow is not made alive unless it dies. [37]That which you sow, <u>you don't sow the body that will be,</u> *but a bare grain,* maybe of wheat, or of some other kind... [42]So also is the resurrection of the dead. It is sown in corruption; it is raised in incorruption... [45]So also it is written, "The first man, Adam, became a living soul." *The last Adam <u>became a life-giving spirit</u>.* [46]However *that which is spiritual isn't <u>first</u>, but that which is natural, <u>then that which is spiritual</u>.* [47]The first man is of the earth, made of dust. The second man is the Lord from heaven. (1 Corinthians 15: 35–37, 42, 45–47)

When Paul wrote, "you don't sow the body that will be," he was talking about Christ. It is very revealing to read verse 45 in a word-to-word translation of the Greek. In English, this passage literally says: "And so it is written the first man Adam was made into a living soul; the last Adam into a quickening spirit." In the Greek it clearly says that Christ *was made* a life giving spirit using the same word he used to say Adam was made. Adam didn't just "become" a living soul; God made him that. In the same exact way, Christ didn't just become a life-giving spirit; God made him that! This whole passage refutes the idea that Jesus actually preexisted his human birth.

Next, Colossians and Romans give us more details...

> He is the head of the body, the assembly, who is *the beginning, <u>the firstborn from the dead</u>; that in all things he might have the preeminence.* (Colossians 1:18)

> We know that all things work together for good for those who love God, to those who are called according to his purpose. For whom he foreknew, he also predestined to *be conformed to the image of his Son, <u>that he might be the firstborn among many brothers</u>*. (Romans 8:28–29)

> He is the head of the body, the assembly, who is the beginning, *the firstborn from the dead; <u>that in all things he might have the preeminence</u>*. (Colossians 1:18)

What we learn from these verses, and many others, is the context in which Jesus was talking when he said, "before Abraham comes to be, I am." That context is the marvelous truth that Jesus is the first-begotten from the dead *and all that implies!* That is to say, the Bible is very clear that a) Jesus became a life-giving spirit that did not exist before Adam, and b) in regard to the resurrection of the dead, he was the firstborn of that brotherhood, and just importantly, this was God's plan all along through which he put creation into existence in the first place!

When we see this "master plan" of God's as the cause, effect, and results of what Jesus accomplished, then we can understand that this was God's only plan that all this happen. When we see this, then Jesus' words take on a completely different meaning that is in line with all the other teachings about God and His Anointed One.

That is to say, in John 8:58, Jesus was asserting his superiority (or preeminence) as a human above that of Abraham, or any other man for that matter.

Jesus was not at all unaware or in denial that he was anointed by God his Father to be the savior of the world and was to be given preeminence over the brotherhood of the redeemed.

The hard part for many people to keep in mind is that Jesus "preexisted" before his beginning (genesis) in Bethlehem *only in God's "plan"* (or Greek *logos*). That is to say that in John 1:1–2, 14, we have "it is written again" Scriptures that qualify and describe the way in which the Son of God "existed," which was, simply, as God's plan (as we covered in Chapter Sixteen).

> In the beginning was the plan, and the plan was with God, and the plan was God... The plan became flesh, and lived among us. We saw his glory, such glory as of the one and only Son of the Father, full of grace and truth. (John 1:1, 14)

We know that Jesus understood and taught this because he clearly stated the following:

> ...I have come down from heaven, <u>not to do my own will, but the will of Him</u> who sent me. (John 6:38)

> No one has ascended into heaven, but he who descended out of heaven, the <u>*Son of Man*, who is in heaven</u>. (John 3:13)

So here, first, we have Jesus himself refuting the idea that he was supposedly God in heaven before becoming a human, because he didn't come "down from heaven to do his own will." Second, when referring to the one who descended, he describes himself as the son (offspring) of man (humanity) *even while he was in heaven.* Recall again this Scripture we've quoted before:

> *God is not a man*, that he should lie, *Neither the son of man...* (Numbers 23:19)

So Jesus was not trying to imply that he had been God in heaven, only that he, as a son of man, had been sent from heaven. In that regard, let's talk about these two phrases:

> ⁴⁷...The second man is the Lord from heaven. (1 Corinthians 15:45–47)

> ...I have come down from heaven... (John 6:38)

How are we to understand these phrases? Are these hints from Jesus that he is actually "god come down to earth in the likeness of men" like the pagans believe? No. Once again, the correct way to interpret Jesus is to search the Scriptures for clearer passages like Jesus taught us to do. For example, let us hear what we are taught through the following passages about the bread coming down from heaven.

> ³⁵Jesus said to them, "*I am the bread of life*. He who comes to me will not be hungry, and he who believes in me will never be thirsty..." ⁴¹The Jews therefore murmured concerning him, because *he said, "I am the bread which came down out of heaven."* ⁴² They said, "Isn't this Jesus, the son of Joseph, whose father and mother we know? How then does he say, *"I have come down out of heaven?*... ⁴⁷Most assuredly, I tell you, he who believes in me has eternal life. ⁴⁸*I am the bread of life.* ⁴⁹*Your fathers ate the manna* in the wilderness, and they died. ⁵⁰This is the bread which comes down out of heaven, that anyone may eat of it and not die. ⁵¹*I am the living bread which came down out of heaven.* If anyone eats of this bread, he will live forever. Yes, the bread which I will give for the life of the world is my flesh.' (John 6:35, 41–42, 47–51)

Here we have Jesus clearly explaining to us how it is that he has "come down out of heaven." He explains that he is the bread of life that came down out of heaven *just like the manna that the Israelites ate* in the wilderness. That bread also came down out of heaven.

> [31]Our fathers ate the manna in the wilderness. As it is written, *"He gave them bread out of heaven to eat."* [32]Jesus therefore said to them, "Most assuredly, I tell you, it wasn't Moses who *gave you the bread out of heaven*, but my Father gives you the true bread out of heaven. [33]For the bread of God is that which comes down out of heaven, and gives life to the world." [34]They said therefore to him, "Lord, always give us this bread." [35]Jesus said to them, "I am the bread of life." (John 6:31–35; with Psalms 78:24–25)

So then, as we can see, Jesus has plainly taught us exactly in what way he "came down out of heaven." It was the same way that God fed the Israelites in the desert with manna from heaven. It is simply an idiom meaning that it was ordained and directed to come to pass, and put into motion by God in heaven.

Did the manna actually, physically exist in heaven before coming down out of heaven? Absolutely not. So also with the Son of Man that was in heaven but came down out of heaven, not to do his own will but the will of the Father. Saying that he came down from heaven does not mean, biblically, that he preexisted in the spiritual realm and eventually "came to earth in the likeness of man" in the pagan sense of incarnation. It means that God in heaven directed it to be so; thus, "out of heaven."

Take, for example, John's baptism: "The baptism of John, where was it from? *From heaven or from men?*" (Matthew 21:25). Obviously John's baptism didn't preexist in heaven, other than in God's foreknowledge of His plan. So it is also with the "Son of Man" who came down out of heaven, not to do his own will but the will of Him who sent him. This means it wasn't man who directed John, or Jesus; it was God in heaven who directed and ordained John's baptism, just as God also directed Jesus to be the bread of life that came down out of heaven.

Again, keep in mind that Jesus spoke and taught in parables. In Matthew 5:29–30, Jesus said that if your eye or hand offends you, you should cut if off, "for it is more profitable for you that one of your members should perish, than for your whole body to be cast into Gehenna" (Matthew 5:29). Was Jesus being literal? Absolutely not, for he who destroys the temple of God, which temple you are, him will God destroy (1 Corinthians 3:17). The point is, we need to look to where the Scriptures explicitly explain these things, rather than jumping to conclusions that make what is explained of no effect. And that is what happens when people insist that Jesus literally preexisted his beginning in Bethlehem: they build their doctrines on the parabolic meanings of texts rather than accepting the literal explanations given throughout Scripture.

The simple fact is that if people weren't so quick to interpret the Bible after pagan mythology, they would be able to hear Jesus' explanation of what he meant by saying, "Before Abraham's coming—I am" (John 8:58 YLT).

With this understood, look how clear Jesus' words become:

> No one has ascended into heaven, but he who descended out of heaven, the *Son of Man, who is in* heaven. (John 3:13)

Jesus didn't claim to be Yahweh in heaven, or "I am that I am" in heaven, but he did describe himself as something. And that something, explicitly and clearly, was "the offspring of humanity." How did the offspring of humanity come to be in heaven? Because God always had His Plan that Jesus would be the Son of God and the Son of Man. So Jesus was referring to God's foreknowledge by the fact that Jesus was God's "plan." This is also what the apostles preached!

In Chapter Sixteen we presented the following graphic as a representation of God's foreknowledge. In the top view we see God's foreknowledge of Christ dying for the sins of man as expressed in Revelation 13:8: "The Lamb slain from the foundation of the world." In contrast, on the bottom half, we have the actual scene in which Christ was crucified "once at the end of the world," according to Hebrews 9:12, 25, 26, 28; 10:10, 12, and 14. That is to say, the bottom event was the actualization and realization of God's plan, which was always with God, when it came to pass in our world.

"The Lamb slain from the foundation of the world." (Revelation 13:8)

"The Son of Man, who is in heaven." (John 3:13)

"He offered one sacrifice for sin forever." (Hebrews 10:5-20)

"Came down from heaven, not to do his will." (John 6:38)

This graphic simply illustrates this truth:

> In the beginning was the plan, and the plan was with God, and the plan was God... The plan became flesh, and lived among us. We saw his glory, such glory as of the one and only Son of the Father, full of grace and truth. (John 1:1, 14)

In this way we can see how to use John 1 as a qualifying passage. We saw that, when viewed alone in John 1 as an excuse for adopting pagan ideas of incarnations of deity, it was very much a "gray area" Scripture. But now, when we use John 1:1–2, 14 as our qualifying passage for interpreting it, we find that John 1 was very precisely descriptive indeed! John tells us so plainly that what was actually with God before the foundation of the world was God's *logos*, His plan, which predominantly contained what Christ was ultimately to become and to fulfill.

Since Jesus was the fulfillment of God's plan made flesh, Jesus was correct in that sense to claim to exist before Abraham. The key to understanding this is context: grammatical, historical and theological.

When Does Abraham Come to Be?

The real issue, which many English translations hide and obscure, is the grammatical fact that in the Greek Jesus did not speak of Abraham in the past tense. Jesus was talking about the truth that Jesus was to come before Abraham who is yet to come in the resurrection of the dead!

To explain this, I will refer my readers to an article found online and easily verifiable.

> What is happening in John 8:56–59 is about establishing Jesus' rights as firstborn over Abraham and the patriarchs.
> John 8:58 Before Abraham becomes, I exist.
> John 14:6 Jesus said to him, 'I am the way, and the truth, and the life. No one (including even Abraham) comes to the Father except through me.'
> Heb 11:13 'These all died in faith, not having received the things promised, but having seen them and greeted them from afar, and having acknowledged that they were strangers and exiles on the earth.'
> So this is the day that Abraham rejoiced to see, but which we have seen and Abraham has not yet. Hence Jesus is before Abraham. Not that Jesus "was" before Abraham became, but Jesus "is" before Abraham becomes.[1]

What the cited writer is referring to, for one thing, is the fact that the Greek grammar in John 8:58 does not at all support the idea that Jesus was referring to Abraham in the past tense. Where John 8:58 says (according to versions like the KJV) "Before Abraham was," it really says, and means, "before Abraham's [future] coming..." What we are dealing with in the verb regarding Abraham in John 8:58 is not the aorist indicative, but the aorist infinitive! Therefore, Young's Literal Translation renders it correctly, as such:

---

[1] Steven, What did Jesus mean when he said "before Abraham was, I am"?, accessed 9/12/2016, http://bibleq.net/answer/447/

Before Abraham's coming—I am. (John 8:58 YLT)

Thus Jesus was not claiming to have "literally preexisted" Abraham; rather, he was simply reiterating his preeminence even regarding father Abraham. The Jews who listened to Jesus, just as many do today, apparently misunderstood Jesus (as they did in many other places) and jumped to false conclusions about his meaning.

As we see, if and when we truly let the Scriptures speak, then, and only then, do we see one truth emerge dominant over all other theories and jumped-to conclusions. The simple fact remains that there are no verses that either Onenessians or Trinitarians can turn to that actually "explain" in detail that Jesus preexisted as God (or as a literal separate person from God) and in the process of time became incarnate as a human. Rather, when we look to the Scriptures for actual explanations, we find Jesus described in completely different terms. Furthermore, we find that the passages typically relied upon to support the incarnation theories are far from being clear, explanatory, or conclusive. Rather, such conclusions are built on human interpretation and predicated upon personal biases or preconceptions, rather than what the Scriptures actually state and elsewhere clearly explain.

This explains what the Incarnationists do in order to make John 8:58 appear to support their theories. In order to have one God in three persons, Trinitarians adopt the "same substance" (*homoousios*) doctrine of the Gnostics and pagans, and then interpret John 8:58 as if Jesus was referring to his eternal sonship, which is a concept Onenessians obviously reject. As for Onenessians, in order to deny the two persons of God the Father and His Son, Jesus the Anointed One, they adopt the Gnostic and pagan idea of speaking of the persons as dual natures instead of two persons, and in this way, they interpret John 8:58 to mean that Jesus was speaking of his deific nature. Thus, they make void the word of God through their tradition (Mark 7:13), because Jesus was clearly speaking of his "self." This is how Onenessians reveal the anti-christian nature of their position: at its root, Onenessianism is a rejection of Christ's true and full humanity. Onenessians have Christ arbitrarily switching from being human and personally separate from God one minute, to being God the next, simply depending on his manner of speech.

Arriving at their respective conclusions, both groups use their preconceived ideas to interpret other passages that seem to them to fit their theory. And then they make of no effect, or explain away, the passages that clearly contradict their contrabiblical idea that Jesus is an incarnation of deity. This leaves it in their hands to interpret which nature is doing the talking at any given point in the narrative, regardless of the context that Jesus had provided up to that point! This is contrary to Jesus' words:

> They said therefore to him, "Who are you?" Jesus said to them, "Just what I have been saying to you from the beginning." (John 8:25)

What he had been saying all along are things like the following, that absolutely contradict the false notion that he was claiming to be an incarnation of the person of God:

> Most assuredly, I tell you, the Son *can do nothing of himself*... (John 5:19)
> *I can of myself do nothing.* (John 5:30)

What he never said, nor did the apostles, was that only a select few would be able to understand him based on hidden meanings in clues that he dropped. This is completely different than speaking in parables; the parables were actually pretty clear, especially since quite often he gave the meaning of them to his disciples, who then wrote them down for us. The problem with the theories of both Trinity and Oneness is that their particular teachings are not anywhere spelled out in the Bible and were never preached on for salvation, and they go against particular explanations that are made in the Bible. The simple fact remains that the details of the Son of God doctrine are spelled out all over the place in the Bible!

The Snake-Handler Factor: The whole point of introducing the snake-handler factor is that the snake handlers actually believe that their Scriptures are very clear and irrefutable. The Bible says believers will take up serpents, which won't hurt them. Therefore, snake handlers feel they are being totally scriptural in purposely taking up venomous snakes to prove their faith is genuine. The problem isn't that such Scriptures don't speak of protection. The problem is that the snake handlers must ignore and negate other Scriptures, which are just as authoritative, that speak against the practice of tempting God.

The same holds true for the way Christian Incarnationists interpret John 8:58. First they completely ignore the context in which Jesus made this statement, wherein he had already made it clear that he could do nothing of himself, that he was not alone, and that he was only claiming to be the Son of God, not God himself. Then Incarnationists further disregard and negate the Scriptures that clearly teach that Jesus had his beginning (genesis) when he was born in Bethlehem, that he was the second Adam who did not come first, but that he was made a quickening spirit, and, as Romans says, that justification to life came by the obedience of one man. Third, they change the Greek grammar and interpret the passage rather than simply translate it. All of these tactics are extremely dishonest.

Following, then, are the Scriptures that explicitly teach that Jesus was made in the process of time and did not actually preexist his human conception and birth other than in the plan of God. These Scriptures are not compatible with the interpretation of John 8:58 that claims he personally and actually preexisted Abraham in his life as recorded in the Book of Genesis.

> [12]When your days are fulfilled, and you shall sleep with your fathers, I will set up *your seed after you*, who shall proceed out of your bowels, and I will establish his kingdom. [13]He shall build a house for my name, and I will establish the throne of his kingdom forever. [14]*I will be his father, and he shall be my son*... (2 Samuel 7:12–14)

Here, during the time of King David, God explicitly speaks of His Son in the future tense. This same truth is reiterated in these next two passages:

> I will tell of the decree. Yahweh said to me, "You are my son. *Today I have become your father.*" (Psalms 2:7)

> For to which of the angels did He say at any time, 'You are my Son, *Today have I become* your father?' and again, "*I will be to him* a Father, And he will be to me a Son?" (Hebrews 1:5)

Here in Hebrews 1:5, both 2 Samuel 7:12–14 and Psalms 2:7 are interpreted for us as the same event: the timing of Christ becoming as a son to the Father, which was after the time of King David. Thus the NT opens with the beginning of Jesus:

> The book of the generation [Gr. *genesis* = beginning] of Jesus Christ, the Son of David, the Son of Abraham... (Matthew 1:1)

> But *when the fulness of the time* was come, God sent forth *his Son, made of a woman*, made under the law (Galatians 4:4)

Galatians explicitly tells us that God's Son was made in the fullness of time and made of a woman. Then 1 Corinthians 15 explains why this was so:

> [21]For since death came <u>by man</u>, the resurrection of the dead also <u>came by man</u>. [22]For as in Adam all die, <u>so also in Christ</u> all will be made alive...
> [45]So also it is written, "The first man, Adam, became a living soul." *The last Adam <u>became a life-giving spirit</u>*. [46]However <u>that which is spiritual isn't first</u>, but that which is natural, <u>then that which is spiritual</u>. [47]The first man is of the earth, made of dust. The second man is the Lord from heaven. (1 Corinthians 15: 21–22; 45–47)

These are "it is written again" Scriptures that explicitly refute the false interpretation of John 8:58 claiming Jesus literally preexisted. Either Onenessians are mistaken or lying about Jesus' identity, or Jesus was lying and what the Bible explains Jesus to be is also misleading and untruthful. There simply is no middle ground. The reason people come to such false conclusions is because they neglect the biblical rules of interpretation; that is, they don't let Scripture explain Scripture. They use their own reasoning and claim their reasoning for their authority! That is humanism, not faith that comes from hearing the word of God! But worst of all, they go to pagan ideas (such as incarnation) to get the words and concepts by which to view and describe Christ. That is idolatry.

References:

Following are some sites that will explain the grammatical meaning of the Greek aorist and Infinitive verbs. These will help support the fact that in John 8:58 Jesus was not speaking about Abraham in the past tense, but was referring to what he is to be in the future. These grammatical definitions show that this verse should read, "before Abraham *comes to be*, I am" and not, "Before Abraham *was,* I am."
http://ntgreek.org/learn_nt_greek/verbs1.htm
https://greeklinguistics.com/grammar/14.html

CHAPTER THIRTY

John 20:28 Thomas answered him, "My Lord and my God!"

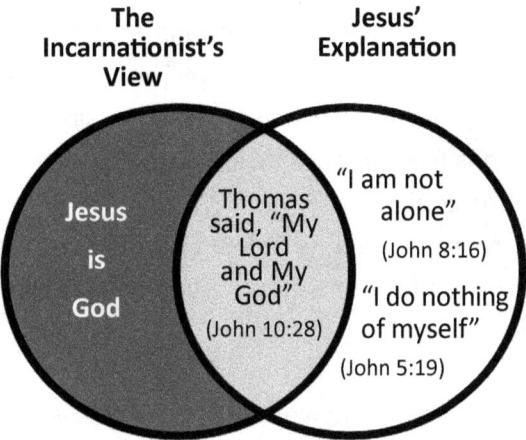

²⁷Then he said to Thomas, "Reach here your finger, and see my hands. Reach here your hand, and put it into my side. Don't be unbelieving, but believing." ²⁸*Thomas answered him, "My Lord and my God!"* ²⁹Jesus said to him, "Because you have seen me, you have believed. Blessed are those who have not seen, and have believed." (John 20:27–29)

Did Thomas make a confession that Jesus himself was his God? That is what many people conclude, and if this verse were all we had of the whole story, it would appear to be justified and clear as day. But would Thomas have made that confession from what he had learned by being with Jesus for three-and-a-half years? The answer is no. Instead, his confession is a very logical and reasonable reaction to what Jesus had been teaching him, such as:

> Even if I do judge, my judgment is true, for *I am not alone*, but I am with the Father *who* sent me. (John 8:16)

He who sent me is with me. *The Father hasn't left me alone, for I always do the things that are pleasing to him.* (John 8:29)

You will leave me alone. Yet <u>*I am not alone*</u>, because the Father is with me. (John 16:32)

Now, if Thomas really believed Jesus was "not alone," it would be perfectly fitting upon seeing Jesus for Thomas to recognize that where Jesus was, there God also was. The key, again, is in not jumping to conclusions like the devil does, but in hearing the rest of the Scriptures on the topic.

For a little more context, let's keep in mind that Jesus had just recently been raised from the dead. Let's consider the ramifications and implications of that.

> [18]The Jews therefore answered him, "What sign do you show us, seeing that you do these things?" [19]Jesus answered them, "<u>*Destroy this temple, and in three days I will raise it up*</u>." [20]The Jews therefore said, "Forty-six years was this temple in building, and will you raise it up in three days?" [21]But <u>*he spoke of the temple of his body*</u>. (John 2:18–21)

> [19]Jesus therefore answered them, "Most assuredly, I tell you, the Son can do <u>*nothing*</u> of himself, ... [26]For as the Father has life in himself, even so <u>*he gave to the Son also to have life*</u> in himself. [27]He <u>*also gave him authority*</u> to execute judgment, because he is a son of man... [30]<u>*I can of myself do nothing*</u>." (John 5:19–30)

> [17]Therefore the Father loves me, because *I lay down my life, that I may take it again.* [18]No one takes it away from me, but I lay it down by myself. I have power to lay it down, and I have power to take it again. <u>*I received this commandment*</u> from my Father. (John 10:17–18)

Jesus had been teaching about his resurrection in the context of his body being a temple. In this context, we see that Jesus clearly denied inherent authority. He would raise the temple of his body by a commandment.

We covered this topic in some depth in Chapter Nineteen. Jesus was very clear in stating that he could do nothing of himself, but that the Father gave him authority by commandment to take up his life again. Thus, in his confession, Thomas was acknowledging *exactly and precisely that: Jesus was not alone.*

Now keep in mind that the temple of the Lord signified God's dwelling presence.

> ¹Now when Solomon had made an end of praying, the fire came down from heaven, and consumed the burnt offering and the sacrifices; and the glory of <u>Yahweh filled the house</u>. ²The priests could not enter into the house of Yahweh, because the glory of <u>Yahweh filled Yahweh's house</u>. (2 Chronicles 7:1–2)

The idea of God's presence actually dwelling in the temple and being with the children of Israel was a major part of the significance of the temple. But that never meant that the temple itself was God! This same truth was carried over into the NT, with the major difference being that God would no longer dwell in temples made with hands, but within us humans!

> For <u>you are a temple</u> of the living God. Even as God said, '<u>I will dwell in them</u>, and walk in them; and I will be their God, and they will be my people.' (2 Corinthians 6:16)

> ²⁴...The God who made the world and all things in it, he, being Lord of heaven and earth, *doesn't dwell in temples made with hands,*... ²⁶He made from one blood every nation of men... ²⁷that they should seek the Lord, if perhaps they might *reach out for him and find him, though he is not far from each one of us.* ²⁸"For in him we live, and move, and

have our being." As some of your own poets have said, "For we are also his offspring." ²⁹Being then the offspring of God, we ought not to think that the Divine Nature is like gold, or silver, or stone, engraved by art and design of man. ³⁰*The times of ignorance therefore God overlooked. But now he commands that all people everywhere should repent,* ³¹because he has appointed a day in which he will judge the world in righteousness *by the man whom he has ordained; of which he has given assurance to all men, in that he has raised him from the dead.* (Acts 17:24–31)

Now let's consider Thomas' reaction with the bigger NT picture in mind.

As Jews, the disciples had been looking for an heir of David to deliver them from bondage under Rome. It just wasn't "right" that God's chosen people should be held under the authority of a pagan empire: they desired and hoped for a return to the previous glory of Israel under God, as led by a Jewish king!

But Jesus' resurrection from the dead was something way beyond their expectations of a restored Davidic kingdom! What had actually come to pass, and which they were called to be witnesses to, was that Jesus, who had claimed to be a human temple of God, had been raised from the dead by God!

For Thomas to exclaim, then, "my Lord *and* my God," was simply to confess that Jesus is and was who he had been saying he was all along: an anointed man with whom God was always present!

Jesus did not claim to have resurrected himself by his own inherent power or authority! Rather, he had explicitly explained, as we saw above, that he was operating under direction, authority, and command of God!

So then, Thomas, in his confession and declaration, was affirming and recognizing both Jesus as his Lord, *and* the God who was with him. That is, Jesus wasn't merely a man who had been given an anointing and all authority from God and who then set about using his power and authority and unction wherever and however he saw fit on his own. Rather, everything that Jesus said and did, he did by direction and commandment from God within him and working through him. So, far from being "equal" to God, Jesus remained under authority to God in everything he did, because God was always with him. *Therefore, it was most fitting that Thomas would proclaim, "my Lord and my God."* Not just my Lord acting alone, but the one whom God had made Lord and Messiah acting completely within the very presence of God, and to an extent better than was ever realized in the temple presence of the Old Covenant! This is, after all, the ultimate hope and destiny of all true Christians: that God would be all in all (1 Corinthians 15:28).

The question is, does the Scripture state and support this view and understanding of Thomas' confession?

Indeed, our understanding of the verse is exactly what all the apostles, speaking in one mind and accord, preached Christ to be on the day of Pentecost; that is, a man whom God raised from the dead and anointed to be the Son of David and whom God *made* Lord and Messiah:

> [29]...*The patriarch David...* [30]...being a prophet, and *knowing that God had sworn with an oath* to him that of the fruit of his body, according to the flesh, *he would raise up the Christ to sit on his throne,* [31]he foreseeing this spoke about the resurrection of the Christ, that neither was his soul left in Hades, nor did his flesh see decay. [32]*This Jesus God raised up*, to which we all are witnesses. [33]Being therefore *exalted by the right hand of God*, and having *received from the Father the promise* of the Holy Spirit, he has poured out this, which you now see and hear. [34]For David... says himself, "The Lord [Yahweh] said to my Lord [*Adoni*], 'Sit by my right hand, [35]Until I make your enemies a footstool for your feet.'" [36]Let all the house of Israel therefore know assuredly that *God has made him both Lord and Christ*, this Jesus whom you crucified. (Acts 2:29–36)

This is how the apostles explained and preached their confession of Jesus: as a man who was anointed and sent by God. This isn't jumping to conclusions, this is the apostle's express position. This was the apostles all together in one accord proclaiming what they witnessed and believed.

And what confession regarding Jesus were the apostles prompting from the Jews? That Jesus was God? No, not at all. Not here or anywhere else. Rather, they proclaimed that it was God who raised Jesus from the dead and *made* him Lord and Messiah (Anointed One).

We've seen Jesus saying that God hadn't left him alone. We've also seen that the apostles never, ever *clearly* concluded or proclaimed that Jesus actually was God Himself. These Scriptures are all very clear and to the point. And yet there is still more that could be quoted in this regard. So next we'll look at Scriptures explaining that we are always to view God and his Christ together and not separately (that is, not one in person, but one in purpose, and that purpose being the salvation of mankind):

> [21]I have not written to you because you don't know the truth, but because you know it, and because no lie is of the truth. [22]Who is the liar but he who denies that Jesus is the Christ? This is the Antichrist, he who denies <u>the Father and the Son</u>. [23] Whoever denies the Son, the same doesn't have the Father. He who confesses the Son has the Father also. [24]Therefore, as for you, let that remain in you which you heard from the beginning. If that which you heard from the beginning remains in you, you also will <u>remain in the Son, and in the Father</u>. (1 John 2:21–24)

> [9]Whoever transgresses and doesn't remain in the teaching of Christ, doesn't have God. *He who remains in the teaching, the same has both the Father and the Son.* [10]If anyone comes to you, and doesn't bring this teaching, don't receive him into your house, and don't welcome him... (2 John 9–10)

> Jesus said to him, "I am the way, the truth, and the life. *No one comes to the Father, except through me.*" (John 14:6)

These verses explain that the Father and son are a "package deal." No one comes to the Father "except through" the Son. This means there is no salvation in any other man-made forms of religion! Neither Buddhism, Islam, or any other form of religion will bring anyone to the Father.

What these verses also make clear is that the Father is not the person of the Son, and the Son is not the person of the Father. These also don't "redefine" the terms father and son. These aren't saying that son equals the flesh of the person of Jesus, and the Father equals his deity. We covered this topic thoroughly in Chapter Twelve, and those concepts apply here also.

The Bible is very clear that Jesus is not God. It is therefore a misrepresentation of the biblical record to interpret Thomas' confession in a way that makes it appear that is what he believed.

The key is to interpret in the manner of Jesus, the true witness, rather than Satan, the known liar. In all our efforts, we've used clear "it is written again" Scriptures. Onenessians take John 20:28 and re-interpret it in a way that makes all the other *explanatory* Scriptures of no effect, just like the devil does.

That is to say, those who claim that Thomas was confessing Jesus to be God, rather than "the Son of God in truth," who the Father was with, by being in the son, are lying about the biblical testimony. In fact, that is exactly what John was saying when he wrote, *"[22]Who is the liar but he who denies that Jesus is the Christ? This is the Antichrist, he who denies the Father and the Son"* (1 John 2:22).

Jesus Disagrees with Pharisee Conclusions

Let's look at the following example where the Jews concluded that Jesus must have been claiming to be God. Ask yourself as you read whether Jesus felt these Jews had correctly understood him or not.

> [5]Jesus, seeing their faith, said to the paralytic, "Son, your sins are forgiven you." [6] But there were some of the scribes sitting there, <u>and reasoning in their hearts</u>, [7]"Why does this man speak blasphemies like that? Who can forgive sins but

> God alone?" ⁸Immediately Jesus, perceiving in his spirit that *they so reasoned within themselves,* said to them, "<u>Why do you reason these things in your hearts</u>? ⁹Which is easier, to tell the paralytic, 'Your sins are forgiven;' or to say, 'Arise, and take up your bed, and walk?' ¹⁰ But that you may know that <u>the Son of Man has authority</u> on earth *to forgive sins*"—he said to the paralytic— ¹¹"I tell you, arise, take up your mat, and go to your house." (Mark 2:5–11)

Clearly, Jesus did not agree with these Jews! While some claim these Jews were correct in their reasoning, Jesus didn't. Instead, he criticized them for *"reasoning in their hearts,"* which is what they were doing that caused them to think he was claiming to be God! Jesus didn't say, "You're right, I'm claiming to be God the Father incarnate!" To the contrary, he explained to them something completely different. He said, "But that you may know that *the son of man has authority* on earth *to forgive sins..."*

The phrase "son of man" literally means the *offspring of humanity*! Jesus was simply demonstrating the authority, as he said later, in Matthew 28:18, that, *"all authority* has been *given to me* in heaven and earth!" Jesus was claiming this authority as to his personal humanity that was a separate personality from that of God who gave him such authority.

Does the Scripture say that only God can forgive sins? That is what many presume. Well, what does the Scripture say? If that is so, what do we do with this next Scripture and others like it?

> ²²When he had said this, he breathed on them, and said to them, "Receive the Holy Spirit! ²³*Whoever's sins <u>you</u> forgive, they are forgiven* them. *Whoever's sins <u>you</u> retain, they have been retained."* (John 20:22–23)

If only God can forgive sins, then how was Jesus able to give men the power to forgive sins? The answer is, the same way in which Jesus was given the authority by his Father. It comes from God through men when they are acting on behalf of God, just as the Jews did in the OT temple! So it is just a false dilemma type argument to claim that only God can forgive sins.

Let's look at a couple of biblical commentators who explain what Jesus was telling these disciples.

> John 20:23. The authorisation of the Apostles is completed in the words: ... "Whosoever sins ye forgive, they are forgiven to them: whosoever ye retain, they are retained."... The announcement is unexpected. *Yet if they were to represent Him, they must be empowered to continue a function which He constantly exercised* and set in the forefront of His ministry. They must be able in His name to pronounce forgiveness, and to threaten doom. This indeed formed the main substance of their ministry, and *it was by receiving His Spirit they were fitted for it. The burden was laid upon them of determining who should be forgiven, and who held by their sin*. Cf. Acts 3:26; Acts 5:4.[1]

> 23. Whose soever sins, &c.] *This power accompanies the gift of the Spirit* just conferred. It must be noticed (1) that *it is given to the whole company present; not to the Apostles alone*. Of the Apostles one was absent, and there were others who were not Apostles present: *no hint is given that this power is confined to the Ten*. The commission therefore in the first instance is *to the Christian community as a whole*, not to the Ministry alone...
> It follows from this (2) that the power being conferred on the community and never revoked, the power continues so long as the community continues. While the Christian Church lasts *it has the power of remitting and retaining*

---

[1] W. Robertson Nicoll, M.A., LL.D. (Editor), *The Expositor's Greek Testament* (New York: Doran), as quoted at http://biblehub.com/commentaries/john/20-23.htm.

along with the power of spiritual discernment which is part of the gift of the Spirit. That is, it has the power to declare the conditions on which forgiveness is granted and the fact that it has or has not been granted.[2]

So, no, it isn't *only* God who can forgive sins like the unbelieving Jews wrongly assumed! While it is true that Isaiah had God saying he blots out sins (i.e., Isaiah 43:25), verses such as that do not say that **only** God can and/or ever will be the only one with the authority to do so!

In his book, David Bernard[3] attempted to use Luke 5:20–26, above, to try to prove Jesus claimed to be God. He also referred to the following for the same purpose:

John 8:19–27. This is where Jesus said that to know him and to see him is to know and see the Father. We covered this in Chapter Two, where we saw that Jesus refuted this interpretation by claiming he was **not** alone and could do nothing of himself.

John 5:17–18. In this passage the Jews sought to stone Jesus because he called God his Father. Calling God his Father is not grounds for biblically accusing Jesus of claiming to be God (see Chapter Six).

John 8:56–59. We dealt with this passage in the last two chapters. Jesus said, "Before Abraham comes to be, I am." The Scriptures are very clear that the term "I am" is not equal to saying "I am that I am," as God says of Himself, and that in the fullness of time Jesus was made of a woman. Thus Jesus did not claim to be God the Father in this passage either, as Mr. Bernard "reasons in his heart" him to be.

John 10: 30–33 and 38–39. This is where we turn our attention now...

---

[2] Alfred Plummer, *The Gospel According to S. John, with Maps, Notes and Introduction* (London: C. J. Clay and Sons, Cambridge University Press Warehouse, 1896), 344.

[3] See David Bernard, *The Oneness of God*, 75–76.

Did Jesus claim to be God, and did the Jews understand him correctly in John 10:30–33 and 38–39?

> ³⁰"I and the Father are one." ³¹Therefore Jews took up stones again to stone him. Jesus answered them, "I have shown you many good works *from my Father*. For which of those works do you stone me?" ³³The Jews answered him, "We don't stone you for a good work, but for blasphemy: because you, being a man, make yourself God." ³⁴Jesus answered them, "Isn't it written in your law, 'I said, you are gods?' ³⁵If he called them gods, to whom the word of God came (and the Scripture can't be broken), ³⁶do you say <u>of him whom the Father sanctified and sent into the world</u>, 'You blaspheme,' <u>because I said, 'I am the Son of God?'</u> ³⁷If I don't do the works of my Father, don't believe me. ³⁸But if I do them, though you don't believe me, believe the works; that you may know and believe that the Father is in me, and I in the Father." ³⁹They sought again to seize him, and he went out of their hand. (John 10: 30–33 and 38–39)

In what verse did Jesus say, "You're right. I am claiming to be God the Father because that is who I am." Somehow, that is what Onenessians believe he meant and said here. The problem is, he didn't say any such thing. In fact, he challenged, criticized, and corrected their faulty reasoning as not being in line with the Scriptures.

False teachers want you to go along with the faulty *"reasoning in their hearts"* that the Jews were practicing, rather than to hear what Jesus was trying to explain to them.

To understand what Jesus was telling these Jews, let's look at the context. Jesus was actually referring to Scriptures that the Jews should have understood. And by Jesus' reference, they should have understood that God did set men in the place of God over other men.

To see this, let's first look at the passage Jesus quoted. The verse says:

> I said, "You are gods, *All of you are* sons of the Most High." (Psalms 82:6)

This is the context in which Jesus *claimed himself to be the Son of God*. In other words, Jesus said he was only claiming himself to be a child of God in the sense that Israelites were "sons of the Most High." The difference between Jesus and the rest of them is that he did claim to be *The* Son. But that certainly wouldn't have been enough for them to accuse him of blasphemy. After all, God had also sworn with an oath that David's offspring would be God's Son!

So what Jesus actually said to the Jews was simply that his personal authority came from the same context of authority that God had given corporately to the leaders of the Israelites. The OT clearly taught this authority in the corporate body of Israel, and it did so, in the Bible, by calling them "gods."

> *God presides in the great assembly. He judges among the gods.* (Psalms 82:1)

In this verse we find an explanation of how God dwells in the congregation of His people. That is, when they follow His law and stand in judgment (according to His commandments) of the wrongs people do against each other, God Himself is among them. Passages such as Exodus 21:6 and Exodus 22:8–9 express the commandments for the Sons of God to sit in judgment with God in their midst. Here is how the King James Version translates the passages:

> If the thief be not found, then the master of the house shall be brought unto *the judges (elohim = gods)*, to see whether he have put his hand unto his neighbour's goods. For all manner of trespass, whether it be for ox, for ass, for sheep, for raiment, or for any manner of lost thing, which

> another challengeth to be his, the cause of both parties shall come before the judges; and whom *the judges (elohim)* shall condemn, he shall pay double unto his neighbour. (Exodus 22:8–9, KJV)

> Then his master shall bring him unto the *judges (Elohim = gods)*; he shall also bring him to the door, or unto the door post; and his master shall bore his ear through with an awl; and he shall serve him for ever. (Exodus 21:6, KJV)

In both of the above passages, the phrase *"the judges"* comes from the Hebrew word *elohim*. That is a word used non-exclusively for "God" in the OT. These passages represent what Jesus was referring to in saying that God Himself called His people "gods" (*elohim*). According to the interpretation of these verses in Psalms 82:1 (the Scripture interpreting Scripture), when the children of Israel sat in judgment according to God's commandments, *there was God Himself in the midst of them presiding over the assembly.*

As if to address this very issue, Paul wrote: "[5]For though there are *things that are called "gods,"*... [6]yet to us there is one God, the Father, of whom are all things, and we for him; and one Lord, Jesus the Anointed..." (1 Corinthians 8:5–6).

So then, just as Jesus pointed out, the concept that God bestows authority on people and resultantly, in that context, calls them "gods" (*elohim*) is biblically established. But that does not make them "true God." Jesus was clearly telling them that his authority was a derived authority, as was the case with the Israelite judges/*elohim*, and thus not an authority that was inherent to his person. The Jews refused to accept Jesus in this context out of their own Scriptures. The Onenessians also refuse to hear Jesus when he proclaims that he himself is not the "true God": "[3]This is eternal life, that they should know *you, the only true God*, and *him whom you sent, Jesus Christ*" (John 17:1–3).

Thus, to assign inherent deity to the person of the Son is to take Jesus' words totally out of his own context and reject Jesus' clear explanation of himself.

The Jews' problem wasn't in understanding Jesus' claim of god-like authority over them. It was in not accepting that he was just what he said he was: a man exalted in God's plan before time began and who had been <u>*given*</u> <u>*all*</u> authority in heaven and earth (just as he had said). Therefore, the problem many Christian people have is *exactly the same problem the Jews had—they cannot understand, believe, or accept that this man Jesus could be made to appear equal to God because he was sent by God and thus came in all of God's authority! This is what is literally meant by being anti-christ: being against an anointed man being given and exercising such authority!*

Jesus emphatically did not deny that he was a man who was exercising what previously would have been considered god-like authority. Instead, he justified and explained his authority through the Scripture! Even though Jesus explained it, most people still can't simply accept it. People will not hear Jesus' explanation of himself: "<u>*All*</u> authority has been <u>*given*</u> to me in heaven and on earth" (Matthew 28:18).

We simply need to hear what Jesus explained, rather than jumping to conclusions about what he meant.

The False Witnesses at Jesus' Trial

Most Oneness preachers adamantly contend that the Jews knew and correctly understood that Jesus was claiming to be God. As we've seen above, Jesus clearly refuted the idea that he was claiming to be God incarnate and explained himself to the contrary from their own Bible.

When we take a look at the biblical testimony around Jesus' trial and condemnation, we find that no Jew *directly* accused Jesus of being God during this time. That is, they ultimately didn't consider his "I am" statements to be grounds for accusing him of claiming to be God, so they had to look elsewhere for condemning material.

So now, let's look at the passages relating to Jesus' trial.

SECTION FIVE - REFUTING ONENESS

⁵⁹Now the chief priests, the elders, and the whole council <u>sought false testimony</u> against Jesus, *that they might put him to death;* ⁶⁰*and they found none.* Even though <u>many false witnesses came forward</u>, they found none. But at last *two false witnesses came forward,* ⁶¹and said, *"This man said, 'I am able to destroy the temple of God, and to build it in three days.'"* ⁶²The high priest stood up, and said to him, "Have you no answer? What is this that these testify against you?" ⁶³But Jesus held his peace. The high priest answered him, "I adjure you by the living God, that you tell us whether you are the Christ, the Son of God." ⁶⁴Jesus said to him, "You have said it. Nevertheless, I tell you, henceforth you will see the Son of Man sitting at the right hand of Power, and coming on the clouds of the sky." ⁶⁵Then the high priest tore his clothing, saying, "He has spoken blasphemy! Why do we need any more witnesses? Behold, now you have heard his blasphemy." (Matthew 26:59–65)

⁵⁵Now the chief priests and the whole council sought witnesses against Jesus to put him to death, and found none. ⁵⁶For <u>many gave false testimony against him</u>, and *their testimony didn't agree with each other.* ⁵⁷Some stood up, and gave *false testimony* against him, saying, ⁵⁸*'We heard him say, 'I will destroy this temple that is made with hands, and in three days I will build another made without hands.''* ⁵⁹Even so, their testimony did not agree. ⁶⁰The high priest stood up in the midst, and asked Jesus, 'Have you no answer? What is it which these testify against you?' ⁶¹But he stayed quiet, and answered nothing. Again the high priest asked him, *'Are you the Christ, the Son of the Blessed?'* ⁶²Jesus said, *'I am.* You will see *the Son of Man* sitting at the right hand of Power, and coming with the clouds of the sky.' (Mark 14:55–62)

What did Jesus confess here? That he was God? No, rather, that he was "*the Son of the Blessed... I am...*"

> ⁶⁶As soon as it was day, the assembly of the elders of the people was gathered together, both chief priests and scribes, and they led him away into their council, saying, ⁶⁷"<u>*If you are the Christ, tell us*</u>." But he said to them, "If I tell you, you won't believe, ⁶⁸and if I ask, you will in no way answer me or let me go. ⁶⁹From now on, *the Son of Man* will be seated at the right hand of the power of God." ⁷⁰They all said, "<u>*Are you then the Son of God?*" He said to them, "You say it, because I am</u>." ⁷¹They said, "Why do we need any more witness? For we ourselves have heard from his own mouth!" (Luke 22:66–71)

What did Jesus confess here? Once again, "the Son of God... I am..." "son" does not equal "father"! A son and a father are never, ever a son to themselves or a father to themselves. This is the "I am" of Jesus: he is the son of God. God is not a man...neither the son of man (Number 23:19)!

These are the "official" accusations that were brought against Jesus, and his replies. He was put to death for claiming to be the Son of God, not God Himself.

In not one of these accusations was Jesus accused of directly claiming to be God the Father. If Jesus had been so plain, as some claim, then they would not have needed to seek other witnesses. Apparently even these Jews were shrewd enough to realize that "reasoning in their hearts" alone wasn't enough to accuse Jesus of claiming to be God incarnate.

In these passages, Jesus agreed with them that *he called himself the Son of God and the Son of Man*. And yet, the apostles, in the Scriptures that cannot be broken, *referred to his accusers as false witnesses over and over again*.

Why is that so? It is simply because the things Jesus did claim of himself were not crimes that were worthy of death. They had "*sought false testimony against Jesus, that they might put him to death; and they found none"* (Matthew 26:59–60). *That is, they found no testimony worthy to put him to death over!* You see, it was a two-part proposition. Just finding testimony is one thing; finding testimony of a crime worthy of death is quite another.

We must keep in mind that Judea was under Roman occupation. Claiming *any* other type of authority, at that time, *was* a capital crime ("worthy of death") under Roman law. The Romans killed people for a lot less, as Josephus and other contemporary sources make clear. The issue with the Jews was not whether Jesus thought he was God; the issue was whether the role he claimed was a challenge to the existing authority and could bring down the wrath of Rome upon the populace, and there is no question that it was. Any anointing going on was in the control of Rome, which is to say, no kings, and *the high priest was a Roman appointee* who could and was deposed at Roman will. The charges against Jesus likely had more to do with Roman context than scriptural content.

Another thing we need to keep in mind is that, according to the testimony of the apostles, the Romans didn't find Jesus guilty; they wanted to release him. This seems to lend further support to the idea that the Jews were merely offering trumped up charges by which they could get rid of him.

That is the religious, political, and historical context in which Jesus was forcefully rejected by the religious leaders of his day. They accused him, primarily, of two things: a) he claimed that he would destroy the temple and in three days he would raise up a temple made without hands; and b) he claimed he was the Christ, (meaning the Messiah, or the Anointed One), and the Son of God (meaning the heir to David's kingdom), or in other words, king of the Jews.

So what makes these accusations false? It wasn't that he didn't make these claims, because he did. Rather, it is simply that his claims didn't break any biblical laws as the Jews were implying they did.

> ...Where there is no law, neither is there disobedience. (Romans 4:15)
> Or, as the King James put it: "...Where no law is, there is no transgression." (Romans 4:15)

The simple fact is that there were no OT laws that said what Jesus was doing were things that *"only"* God could do or say. He simply wasn't guilty of any sin! He didn't claim to be God! He had transgressed no commandment that the Pharisees pointed to, so apparently they had to make up some accusations!

Let's look at the Scriptures that these accusations are typically said to be based upon and see what they tell us.

A) Scriptures that speak about God and the temple.

> [17]The place, Yahweh, which you have made for yourself to dwell in; The sanctuary, Lord, which your hands have established. [18]Yahweh shall reign forever and ever. (Exodus 15:17–18)

Although the Scriptures do teach that God "made" the sanctuary, we know that in actuality it was the *workers who were enlisted for the work who actually constructed the buildings*. So did God build the temple alone? Absolutely not! When Jesus said that he would raise up the temple in three days, as we have seen previously in Chapter Nineteen, he claimed to have been given the power to take up his life again *by commandment*. Such are not the words of God! God doesn't need to command himself to do something! It was specifically in regard to raising from the dead that Jesus explained *he could do nothing of himself...*

> [19]Jesus therefore answered them, "Most assuredly, I tell you, *the Son can do nothing of himself...* . [26]... as the Father has life in himself, even so *he gave to the Son also to have life* in himself. [27]He *also gave him authority* to execute judgment, because he is a son of man... [30]*I can of myself do nothing.*" (John 5:19–30)

So then, for later Incarnationists to assert that Jesus was claiming to be God, or even claiming to be equal to God, because he prophesied that he would raise the temple of his body in three days, *is to bear false witness against Jesus just like the Pharisees had done.* This is exactly what the Jews who crucified him were guilty of! Let anyone who claims this produce the Scripture that says, "anyone who claims he can destroy the temple and build it again in three days (while also claiming he can do nothing of himself) is claiming himself to be equal to God and is worthy of death." Where is that Scripture? Such a scriptural commandment simply does not exist, and where there is no commandment there is no transgression. The Jews were making up their own rules by which to judge Jesus. And the Onenessians and Trinitarians just love them for doing so! Of course, there is always the option that the apostles were the ones who were making things up against the Jews; but that isn't my position or, in general, the position of those for whom this book is intended.

B) He claimed he was the Christ, the Messiah, the Son of God.

We covered each of these three titles in Chapters Six and Seven. Here are the basic conclusions:

David's son was to be the Son of God by sworn oath from God:

> [8]Now therefore thus shall you tell my servant David, <u>Thus says YHWH</u>... [12]*When your days are fulfilled*, and you shall sleep with your fathers, *I will set up <u>your seed after you,</u> who* shall proceed *out of your bowels*, and I will establish his kingdom... [14]<u>*I will be his father, and he shall be my son*</u>... (2 Samuel 7:8–14)

Note that God explicitly said that David's son would be God's Son: "I will be *his* father, and *he* shall be my son." This, coupled with other Scriptures like it, is the biblical source for calling the Messiah *the Son of God*.

> Brothers, I may tell you freely of the patriarch David, that he both died and was buried, and his tomb is with us to this day. Therefore, being a prophet, and knowing that <u>God had sworn with an oath to him that of the fruit of his body, according to the flesh</u>, he would raise up the Christ to sit on his throne. (Acts 2:29–30)

Let us also recall that God Himself made Moses a "god" by making him a redeemer (Exodus 7:1). Certainly no Jew would have accused Moses of claiming to be God Himself because God had made him a god to Pharaoh.

All of this means that those asserting that Jesus claimed to be "God" are *guilty of the same false accusations that the Jews who put Jesus to death were guilty of:* claiming he blasphemously claimed to be God by claiming to be the Son of God and that he would raise himself (by commandment from God) in three days after they crucified him.

The apostles said the accusers of Jesus were false. To the contrary, false teachers would have us believe the apostles were false and the unbelieving Jews were telling the truth!

In fact, if Incarnationists are right, and telling the truth, then the apostles were the ones who were the liars for claiming the Jews bore "false witness" against Jesus! Remember, we've heard such teachers claim the Jews knew what Jesus meant. The Incarnationists have thus checkmated themselves by their doctrine. If they are right, then that means the apostles lied and aren't to be trusted (i.e., 1 Corinthians 15:14–17). This, of course, would invalidate all of Christianity, which is built on the testimony of the apostles! (See, for example, John 17:20; Ephesians 2:20.) This then would also nullify their position as "apostolics," and they should condemn Jesus along with the apostles since they have taken up sides with the Jews against the apostle's testimony!

Onenessians and Trinitarians side with the Accusers of Jesus!
Against the Apostles!

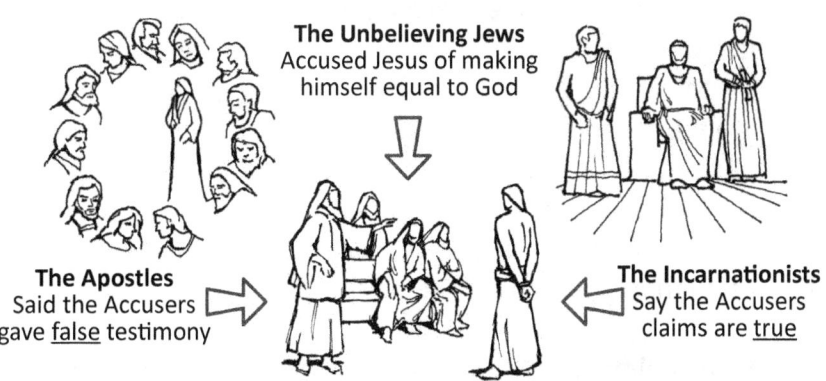

According to Onenessians and Trinitarians,
the Apostles bore false witness against the Accusers of Jesus!

Dear Oneness reader, how are you going to justify agreeing with the Jews' false accusations? By "reasoning in your heart"? Will that work for you better than it worked for the Jews who falsely accused him of making himself equal with God? No!

We have chosen to believe the apostles and thus to be apostolic. Since Onenessians don't believe the testimony of the apostles, they should stop calling themselves "apostolic," because, in fact, they actually deny the apostle's doctrine and make the apostles out to be liars.

The Snake-Handler Factor: The idea that Jesus claimed to be "God," and the Jews understood him correctly, even though he refuted the accusation, is yet another classic case of handling the Scriptures the way the snake handlers do. When Jesus is given the opportunity to explain himself, and his explanation is actually heeded, we find him explaining himself completely otherwise than the Oneness conclusion.

Jumping to Conclusions. In this chapter we've learned a new expression for jumping to conclusions: "reasoning in their hearts." The Bible teaches that the heart is desperately wicked above all things (Jeremiah 17:9). This is why "heart-reasoning" is most often contrary to biblically stated concepts. Thus, ignoring what the Bible explains in order to hold a teaching that is never clearly stated in the Bible but is actually refuted over and over again, is just more jumping to conclusions the way the devil interprets the Bible. Finally, we found out that the conclusions that Onenessians jump to just happen to be *the same* type of *false accusations* that the Jews who murdered Jesus were guilty of: *accusing Jesus of claiming to be equal to God by the things he said, which was the primary false accusation that sent Jesus to the cross!*

The OT Schoolmaster. The OT never taught, and no true Jew ever believed, that the Messiah would be God the Father Himself incarnate. Furthermore, the NT account of the "official" trial of Jesus doesn't present the Jews as accusing him of claiming to literally "be" the person of God (as Incarnationists falsely claim). Besides, Jesus had clearly and effectively refuted their false accusation that he was trying to make himself "equal" with God head-on when they had tried to pin it on him earlier (John 10:30–39). Their accusation that he was a "man" making himself "equal" to God is a completely different idea than the Incarnationist view. So now we have a case of the Incarnationists falsely accusing the false accusers of Jesus! The Jews no more assumed Jesus to be saying that he was God than they understood God to be a Trinity! It is the same with claiming the Jews were accusing Jesus of being God incarnate: it didn't happen, and it is dishonest for Incarnationists to make such a false claim.

On the other hand, one thing that was a real concern would be someone claiming to be the king of the Jews. This would bring the whole community of Jews into danger. It was the Romans who oversaw all leadership in Judea at that time. For a Jew like Jesus to claim himself king would have been regarded as treason by the Romans. However, the Roman officials, according to what we read in the NT, found no guilt in Jesus (Luke 23:4). So, the condemnation of Jesus did fall back upon the Jews at that point. They let a known criminal go free, and had a man considered guilt-free by Rome, crucified at the hands of the Romans.

Teach no other doctrine. Nowhere did the apostles expound on the idea that Jesus claimed to be God the Father incarnate; nor did Jesus.

References:

Here is another site that does a good job of dealing with John 20:28: http://www.angelfire.com/space/thegospeltruth/TTD/verses/john20_28.html

CHAPTER THIRTY-ONE

Colossians 2:9
For in Him All the Fullness of the Godhead Dwells Bodily

> ⁸Beware lest any man spoil you through philosophy and vain deceit, after the tradition of men, after the rudiments of the world, and not after Christ. ⁹*For in him dwelleth all the fulness of the Godhead bodily.* ¹⁰And ye are complete in him, which is the head of all principality and power." (Colossians 2:8–10, KJV)

Does the phrase "in him *dwells all the fullness* of the godhead bodily" mean that Christ is an incarnation of the person of the Father? That is the Onenessian idea that we want to address, and refute, here.

In Chapter Two and again in Chapter Thirteen, we discussed what "indwelling" means. Indwelling means precisely the opposite of identity. We are told that we are indwelt by the Spirit of God, and this specifically means that we are not to confuse the "Spirit of God in us" with us being able to do the things of God by ourselves.

What is this verse actually saying? For that, as usual, we will search the Scriptures to see how it aligns with scripturally stated teachings and truths.

So what does the Scripture mean by the word "fullness"? Let's begin with these passages:

> ...*Until we all attain to* the unity of the faith, and of the knowledge of the Son of God, to a full grown man, to the measure of the stature of *the fullness* of Christ. (Ephesians 4:13)

Does saying that we will eventually attain to "the fullness of Christ" mean that we will eventually become incarnations of the person of Christ himself? No. It simply means that we will be brought to a point where we can walk completely, or fully, in the goodness, holiness, and righteousness that Christ attained through faith in God. So the word "fullness" itself is not equal to "personality," as if to say Christ was the "personality" of God.

Earlier in Ephesians, Paul had written this:

> [17]...That Christ may dwell in your hearts through faith; to the end that you, being rooted and grounded in love, [18]may be strengthened to comprehend with all the saints what is the breadth and length and height and depth, [19]and to know Christ's love which surpasses knowledge, <u>that you may be filled with all the fullness</u> of God. (Ephesians 3:17–19)

So the goal for us is to *also* be filled with all fullness, *even as Christ was*! Was Paul exhorting us to become incarnations of the person of God, since he exhorted us to come to the point where we would be "filled with all the fullness of God"? Obviously not. *Being "filled" with the fullness of God means the opposite of being the identity of God.* It means, though you aren't God, you allow God to fully influence your life, thoughts, and actions!

Thus, in Colossians 2:9, Paul was plainly saying the opposite of what Onenessians think he meant!

Even earlier in Ephesians, Paul made another reference to "fullness":

> [17]...The God of our Lord Jesus Christ, the Father of glory... [22]He put all things in subjection under his feet, and *gave him to be head over all things for <u>the assembly,</u> [23]<u>which is his body, the fullness of him</u>* who fills all in all. (Ephesians 1:17–23)

Now here is a remarkable thing! Was Paul describing the body of Christ, the assembly, as the fullness of Him who fills all? We can properly understand this passage when we read it in harmony with these other verses on the same topic:

> When all things have been subjected to him, then the Son will also himself be subjected to him who subjected all things to him, *that God may be all in all*. (1 Corinthians 15:28)

> There are various kinds of workings, but the same God, who works all things in all. (1 Corinthians 12:6)

This means that in Ephesians, Paul was saying the body of Christ, the believers, will attain to being filled with all the fullness of God to the same extent that Jesus was!

Now notice what Paul said leading up to the statement in Colossians 2:9:

> [14]...In whom (the Son) we have our redemption, the forgiveness of our sins; [15]who is the image of the invisible God, <u>the firstborn of all creation</u>. [16]For by him were all things created, in the heavens and on the earth, things visible and things invisible, whether thrones or dominions or principalities or powers; all things have been created through him, and for him. [17]He is before all things, and in him all things are held together. [18]*He is the head of the body, the assembly*, who is the beginning, *the firstborn from the dead*; <u>that in all things he might have the preeminence</u>. [19]For <u>all the fullness was pleased to dwell in him</u>; [20]and through him to reconcile all things to himself, by him, whether things on the earth, or things in the heavens, having made peace through the blood of his cross. (Colossians 1:14–20)

Now here we have the "fullness" being "pleased to dwell in him [the Son], and through him to reconcile all things to himself, by him." These are two "hims," or two "whos" if you will. The one in whom the other One is dwelling, and the One who dwells within the one, who also reconciled all things through the other who or him. This is simply language that is describing God in Christ.

These Scriptures are not saying that God is Christ or Christ is God. Rather, these Scriptures are simply talking about what is clearly taught in other passages. For example:

> ¹Jesus... lifting up his eyes to heaven, he said, "Father... ⁹I pray for them... for those whom you have given me, for they are yours... ¹¹... Holy Father...*that they may be one, <u>even as we are</u>...* ²⁰Not for these only do I pray, but for those also who believe in me through their word, ²¹That they *may all be one; <u>even as</u> you, Father, <u>are in me, and I in you</u>, <u>that they also may be one in us</u>...* ²²The glory which you have given me, I have given to them; *that they may be one, even as we are one."* (John 17:11, 21–22)

In other words, God is in Christ, and Christ is in God, *in the same way* that we are to be in Christ and God, and that God and Christ are to be in us. This is indwelling, not identity. It is unity of mind and purpose, but not identity of person ("that they may be one even as we are one"). This is true (expressed and defined) biblical oneness that has no relation to the modalistic Monarchian "Oneness." Christ is no more God Himself because all fullness dwells in him than we are God because we dwell in him and God dwells in us! Both are specified so that there is no confusion for those who have ears to hear, rather than those who simply want to "reason these things in their hearts" contrary to what the Scriptures actually, and clearly, teach.

Here are some interesting passages that are referring to this same interchangeable unity of Christ in us and us in Christ:

> ¹⁰...Put on the new man, that is being renewed in knowledge after the image of his Creator, ¹¹where there can't be Greek and Jew, circumcision and uncircumcision, barbarian, Scythian, bondservant, freeman; **but Christ is all, and in all**. (Colossians 3:10–11)

> ¹⁵Don't you know that your bodies are members of Christ?... For, 'The two,' says he, 'will become one flesh.' ¹⁷But *he who is joined to the Lord is one spirit*. (1 Corinthians 6:15–17)

> ¹¹But the one and the same Spirit works all of these, distributing to each one separately as he desires. ¹²For as the body is one, and has many members, and all the members of the body, being many, are one body; so also is Christ. ¹³*For in one Spirit we were all baptized into one body, whether Jews or Greeks, whether bond or free; and were all given to drink into one Spirit.* ⁹For the body is not one member, but many. (1 Corinthians 12:11–14)

The Snake-Handler Factor: The idea based on Colossians 2:9 that Jesus is God bodily incarnate can't even really be given the benefit of being a snake-handler factor. Even the actual snake-handler proof texts actually do say what the snake handlers say they say. Colossians 2:9 does not at all say what the Onenessians imply that it means. Their position on this verse is nothing but...

Jumping to Conclusions. In this chapter we've reiterated that "indwelling" does not mean "identity"; in fact it means the opposite. We also saw that fullness can mean being full of the attributes of God, such as saints are exhorted to be filled with the fullness of God, but that doesn't mean we will be God incarnate ourselves. So using Colossians 2:9 as a proof text for modalistic monarchian "Onenessianism" is definitely jumping to conclusions in a very big way; that is, it is a very big jump over a very big gap in ideas!

The OT Schoolmaster. The OT never taught, and no true Jew ever believed, that the Messiah would be God Himself bodily incarnated.

Teach No Other Doctrine. Nowhere did the apostles expound on the idea that Jesus claimed to be God the Father personally, nor did Jesus. However, Jesus is the body of God in the same way that we are the body of Christ, which doesn't mean we are personally Jesus. The same goes for Jesus and God. To claim otherwise is teaching a doctrine the apostles never preached or taught.

CHAPTER THIRTY-TWO
1 Timothy 3:16 God was Manifest in the Flesh

> [14]These things write I unto thee... [15]... *that thou mayest know how thou oughtest to behave thyself in the house of God*, which is the church of the living God, the pillar and ground of the truth. [16]And without controversy great is the mystery of godliness: *God was manifest in the flesh*, justified in the Spirit, seen of angels, preached unto the Gentiles, believed on in the world, received up into glory. (1 Timothy 3:14–16, KJV)

This interpretation of 1 Timothy 3:16 is highly touted by Onenessians as a proof text that Jesus is a personal incarnation of God the Father. This chapter will address the many errors in the Oneness interpretation and respond with a view that is in harmony with the subject in the rest of the Bible.

The first thing we need to ask is, does this passage mean that, in some way, *God was made into* the human being named Jesus Christ, as Trinitarians and Onenessians believe? The biblical answer is a resounding no!

The first and most important thing we need to bring into focus is the *context* of this passage; namely, that Paul was writing to his disciple Timothy for the purpose of teaching people how they "ought to behave." Paul's stated purpose was not to teach that God became a man. Rather, his topic was that Jesus made known to us (which is what "manifested" means) *a life of godliness that we could all see and pattern our lives upon.* And Paul stressed that it was made sure because that godliness was revealed, justified, preached, believed, and received up in glory. Here's how Paul explained this same concept elsewhere, as if to say, "in other words..." or, "it is written again"...

> [5]For we don't preach ourselves, but Christ Jesus as Lord, and ourselves as your servants for Jesus' sake; [6]seeing it is God who said, 'Light will shine out of darkness,' who has shone in our hearts, *to give the light of the knowledge of the glory of God* in the face of Jesus Christ. [7]But we have this treasure in clay vessels, that the exceeding greatness of the power *may be of God, and not from ourselves*... [10]...<u>*that the life of Jesus may also be revealed (manifested) in our body*</u>. [11]For we who live are always delivered to death for Jesus' sake, that the life also of *Jesus may be <u>revealed (manifested)</u> in our mortal flesh*. (2 Corinthians 4:5–11)

The word translated here as "revealed" is the same Greek word used for "manifested" in 1 Timothy 3:16. Is this passage saying that when we make Jesus known through us that it is evidence we are incarnations of Jesus Christ? Absolutely not! And yet that is what certain people read into 1 Timothy 3:16 as it applies to Christ. This is inconsistency and double-mindedness.

Rather, the point in this passage is simply that when we make the life of Jesus Christ *manifest*, we make him *known* or, we could say, *"clearly understood."*

Thus, we see that an interpretation that imposes the idea of Christ as an incarnation on 1 Timothy 3:16 actually hides and replaces the original intent of what Christ "made known" to us, which is "godliness." The simple truth is that Christ made God and godliness known in the exact same way that we are to turn and make Christ and his righteousness known to others through our "godliness." This view is also totally in harmony with Paul's stated context in 1 Timothy 3:14–15, where his purpose was to teach how we ought to behave.

Second, the word "godliness" (Greek *eusebia*) is about "behavior." It means, "that piety which, characterized by a Godward attitude, does that which is well-pleasing to Him (God)."[1]

---

[1] *Vine's Expository Dictionary of Biblical Words* (Old Tappan, NJ: Thomas Nelson, 1985.

Did God need to be pious toward Himself? No. Did God need to be justified? No. Did God need to be received up into glory? No. However, in each case, the mystery of how mankind ought to behave in the sight of God certainly did need to be made known to us through the example of Christ and the teachings of the apostles. Otherwise it would still be a mystery to us. The way John put this in 1 John 1:2 was that Jesus manifested "the life" to us. That is to say, Jesus lived the life that God had in mind for mankind from the very beginning. Paul put it as a mystery to us, until Jesus made it known. And God confirmed that life by justifying it and receiving it up into glory. Taking a phrase out of the context of what Paul was teaching makes the whole passage rather unclear, if not questionable, and actually changes and negates the true topic that Paul was trying to make clear to us: that Jesus lived the type of life that pleases God.

Third, the use of the word "God" in this verse is, beyond controversy, a scribal error. Based on the earliest available ancient copies (including the Peshitta, and Coptic, Ethiopic, Sahidic, and Gothic manuscripts), as well as citations from the most ancient writers, scholars have concluded that 1 Timothy 3:16 should be translated as "**who** was manifest in the flesh" or most likely, "**which** was manifested in the flesh." It is beyond suspicious, we should say, even scandalous, when people are using a word known to be corrupt to "prove" their doctrine. But Onenessians don't just use this as a proof text—it is one of their very mantras!

To preserve and perpetuate a lie is a grievous error. To knowingly justify, condone, and even to exalt and celebrate that lie by immortalizing a known corruption of Scripture is to be a partaker in the sin of the corrupters, right along with the original perpetrators. While we aren't sure whether the copyist simply made a mistake (although it is highly doubtful), passing on an obvious error is unethical by anyone's standards. Yet that is the extent to which Onenessians are willing to go to hold onto their man-made idea that "Christ is God Himself incarnate."

Scholars can even point out exactly how that corruption came to be: it only took the slightest of a pen stroke to change the whole meaning of one word. The reader is encouraged to do a little research on their own to verify the truth of this point. One place to start is at the Trinity Delusion web site.[2]

Fourth, even if the third point weren't true, the passage still *does not say* that "God was *made* flesh" or that "God was *incarnated.*" This shows that the Oneness doctrine rests on how they interpret it, as opposed to what the Bible clearly says otherwise in a good many places. Being "manifested" merely means that Jesus Christ *revealed (made known)* what being godly (good, holy, and righteous) looks like. The same word for "manifest" is used in other passages, such as Romans 1:19, John 3:21, and John 21:14 (see below). In these passages we can also see that the word "manifest" simply means "made known" or "revealed." It certainly does not mean being made into something, so it absolutely is not saying that "God was *made* flesh."

> Because that which is known of God is revealed [manifested] in them, for God revealed [manifested] it to them. (Romans 1:19)

> But he who does the truth comes to the light, that his works may be revealed [manifested], that they have been done in God. (John 3:21)

> This is now the third time that Jesus was revealed [manifested] to his disciples, after he had risen from the dead. (John 21:14)

Other writers of Scripture say the same thing Paul was saying in different ways. For example:

> No one has seen God at any time. The one and only Son, who is in the bosom of the Father, *he has declared him.* (John 1:18)

---

[2] Located here: http://www.angelfire.com/space/thegospeltruth/trinity/verses/1Tim3_16.html.

John 1:18 presents a clear, "it is written again" quote in which Jesus is one "who" and he declared another "Him" than himself. These are personal pronouns that explicitly identify two different individuals, not mere "natures," as Onenessians make them out to be.

> ¹That which was from the beginning, that which we have heard, that which we have seen with our eyes, that which we saw, and our hands touched, concerning the Word of life ²(and *the life was <u>revealed</u>, and we have seen, and testify, and declare to you the life, the eternal life*, which was with the Father, and *was revealed to us*); ³that which we have seen and heard <u>*we declare to you*</u>, that you also may have fellowship with us. Yes, and our fellowship is with the Father, and with his Son, Jesus Christ. (1 John 1:1–3)

In the above passage we are said to manifest (or declare, the same word in the Greek) eternal life. This no more says that we are incarnations of Jesus or of God than does 1 Timothy 3:16 teach that Jesus was an incarnation of God the Father.

> ¹God, having in the past spoken to the fathers through the prophets at many times and in various ways, ²*has at the end of these days spoken to us by his Son*, whom he appointed heir of all things, through whom also he made the worlds. (Hebrews 1:1–2)

This passage provides an explanation of how Jesus manifested God and godliness: it's because God has spoken to us through His Son in the same way that he used to speak through prophets!

We believe that if anyone makes an honest effort to compare these verses with 1 Timothy 3:14–16, they will see they are all saying essentially the same thing, just in different ways. These are some of our "it is written again" passages against the Onenessian interpretation, just like they and we use such parallel passages as Mark 16:15–17; Luke 24:47; and Acts 1:8 and 2:38 against the Trinitarian interpretation of Matthew 28:19.

Fifth, both Onenessians and Trinitarians seem to forget that Christ is what we are to be. In particular, Christ was made in all things like his brothers; that is, us (Hebrews 2:17)! He can never honestly be said to be made like us if he is actually God made into a man. The idea that Jesus was God made into a man suggests that the serpent was right all along and that it was God's intent to transform mankind into being "like gods." Looking at the subject in this light makes the idea that Jesus was somehow God made into a man both devilish and antichristian (Gnostic). Therefore, the idea that 1 Timothy 3:14–16 means that God was made into a man twists, obscures, and ultimately negates the ultimate promise of Christianity!

> [2]...*We will be like him*; for we will see him just as he is. [3]Everyone who has this hope set on him purifies himself, even as he is pure. (1 John 3:2–3)

Sixth, and finally, the idea of Jesus being called "God manifest" in the flesh would have been, in Jewish estimation, just as much an abominable doctrine as the Trinity would have been. And that is because there was an infamous, pagan character in the annals of Jewish history who gave himself that very appellation: Antiochus Epiphanes. This man was so vile as to offer swine on the Jewish altar in Jerusalem after ransacking the city.

> Antiochus regarded himself as Zeus (hence his title, *epiphanes*, meaning "manifestation of"), the Greek God... His self-view as the supreme God meant that he saw himself as having power over all the religions in his realm. He thus tried to systematically change the traditions of the Jews, based on the laws of Moses, to make them conform to Greek beliefs.[3]

---

[3] "Antiochus IV Epiphanes," New World Encyclopedia, http://www.newworldencyclopedia.org/p/index.php?title=Antiochus_IV_Epiphanes&oldid=1001584 (accessed 8/9/2017).

Antiochus Epiphanes was perhaps the closest forerunner and prototype of the coming antichrist as we've ever seen in history. When Jesus spoke of the "abomination of desolation spoken by Daniel the prophet," this man Antiochus Epiphanes probably fit the bill more closely than any previous character in history. In many important ways, he did ultimately fall short of being "the man of sin" who is to come into the world, but he was a very close simile.

The idea that "God was manifest in the flesh" seems so ready-made for those who want to adopt the antichristian doctrine of dual natures in Christ. The very notion of an incarnated deity is totally foreign to the sacred writings we call Scripture. And 1 Timothy 3:16 is, in the final analysis, another piece of evidence showing how far Incarnationists are willing to go to justify a false and pagan doctrine: even to the point of supporting a blatant corruption and mistranslation of the word of God.

The Snake Handler Factor: The snake-handler factor is when someone takes a Scripture and jumps to a conclusion that is clearly contradicted by other Scriptures. There are no clear Scriptures that teach, as Onenessians claim, that "God was made flesh." When we look at all the other parallel verses to 1 Timothy 3:16 we find a consistent theme and message: *Jesus made known to us* what a godly life is supposed to look like. To take that passage beyond what it says and contrary to what a host of other Scriptures say, is to enter the *Snake Handler School of Theology*. Taking any number of such passages and jumping to conclusions doesn't transform anyone into a biblical scholar or student, it just means they are more sophisticated at the wiles of error than most other people.

> [12]Yes, and all who desire to live godly in Christ Jesus will suffer persecution. [13]But <u>evil men and impostors will grow worse and worse, deceiving and being deceived</u>. [14]But you remain in the things which you have learned and have been assured of, knowing from whom you have learned them. [15]From Infancy, you have known *the sacred writings which are able to make you wise for salvation through faith,*

> *which is in Christ Jesus.* ¹⁶Every writing inspired by God is profitable for teaching, for reproof, for correction, and for instruction which is in righteousness, ¹⁷that the man of God may be *complete, thoroughly equipped for every good work.*
> (2 Timothy 3:12–17)

For evil men to grow worse and worse means they will grow more sophisticated and effective in their deceptions. Dear reader, you don't need experts to teach you what the hidden meanings are in the Bible. Instead, we need to let what the Bible clearly says speak to our hearts!

Yes, we all needed a preacher at one time to proclaim to us the Good News of salvation (Romans 10:14). But that time, for many of us, has come and gone and we are still, like children, being "tossed back and forth and carried about with every wind of doctrine, by the trickery of men, in craftiness, after the wiles of error."

> ⁵So also <u>Christ didn't glorify himself to be made a high priest</u>, but <u>it was he who said to him</u>, 'You are my Son. Today I have become your father.' ⁶As he says also in another place, 'You are a priest forever, After the order of Melchizedek.' ⁷He, in the days of his flesh, having *offered up prayers and petitions with strong crying and tears* <u>to him who was able to save him</u> *from death*, and having been *heard for his godly fear*, ⁸though he was a Son, *yet learned obedience by the things which he suffered.* ⁹<u>Having *been made perfect, he became*</u> to all of those who obey him the author of eternal salvation, ¹⁰named by God a high priest after the order of Melchizedek. ¹¹About him we have many words to say, and hard to interpret, seeing you have become dull of hearing. ¹²For <u>*when by reason of the time you ought to be teachers*</u>, you again need to have someone teach you the rudiments of the first principles of the oracles of God. *You have come to need milk, and not solid food.* ¹³For everyone who lives on milk is *not experienced in the word of righteousness*, for he is a baby. ¹⁴But solid food is for those who are full grown, who by reason of

use *have their senses exercised to discern good and evil.* ⁶:¹Therefore leaving the doctrine of the first principles of Christ, *let us press on to perfection*—not laying again a foundation of repentance from dead works, of faith toward God, ²of the teaching of baptisms, of laying on of hands, of resurrection of the dead, and of eternal judgment. *³This will we do, if God permits.* (Hebrews 5:5–6:3)

Jumping to Conclusions: The idea that 1 Timothy 3:16 means God was "made" man is definitely jumping to conclusions. Using Jesus' method of interpretation, we can say, it is written again:

> No one has seen God at any time. The one and only Son, who is in the bosom of the Father, he has declared him. (John 1:18)

> No one has seen God at any time. If we love one another, God remains in us, and his love has been perfected in us. (1 John 4:12)

> The Father himself, who sent me, has testified about me. You have neither heard his voice at any time, nor seen his form. (John 5:37)

If Jesus believed for a moment that he was God the Father, then his statement in John 5:37 would be a blatant lie. According to the Oneness doctrine, it was the person of God the Father Himself who was visibly standing there and talking to these Jews. We can't have it both ways. The ends do not justify the means. If we are going to preach the truth of Christ, it is not seemly that we have to make a liar out of Christ in order to preach the truth of who he is.

> But [we] have renounced the hidden things of dishonesty, not walking in craftiness, nor handling the word of God deceitfully; but by manifestation of the truth commending ourselves to every man's conscience in the sight of God. (2 Corinthians 4:2)

The OT Schoolmaster: The idea that Messiah would be "God made flesh" was simply never taught in the OT. Thus the idea that 1 Timothy 3:16 means that he was God made flesh negates the truth of the OT being our Schoolmaster to bring us to Christ.

Teach No Other Doctrine: The idea that 1 Timothy 3:16 means "Jesus was God" is definitely adding to the word of God. Note what this following writer has to say about why it wasn't used for argumentation in the early years of Christianity when the Trinity was being formulated:

> When the Christological controversies were occurring in the fourth century, we do not see even one solitary person making a reference to the 'God was manifested in the flesh' version of this verse as evidence for identifying Jesus as 'God.' This fact does itself undeniably demonstrate it was unknown to them. If indeed 1 Timothy 3:16 really said 'God was manifest in the flesh,' we can most definitely be sure this passage would have most been brought forward as 'Exhibit A.' Yet, not one soul mentions it even though this passage more than any other would have supported the teaching that the incarnate Christ was 'God.' But the facts remain as they are and it was never mentioned once in the myriads of documentation that exist illustrating what was argued in these debates. There is a good reason that no one in the fourth century church ever mentioned the passage. The word 'God' did not appear in 1 Timothy 3:16 until much later. It first appeared in manuscripts after Trinitarian dogma was developed and canonized and is an obvious later alteration.[4]

---

[4] The Trinity Delusion," 1 Timothy 3:16, http://www.angelfire.com/space/thegospeltruth/trinity/verses/1Tim3_16.html, accessed 9/12/2016.

This shows how double-minded Onenessians are. They are quick to renounce changes in the Bible during the Trinitarian controversies. But this particular change fits their preconception, so they are silent in renouncing it, and choose to exalt it instead, regardless of how it fits with the rest of the Scriptures.

Other References

The Most Notable Corruptions of Scripture
http://www.thenazareneway.com/textual_analysis/most_notable_corruptions.htm

1 Timothy 3.16–Who Was Manifested?
http://lhim.org/blog/2008/08/13/1-timothy-316-who-was-manifested/

CHAPTER THIRTY-THREE
Conclusive Summary of Onenessianism

So what have we learned and what can we conclude about the Oneness theory in comparison to the "Son of the Father in truth"?

1) We've learned that there are Scriptures (e.g., Psalms 91:9–12) that can seem to imply certain teachings, but those teachings are untrue when clearly contradicted by other Scriptures.

2) We've learned that Christ taught through his temptations (Matthew 4:1–7) that the clearer Scriptures must be applied and not compromised when there appears to be a conflict of ideas.

3) We've seen examples of these conflicts in the way the devil interpreted Genesis 2:17 at Genesis 3:1–5, and again regarding Psalms 91 at Matthew 4:6. We've seen this same example repeated in the way snake handlers interpret Mark 16:18 and Luke 10:19 while ignoring Deuteronomy 6:16. We've seen that Trinitarians use this same method in interpreting such passages as Genesis 1:26 while ignoring the context of Genesis 1:27 (as they also do with Matthew 28:19 while ignoring all the other Scriptures pertaining to the name of Jesus in baptism). We've also demonstrated that Satan's method is the sole method of interpretation used to arrive at the Oneness conclusion that Jesus is an incarnation of the person of the Father.

4) We've provided a many-to-one ratio of Scriptures that plainly and clearly declare and describe:
   a) God's sworn oath that His Son would be born of David's flesh (and Eve's, and Abraham's).
   b) Christ's actual beginning at Bethlehem, where he was born.
   c) Christ's personal denial of any self-reliant authority, power, and even doctrine.

5) We've demonstrated just how unclear the Onenessian "proof texts" are upon closer examination.

6) We've demonstrated that the following essential core tenets of Onenessianism are false, and that they were never explained or articulated as such until well after the apostles:
   a) Jesus is an incarnation of God the Father (which is a pagan belief according to Acts 14:11)
   b) Jesus consists of dual natures of deity and humanity (invented by antichristian Gnostics).
   c) The phrase "Son of Man" is supposedly code for his human "nature," and the phrase "the Father" and "the Spirit" are code words for Jesus' deity (an idea first put forth by Praxeus, Noetus, and Sabellius).

7) Thus Onenessianism is a "new teaching" (as far as the apostles would be concerned) that has been adapted, revised, and refined from Paganism, Gnosticism, and Trinitarianism. This also means that Onenessianism is something that is "read into" the Bible, not something that is simply given to us by and through it.

8) We've demonstrated that what Onenessians call a "revelation" is actually an extrabiblical, jumped-to conclusion and not a proper biblical confessional response to the proclamations in the Scriptures about who and what Christ is. No one in the Bible was ever led to or made such a confession. Rather, they consistently testified that Jesus was the Son of God (but never "God incarnate").

9) We've demonstrated, on the other hand, that the true "Son of God" doctrine soundly outclasses both the Trinity and Oneness doctrines in the areas of:
   a) Source in the Old Testament law as Schoolmaster.
   b) Original apostolic faith as was consistently preached and taught.
   c) Rejection of extrabiblical traditions of men.
   d) Clear explanation and descriptions in Scripture.
   e) Sheer volume of explanations in Scripture.
   f) Consistency of confession ("Jesus the Anointed, the Son of God")!

Thus, in quantity, quality, source, expression, and method of interpretation, the Son of God doctrine stands unassailable. How much more completely biblical would a teaching have to be to prove its superiority over any other before being held as true? What else would we have to provide in order to "prove" this is the true biblical position and persuade you to accept it?

Here then, in light of all the positive and negative points we've summarized in this chapter, is the actual, total solution that should put to rest both the Trinity and the Oneness and establish the truth of the Son of God Doctrine:

> But he answered, 'It is written, 'Man shall not live by bread alone, but *by every word* that proceeds out of the mouth of God.' (Matthew 4:4)

> Teach no other doctrine (1 Timothy 1:3)

> Grace, mercy, and peace will be with us, from God the Father, and from the Lord Jesus Christ, the *Son of the Father, in truth* and love. (2 John 3)

> I rejoice greatly that I have found some of your children walking *in truth, even as we have been commanded* by the Father. (2 John 4)

¹⁹Jesus therefore answered them, 'Most assuredly, I tell you, <u>the Son can do nothing of himself</u>, but what <u>he</u> sees the Father doing. For whatever things <u>he</u> does, these <u>the Son</u> also does likewise. (John 5:19)

Even if I do judge, my judgment is true, for *<u>I am not alone</u>*, but I am with the Father *<u>who</u>* sent me. (John 8:16)

You will leave me alone. Yet *<u>I am not alone</u>*, because the Father is with me. (John 16:32)

APPENDICES

APPENDIX - I

We are not Arians or Jehovah's Witnesses ("Preexisters")

Arians and Jehovah's witnesses are among those who believe that Jesus was somehow created or came to be at some point before the rest of creation. That is, they believe Jesus "preexisted" his human existence, so we'll refer to them here as "Preexisters." The idea of literal preexistence did not originate with the apostles. The problem, quite simply, is that people have been spoiled by the philosophical and pagan ideas of preexistence so that they do not accept the biblical truth of God's utter foreknowledge.

Irenaeus (ca. AD 120–200) was one of the best witnesses outside of the Bible, and within early Christian writings, against the preexistence doctrine. He wrote against those same ideas that Tertullian (AD 160-220) adopted and reintroduced. Trinitarians today hold many of the same beliefs that were once only Gnostic but were made "acceptable" by Tertullian. Unlike Tertullian, Irenaeus refuted, rebuked, and rejected Valentinus' *"projection of one thing [god] out of another."* Although Irenaeus was writing against the antichristian Gnostics, his words apply equally well to these same ideas when held by Tertullian, Trinitarians, Arians, Jehovah's Witnesses, or anyone else who believes the Son of God literally existed before the rest of creation.

> If, again, they affirm that that (intelligence) was not sent forth beyond the Father, but within the Father Himself, then, in the first place, *it becomes superfluous to say that it was sent forth at all.* For how could it have been sent forth if it continued within the Father? For *an emission is the manifestation of that which is emitted, beyond him who emits it.* In

the next place, this (intelligence) being sent forth, *both that Logos* who springs from Him will still be within the Father, as will also be the future emissions proceeding from Logos..."[1]

Here Irenaeus was talking about *the Gnostic idea* of God-Persons, who were "emitted" (begotten) from the Father and yet remained within the fullness of the godhead (or *pleroma*). Irenaeus pointed out how superfluous that would be. If they didn't have anywhere to go, in what sense were they begotten? If they didn't go out from the godhead, what was the point in their being begotten?

It would be like a pregnant mother saying her baby was born while it was still in her womb. You can't have it both ways. Certainly a baby is conceived and has life before birth, but birth speaks of a specific event in the baby's life. Either the baby is born, or it's not; but it isn't yet born while it remains in the womb. First, it would suffocate! Second, it hasn't become its own breathing self yet. This is how ludicrous the Gnostic antichristian projection of one thing *out of another within the godhead* was to Irenaeus. Consequently, he stated that he did not believe in a son that was born before the rest of creation. Likewise, Jesus was neither "conceived" nor born until the time he was "made of a woman, made under the law." There was no mother who also preexisted in heaven whose egg would have been impregnated, and so forth. What did "preexist" was simply God's "plan," his *logos*/word that was part of who God was.

So those who teach that Jesus somehow literally, personally preexisted the rest of creation need to explain into what expanse Jesus was born, who his mother was, and whether David preexisted also since Christ was made of David's offspring. Of course such ideas are as nonsensical as the idea of literal preexistence itself and confirm Irenaeus' contention against the whole idea. For if Christ didn't have a mother and wasn't ever really "born" (in the sense of "emitted" or emerged from a womb, since he never would have left the Father as in the Gnostic view), how is it not superfluous (to use Irenaeus' word) to say he was born?

---

[1] Irenaeus, *Against Heresies*, Book 2, Chapter 13, par. 6.

The real issue is that the Son prophesied in the Bible was to be, exclusively, an offspring of David. Any merging of pagan ideas of incarnations of God and the like would identify such a one as not being the Messiah of biblical prophecy.

> When your days are fulfilled, and you shall sleep with your fathers, I will set up *your seed after you, who shall proceed out of your bowels*, and I will establish his kingdom. He shall build a house for my name, and I will establish the throne of his kingdom forever. *I will be his father, and he shall be my son*: if he commit iniquity, I will chasten him with the rod of men, and with the stripes of the children of men; but my loving kindness shall not depart from him, as I took it from Saul, whom I put away before you. Your house and your kingdom shall be made sure for ever before you: your throne shall be established forever.
> (2 Samuel 7:12–16)

Clearly, God's Son was defined here, by God Himself, as the offspring of David that would proceed out of David's body. If Jesus preexisted his human life, then so must have David (which didn't happen). This shows how that both David and Jesus only "preexisted" in God's plan, or foreknowledge of His Son, but not in reality.

The Biblical Concept of God Calling Things That Are Not As Though They Were

The biblical principle that "Preexisters" ignore and fail to take into account is simply that "God... calls the things that are not, as though they were" (Romans 4:17). This verse agrees with this next one: "...I am God... declaring the end from the beginning, and from ancient times things that are not yet done; saying, My counsel shall stand, and I will do all my pleasure" (Isaiah 46:9–10).

Scholars call this biblical figure of speech by several names; for example, the "prophetic perfect (tense)," or "Already–not yet."

For example:

> In the Hebrew and Aramaic idiom in which the Bible was written, when something was absolutely going to happen in the future, it is *often* spoken of *as if* it had already occurred in the past. Hebrew scholars are familiar with this idiom and refer to it as "the prophetic perfect," "the historic sense of prophecy," and the "perfective of confidence." Students studying Semitic language and thought sometimes call this idiom, "here now, but not yet" or "already—not yet." Unfortunately, *the average Christian has no knowledge of the idiom*. This is due to the fact that in the vast majority of the cases in which it appears in the Hebrew, Greek, and Aramaic texts, the translators have not done a literal translation into English, but have actually changed the tense. Thus, the "prophetic perfect" is rarely apparent in English Bibles.[2]

So, what is unknown to average Christians, but commonly known to scholars who read the Scriptures in their original languages, is that prophetic statements in the Bible *often speak in the past tense.* Thus it would be incorrect and unlearned to claim that Romans 4:17 only applies to one, solitary incident. Rather, it is a generality for a quite common figure of speech in the Bible. In fact, as one writer points out...

> We find in the Bible that *a great deal of* prophetic utterances are *not* written in the future tense, but rather, are written in the PAST, or PRESENT tense. This is why many prophecies are considered to have already taken place. This has *resulted in error, confusion, and bewilderment*. Hopefully, this composition will clear up any misunderstanding

---

[2] Author not provided, "The Prophetic Perfect," accessed 1/29/2017, http://www.truthortradition.com/articles/the-prophetic-perfect.

caused by the inappropriate uses of English grammar—to wit, using past and present tenses in our Bibles instead of the future tense.[3]

So then, in the original languages, the Bible has quite a number of instances of God calling those things that are not as though they were. The writings linked above provide many more examples. When God speaks in such figurative language, we need to understand that He isn't lying; rather, He is simply emphasizing to us the point that what He has settled to come to pass in the future, will come to pass with the utmost of certainty.

Let's take a look at a small sampling of prophecies that would appear to be lies if we didn't view them through the knowledge of "God calling those things that are not as though they were"...

> A shoot will come out of the stock of Jesse, And a branch out of his roots will bear fruit. (Isaiah 11:1)

In the original language, this literally states "And a rod hath come [past tense] out of the stock of Jesse." If we were to take this passage literally, it would be saying that the Messiah had already come out of the stock of David centuries before Jesus was born. Did the prophet lie here and the KJV translators cover up the error? No, the KJV translation has attempted to fix a problem for us by changing the language from the prophetic perfect to a future tense. But an attempt to fix one area has created an inordinate amount of confusion in another area: understanding, recognizing, and accepting God's idioms and figures of speech!

There are many more examples in both testaments that could be provided, but we will limit them here. Take, for example, this next passage and consider the way in which God speaks to Mo-

---

[3] Tom L. Ballinger, "Prophecy: Past Or Present Tense?" accessed 1/29/2017, http://www.plainerwords.com/artman2/publish/2007/Prophecy_Past_Or_Present_Tense.shtm.

ses. Clearly, in giving Moses instructions, God is using language that calls things that had not happened yet as though they already had:

> ¹⁶Go, and thou hast gathered the elders of Israel, and hast said unto them: Jehovah, God of your fathers, hath appeareth unto me, God of Abraham, Isaac, and Jacob, saying, I have certainly inspected you, and that which is done to you in Egypt; ¹⁷and I say, I bring you up out of the affliction of Egypt... ¹⁸And they have hearkened to thy voice, and thou hast entered, thou and the elders of Israel, unto the king of Egypt, and ye have said unto him, Jehovah, God of the Hebrews, hath met with us; and now, let us go, we pray thee, a journey of three days into the wilderness, and we sacrifice to Jehovah our God. And I — I have known that the king of Egypt doth not permit you to go, unless by a strong hand. (Exodus 3:16–19, YLT)

If we read this passage out of context, it gives the impression of being something that God said after Moses had already gone and spoken to the elders of Israel. But in fact, this was the way God spoke to Moses before he even left to go back to Egypt. If you were to reread the passage in the Bible, the context would be obvious: Moses is speaking to God in the famous burning bush incident. This is where God was initially giving Moses direction on what he was to do.

This fact leads us to the internal indicator in the above passage. Note the very first word, *go*. That word is an imperative, a command to Moses. So in this passage we actually have a conflict of tenses: first an imperative indicating what Moses is to do in the near future, and then the past tense, when God declares to Moses what he will do.

When we compare the way this text literally reads, as above, with how it is most often translated in our English Bibles, we can see how our translators have taken their liberty to attempt to clear things up for us. But in doing so, by masking God's actual figures of speech, they have clouded our understanding, which in turn causes unwary and unlearned people to stumble in other areas.

Notice that all the past tense speech in the original language has been rendered into future tense:

> [16]"Go, and gather the elders of Israel together, and tell them, 'Yahweh, the God of your fathers, the God of Abraham, of Isaac, and of Jacob, has appeared to me, saying, 'I have surely visited you, and seen that which is done to you in Egypt; [17]and I have said, I will bring you up out of the affliction of Egypt...'" [18]They will listen to your voice, and you shall come, you and the elders of Israel, to the king of Egypt, and you shall tell him, 'Yahweh, the God of the Hebrews, has met with us. Now please let us go three days' journey into the wilderness, that we may sacrifice to Yahweh, our God.' [19]I know that the king of Egypt won't give you permission to go, no, not by a mighty hand." (Exodus 3:16–19, WEB)

When we continue the passage in the literal interpretation, we can clearly see, by Moses' response to God, that this conversation was taking place before Moses left God's presence to return to Egypt. That is because Moses has questions about what to do if things don't go as expected:

> And Moses answereth and saith, 'And, if they do not give credence to me, nor hearken to my voice, and say, Jehovah hath not appeared unto thee? (Exodus 4:1, YLT)

Repetitive expressions occurring as a pair is called a "couplet." This is a poetic device that is common in Semitic languages. Sometimes couplets are paired with mix tenses. When tenses are mixed in pairs of passages regarding the same topic, this can be a good indicator of figurative language mixed with literal, because we can't actually have the past tense and the future tense occurring simultaneously except in God's foreknowledge.

Further along in their conversation, we see another example of God mixing an imperative tense with a past tense:

> ²¹And Jehovah saith unto Moses, "In thy going to turn back to Egypt, see — all the wonders which I have put in thy hand — that thou hast done them before Pharaoh, and I — I strengthen his heart, and he doth not send the people away." (Exodus 4:10, YLT)

The mixing of tenses are the key, in addition to the context of the conversation.

Now let's look at a few more samples provided in E. W. Bullinger's book, *Figures of Speech Used In The Bible Explained and Illustrated*.[4] The parenthesis are found in the source:

> Heb. ii:7.– "Thou hast made (i.e., Thou wilt make) him for a little while less than the angels." For this prophecy was spoken of Christ long before, in Ps. viii. (page 519).

> Heb. iii:14 We have been made (i.e., we shall become) partakers of Christ, if we hold, etc. (Page 519).

> Mark ix:31.–The Son of man is delivered (i.e., will be delivered) unto the hands of men. (Page 521).

> 2 Pet. iii:11.–Seeing that all these things are (i.e., shall be) dissolved. (Page 521).

Here's how Bullinger explained these:

> The Past for the Future. This is put when the speaker views the action *as being as good as done*. This <u>is very common</u> in the Divine prophetic utterances: where, though *the sense is literally future, it is regarded and spoken of as though it were already accomplished* in the Divine purpose and

---

[4] (Mansfield Centre, CT: Martino Publishing, 2011, reprint of 1898).

determination: the figure is to show the absolute certainty of the things spoken of... nearly all the prophecies are thus written.[5]

Or, as the Bible says, God calls things that are not as though they were!

The Son Was Born in Process of Time

When the Bible defines Christ's birth, it is defined as occurring in the process of time in our world. There is never an "explanation" given of an incarnation of a preexistent son of God.

The idea of the "couplet" was mentioned above. This is the key to understanding and identifying when the prophetic perfect is being used. It is important to keep in mind that the "couplet" doesn't have to be within the context of the event being described in the past tense, or even adjacent to it.

Understanding and accepting the concept of the couplets used with the prophetic perfect helps us to understand how the Bible seems to talk of Christ as both preexisting and also being born in process of time.

The wrong way of interpreting the Scriptures, which people often resort to, is to jump to pagan ideas of actual, literal preexistence. But, again, no Scripture goes into such types of explanations. And that is why understanding the use of the prophetic perfect, and the use of the couplets in the Bible, is the way to show that a non-literal-preexistent view of Christ is the only true biblical position.

These next verses should be used as the couplets to verses that appear to present a preexistent Christ. These verses are the "it is written again" Scriptures that neutralize the jumped to conclusion of a literal preexistent Christ:

---

[5] E.W. Bullinger, *Figures of Speech Used In The Bible*, 518–521.

> For to which of the angels did He say at any time, "You are my Son, *Today have I become* your father?" and again, "*I will be to him* a Father, And he will be to me a Son?" (Hebrews 1:5)

> I will tell of the decree. Yahweh said to me, "You are my son. *Today I have become your father.* Ask of me, and *I will give* the nations for your inheritance, The uttermost parts of the earth for your possession. You shall break them with a rod of iron. You shall dash them in pieces like a potter's vessel." Now therefore be wise, you kings. Be instructed, you judges of the earth. (Psalms 2:7–10)

These two verses explicitly assign a point in time to Christ's sonship and the Father's fatherhood: *"Today I have become your father."* Note that the writer of Hebrews contrasts the prophecy from 2 Samuel (above) with the exclamation of God that "today I have become..." This again shows that the time of the Son had a beginning that came after David.

> But when the fulness of the *time* was come, God sent forth *His Son, made of a woman*, made under the law. (Galatians 4:4, KJV)

Here we have yet another passage that tells us the Son was made when the time came and that he was made of a woman. He was also made "under the law," which tells us two things: he was made during the period that the law was in force; and secondly, he was made according to the law. God was legally wed to Israel and had every right to have a child by His legal "wife" (Jeremiah 31:32).

And finally, we know that Jesus wasn't made and didn't exist before his birth (in Bethlehem by his mother Mary) because the Bible explicitly tells us so:

> So also it is written, "The first man, Adam, became a living soul." *<u>The last Adam</u> <u>became</u> a life-giving spirit.* However *that which is <u>spiritual isn't first</u>, but that which is natural,*

then that which is spiritual. The first man is of the earth, made of dust. The second man is the Lord from heaven (1 Corinthians 15:45–47).

Saying, "That which is spiritual isn't first, really should settle the matter.

Those Scriptures explicitly teach that the Son was made in the process of time and did not literally preexist his human existence. It was not until being human that he "became a life-giving spirit."

The problem people have in accepting these Scriptures is that they have been spoiled by the pagan doctrine of literal preexistence and have not come to the understanding of God's awesome power of foreknowledge and the use of the "prophetic perfect." That is, when they read the passages where Jesus appears to preexist his human life, they aren't reading them in the context of God calling those things that are not; rather, they read them in the context of the pagan idea of God's coming to earth in the form of man. This is exactly what "being spoiled by philosophy" means. This topic was covered in Chapter Sixteen of this book.

Christ Had Faith, and Faith That is Seen is Not Faith!

Another point that does not harmonize with the literal preexistent Christ theory is the fact that Christ had faith in God and was tempted in all things just as we are. This topic was covered under the subheading "Jesus was, above all things, the epitome of a faithful man!" in Chapter Thirty-Four. Essentially, in no way could Christ have been tempted as we are in all things if he hadn't had the same faith as we have. Faith is the substance of things <u>not seen</u>. If Christ had been alive even for a moment in eternity before coming to this earth, then his obedience would not be the obedience of faith; rather, it would be the obedience of having seen God firsthand. That would mean every saint of God that ever lived would have had more faith than Christ himself! The idea is utterly foolish and would practically make void the whole basis of Christianity. That's how wrong, bad, and evil this doctrine is!

All of this is why, when the apostles preached Christ on the day of Pentecost, they preached him as a *man who was <u>foreknown</u> of God*, not a man that preexisted his human existence.

> ²²Men of Israel, hear these words! Jesus of Nazareth, a man approved by God to you... which *God did by him*... even as you yourselves know, ²³him, being *delivered up by the determined counsel and <u>foreknowledge</u> of God*, you have taken by the hand of lawless men, crucified and killed... (Apostle Peter, Day of Pentecost, Acts 2:22–23)

> ¹Peter, an apostle of Jesus Christ, to the chosen ones... ²according to the <u>*foreknowledge*</u> *of God the Father*... ¹⁸knowing that you were redeemed... ¹⁹...with precious blood, as of a faultless and pure lamb, the blood of Christ; ²⁰*who was <u>foreknown</u> indeed before the foundation of the world*, but was revealed at the end of times... (1 Peter 1:1–2, 18–20)

Note carefully that "foreknowledge" is a biblical word that was used in preaching the Christ. The word "preexistence" is not a biblical word; in fact, it is nonsensical. To preach a literally preexistent Christ is to preach a different Christ than the apostles preached him to be. That in itself is a very grave error.

> I fear, lest... your minds may be corrupted from the simplicity that is in Christ. For if he who comes preaches *another Jesus whom we have not preached*, or if you receive a different spirit which you have not received, or a different gospel which you have not accepted—you may well put up with it! (2 Corinthians 11:3–4, NKJV)

The preexistence doctrine is, therefore, a doctrine that is "against" the true Son of God and should not be either preached or supported!

Another fine article that helps refute the idea of a preexistent Christ is J. Dan Gill's article on Philippians 2:5–8.[6]

---

[6] J. Dan Gill, "21st Century Reformation Commentary: Philippians 2:5–8," accessed 1/29/2017, http://www.21stcr.org/21stcr_commentary/phil2_5-8-page3.html.

APPENDIX - II

We are Pentecostal

As I've stated, I came into the knowledge of the Son of God doctrine from a Oneness Pentecostal background. One of the things I discovered is that there are a good number of Son of God believers who, for one reason or another, do not hold the same "Pentecostal" view as I (and a number of others) do. Accordingly, I thought it would be useful to make this position known, in brief, and answer some views against it.

The word "Pentecostal," like most titles, is described in different ways by different Christian groups. For our purposes, the term Pentecostal means the belief that the gift, or baptism, of the Spirit, accompanied by speaking in other languages just as on the day of Pentecost, is considered to be the normal and expected experience to this day. This appendix briefly explains why many of us strongly support the Pentecostal experience, and expounds on a few of its often overlooked significances.

To begin with, a number of verses clearly state this position...

> The wind blows where it wants to, and you hear its sound, but don't know where it comes from and where it is going. *So is everyone who is born of the Spirit.* (John 3:8)

> [1]Now when the day of Pentecost had come, they were all with one accord in one place. [2]Suddenly there came from the sky a sound like the rushing of a mighty wind, and it filled all the house where they were sitting. [3]*Tongues like fire*

appeared and were distributed to them, and one sat on each of them. *⁴They were all filled with the Holy Spirit, and began to speak with other languages*, as the Spirit gave them the ability to speak. (Acts 2:1–4)

...and having received from the Father the promise of the Holy Spirit, he [Jesus] has poured out *this, which you now see and hear*. (Acts 2:33)

³⁸Peter said to them, "Repent, and be baptized, everyone of you, in the name of Jesus Christ for the forgiveness of sins, and *you will receive the gift of the Holy Spirit*. ³⁹For *to you is the promise, and to your children, and to all who are far off*, even as many as the Lord our God will call to himself." (Acts 2:38–39)

¹²But when *they believed* Philip preaching *good news concerning* the Kingdom of *God and the name of Jesus Christ, they were baptized*, both men and women. ¹³Simon himself also believed. Being baptized, he continued with Philip. Seeing signs and great miracles occurring, he was amazed. ¹⁴Now when the apostles who were at Jerusalem heard that Samaria had received the word of God, they sent Peter and John to them, ¹⁵who, when they had come down, *prayed for them, that they might receive the Holy Spirit*; ¹⁶*for as yet he had fallen on none of them. They had only been baptized* in the name of Christ Jesus. ¹⁷Then they laid their hands on them, and *they received the Holy Spirit*. ¹⁸Now when *Simon saw that the Holy Spirit was given through the laying on of the apostles' hands, he offered them money,* ¹⁹saying, "Give me also this power, that whoever I lay my hands on may receive the Holy Spirit." (Acts 8:12–19)

⁴⁴ While Peter was still speaking these words, the Holy Spirit fell on all those who heard the word. ⁴⁵They of the circumcision who believed were amazed, as many as came with

Peter, because the gift of the Holy Spirit was also poured out on the nations. *⁴⁶For they heard them speaking in other languages and magnifying God*. Then Peter answered, ⁴⁷ "Can any man forbid the water, that *these who have received the Holy Spirit as well as we* should not be baptized?" ⁴⁸He commanded them to be baptized in the name of Jesus Christ. Then they asked him to stay some days...
¹¹:²When Peter had come up to Jerusalem... ⁴...Peter... explained to them in order, saying... ¹²The Spirit told me to go with them, without discriminating. These six brothers also accompanied me, and we entered into the man's house. ¹³He told us how he had seen the angel standing in his house, and saying to him, "Send to Joppa, and get Simon, whose surname is Peter, ¹⁴who will speak to you words by which you will be saved, you and all your house." ¹⁵As I began to speak, *the Holy Spirit fell on them, even as on us at the beginning*. ¹⁶I remembered the word of the Lord, how he said, 'John indeed baptized in water, but *you will be baptized in the Holy Spirit*.' ¹⁷If then God gave to them the same gift as us, when we believed in the Lord Jesus Christ, who was I, that I could withstand God?" (Acts 10:44–11:17)

¹It happened that, while Apollos was at Corinth, Paul, having passed through the upper country, came to Ephesus, and found certain disciples. ²He said to them, *"Did you receive the Holy Spirit when you believed?"* They said to him, "No, we haven't even heard that there is a Holy Spirit." ³He said, "Into what then were you baptized?" They said, "Into John's baptism." ⁴Paul said, "John indeed baptized with the baptism of repentance, saying to the people that they should believe in the one who would come after him, that is, in Jesus." ⁵When they heard this, they were baptized in the name of the Lord Jesus. ⁶When Paul had laid his hands on them, *the Holy Spirit came on them, and they spoke with other languages and prophesied*. (Acts 19:1–6)

What can't be denied in these passages is that some converts clearly displayed "other tongues" (or languages) when they received the gift or baptism of the Spirit, and those other languages were taken as a sign by the apostles. The questions that arise, then, are whether or not such an experience is or was normal for all, and whether or not these experiences were only for that time period.

We *Pentecostals generally believe these passages represent the normal process* of events that accompanies conversion. As Peter said, we are to repent, be baptized into the name of Jesus Christ unto the remission of sins, and we *shall receive* the gift of the Holy Spirit, for the promise is unto all that believe. Jesus had claimed that there would be a *sound* evident in everyone who was born of the Spirit (John 3:8), and Peter claimed that the gift of the Spirit was both seen and heard.

As we see through later outpourings in the book of Acts, the single event in Acts 2 did not automatically apply to all, as, for example, the giving of the law on Mt Sinai did. The giving of that law was one event in which all future children of Israel partook indirectly. Such was not the case in Acts, where the event did reoccur with later conversions. As we also see in Acts, the apostles stated specifically that they knew their new converts had received the Spirit, "for they heard them speaking in tongues and magnifying God." These verses seem to be rather conclusive.

There is no other corresponding statement to the contrary. Those who deny that speaking in tongues is "the" initial, outward sign of receiving the gift of the Holy Spirit are left to their own imaginations. Certainly, the fruits of the Spirit must and will manifest themselves in all believers, but we don't find anyone in the Scriptures stating, "They received the Holy Spirit for we witnessed them..." exercising the gift of faith, or the word of knowledge, or the fruit of goodness or gentleness. Only the *sound* of speaking in other tongues was ever clearly and specifically given as *the* sign of the initial gift, or baptism of the Holy Spirit.

We are talking about a specific sign that is meant to accompany a particular event and experience. Jesus called that particular event a new birth, or more literally, a birth from above. Thus, Jesus gives us a reason to explore the metaphor of a natural birth in comparison. When a baby is born, we don't say it is born the moment we can hear its heart beating, or when it has sensory perception like feeling or hearing, or because it seems to be thinking on its own or reacts to stimuli. All of these things are discernible in babies both before they are born and after. Rather, the one sign that indicates immediately and conclusively that a human birth has taken place is when a baby takes its first breath, which is usually accompanied by the definitively audible sound of crying. This is a specific sign that accompanies a specific event, and that is how tongues were used in the explanation and example of the apostles. That isn't to say, either in the natural or spiritual realms, that this is the only time or reason a baby or child would ever breathe or cry. So it is with tongues, where the initial sign isn't the only purpose that speaking in tongues serves.

Through the verses we've quoted, we can also see that the apostles did not consider *belief* or *confession* to be synonymous with having received the promised Spirit. In Acts 8, Philip made converts who believed and were promptly baptized, and yet the apostles still came down to pray with them that they might receive the Holy Spirit, because they hadn't yet received the promise! In practice, none of the elements of belief, repentance, water baptism, or Spirit baptism, were necessarily considered to be the same event. Just because one had happened, it didn't necessarily mean the others had happened. Sometimes a person was water baptized first, whereas others were water baptized after having received the Spirit. In fact, the gift of the Spirit is something a believer should ask for, according to Jesus: "If you then, being evil, know how to give good gifts to your children, how much more will your heavenly Father give the Holy Spirit to those who ask him?" (Luke 11:11).

A Sign of the Rest and Refreshing

Furthermore, the Scriptures even state *that tongues are a sign,* and *what they are a sign of*. Note carefully what both these passages explain for us...

> ¹¹But he will speak to this nation with stammering lips and in another language; ¹²to whom he said, *"This is the resting place. Give rest to weary;"* and *"This is the refreshing;"* yet they would not hear. (Isaiah 28:11–12)

> ²¹In the law it is written, 'By men of strange languages and by the lips of strangers I will speak to this people. *Not even thus will they hear me, says the Lord.*' ²²Therefore other languages are for *a sign, not to those who believe, but to the unbelieving*; but prophesying is for a sign, not to the unbelieving, but to those who believe. (1 Corinthians 14:21–22)

When we read these passages together, we obtain a more complete picture and explanation (just as we do when reading the synoptic gospels, for instance). These verses clearly state that stammering lips (called "languages like as of fire" in Acts 2:3) and another tongue would be a sign of "the rest" and "the refreshing," which the nation who is supposed to receive "would not hear." Those are the "unbelievers," who are clearly identified in Isaiah 28:11–12: those who don't believe that this is the rest and refreshing. This is why Paul said "tongues are for a sign, not to those who believe, but to the unbelieving."

Now, notice what Paul says in this passage:

> ²³If therefore the whole assembly is assembled together and all speak with other languages, and unlearned or unbelieving people come in, won't they say that you are crazy? ²⁴But if all prophesy, and someone unbelieving or unlearned comes in, he is reproved by all, and he is judged by all. ²⁵And thus the secrets of his heart are revealed. So he will fall

down on his face and worship God, declaring that God is among you indeed. (1 Corinthians 14:23–25)

Paul had said, above in 14:22, that speaking in other tongues was a sign to the unbelievers, whereas prophecy was a sign to believers. But then he turns right around and says that if you speak in other languages to the unlearned and unbelieving, they will think you are crazy. So which is it? Paul lived in a multicultural world, so most people would have been exposed to speakers of other languages. Judea itself was overrun by soldiers of the Roman army. So why would anyone presume that speaking in another language was crazy? However, it would be a different story if someone tried speaking to you in a language you didn't know and expected you to understand. It's not hard to imagine that would cause you to think they were a little crazy. And that is why Paul provided the following explanation:

> [2]For he who speaks in another language *speaks not to men, but to God*; for *no one understands*; but *in the Spirit he speaks mysteries*. [3]But *he who prophesies speaks to men for their edification, exhortation, and consolation*. [4]He who speaks in another language *edifies himself*, but he who prophesies edifies the assembly. [5]Now I desire to have you all speak with other languages, but rather that you would prophesy. For he is greater who prophesies than he who speaks with other languages, unless he interprets, that the assembly may be built up. (1 Corinthians 14:2–5)

So here Paul explicitly says that he who speaks in another language speaks not to (or toward) men but to, or toward, God. This is a spiritual principle. There is another that goes along with it:

> [27]"If any man speaks in another language, let it be two, or at the most three, and in turn; and let one interpret. [28]But if there is no interpreter, let him keep silent in the assembly, and let him speak to himself, and to God." (1 Corinthians 14:27–28)

So then, the biblical standard for speaking in tongues *within the assembly* is not to speak as if *unto* men in tongues unless it is interpreted, and not to speak *unto* the assembly except by two or at the most three, and only if it is interpreted.

The way non-Pentecostals often interpret 1 Corinthians 14 implies that the saints in Acts 2:1–4 were out of order and acting against these biblical standards! Why? Because they point to Paul's instructions in the assembly and claim that anything other than two or three speaking with an interpreter is out of order. But in Acts 2 all 120 of them were speaking in other languages, and there was no interpreter; the unbelievers all understood in their own languages! So then, it is ridiculous to interpret 1 Corinthians in a way that makes Paul out to be condemning or correcting the actions of the saints on the Day of Pentecost! And yet that is what they do who claim 1 Corinthians 14:27–28 applies to all circumstances of speaking in tongues.

The point is, what was happening in Acts 2 was not the only type of speaking in other tongues that Paul was addressing. The sign of speaking in other tongues when receiving the gift of the Holy Spirit is simply not the same particular event or circumstance as ministering the gifts to other believers in a Christian assembly.

The Law Written on the Heart

One significance of the NT gift of the Holy Spirit is to represent the law being written on our hearts:

> You are a letter of Christ, ministered by us, written not with ink, but with the Spirit of the living God; *not in tablets of stone, but in tablets that are hearts of flesh.*(2 Corinthians 3:3)

> "For *this is the covenant* that I will make with the house of Israel. After those days," says the Lord, "I will put my laws into their mind, I will also write them on their heart. I will be to them a God, And they will be to me a people." (Hebrews 8:10)

Can anyone then actually be of "His people" if His laws are not written in their heart? This is important because of the components (turbulence, fire, voice, lawgiving) that were involved in the law being written on stone and what the Bible has to say about that event:

> [17] Moses led the people out of the camp to meet God; and they stood at the lower part of the mountain. [18] Mount Sinai, the whole of it, smoked, because Yahweh descended on it in fire; and its smoke ascended like the smoke of a furnace, and the whole mountain quaked greatly. [19] When the sound of the trumpet grew louder and louder, Moses spoke, and God answered him by a voice. [20] Yahweh came down on Mount Sinai, to the top of the mountain. Yahweh called Moses to the top of the mountain, and Moses went up... [20:1] God spoke all these words, saying... (Exodus 19:17–20:1) [and thus the law was given by God to Moses who delivered the words to the people of Israel].

Consider how that experience is described in the following passages through key statements highlighted in italics below:

> [3] Our God comes, and *does not keep silent*. A *fire* devours before him. It is very *tempestuous* around him. [4] He calls to the heavens above, To the earth, that he may judge his people: [5] "Gather my saints together to me, Those who have *made a covenant* with me by sacrifice." (Psalms 50:3–5)

> Out of heaven he made you to *hear his voice*, that he might *instruct* you: and on earth he made you to see his great *fire*; and you heard *his words* out of the midst of the fire. (Deuteronomy 4:36)

> [2] He said, Yahweh came from Sinai... At his right hand was *a fiery law* for them. [3] Yes, he loves the people; *All his saints* are in your hand: They sat down at your feet; Everyone shall

receive of your words. ⁴ Moses *commanded us a law*, An inheritance for the assembly of Jacob. (Deuteronomy 33:2–4)

Now let's compare the sequences of events (from the above). The best way to demonstrate and compare the elements involved is to show them in a table and compare them alongside each other as follows.

The Like Element	In Exodus	In Acts	Supporting Verses
A. God Brings the People Before Him	"Moses led the people out of the camp to meet God" Ex. 19:17	"They were all with one accord in one place" Ac. 2:1	"Gather my saints together to me" Ps. 50:5; "All his saints...sat down at your feet" De. 33:3
B. There are Physical Manifestations	"The whole mountain quaked greatly" Ex.19:18	"There came from the sky a sound like the rushing of a mighty wind, and it filled all the house where they were sitting" Ac. 2:2	"It is very tempestuous around him" Ps. 50:3
C. There is the Presence or Likeness of Fire	"Yahweh descended on it in fire" Ex. 19:18	"Languages like fire appeared and one sat on each of them" Ac 2:3	"A fire devours before Him" Ps. 50:3; "On earth he made you to see his great fire" De. 4:36; "At his right hand was a fiery law for them" De. 33:2

The Like Element	In Exodus	In Acts	Supporting Verses
D. Man Begins to Speak and God Replies with a Voice or Words	"Moses spoke, and God answered him by a voice" Ex. 19:19	"They... began to speak with other languages, as the Spirit gave them the ability to speak" Ac. 2:4	"Our God comes, and does not keep silent" Ex. 50:3; "You heard his words out of the midst of the fire" De. 4:36; "Everyone shall receive of your words" De. 33:3
E. Communion with God where Law Is Written On Tables Of Stone/Flesh	"Yahweh came down on Mount Sinai... and Moses went up" Ex. 19:20	"They were all filled with the Holy Spirit" Ac 2:4	"Our God comes... that he may judge his people" Ps. 50:3–4; "That he might instruct you" De. 4:36

While considering the chart, let's now look at these passages in Acts:

> Being therefore exalted by the right hand of God, and having received from the Father the promise of the Holy Spirit, he has poured out this, *which you now see and hear*. (Acts 2:33)

> [45]They of the circumcision who believed were amazed, as many as came with Peter, because the gift of the Holy Spirit was also poured out on the nations. [46]For they heard them speaking in other languages and magnifying God. (Acts 10:45–46)

> ⁷Don't marvel that I said to you, You must be born anew. ⁸The wind blows where it wants to, and *you hear its sound*, but don't know where it comes from and where it is going. So is everyone who is born of the Spirit. (John 3:7–8)

> When Paul had laid his hands on them, the Holy Spirit came on them, and they spoke with other languages and prophesied. (Acts 19:6)

> ¹¹But he will speak to this nation with stammering lips and in another language; ¹²to whom he said, "This is the resting place. Give rest to weary;" and "This is the refreshing;" yet they would not hear. (Isaiah 28:11–12)

> ²¹In the law it is written, "By men of strange languages and by the lips of strangers I will speak to this people. Not even thus will they hear me, says the Lord." ²²Therefore other languages are for a sign. (1 Corinthians 14:21–22)

In light of the aforementioned scriptures, in addition to asking you the scriptural question (Acts 19:2)— "have you received the Holy Spirit"—allow me to ask you this:

Have you had *the law written on your heart*?

Don't be deceived. This Law being written on the heart is to be a glorious experience in the heart and soul, of which, as the scripture says, the other languages are only an outwardly sign:

> ⁷But if the service of death, written engraved on stones, came with glory, so that the children of Israel could not look steadfastly on the face of Moses for the glory of his face; which was passing away: ⁸won't service of the Spirit be with much more glory? ⁹For if the service of condemnation has glory, the service of righteousness exceeds much more in glory. ¹⁰For most assuredly that which has been made glorious has not been made glorious in this respect, by reason

of the glory that surpasses. ¹¹For if that which passes away was with glory, much more that which remains is in glory. (2 Corinthians 3:7–11)

This passage in particular is why we must remain adamant that speaking in tongues is just an outward sign. Being born again by the baptism of the Spirit is analogous to being born in the natural; speaking in tongues is analogous to the sound of a baby's cry. In the natural, as with the spiritual, the outward cry isn't what is notable or spectacular; it is the life that the sound represents that is the true substance of the miracle! A midwife doesn't tell the father, "your baby cried," she says, "you now have a daughter" or "your daughter was born perfectly healthy." It is what is happening in the life of the newborn that is significant, just as it is in the spiritual new birth.

On the other hand, medics can take a stillborn and put it on artificial respiration for as long as they like, but that doesn't necessarily mean they have instilled new life into the baby. Unfortunately, in the same way, in the spiritual, tongues can be artificially induced, and imitated. The problem, or shortcoming with that, is, that the Bible describes the baptism of the Holy Spirit as a truly glorious experience:

> ⁷But if the service of death, written engraved on stones, *came with glory*, so that the children of Israel could not look steadfastly on the face of Moses for the glory of his face; which was passing away: ⁸won't service of *the Spirit be with much more glory?* ⁹For if the service of condemnation has glory, *the service of righteousness exceeds much more in glory.* ¹⁰For most assuredly that which has been made glorious has not been made glorious in this respect, by reason of the glory that surpasses. ¹¹For *if that which passes away was with glory, much more that which remains is in glory.* (2 Cor 3:7–11)

Those who say the spirit comes without observation have no real explanation for this glory that Paul is explaining here.

Born of Promise Versus Born of the Flesh

We have given scriptural examples, explanations, and even prophecy regarding the use of speaking in other tongues as an initial, outward sign of receiving the promised gift of the Holy Spirit. It is notable that there are no other corresponding signs, nor any other Bible verses in prophecy or explanation, that express an alternative view, and that is yet another shortcoming with any non-Pentecostal position.

When God told Abraham that he would have a son and become the father of many nations, Abraham got impatient and figured out a way to receive a son outside of God's perfect plan. This method is called humanism, and biblically it is called "of the flesh." This isn't to say something isn't or can't be obtained in this manner; it is to say that what is obtained by the flesh is not what God intends.

> [21]Tell me, you that desire to be under the law, don't you listen to the law? [22]For it is written that Abraham had two sons, one by the handmaid, and one by the free woman. [23]However, the son by the handmaid was born according to the flesh, but the son by the free woman was born through promise. [24]These things contain an allegory, for these are two covenants. One is from Mount Sinai, bearing children to bondage, which is Hagar. [25]For this Hagar is Mount Sinai in Arabia, and answers to the Jerusalem that exists now, for she is in bondage with her children. [26]But the Jerusalem that is above is free, which is the mother of us all. [27] For it is written, "Rejoice, you barren who don't bear. Break forth and shout, you that don't travail. For more are the children of the desolate than of her who has a husband." [28]Now we, brothers, as Isaac was, are children of promise. [29]But as then, he who was born according to the flesh persecuted him who was born according to the Spirit, so also it is now. (Galatians 4:21–29)

Inasmuch as the gift of the Spirit is a promise, it should be received as a gift and as a promise and not as if it were automatically inherent, nor should it be taken according to man's inherent ability within his natural means. In the biblical record, the apostles simply did not presume people had received because they believed, and thus neither should we.

> Being therefore exalted by the right hand of God, and having received from the Father the promise of the Holy Spirit, he has poured out *this, which you now see and hear*. (Acts 2:33)

> [38]Peter said to them, 'Repent, and be baptized, everyone of you, in the name of Jesus Christ for the forgiveness of sins, and you will receive the gift of the Holy Spirit. [39]For *to you is the promise*, and to your children, and to all who are far off, even as many as the Lord our God will call to himself.' (Acts 2:38–39)

> [1]It happened that, while Apollos was at Corinth, Paul, having passed through the upper country, came to Ephesus, and found certain disciples. [2]He said to them, "Did you receive the Holy Spirit when you believed?" (Acts 19:1–2)

APPENDIX - III

We Believe God is Spirit and Incorporeal

It is written: "You worship what you do not know; *We know what we worship, for salvation is of the Jews*" (John 4:22).

These words of Jesus are simple, profound, and absolutely authoritative. We may look to a lot of practices that Jesus strongly rejected and rebuked, but the Jewish knowledge of the "what" of God was not one of them. Unfortunately, there are certain Son of God advocates who have concluded a strange view of God that we want to address; namely, the false notion that God is corporeal and has a body, expressed in the following quote:

> Our Father God is a person (Job 13:8, Heb. 1:3), who has a will (Luke 22:42; John 5:30), a personality (Zeph. 3:17), a shape (Num. 12:8; James 3:9)... He is not in any way human, but he has a heavenly body (as do angels–Ps. 104:4; 1 Cor. 15:40, 44; Heb. 12:9; 1 Kings 22:19)... Note: Do not be confused by the Bible verses that make reference to the Almighty's wings. This is speaking figuratively as the nations of Assyria and Moab are also said to have wings (Isa. 8:8; Jer. 48:9; and the Messiah, Jesus Christ is promised to 'arise with healing in his wings' Mal. 4:2).[1]

We must disagree. God, being incorporeal, simply does not have a literal "shape" as the above writer contends. Ironically, the writer has provided us with the very answer to such a dilemma: these are

---

[1] Joel W. Hemphill, *God and Jesus: Exploring The Biblical Distinction* (Joelton, Tennessee: Trumpet Call Books, 2013), 88.

figures of speech. There is no scripture clarifying that only God's wings are figurative but all these other descriptors are to be understood literally. Thus, each of these attributes is to be understood as a figure of speech designed to help us understand that God isn't just some impersonal, impassive mass of computational energy.

It really comes down to a simple issue of interpreting the Bible through the lens of Jesus' authorized Jewish view, rather than through the lens of pagan ideas of metaphysics. Here then is the typical Jewish view:

> G-d is Incorporeal: Although many places in scripture and Talmud speak of various parts of G-d's body (the Hand of G-d, G-d's wings, etc.) or speak of G-d in anthropomorphic terms (G-d walking in the garden of Eden, G-d laying tefillin, etc.), Judaism firmly maintains that G-d has no body. Any reference to G-d's body is simply a figure of speech, a means of making G-d's actions more comprehensible to beings living in a material world. Much of Rambam's Guide for the Perplexed is devoted to explaining each of these anthropomorphic references and proving that they should be understood figuratively. We are forbidden to represent G-d in a physical form. That is considered idolatry. The sin of the Golden Calf incident was not that the people chose another deity, but that they tried to represent G-d in a physical form.[2]

This is a typical Jewish view of God: He is incorporeal and non-compound. Any description of God that attempts to make God out to be otherwise, is simply influenced by pagan ideas of corporeality and not the Bible. Note well, therefore, the last sentence cited: the golden calf wasn't a different God; it was an attempt to represent God in physical form. Thus, the name of this theological error we are addressing is *idolatry,* after the manner of the golden calf.

---

[2] Tracey R. Rich, "Judaism 101: The Nature of G-d," accessed 1/29/2017, http://www.jewfaq.org/g-d.htm.

The idea of God's incorporeality can be seen in God coming to Solomon's temple and the revelatory answer to Solomon's question: "But will God in very deed dwell on the earth? Behold, heaven and the heaven of heavens can't contain you; how much less this house that I have built!" (1 Kings 8:27). Solomon goes on to answer his own question in the form of a prayer of worship.

> Yet have respect for the prayer of your servant...Yahweh my God... that your eyes may be open toward this house night and day, even toward the place of which you have said, My name shall be there; to listen to the prayer which your servant shall pray toward this place. Listen you to the supplication of your servant, and of your people Israel, when they shall pray toward this place: yes, hear in heaven, your dwelling place; and when you hear, forgive. (1 Kings 8:28–30)

Solomon's temple eventually became one of the cornerstones of the Jewish religion. It was to be the place where God's name dwelt. It was the place where God's people would direct their prayers and meet and commune with God. And yet Jewish tradition consistently maintained that all anthropomorphic ideas were entirely figures of speech. If God had a body, then that body would necessarily have abode in the temple, and the priests that served the temple would have testified of such; but they did not, they consistently maintained that God is incorporeal (bodiless/formless). This is the Jewish view of the "what" of God that Jesus affirmed. For those to teach otherwise is to claim they know better than Jesus!

Early Christians continued to view God in non-corporeal terms, and they were shocked at Tertullian's inventions to the contrary! It is only with the writings of Tertullian that we begin to find philosophers, such as he, redefining God in pagan terms.

In the following passage, Tertullian was writing against someone named Praxeas. Praxeas was a One God (monarchian) preacher who was in open fellowship with the Roman assembly of his day. In this writing, Tertullian was complaining that Praxeas wouldn't allow God to have a physical substance. Tertullian, writing as if speaking directly to Praxeas, said that Praxeas had asked him if he believed the Word was a certain substance. Tertullian then criticized Praxeas for not allowing God to have a real substance.

> He (the word) became also the Son of God, and was begotten when He proceeded forth from Him. Do you then, (you ask,) grant that the Word is a certain substance, *constructed by the Spirit and the communication of Wisdom? Certainly I do. But you [Tertullian accusing Praxeas here] will not allow Him to be really a substantive being, by having a substance of His own; in such a way that He may be regarded as an objective thing and a person, and so be able (as being constituted second to God the Father,) to make two*, the Father and the Son, God and the Word. For you will say, what is a word, but a voice and sound of the mouth, and (as the grammarians teach) air when struck against, intelligible to the ear, but for the rest a sort of *void, empty, and incorporeal thing. I, on the contrary, contend that nothing empty and void could have come forth from God, seeing that it is not put forth from that which is empty and void; nor could that possibly be devoid of substance which has proceeded from so great a substance, and has produced such mighty substances*: for all things which were made through Him, He Himself (personally) made. How could it be, that He Himself is nothing, without whom nothing was made? How could He who is empty have made things which are solid, and He who is void have made things which are full, and He who is incorporeal have made things which have body?[3]

In this passage, Tertullian showed he still viewed God in a philosophical, metaphysical sense and had departed from, or never accepted, a Jewish, biblically-influenced view of God. He even argued against the idea that the word of God was merely "a voice and

---

[3] Tertullian, *Against Praxeas*, Chapter 7, Ante-Nicene Fathers, Volume 3, PC Study Bible.

sound... *empty, and incorporeal...*" Yet the majority of Christians at this time (that is, other than the Gnostics) held the latter view, which we know from Irenaeus in particular. Irenaeus had taken the time to describe God in terms that Tertullian later rejected, such as he has done here. Note that, for Tertullian, if the word of God does not have some kind of material substance, it can have no real existence. In the same way, for Tertullian, God was material and corporeal, not incorporeal.

The Bible clearly refutes Tertullian's belief that God's nature is an actual material substance. For example, Tertullian compared and likened God's substance to other great substances that God created. Tertullian explicitly said that God had to have substance in order to produce other substances. The Bible refers to these as, "...man—and birds and four-footed animals and creeping things." Of course, Tertullian brought himself, *and all Trinitarians* who ascribe to his reasoning as well, under the condemnation of the Scriptures. For it is written again,

> Professing themselves to be wise, they became fools, And *changed the glory of the incorruptible God into an image made like to corruptible man*, and to birds, and fourfooted beasts, and creeping things. Therefore God also gave them up... (Romans 1:22–24)

Tertullian stood at the forefront of the Trinity's development and led the way by first changing the glory of God into an image made like corruptible man. As seekers of truth, we should not relapse into the pagan views of God that ultimately led to the Trinity.

As a final note against the idea of a corporeal, compound (having body parts) God, let us draw upon the same argument creationists use against evolutionists. The creationist argument is that man had to be created simply due to the complexity and balance of all the parts and pieces, not to mention the supportive ecosystem required to feed and sustain man. On the other hand, we contend with the creationist, that God is uncreated, as proven by the fact that He is eternal and is not compound or corporeal. That is to say, creation requires three elements all to exist at once: time, space and matter. If matter doesn't exist in time and space, when and where does it exist? If there is space, but no time or matter, with which to measure it, it is meaningless. If there is time, but no matter or space, it is just as superfluous. That is why the Bible begins by saying, in the beginning (time) God created the heaven (space) and earth (matter).

God must absolutely transcend time, space and matter to be the Creator of all such, otherwise God is Himself a creation; and if God is a creation, what or who created Him? Who designed the pieces and parts that would make up a corporeal God, and who put them together? Did God Himself have a God? No, God is eternal, incorporeal, non-compound, omniscient, and omnipresent. He absolutely transcends time, space and matter. So let's not profess to be wise and then become foolish by changing this glory of God into an image made like corruptible man!

APPENDIX - IV

Baptism into Jesus' Name

The following is an extract from *The Faith Once Delivered*, a Bible study I put together as a Oneness writer.

Water baptism into Jesus' name produces results and performs functions.

1. By being buried with Christ we participate in His death, burial, and resurrection (the gospel) (Romans 6:3–4).
2. By being baptized in Jesus' name (buried with Christ) we receive remission of sins (Acts 2:38; 22:16).
3. Being baptized in Jesus' name means putting on Christ (Galatians 3:27).

Other Scriptural injunctions for water baptism in the name of Jesus besides Acts 2:38 are listed below:

Six Witnesses

I will introduce the "six witnesses" with the following poem.

> I have six honest serving men,
> They taught me all I knew,
> Their names? What and Why and How,
> And When and Where and Who
> 　　　　　-Author unknown

The Scriptural counterpart for the concept found in the poem is 2 Corinthians 13:1: "In the mouth of two or three witnesses shall every word be established." I will let these six witnesses—What, Why, How, When, Where, and Who—defend baptism in the name of Jesus.

WHAT?

Baptism in/into the name of Jesus Christ

1. Acts 2:38 with Luke 24:47
2. 1 Peter 3:20–21; Mark 16:16; Acts 4:10–12
3. Colossians 2:6,12
4. Acts 22:16; Romans 6:3–4
5. Galatians 3:27
6. Acts 19:4–5
7. Acts 8:5–16
8. Acts 10:48

WHY?

1. Remission of sins: Luke 24:47; Acts 2:38; 22:16
2. To put on Christ: Galatians 3:26–27. (Also see 2 Corinthians 11:2.)
3. Salvation: Mark 16:16; Acts 4:10–12; 1 Peter 3:20–21; Hebrews 11:7
4. To be buried with Jesus: Colossians 2:11–12; Romans 6:3–4
5. In obedience to the gospel: 1 Corinthians 15:1–4; 2 Thessalonians 1:7–9; Mark 8:34–35
6. In obedience to Jesus' command (as opposed to recital of His words): Acts 9:6; 22:16; Romans 6:3–4; Galatians 3:27

HOW?

1. By immersion: Acts 8:38
2. By faith/belief in the name (i.e., not a mere recital of a formula): Acts 8:36–37; 2:38; 10:43; Luke 24:47

3. By invocation of the name: Acts 22:16; 9:5; 26:15
4. In the name of Jesus Christ: Acts 2:38; 8:12–16;19:4–5; Romans 6:3; Colossians 2:6, 12; Galatians 3:27

WHEN AND WHERE?

1. Day of Pentecost at Jerusalem: Acts 2:38
2. In Samaria, after the death of Stephen: Acts 8:5, 16
3. At Joppa, during Peter's second journey from Jerusalem: Acts 10:48
4. At Ephesus, during Paul's third journey: Acts 19:5

WHO?

Who Received baptism in Jesus' name?
1. Jews: Acts 2:38
2. Samarians: Acts 8:16
3. Italian Gentiles: Acts 10:47–48
4. Ephesian disciples baptized by John who needed rebaptizing in Jesus' name: Acts 19:5
5. Romans: Romans 6:3–4

Who Preached And Taught Baptism In Jesus' Name?
1. Jesus: Acts 9:5–6; 22:12–13; Romans 6:3. (See Acts 9:10–15; 19:1–5; Luke 24:47; Acts 2:38; Mark 16:16; Acts 4:10–12; 1 Peter 3:20–21; Hebrews 11:7.)
2. Peter, with *all* the other apostles, including Matthew: Acts 1:14; 2:38, 41
3. Philip: Acts 8:5, 12
4. Peter with six other Jewish believers: Acts:10:45–48; 11:12
5. Paul: Acts 19:5; Romans 6:3–4; Colossians 2:11–12; Galatians 3:26–27

www.ingramcontent.com/pod-product-compliance
Lightning Source LLC
Chambersburg PA
CBHW071106160426
43196CB00013B/2491